MODERN BRITAIN

Title-page

London from the terrace of Richmond House, painted by Canaletto for the second Duke of Richmond, probably in 1746.

MODERN
Life and Work through
T. K. Derry, M.A., D.Phil.(Oxon.) and

John

BRITAIN
Two Centuries of Change
T. L. Jarman, M.A., B.Litt. (Oxon.), A.M. (Harvard)

Murray

Set, printed and bound in Great Britain by Cox and Wyman Ltd, London, Fakenham and Reading

0 7195 3546 8

Preface

This book reproduces the earlier chapters of *The Making of Modern Britain*, where we stated our aim as follows: 'We try to show, not only the growth of the Industrial Revolution down to our own time, but how the Welfare State has emerged from the individualistic society of the days of Arkwright and Adam Smith; we try to show, also, the stages by which the rustic Englishman of the Woodforde Diary developed the character and way of life appropriate to an urban civilization in an overcrowded island.' As far as the close of the Victorian Age this still describes our theme, though the story is now told with various amplifications and revisions, a much fuller equipment of illustrations, a new appendix of 'Social History in Figures', additions to the Book List, and an expanded index to provide for topic studies. In all these matters, the authors wish to express their gratitude to Miss Tessa Tulk-Hart, of John Murray's, for her assiduous assistance, especially in the selection of illustrations.

But the course of events in recent years has led schools of all kinds to pay increasing attention to the history of our own century. This is because a knowledge of political and international as well as of social and economic developments is needed for the light it sheds upon the pathway from the recent past to the present with its many contrasts. *Modern Britain* accordingly deals with such subjects as the two World Wars, British adhesion to the European Community, and the background of twentieth-century domestic politics as directly influencing life, work, and society today. The authors point also to the emergence of big problems, not only socio-economic but moral, with which we have so far failed to grapple. Such deviations from our proper field into that of citizenship are very brief, and may in any case be justified by the words of an eminent historian and educational reformer who numbered one of us among his pupils: 'The fact of progress is written plain and large upon the page of history: but progress is not a law of history. The ground gained by one generation may be lost by the next.'[1]

T.K.D.
T.L.J.

[1] H. A. L. Fisher: *A History of Europe* (3 vols., 1935), I, p. vii.

Acknowledgements

Thanks are due to the following who have kindly permitted the reproduction of copyright illustrations:

Adprint Ltd (p. 2); Aerofilms Ltd (p. 63); Architectural Press (p. 313); The Governor and Company of the Bank of England (p. 36); The Bodleian Library (p. 54); British Airways (p. 291); British Gas Corporation (p. 296); British Hovercraft Corporation (p. 318); British Leyland (p. 236); British Library of Political and Economic Science (p. 142); Trustees of the British Museum (pp. 8, 13, 16, 37, 50, 58, 81, 104, 108, 114, 118, 139); British Steel Corporation (p. 289); Central Electricity Generating Board (p. 293); Co-operative Union Ltd (p. 149); Cumbernauld Development Corporation (p. 315); The *Daily Mail* (p. 189); Elliott and Fry (p. 284 (bottom)); Gareth Photography (p. 317); Gernsheim Collection (p. 195); from Goodwood House by courtesy of the trustees (title-page); The *Illustrated London News* (pp. 155, 182); Imperial War Museum (p. 198); Josiah Wedgwood and Sons Ltd (pp. 86, 88); Keystone Press (pp. 284 (top), 301); London County Council (pp. 304, 305); Mansell Collection (pp. 14, 23, 29, 41 (bottom), 83); Mary Evans Picture Library (pp. 10, 41 (top), 53, 76, 95, 116, 135, 187, 207); Massey-Ferguson (p. 241); National Portrait Gallery (p. 109); National Trust (p. 244); Platt Bros Ltd (p. 44); Popperfoto (pp. 257, 261); Radio Times Hulton Picture Library (pp. 34, 60, 68, 70, 75, 91, 106, 124, 159, 165, 168, 185, 190, 202, 214, 217, 220, 229, 268); Royal Academy of Arts (p. 145); The Science Museum (pp. 47, 73, 122, 126); Shell International Petroleum Co. Ltd (p. 340); University of Reading, Museum of English Rural Life (p. 59); Vickers (p. 237); Crown Copyright: Victoria and Albert Museum (p. 158); Walker Art Gallery, Liverpool (p. 4).

In Appendix 1, poem no. 7 by W. H. Davies is reproduced by permission of Mrs H. M. Davis. Poem no. 9 by William Plomer is reproduced by permission of the Estate of William Plomer. Both poems are published by Jonathan Cape Ltd.

Contents

An Eventful Half-Century

Since 1945: A Different Britain

Illustrations

BEFORE THE GREAT CHANGES

I Village life in the eighteenth century

Just over two hundred years ago England was still mainly a land of countrymen leading country lives. Let us then begin by looking at the England of those days through the eyes of a countryman—the Rev. James Woodforde, a bachelor and the newly appointed parson of Weston Longeville in the county of Norfolk. His diary, happily preserved through a century and a half, enables us to observe the life of his own day and district, hum-drum and far from the madding crowd. The portrait (taken in the gown, bob-wig, and bands appropriate to his profession) shows us the sort of man his parishioners were staring at: for the arrival of a stranger was a great event in a country village.

In the opening months of 1776, Parson Woodforde has been busy moving into his Rectory; then, as now, a tiresome business—what with the buying of furniture, house repairs and, in this case, the destruction of a plague of rats, requiring the services of a rat-catcher at what was then the high price of 10s. 6d. (52½p). By early summer he appears to be settled, and on 3 June two servant maids come and offer their services. He engages them—the more experienced for £5 5s. a year and tea twice a day, the less experienced for £3 3s. a year. Then there is a disagreeable interruption: he is racked with toothache. On 4 June he rises at 5 a.m. after a sleepless night: 'Sent for one Reeves a man who draws teeth in this parish, and at about 7 he came and drew my tooth, but shockingly bad indeed: he broke away a great piece of my gum and broke one of the fangs of the tooth: it gave me exquisite pain all the day after, and my face was swelled prodigiously in the evening and much pain. Very bad and in much pain the whole day long. Gave the old man that drew it, however, £0 2s. 6d. He is too old, I think, to draw teeth; can't see very well.'

Parson Woodforde, wearing a bob-wig and the gown and white bands of his profession.

Next day he pays his bills for '2 cows, 3 Pigs, 3 pr. Shoes, Flour, Tea, Sugar, News Papers, Pipes, Candles, Pan, Tobacco, Beer, Mustard, Salt, Washing, Halters, Comb and Brush, Crabs, Bread and Porterage,' in all £14 9s. 3d. After that life goes more quietly. Like many other clergy in those days Parson Woodforde farmed his own land, the glebe, so in September he is busy with his harvest—mostly barley—and on 14 September he entertains his 'Harvestmen with some Beef and some Plum Pudding and as much liquor as they could drink'. That done, he goes for a pleasant jaunt to Yarmouth with his nephew. The fees at the turnpike gates[1] on the roads cost him 1s. 6d. They watch the Dutch herring boats come in. He notes that 'The Dutch are very droll fellows to look at, strange, heavy, bad dressed People with monstrous large Trousers, and many with large wooden shoes.' But

[1] See page 50.

the two holiday-makers have a very good time and are entertained 'with Wine, Gin etc.' on board a collier about to return to Sunderland.

Later in the autumn, Woodforde feels that he ought to do something about a local smallpox scare; and at 11 o'clock on 3 November a Dr Thorne comes to the house and inoculates two of the servants.[1] This was a complicated business unlike our modern vaccination, involving careful dieting and physicking during recovery, and the Parson writes anxiously in his diary: 'Pray God, my people and all others in the Small Pox may do well; several Houses have got Small Pox, at present 9 in Weston.'

But the year ends well. There was generally a good congregation at church, and they seemed to like certain changes the new Rector had made. On 3 December his people come to pay him their tithes—one-tenth of the yearly farm produce, which was the proportion that had always been given to the support of the clergy. Parson Woodforde in return gives them a good dinner: 'sirloin of beef roasted, a leg of mutton boiled and Plum Puddings in Plenty'—not to mention, later in the day, 'Wine, Punch and Ale as much as they pleased; they drank of wine 6 Bottles, of Rum 1 gallon and a half, and I know not what ale'. There were only seventeen of them, so they must have drunk plenty.

On 10 December he arranges for Mr Chambers, the schoolmaster, to teach his two men-servants, Ben and Will, 'to write and read at 4s. 6d. a quarter each'. 13 December 'was appointed a Fast on our Majesty's arms against the rebel Americans', and there was a full congregation that day, but their prayers were uneog. As we know from other sources, those 'rebel Americans' soon ceased to be British subjects and became citizens of the new United States.

Yet life at the village of Weston continued almost undisturbed by upheavals in the great world. On Christmas Day the Rector entertains seven poor old men to dinner. He gives to each a shilling, and to one an old black coat and waistcoat. In the afternoon he goes to church. 'It was very dark at church.' He could 'scarce see'. So, with the year moving to its end, let us there take leave of him—in a church where people still worship—reading the services still familiar to many, on one of those dark winter afternoons which are familiar to us all.

The Old Village

Most villages in England, and many in Wales and Scotland as well, have not only an ancient parish church but other buildings dating far back into the Middle Ages. Much of the past history of a village can

[1] See page 11.

Village fair, by Rowlandson—Cuckfield, Sussex.

also be learnt from the names of the old fields; we may even be able to trace in the rise and fall of the ground something of the strip system of farming[1] as it was in the days before modern methods of agriculture came into use. Broadly speaking, there is most to be seen from the old days in counties south of the Trent; southern and eastern England were then the most prosperous areas and the areas in which most people lived. Two hundred years ago the northern counties were thought of as a remote district of infertile moors and Wales as poorer still, while the Highlands of Scotland would be regarded by Parson Woodforde as almost entirely uncivilized.

Thus a sleepy village street somewhere in England south of the Trent, with one or two comfortable-looking, red-brick Georgian houses, some rows of thatched cottages, orchards, and gardens, represents the world that many, perhaps most, of our ancestors knew well. For the poor, who in those days hardly ever travelled more than a few miles from home, it was their only world.

The Manor House

But we must not forget the houses of the great. They are still one of the chief glories of the English countryside, those castles and mansions and manor houses, in some cases built in the time of the Normans.

[1] See page 14.

Even nowadays, when their owners have been greatly impoverished by high taxation and other causes, these places more often than not still cherish, besides their excellence as specimens of architecture and historic buildings, the loveliest gardens, the finest furniture, and even the best pictures to be seen in their district. How much more true was this in the eighteenth century! There were no newspapers for the masses, and the Sunday sermon in the parish church was the nearest thing the villager knew to all we get from radio or television.

A nobleman's palace, like Chatsworth in Derbyshire or Woburn Abbey in Bedfordshire or Knole in Kent, used to be the centre from which ideas about politics, society, arts and manners would spread through the whole county. As for the 'big house' in the village—the Hall or Manor where the squire (and still more important, often, the squire's lady) resided—it was the one link with the outside world. A Georgian wing, or even a couple of bow windows, added to the mansion would spread the sound knowledge of structural proportions which made eighteenth-century buildings of all kinds so satisfying to the eye. A landscape gardener, called in to make the park or gardens more 'natural' in accordance with the new eighteenth-century taste, would create years of discussion for the frequenters of the local inn. The contents of the picture gallery or the library, new styles of furniture and new patterns of china, even the costlier kinds of food and drink—these things which were not bought locally but came from London or the larger towns, had some effect, at least through hearsay, in making country life as a whole less isolated and brutish than we might suppose.

It was, of course, an age of class-distinction, when everybody in the village 'knew his (or her) place'—or was constantly reminded of it. But it was also the age of 'Merry England', as people called it after it was over. The eighteenth century was the time when fox-hunting, which gave pleasure as a spectacle and an excitement to thousands who could not afford a horse, became established as the fashionable winter sport of the English countryside. It was also the time when cricket matches began to be of more than local interest and it saw the start of professional boxing (bare-fist)—two interests which, even more than the meet, brought together all classes to share a common pleasure. The people who in 1740 first sang the strains of 'Rule Britannia!' were very far from regarding themselves as slaves or their island-home as a prison.[1]

---

[1] Crabbe's contemporary account of *The Village* emphasizes other sides of its life (see Appendix I, No. 1).

2 Town life in the eighteenth century; London

London, as the painter Canaletto saw it from the terrace of a noble-man's West End mansion on a bright morning in 1746, might well be called 'the hub of England's universe'.[1] Count the towers and spires of Sir Christopher Wren's churches, which belong to the rebuilding after the Great Fire of 1666; examine the fine buildings which line the river bank; notice the traffic on the river and the elegant costumes of the onlookers. There can be no disputing the greatness of mid-eighteenth-century London—its West End, where Robert Adam (architect to King George III) and his three brothers were about to create the fine terrace of houses known as the Adelphi, and other monumental works; the City, with the endless bustle of business in its ancient jumble of narrow, huddled streets; and the shipping of the Pool below London Bridge, that great medieval structure with both sides of its narrow roadway still lined by shops and houses.

In 1738 London had obtained its second bridge, at Westminster, near Parliament, the Abbey, and the Palace of St James's, and it was indeed to the west of the City that most of the spectacular new building was done; east of Aldgate the houses of the poor were merely allowed to spread themselves without plan or comfort towards the green fields of Essex. The West End was admired by every visitor, as estate-owners and speculative builders joined efforts to extend the network of gracious squares and dignified streets northwards across Tyburn Road (that mournful road for condemned criminals) on to the Duke of Bedford's lands at Bloomsbury or in the direction of Marylebone Fields, and westwards to Hyde Park, across which one could walk to Kensington village with its royal palace.

It was indeed fortunate that this golden age of London 'improve-ment' was also the age which produced the greatest of the Georgian architects—and rich men with sufficient taste to employ them. Many

[1] See title-page.

of the new houses were the town residences of country gentlemen; but others were occupied by City businessmen, for it was now no longer so usual to live on the top of one's business premises in the City. It was pleasanter to be within easy reach of the West End parks: St James's and Green Park and Hyde Park. For those who sought more glamorous amusement, there were the pleasure gardens of Ranelagh to the north of the river beyond Westminster; or Vauxhall on the south bank beyond Lambeth Palace. Both on summer nights were full of music and ablaze with lights among the trees. Ranelagh was the great marvel of the age, with its resplendent 'Rotunda' (circular hall) and its ornamental boxes where one could listen to the music, and eat and drink and talk, and watch the people of rank and fashion meeting and promenading and 'quizzing' one another. It was indeed so popular in fine weather that on one occasion Horace Walpole—son of the famous statesman—was held up for thirty-six minutes in a traffic block of four-horse coaches on the road from town.

Foreign visitors were naturally impressed with all this, but a little surprised at the wealthy Londoner's preference for living 'vertically', in houses where rooms were built one on top of the other and connected by steep staircases. Foreign visitors might well be impressed, too, by the enterprise of public-spirited citizens who, since the government would do nothing to help, had got together to begin schemes for policing, lighting and paving their neighbourhood.. Cavendish Square, which was the first square built north of Oxford Street, is shown in our illustration overleaf with street lamps and a pavement. But the carriages are moving at a slow walk over the rough roadway, and the fact that the two pillared houses in the foreground were originally designed for a duke cannot altogether have made up for their hideous inconvenience. There would be no water on the upper floors and no proper sanitation; the domestic staff would be lucky if they were allowed to sleep in the attics (which are nearly hidden by the pediment).

The Life of the Poor

For the houses of the well-to-do, however, 'Improvement' was in the air. But there was far more that needed to be done in the older parts of London and the regions beyond Aldgate in the east. Men were still talking of the bad old days of unrestricted gin-drinking before the Act of 1751, which limited its sales and made it more expensive. They were reminded of those disreputable scenes by prints of Hogarth's famous picture, *Gin Lane*, painted in the same year as the Act. But there was

The north side of Cavendish Square, showing the mansion designed for the Duke of Chandos in 1720.

still much heavy drinking, and all that goes with it of crime, poverty and disease. Yet the Bow Street magistrate of the time considered 'the rabble much mended within the last fifty years, though still very insolent and abusive, sometimes without the least appearance of a cause'. Certainly the London death-rate had fallen, and something was being done to keep foundlings and workhouse children alive.[1]

London was surely a noble city, to which the rich went then in search of company and culture and the poor in search of service with the rich. To its busy river port came Welsh slates and Portland stone and Baltic pines for building, coal from Newcastle for domestic hearths and bakehouses and distilleries, sugar and tobacco from across the ocean, and much else for use or sale in London.

But it was not very safe to walk through the 'rookery of St Giles' (on the site of New Oxford Street) after nightfall, and all round the City there were streets and courts and alleys where open sewers and back-garden cess-pools bred disease. Nearer the river one shut one's window at low tide because of the stench of sewage which Father Thames was expected to carry to the sea.

There was as yet nothing like our modern councils and Ministry of Health to challenge the onslaughts of sickness that come from dirt. Nor was there any Unemployment Insurance or National Assistance to help men tide over the periods of trade depression, which caused

[1] See page 20.

great hardship to many groups of citizens, such as the big population of silk-weavers, who in those days still plied their craft—or rioted for more wages—in the congested district of Spitalfields, east of the City boundary.

Provincial Towns

So much for the 'hub of England's universe'. For London was then about fifteen times as large as the largest provincial towns, which were Bristol and Norwich—the great West of England port and the great centre of the East Anglian cloth manufacture. These two had held their proud position for hundreds of years, but in the eighteenth century they were beginning to be caught up by the towns we think of as the biggest. Birmingham, for instance, with its metal trades—chains, locks, bolts, nails, pins, buttons and buckles—in which much of the work was done by women and children in little home-workshops, was already something more than a quiet market-town. Birmingham also had a considerable industrialized hinterland in the Black Country. Liverpool and Manchester likewise grew fast from humble origins, Liverpool rivalling Bristol in trade with Africa and across the Atlantic, Manchester beginning to expand a little later and helped by the money of the Liverpool merchants to develop the cotton industry of which it was to become the world-centre. Equally remarkable was the growth of Glasgow.[1] Up to the union of the English and Scottish parliaments in 1707 it was quite unimportant; the Union threw the trade of the colonies open to Scottish tobacco-importers and merchants of every kind, with the result that in the course of the eighteenth century the population of the town at the mouth of the Clyde was multiplied by six.

Nevertheless, to complete our general picture of where people mostly lived before the modern industrial towns which most of us know so well had come into existence, we must emphasize the importance of certain traditional local centres, to which the well-to-do resorted for business and pleasure. Besides Bristol, which had a fashionable residential area at Clifton, well away from the busy riverside, and Norwich, with its famous cathedral, the best examples might be York, capital of the north even in the far-off days of Roman Britain, and Exeter for the south-west. But any county town was attraction enough for the squires and their families. Quarter sessions, military duties and the buying and selling of lands and houses could be pleasantly combined with dances, theatre visits and concerts, so that there

[1] See illustration, p. 27.

was often little desire to attempt a long and perilous journey over bad roads, possibly infested by highwaymen, in order to join in the pleasures of the London season.

The most important people went to London every year, when Parliament met, as a matter of course. Others, if they ventured far afield, were more likely to take the road to Bath, which since the beginning of the century had become increasingly famous as a holiday resort. In theory, people went there to drink the waters, which are good for various ailments; in practice, they found society and amusements there—it was a great place for courtships, and for duels. Scotland, too, had its special resort in the Edinburgh 'new town', as they called the district of fine new houses and squares, worthy of the West End of London, which started to grow up about 1760, when Edinburgh was becoming a great centre for literature and learning. Even earlier in the century, Edinburgh and the other three Scottish university towns compared favourably as places of serious study with the Oxford, and even Cambridge, of that period.

Like London, which for a long time depended on the steady flow of new arrivals from the country to maintain its population, the towns were all unhealthy by modern standards, though the smaller ones had the advantage of the breeze blowing in from the country to purify the tainted air and less difficulty also in getting rid of their refuse. But the death-rate was usually very high, particularly among infants and from the smallpox which so alarmed Parson Woodforde even in his little rural parish. It is therefore a most important fact that there was a widespread enthusiasm among charitable people in the eighteenth century for the establishment of hospitals.

Eighteenth-century York with the cathedral in the background.

Hospitals and Medicine

Out of the seven most famous hospitals in London, no fewer than five were founded in the years 1720–45: Guy of 'Guy's', for example, was a bookseller of that period who had made a fortune out of Bibles. The provincial towns, led by Bristol, imitated London, which in 1769 added to its hospital system the first dispensary, forerunner of the modern clinic. Over the whole period 1700–1825 new hospitals and dispensaries were being founded at the rate of one a year. The doctors worked with primitive instruments and very few medicines; antiseptic surgery was unknown; nurses and midwives were not well trained. It remained something of an achievement to have managed to survive the first few years of childhood; but in fact year by year a good deal was being done to encourage survival.

Scotland was in advance of England, and Edinburgh University was the leading centre of medical studies, though knowledge came also from Holland and Italy. In London individual doctors and surgeons trained pupils, and apprenticeship of this kind was a common road to medical practice. From Scotland to London came a number of famous doctors, William Smellie (1697–1763), and the brilliant brothers, William Hunter (1718–83) and John Hunter (1728–93). These men did much by their careful dissecting and teaching of anatomy, and John Hunter, famous for his writings and his museum of specimens, is regarded as the founder of scientific surgery. Not long before it had been part of 'the art and mystery of barbers'; he made it a regular profession.

Results were to be seen in a considerably reduced loss of life in childbirth and a less unscientific treatment of infectious diseases: attempts were made to get smallpox patients into isolation hospitals. This deadly scourge was then being treated by the direct-inoculation process, a mild form of the disease being injected into the human body, which then develops its own organisms of defence. Lady Mary Montagu, the famous letter-writer, had introduced this to England from Constantinople in 1718. At the very end of the century, however, Dr Edward Jenner, who was a pupil of John Hunter, discovered that inoculation with cowpox gives immunity from smallpox. This new process of vaccination proved so successful that within fifty years it had been made virtually compulsory—and deaths from smallpox had virtually disappeared. This is a small but dramatically successful example of the public services, which the crowding of population into towns made it both necessary and possible to provide.

3 Eighteenth-century people at work

So far we have been picturing where people lived before the great modern industries began—in the south more than in the north, in villages rather than in towns, and if in towns then in a kind of town which was altogether smaller and quieter than the industrial areas of today. London alone was already big by modern standards. We can also form some idea of the houses they lived in: the country seats of the nobility and gentry, from which they moved for the season to their town houses in the newly built streets of the West End of London or some local centre; the solid-looking homes of the middle class, scattered about the larger villages, but chiefly forming dignified streets in the middle parts of towns (and nowadays often converted into shops); the farmhouses and clustering cottages of the countryside; the lanes and courts and alleys where the poorer townspeople lived and worked in noisy crowds. But it is also important to picture what the men and women (and children) of those days did for their living, since without knowing this we cannot understand how modern Britain began.

Farming

The main occupation was agriculture, for Britain in those days produced all its principal foodstuffs, except sugar, and in fact not only grew enough corn for its own needs, but some to export to the Continent as well. Wheat and the darker rye were grown for bread; barley and hops for beer; and oats, the staple food of the Scots. The meat was also 'home-killed', though beef and mutton were luxuries which seldom reached a working-class family; their meat came in one form or another from the humble pig or else they made do with cheese, of which nearly every county then produced its own variety—Cheddar, Cheshire, double-Gloucester, Wensleydale, etc. All this gave work in the thousands of villages and even in the smaller market-towns, which often had farms entangled among their streets; but it was work that was not very efficiently organized.

The Plate of Rural Occupations is an eighteenth-century design, intended as decoration for the three beautifully written Whitsuntide

Plate of Rural Occupations. The text was written by Joan Stainton in 1778.

texts. It shows at the top a typical thatched farmhouse and busy farmyard; then the six main seasonal tasks familiar to the farm workers and, in the bottom right-hand corner, the water mill. The river turning the great mill-wheel to grind their corn would be the nearest thing these villagers knew to the power-driven machinery which frees us from their narrow life of toil.

New ideas, such as the sowing of seed in drills instead of broadcast or the growing of turnips for winter fodder, spread very slowly, because in the eastern counties and east Midlands, and in large patches elsewhere, the medieval three-field system still prevailed. That is to say, the farmer had his land scattered in small strips over three huge village fields, which were cultivated on a cropping plan agreed to by all the farmers, and his livestock grazed the common in company with all the livestock of the village. The north and west and the southern seaboard had more usually separate farms, such as we are familiar with today, but the soil being poorer for the most part, those areas could not usually afford to try out new ideas. Another difficulty was the badness of the roads. To save the cost of transport corn was usually ground locally—every stream in those days had its mill—and sold in the nearest market-town. The meat supply might, indeed, come from farther afield, but the Scottish and Welsh cattle made their way along the old drove-roads leading to London on their own hoofs.

The badness of the roads had another effect—it compelled every village to make for itself many of the things which are now bought as a

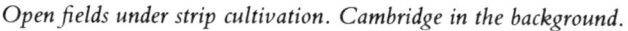

Open fields under strip cultivation. Cambridge in the background.

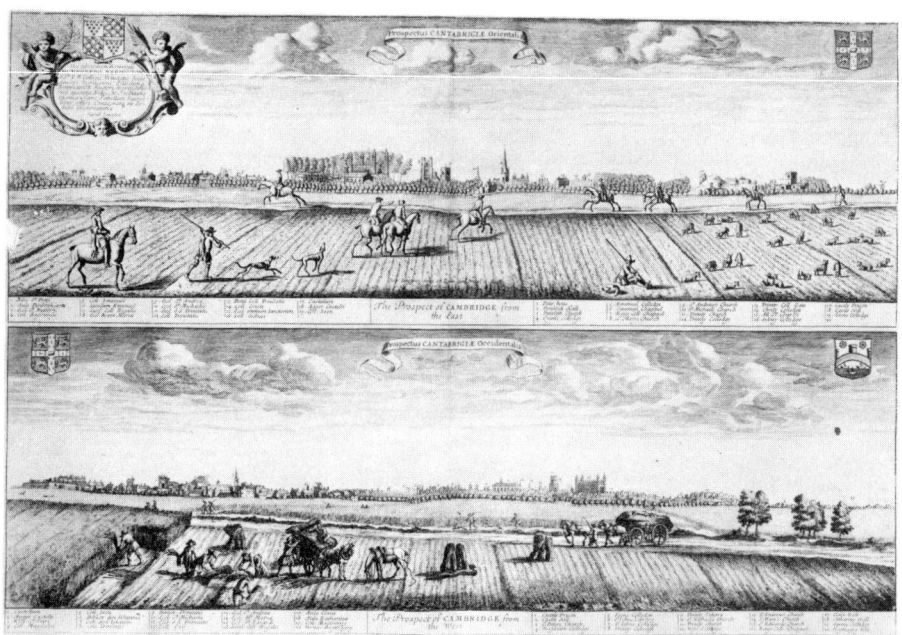

matter of course from shops in the towns or, if there is no town near, by mail-order purchase. In those days the village would be as likely to have its own carpenter and cabinet-maker, shoemaker and tailor, builder and harness-maker as it is now likely to have its post office or garage. Not only so, but a long list could be constructed of articles of everyday use which most village families made for themselves—bread, sausages, and all kinds of preserves, the simpler kinds of furniture, and the less stylish forms of clothing, such as smock frocks and flannel petticoats. And besides all this which the village produced for its own use, there was also the contribution its wool-spinners—this was the typical job for the unmarried woman or 'spinster'—made to the great national export of woollen cloth.

Domestic and other Industries

English cloth was sold all over Europe and as far afield as India, Africa, and America; it was also of course used in large quantities at home. Its manufacture for local use took place in almost every county where sheep were to be found, but the three main districts were East Anglia, the West of England, and the West Riding of Yorkshire. The last-named of these was famous for its small-scale organization, with master weavers whose wives spun their own wool, which the men wove on the loom, a piece at a time, and took for sale to the weekly market. But more commonly a rich merchant bought wool in large quantities, sent it round villages for cottagers to spin in their homes, collected the yarn, employed the weavers (who received so much for each piece they wove), paid for all the finishing processes, such as dyeing, and finally sold the cloth wholesale. In some parts of the country cottages can still be seen with a large, well-lighted room or attic which was built originally to hold the loom. Hogarth's famous drawing shows two silk looms—indeed, the Spitalfields address can be seen on the quart pot which the Idle Apprentice keeps handy, as his employer has no doubt just observed; but the wool-weaver's equipment was very similar. The spinning-wheel, on the other hand, was much smaller and stood in the corner of the cottage kitchen during the rare hours when it was not in use.

But perhaps the most important things to notice, because of their bearings on later developments, are these. The cloth trade was a great source of wealth, making eighteenth-century England wealthier than many of her neighbours. It was a great source of employment, enabling women to earn money in their own homes by spinning, men to combine a smallholding with work at the loom, and even giving a job to reluctant children of four—the age at which they might be set to

The first of twelve Plates in which Hogarth contrasted the careers of Industry and Idleness, personified by the two apprentices of a Spitalfields silk weaver. The series was published on 30 September 1747; the originals were bought by Horace Walpole, the collector and letter-writer referred to above (p. 7).

clean wool by treading it barefoot in a tub. It was also one source of experiment in more modern methods of industrial organization, for sometimes a big employer had a weaving-shed full of weavers working for him in what were almost factory conditions.

There were some industries, less important than the textile manufactures (which included silk and linen and a little cotton as well as the great traditional trade in woollen cloth), where the nature of the work required a large workplace with a large number of workers. Such were the mines—of Cornish tin, Durham coal, and iron ore which was mined or worked in half the counties of England. They provided the material for the metal manufactures of Birmingham, Sheffield and elsewhere, in which people had found another reason to organize the work on a fairly large scale, namely the advantage of specialization.

A very famous writer on trade, Adam Smith, mentions this in 1776 in his book *The Wealth of Nations*, describing what had then been common for a generation or more. He writes about a pin factory—with the same sort of admiring enthusiasm that a twentieth-century observer might experience on seeing a Ford car assembled by a series of simple hand-turns on a moving conveyor belt. 'One man (he writes) draws out the wire, another straightens it, a third cuts it, a fourth points it, a fifth grinds it at the top for receiving the head; to make the head requires two or three distinct operations; to put it on is a peculiar business, to whiten the pin is another; it is even a trade by itself to put them into the paper.' Indeed he had actually seen a factory in which, by means of such organized division of labour, ten persons could make 'upwards of forty-eight thousand pins in a day', though working with quite primitive equipment. Had they worked independently, he points out, 'they certainly could not each of them have made twenty, perhaps not one pin in a day.'

Local Trade and Transport

So much for the bigger industries. But for the most part the boy who was apprenticed to a trade or handicraft in those days would be serving a small master who worked with his own hands, in a shop or workplace attached to his master's home, and most probably in what we should call a very small town. What would the trades of such a place be? There might be some luxury trades, which helped with the furnishing and equipment of the mansions of the nobility and gentry—cabinet-makers or carriage-builders, upholsterers, bookbinders, saddlers, etc. There would also be many small firms which made things in a cheaper way for humbler homes. But chiefly the average town would live by the business of shop-keeping in the modern sense, selling the sugar and tea which were the imported luxuries now in demand by all classes of the population, and everything else which the surrounding villages did not produce in their own fields and gardens. The shops were no doubt busiest on the weekly market day, when the country people came in with their eggs and fowls and butter and went away with their haberdashery or groceries. In a few favoured localities there was also a great annual fair, when people came great distances to buy and sell on the fairground—and doubtless to visit the shops as well.

But we must not paint too rosy a picture. If we were carried back two hundred years to see our ancestors, what would strike us most would be the terrible isolation of their lives. A good many villagers never saw a town at all. In town and country alike it was difficult for the poor to move in search of work from the parish in which they were born, because the dreaded Settlement Law (1662) entitled the authorities to send them back again for fear they should some day ask for poor relief in the new parish. And all trade and travel was handicapped by the shocking state of the roads, already mentioned. Parson Woodforde, for example, thought it a wonderful thing when (in 1774) he managed to travel from Oxford to Somerset, 'near 100 miles', in one day: it had taken him from 5.30 a.m. to 8 p.m. and the cost (by post-chaise) was nearly a shilling a mile. The ill-constructed road-surfaces were churned into thick mud by the four-horsed coaches which linked up the growing centres of population (much as the motor-coach lines do today but with markedly different time schedules); and by the herds of cattle; and by the commercial travellers on horseback and the gentry in their carriages; and again through the transport of heavy goods (corn, pottery, textiles, coal, metal-work) in rumbling covered wagons or by strings of heavily laden pack-horses picking their way in a single file among the pot-holes, splashing through the puddles, and slithering along the ruts.

Thus without new ideas in transport and communications modern Britain could never have come into existence. In the early eighteenth century a very few of the roads began to be improved by the first Turnpike Trusts, which (as we shall see in a later chapter) relaid a stretch of road and charged users a toll to pay for it. But this was only just beginning, and for heavy goods like coal and timber, bricks and building-stone it remained true, as in earlier centuries, that they could be moved only by the coastal shipping routes and up and down the rivers. That is why towns of any importance were almost invariably situated within easy reach of harbour or river bank—like Bristol on its Avon, Norwich on the Wensum, and all the towns strung along Thames, Severn, and Trent. But the river which flows slowly enough to be navigable easily silts up. Far more important, therefore, than the first turnpikes were the 'new cuts' and the deepening and widening of old river beds, on which since about 1700 the more enterprising towns had been spending much money. These improved river channels were called 'inland navigations', the men who dug them 'inland navigators'; with the introduction of this name, familiar in its shortened form of 'navvy', we are approaching those tremendous labours of con-struction and reconstruction which since about 1760 have changed the face of Britain in achieving the Industrial Revolution.[1]

There are, of course, other aspects of life in eighteenth-century Britain. The religious world of John Wesley, for example—he travelled over 200 000 miles during some fifty years, preaching his own evangelical Christianity and influencing the new industrial workers with a new puritanism. Then there was the London literary world of Dr Johnson, intellectual John Bull and compiler of the famous dictionary, who was immortalized by Boswell. But the con-cern of this book is largely with economic and social history, and at this point we must concentrate on the Industrial Revolution.

[1] Crabbe's description of Aldeburgh, where navigations were not improved, gives the social atmosphere of towns and trade before the 'coming of the machine' (Appendix I, No. 2).

THE GREAT CHANGES: THE IMPACT OF NEW MACHINERY

4 What was the Industrial Revolution? A brief survey

The name 'Industrial Revolution' came into popular use in the 1880s, to describe the transformation of industry which had been changing the face of the country for a century or more. More gradual changes had of course been effected in all earlier generations, ever since men first began to cut down trees, drain swamps, plough fields, and build houses. But the speed of change was now revolutionary, as the impact of new machinery enabled towns and sprawling suburbs; factories, mines, and workshops; canals, docks, railways, trunk roads, and finally airfields—all in combination to create the Britain of today.

Population Changes

To put it another way, the small island which 200 years ago provided for something like 8 million inhabitants now provides for 54 million.[1] Moreover, the provision was such that the very poor were then the great majority of the people, whereas now they are a dwindling minority. The vast and rapid increase in population is in itself one of the most astonishing features of the Industrial Revolution; the increase

[1] For detailed figures, see Appendix II, Table 1.

in population was partly the result of industrial changes and at the same time the cause. If we consider western Europe as a whole, up to the seventeenth and eighteenth centuries its people had been thinly spread out and had increased but slowly, so far as we can tell. Agriculture, relying on primitive methods, could not support large numbers. When crops failed, there would be starvation for some and, more widely, under-nourishment. Under-nourishment brought physical weakness and encouraged disease. Death from starvation, plague and other diseases reduced the number of marriages and hence the number of children born, and also reduced the number of children who would grow up to become parents. War also was an ever-recurrent means of reducing population. Thus the death-rate tended to be very high, and this checked the growth of population. But with improved methods of agricultural production and industry, with longer periods of peace, and with the development of medical services, a great change set in.

The factors making for an increase in population applied, probably more strongly than elsewhere, in Britain. Internal peace and order was a basic condition; with improvements in agriculture and industry and the increase in scientific and medical knowledge the other conditions became increasingly effective. Eighteenth-century Britain took no census, but there appears to have been an increase in the birth-rate from about 1710 onwards, which reached its climax at about the year 1790. With the breakdown of apprenticeship and the demand for workers in new industries such as cotton and iron, men, and in some cases women, began to marry younger, and more children were born.

But what was probably more important than the increase in the birth-rate was the fall in the death-rate, which had always been high, especially among infants and children. Now infant mortality was reduced, and more mothers were saved—and lived longer to have yet more children. Thus, later on, the large family came to be characteristic of Victorian times: in fact, the rate of growth of our population did not begin to slacken until late in the 1870s.

How was the fall in the death-rate brought about? It was due to a number of causes working together. The growth of medical knowledge, the training of doctors, and a more highly skilled care for women in childbirth began to take effect in the eighteenth century, as a sequel to the two centuries in which the ideas of the Renaissance had slowly developed a spirit of scientific inquiry. Humanitarianism also played a part, not only through the establishment of hospitals, already mentioned, but through philanthropic work of many kinds. The Foundling Hospital was opened in London in 1745 through the efforts of Captain Thomas Coram, and saved the lives of thousands of deserted children. The work on behalf of children was continued by Jonas Hanway, who also exposed the appalling conditions and high mortality rate in prisons. The cause of the prisoners in turn was taken up by John Howard (1726–90), who from the study of gaol fever went on to consider how contagious diseases in general might be prevented. This great English philanthropist and citizen of the world was in fact touring the military hospitals of Russia when his examination of a case of camp fever brought him to a distant grave. It is noteworthy that his successor, the famous Quakeress Elizabeth Fry (1780–1845), likewise interested herself in hospital as well as prison conditions.

There were other improvements, in town and country, less spectacular than the improvements which the nineteenth century was to bring—and therefore easily overlooked—which helped to make the people of eighteenth-century Britain longer-lived than their predecessors. The diet of country people above the level of the labourer was probably more nourishing, with wheaten bread replacing a poor quality mixture of barley and rye, more use of vegetables, and—through the introduction of root crops—a more plentiful supply of meat. The towns, which seem to us to have been so pestilential and chaotic, were at any rate on the upgrade at the end of the century, when Parliament passed over 200 Improvement Acts in fifteen years, giving Improvement Commissioners in particular towns legal powers of drainage, street-cleaning, and so forth. At the same time cheap cotton clothing, which could be more easily washed than wool, gave a new impetus to the growth—disgustingly slow in all classes of society—of modern standards of personal cleanliness. Disease was still rampant, but by the end of the century workers in regular employment were the main supporters of more than 5000 local Friendly Societies, obtaining benefits in times of sickness or infirmity. Lastly, we may suppose that a more generous administration of poor relief, which was to make the name of Speenhamland (where it originated in 1795) later notorious, must have helped to keep more poor people alive.

Thus the population of Britain increased. How were the new mouths to be filled and the new hands employed? The adaptable Briton, already eager in pursuit of trade, achieved—or perhaps we should say stumbled upon—the solution which we call the Industrial Revolution. New techniques gave a livelihood to vastly increased numbers of people, first in this country and later elsewhere. For the Industrial Revolution which began in Britain about 1760 spread abroad into foreign countries, slowly at first but with increasing speed, so that today there is scarcely a nation in the world left unaffected by it. It has even been claimed by a modern writer that 'The positive achievements of human ingenuity in the past 150 years overshadow all the previous achievements of mankind since the beginning of the Stone Age 15 000 years ago.'[1]

Changes in World Trade

Until the beginning of the nineteenth century, the industrial history of the vast majority of mankind was largely the record of the way in which they kept their animals, grew their crops, and sheltered their homes. Most of the peoples of the world got their food, clothing and housing material by the same simple means as their ancestors had done from time immemorial. In the more civilized communities some part of the population might live in large towns, but even they relied for food and the raw materials of industry upon the work of countrymen in neighbouring villages and farms. Water-mills and windmills were the most conspicuous, and often the most complicated, machines in common use.

During the nineteenth century—with the coming of the all-powerful machine, as we know it—all this was changed. Today, far fewer men and women live under the simple conditions of earlier generations. Instead, many live in factory towns, and they draw their food and the raw materials of industry not from their immediate neighbourhood but from all parts of the world. Historians describe this vast and gradual social and industrial change as the 'Industrial Revolution'. The word 'revolution' is no exaggeration, for social, political and industrial life is utterly different from what it was before the Industrial Revolution developed. The traditional emblem for Britain was John Bull, the corpulent and prosperous farmer shown in cartoons, but in the nineteenth century the emblem ought really to have been changed to John Bull and Co., since it was no longer the farm but the industrial firm which was typical of our new position as the workshop of the world.

Before the Industrial Revolution, moreover, world trade—that is, the exports and imports of every country—was both smaller in amount and different in its contents. Britain, as we have seen, exported cloth and hardware, but also corn; the bulk of the world's trade, however, was in luxury goods. These did not take up much space in the holds of ships which we should call tiny—spices and silks, coffee, tobacco and tea. Sugar, for which Europe then had no satisfactory home-produced substitute, was the only big food import. The Industrial Revolution changed all this. Raw materials for industry, such as cotton, jute, rubber, skins, and metals, were brought across the world

---

[1] Professor Henry Hamilton, *History of the Homeland* (1947), p. 19.

Sheffield, about 1840.

to the manufacturing countries; so were foodstuffs—wheat and meat, oilseeds and fruit from the tropics, and eventually even dairy produce. Manufactures were sent in return, with the result that almost the whole world became joined together by a network of steamship routes and railway lines, and finally by airways, carrying the goods which distant countries now found it advantageous to buy from one another.

Changes in the Economy of Britain

If the whole world has been reorganized on a basis of trade, so also the industrial map of Britain has been almost completely transformed. Older industrial areas, such as Birmingham and Sheffield, expanded, whilst the many new industrial areas, such as the Lancashire cotton towns, Clydeside and Belfast with their shipyards, the South Wales coal-field, and the factory districts of outer London, gave employment to millions of men and women. In most cases the original reason for this density of population was the nearness of cheap supplies of coal and a convenient situation for transport. Early in the Revolution, canals were cut in order to distribute the raw materials and products of

industry cheaply. Even more important changes came with the invention of the steam locomotive and the building of the great railway
systems. These connected the factory towns with the docks at the
greater ports, and thus made the distribution of food and raw materials
imported into our country from overseas still easier and cheaper.

Following the example of Britain—where the Industrial Revolution
began—other nations imported machines, built railway lines, and
established steamship services, so that in the end they also became fully
industrialized. But partly because, in Britain, coal and iron-ore were
found near to each other and could be cheaply mined, and partly
because British inventors were the first to perfect the railway locomotive, Britain was fifty years ahead of her future competitors in applying machine power to manufacture and transport. And thus it was
British engineers and workmen who started the Industrial Revolution
in many parts of the world, and Britain usually lent the money with
which foreigners bought the equipment to launch their industries. But
during the first half of the Industrial Revolution, Great Britain was
almost alone in the development of world trade, and this in turn meant
that a large proportion of world trade was carried in British ships.

In the period 1821–1911 Britain was continuously on the Gold
Standard, and retail prices in those tranquil days never differed by
more than 20 per cent from the level they reached at mid-century. It is
therefore possible to see how the rise in population compares with the
estimated rise in national income or gross national product (GNP).
After ninety years the United Kingdom—which then included the
whole of Ireland with its declining but impoverished population—had
more than twice as many inhabitants as before, but *on an average* they
were now twice as well off.

Thus for a period of about a century the world situation resulting
from the Industrial Revolution suited perfectly the interests of our
island people. We had the coal, the inventions, and the shipping. We
took the lead, as farmers and planters, merchants and traders,
engineers and industrial experts, in developing new countries overseas. As a result an endless stream of raw materials and foodstuffs was
poured into the island, and the whole world bought our manufactures
at prices which were advantageous to us, because we were then the
principal large-scale suppliers of the cotton goods and hardware, coal
and machinery which the rest of the world needed. Even the industries
slowly developing in other countries added to our wealth, since a good
rate of interest was paid on the capital which British investors lent to
help them buy the machines to start with. The meat from Argentina,
for instance, was bought with dividends on Argentinian railways
which had been built by British capital.

Competition had become serious by 1880, but it is chiefly the two World Wars which have speeded up the process of change and enabled those younger rivals, such as the Americans, who were bound to outstrip us some day (as youth always must overtake age), to outdo us as a manufacturing nation with a rapidity and completeness which seem decisive. Thus the Industrial Revolution has rather suddenly ceased to appear as a special gift of Providence to the British people. But that is no reason why we should neglect the drama of the great changes which introduce us to modern Britain. In Act I a number of inventions and discoveries increase the output of our workers as though by magic. In Act II the people of the island find that as a consequence a rapidly expanding population can be maintained, with the help of imported food, at a slowly improving standard of life. In Act III our magic secret *and* our desire for an improving standard of life are both acquired by other countries, which are therefore less eager to buy our industrial output or to sell us their food. The very size and solidity of our great towns, of which we have been justly proud, begins to be a cause of anxiety. In Act IV—but that is the part of the play which the readers of this book must themselves help to devise and to perform.

5 How the great changes came: trade and empire

We may now consider in more detail why the great changes, which (as we have seen) spelt wealth and growth of population and world leadership, came first to our small island and nowhere else. One great advantage which Britain enjoyed over other countries was the long-established internal peace. When George III became king in 1760—which is about the time when the changes in industry gathered enough speed for us to speak of a 'revolution'—England at least had lived without serious disturbance for exactly a century, while other nations had been torn and distracted by foreign invasion and civil war. There had been several great crises, such as the Revolution of 1688 and the change of dynasty in 1714, but Sedgemoor (1685) and Preston (1715) were the only battles fought on English soil and the march of Prince Charles Edward to Derby in the Jacobite rebellion known as the '45 was the only later occasion when the peace of London and the south-east was even seriously threatened. The Scottish record was rather different, what with the struggles of the Covenanters in the reign of Charles II and the devotion of the Highlanders to the Jacobite cause, but the work of pacifying the Highlands had been begun with the building of the first main roads and bridges by Marshal Wade's soldiers in 1726–37 and completed by the crushing of the clans on Culloden Moor in 1746. The growth of Glasgow and Edinburgh shows that the fear of the Highlanders, who throughout Scottish history had raided the Lowlands for plunder, was already disappearing.

Peace encouraged the growth of trade, and if the trade of our towns and villages was badly hampered (as we know it was) by the condition of the roads, it was helped by the fact that there were no internal customs barriers. In other countries, like France, town was separated from town and province from province by the charges which had to be paid for bringing goods of any kind across the boundary between two areas, whereas in this respect all parts of England, Wales and Scotland

Glasgow from the north-east, 1760.

were a single unit. The numerous spires and towers shown in our view of eighteenth-century Glasgow are evidence of its rapidly growing prosperity; the state of the road in the foreground reminds us that the prosperity was not due to better communications but to the fact that, under the Act of Union of 1707, the customs barrier and all trade restrictions as between England and Scotland had been finally overthrown.

When Daniel Defoe, the author of *Robinson Crusoe*, travelled through Britain early in the century he was much impressed by the evidence of increased trade, the rapid growth of some of the towns, and the general prosperity of the country. It is all set down in his book, *A Tour through the Whole Island of Great Britain*. Defoe noticed that 'the business of export and import in the Port of London is prodigiously increased'. It had become a centre for the collection and distribution of colonial products, and it was also our chief corn market. He saw that corn came to London from the corn-growing districts of East Anglia and the south-eastern counties, some of it for export to European markets; other thriving ports included Newcastle with its coal trade, and Hull trading with the Baltic.

Besides 'the business of export and import', internal trade also flourished in the eighteenth century, as the growth of towns provided new markets. Defoe has much to say regarding the transport of food: for instance, about the commotion made by the flocks of 500 or even 1000 geese which he met on the road to London, and the quaint sight of other poultry sent to town in four-storey wagons, with the driver sitting on the roof. More important, Defoe relates that 'it took thirteen counties to dress the grocer's wife', and that travelling merchants were accustomed 'to go all over England with droves of pack-horses and to call at the fairs and market towns over the whole land'.

The Chartered Companies

Alongside this growth of our internal trade, there had been a big increase in overseas trade by the early part of the eighteenth century, as a result of colonial expansion and the work of the Chartered Companies. These were trading companies, holding charters from the Crown which gave them special privileges as the only British subjects allowed to trade in certain areas. The greatest was the East India Company, founded in 1600 at the close of Elizabeth I's reign, which traded both with India itself and also with China and Persia. From China the Company began in 1660 to bring tea to England, and also 'china' or cups and saucers of fine porcelain. From India came spices, perfumes, precious stones, silks and indigo for dyeing. Cotton goods—muslins, calicoes and chintzes—were also brought to England by the East India Company; but this particular import roused the jealousy of the English woollen workers and was therefore made illegal. The sailing ships belonging to the Company, and known as East-Indiamen, with their huge holds were the largest merchant vessels afloat; and they had a dock to themselves at Blackwall on the Thames. The Company gradually developed settlements in India and employed a small force of soldiers, and they protected their property by fortifying the chief settlements, at Bombay, Madras and Calcutta. The French also had interests in India, and there was great rivalry between them and the British.

Of other early Chartered Companies the most important were the Merchant Venturers, who used to have the sole right of selling English cloth in Germany and the Netherlands. Then there was the Levant or Turkey Company which traded with the Near East and the Mediterranean countries, bringing wines and fruits to England, and finding a market for English cloth and wool as well as for sugar and tobacco from our West Indian colonies. Another company, the Eastland, tried to capture the trade of the Baltic, formerly monopolized by the Hansa—the German League of Merchants—which had had its depot in London (the Steelyard) until the reign of Elizabeth I. West African trade was in the hands of the Royal Africa Company, founded in Charles II's reign; it was largely a trade across the Atlantic in slaves. The Hudson's Bay Company was also founded in Charles II's reign, under the presidency of his cousin Prince Rupert. It was favoured by the government because it was a direct rival to the enterprises of the French, who at that time held Quebec. The English had the advantage of plentiful shipping, and were able to use Hudson Strait and Bay, saving them a long overland route. The Company was mainly engaged in the fur trade, and acquired rights over a huge extent of land. These were retained until 1869 and then sold to the Canadian Government; but the Company still continued as a trading corporation and carries on its business at the present day.

A London dockyard scene in the eighteenth century—a painting by Samuel Scott.

Yet another chartered company was founded in 1710 to develop the commercial advantages which were being gained by our victories in the War of the Spanish Succession. This South Sea Company received the monopoly of trade along the Atlantic coast of South America, and in the Pacific Ocean or South Sea (though in fact it never did trade there). In George I's reign, the Company offered, in return for further privileges, to take over the National Debt, then £51 million. The dazzling promises of enormous profits led to a rush for shares in the Company, and the price of its stock rose to fantastic heights, £100 shares changing hands at £1060. But the enthusiasm for the shares collapsed as quickly as it had risen; the 'South Sea Bubble', as it was called, burst; and confidence in trading companies was badly shaken. The government took back the burden of the National Debt, and although the Company went on trading for another 100 years, its successes were small.

Generally speaking, it was felt by this time that the companies had completed the pioneer work of opening-up new lands to British trade, and from 1688 onwards Parliament was inclined to encourage 'interlopers', the name given to merchants who tried to trade in the territory set apart for a company to which they did not belong. It was claimed that this kind of 'free trade' was often more profitable and varied than what the Company's regulations permitted. In the end only the East India Company and, on a much smaller scale, the Hudson Bay Company were able to hold on to their monopolies, the former up to 1813, the latter to 1869. We may now turn to examine another factor which contributed to the increase of British trade, namely the growth and development of our colonial empire.

Colonies and Colonial Trade

Newfoundland, England's oldest colony, was claimed by Cabot in 1497, but was for centuries the seasonal resort of the men who fished the great cod banks rather than a place of settlement. The first attempt to colonize Virginia in the reign of Elizabeth I, associated with the great Sir Walter Raleigh, produced nothing lasting except the name, given in honour of the Queen. It was not until 1607 that Virginia was established as the earliest permanent settlement under our flag, the leader of the venture being Captain John Smith, whose life was saved by the Red Indian princess, Pocahontas. Other bands of colonists (such as the Pilgrim Fathers in 1620) also settled on the American seaboard, and yet others in Barbados (which had the oldest colonial parliament) and the Bahamas and Bermuda. Cromwell's war with Spain brought the important island of Jamaica into the Empire, and the Treaty of

Utrecht in 1713, at the end of the long wars against Louis XIV of France, marks the moment when Britain became at last a leading colonial power.

During the eighteenth century colonial trade was continually expanding as the resources of the colonies and their population increased. At first the colonies were valued mainly as sources of supply for goods not obtainable at home, but they became more and more important also as markets for British manufactures. In the eyes of our merchants, the most valuable colonies were the islands of the West Indies and the two neighbouring American mainland colonies of Virginia and Carolina. As these lay in tropical or sub-tropical regions, they could supply the homeland with increasing quantities of sugar, tobacco, rice and cotton, while the colonists, waxing prosperous, bought greater quantities of our woollen and (later) cotton goods, iron goods and pottery. A large number of slaves were annually transported, under shocking conditions, by British slave-traders from West Africa to the West Indian islands and also to the southern mainland colonies, where the slaves were employed on the plantations.

The exports of fish, timber and corn from the northern American or New England colonies might be shipped to any market unless they were required as stores for the Navy; but trade with the southern colonies and the West Indian islands was closely guarded. Certain goods, known as 'enumerated commodities', including tobacco, sugar and dyes, had to be sold in Britain and nowhere else; re-exportation to the Continent of what had been brought from our colonies was one of the most profitable trades of all for the merchants of London and other ports, who handled it. Moreover, our old Navigation Laws of the mercantile age—before the days of free trade—allowed goods of colonial origin to be carried only in British or colonial ships, and ship-owners could be compelled to pay forfeits if they did not carry their cargoes to such places as were approved by the government.

During the middle of the eighteenth century England and France were again at war (the Seven Years War). Clive's victory at Plassey in 1757 and Coote's victory at Wandewash in 1760 destroyed the French power in India. General Wolfe's capture of Quebec in 1759 destroyed French power in North America, and by the Treaty of Paris in 1763 Britain gained the whole of Canada and also further advantages in West Africa and the West Indies. Thus the Empire reached a new stage of importance: it included eastern Canada and the whole Atlantic seaboard of North America as far as Florida; in India, the control of Bengal and other smaller possessions; many West Indian islands; slave centres in West Africa; and the Mediterranean key-points of Gibraltar and Minorca.

Growth of Liverpool

The growth of the port of Liverpool is a remarkable instance of the development of overseas trade in the eighteenth century. In 1700, the population of Liverpool was only 5000; by 1773, it had risen to 35 000; by 1801, to 82 000. At first the trade of Liverpool was mainly with Ireland; but the opening-up of trade with the West Indies and the North American colonies, together with the development of the cotton industry in Lancashire, gave a great impetus to the growth of the town; and before it became the chief cotton port, it was already the greatest slave-trading port in Europe. Bristol, which shared prominently in the slave trade and had been for centuries the distributing and collecting centre in the West of England, got great profit from sugar and tobacco, but as the eighteenth century went on it was rapidly being overhauled by Glasgow.

To sum up, in the period 1720–60 British exports more than doubled in value; imports nearly doubled; and it seems safe to suppose that internal trade must have increased equally fast. But population during the same period, though growing, grew much less rapidly. Therefore the increase of trade meant that there was more work waiting to be done than there were workers available to do it. Therefore labour-saving inventions—that is, the sort of inventions which made the Industrial Revolution—were urgently needed and anyone with a practical idea of this kind would be encouraged to experiment. Moreover, the fact that many of our existing exports, such as woollen cloth, were not luxury goods but things which all the world wanted, safeguarded the future. For, as Britain developed her inventions, more rapidly expanding trade might be found to support a more rapidly expanding population.

6 How the great changes came: capital and banking

One of the main reasons why the great change-over to machine industry came first in Britain rather than in any other country was because there was more capital saved up in Britain. Without the help of capital new ideas could never have been developed on a commercial basis. The idea of an invention by itself achieves nothing unless there is the money available to pay for experiments, raw material, buildings, and workers' wages in the long period before the new thing can be sold in large enough quantities to be really profitable. In addition, the best chance of rapidly increasing sales is in a country where it is easy to make payments. In Britain this could already be done by means of notes or bills or even cheques instead of paying in gold and silver coins, which are heavy to carry about and tempting to thieves.

England, as we have seen, by comparison with other lands had for a long time been a very safe place, where it was worthwhile to save for the future and where thrifty people could lend their savings and earn interest on them without being afraid that they would lose it all in invasion or civil war. Hence the important part played by banks, in which savings were deposited for safety and convenience and to earn some interest; the banks in turn lent out the deposits to businesses which could not develop without capital and would readily pay high interest for it.

In the Middle Ages Christians were officially discouraged from lending money at interest, so this was a business largely confined to the Jews. Later on, when the Italians were the chief traders in all Europe, they provided our first banks and gave its name to Lombard Street, which is still at the centre of London's banking system. Then for a time the goldsmiths looked after people's money for them, as they had safes for their gold. Finally, towards the end of the seventeenth century, the most important landmark in our banking history was reached.

The Threadneedle Street frontage of the Bank of England in 1797. The west wing, in the foreground, was built after the Gordon Riots (1780) on the site of a church overlooking the Bank; this was pulled down as a precaution against its use by future rioters.

The Bank of England

William III was in desperate need of money for his wars against Louis XIV of France—for his army fighting in the Netherlands and for the upkeep of the Channel Fleet. His ministers advised him to raise a loan of £1 200 000—this was virtually the beginning of the modern National Debt. But only twenty years earlier there had been an occasion when the King refused to pay interest due on the money he had borrowed, so the public were not eager to lend, and it was realized that some special attraction must be offered in order to obtain the money. In addition to receiving 8 per cent interest, the lenders of the money were to be made by law into a joint-stock company which had the privilege of being sole bankers to the government. The bait was successful, and the whole amount was subscribed within eleven days, 21 June–2 July 1694. A few years later (1709) this 'Bank of England', as it was called, was given a further privilege. In return for a reduction in the rate of interest it charged, and the making of a fresh loan, it came to be the only joint-stock bank allowed to issue banknotes in England and Wales. Scottish joint-stock banks could issue their own notes (as they still do); so could private banks in England, but these were smaller concerns, backed usually by the wealth of a single family, and thus more liable to go bankrupt, in which case their notes would suddenly become worthless. The capital of a 'joint stock', on the other hand, might be subscribed from all over the country and such a bank would have considerable resources.

Thus the Bank of England was given a position of superiority, and in the eighteenth century was doing three things of great importance for the growth of trade. The Bank accumulated wealth, which people deposited there instead of hoarding their money, etc., as before, because the Bank was felt to be safe; it lent out these deposits to big trading organizations like the East India Company, as well as to the government; and its notes (in multiples of £10) were available to the smaller banks and to private individuals as a safe and easy means of keeping and paying out money. In 1734 the first of the present buildings was opened on the present site; the buildings have grown larger in the course of 200 years, but their appearance still suggests security rather than show, and dignity rather than the opulence which we might expect in one of the premier banking institutions of the world.

The eighteenth century also witnessed the growth of two other methods of solving the problem, so important for the growth of trade, of paying money without the transfer of coins or bullion from place to place. Private banks, of which the first was set up by a Bristol soap-dealer in 1716, spread so fast in the second half of the century that 230 could be listed in 1797; they made use mainly of Bills of Exchange. These promises to pay were sent from one district to another, and most often from the provinces to London; they were generally payable in three months, cash being obtainable sooner at a discount; and it was usually possible to cancel out Bills payable *from* a certain district against Bills for a similar amount payable *to* that district. Payment by cheque, on the other hand, which became very common after about 1850, developed slowly. The cheque began in the days of the goldsmith bankers, as a letter telling the banker to pay a named sum out of the writer's account; but it was not until 1770 that the number of cheques used in London was big enough to start a Clearing House system. If two cheques required the transfer of sums from an account in Bank A to an account in Bank B and vice versa, it was obviously convenient for the banks concerned to arrange to transfer no more than the difference between the amounts named in the two cheques: the bank clerks originally met to 'clear' all such transactions at a public-house in Lombard Street, already mentioned—close to the Bank of England, from which modern banks still draw the differences for transfer at their regular daily clearances.

Dividend Day at the Bank—a Victorian painter portrays a busy scene at the Bank of England.

The facilities we have described grew up in the eighteenth century to make easier the business of payment, which became more complicated with the growth of trade, abroad as well as at home. Abroad, there was the difficulty that no nation parted lightly with any of its stock of gold. But the high reputation of the Bank of England and the general stability of the country also made easier the business of payment in overseas commerce, for Bills of Exchange on London now began to take the place of Bills on Amsterdam, which was the traditional centre of European finance (and still held a part of our National Debt). But a still more important requirement for the development of British industry was the provision of capital.

Business Capital

It is probably true to say that the personal savings of the owner, his family, and friends were the main source from which businesses got the means to pay for buildings, machinery, raw material, and the wages of work-people in anticipation of the profits that some new enterprise would eventually earn for them. But the early banks also played a part, by collecting people's savings, on which the bank undertook to pay interest, and then lending those savings—of course at a higher rate of interest—along with the bank's own 'credit', to any new venture of which the bank approved. For example, we know that money borrowed from the banks helped to build the first canal, paid for the earliest factory spinning-machines, and kept the pioneer steam-engine at work.

Cash for wages was a special problem in this period. The coinage, based originally on the silver penny, which was 1/240th of a pound weight of silver, had been renewed in 1696, but there was a chronic shortage of small change. Farm labourers had been paid partly in kind and their numbers in any one place were small, but factory workers and others expected to be paid in cash, however numerous they might be. The shortage of coin became so great that some large employers struck token coins of their own, which circulated locally and were exchanged for proper money if and when it became available. This difficulty over cash led to the prevalence of the Truck system. A 'truck shop' was an establishment owned by the employer, where the employees were obliged to exchange their due wages for food or other things which they might or might not want, at prices which were often exorbitant. In 1701, a Truck Act was passed for the textile and iron industries, expressly forbidding the payment of wages in 'clothes, victuals or commodities'. Other laws followed, including a General Truck Act in 1831; but something of the system survived, though

Token money made during the period of great financial stringency, 1797–8 (see p. 97).

denounced by a Royal Commission in 1871–2, until the trade unions became really powerful. There were, of course, some industrial undertakings situated in very lonely places where the employer's shop was a necessity, but in the main 'truck' provided a long-standing grievance for the workers.

The Gold Standard

Meanwhile in 1819, after the Napoleonic Wars, during which the pound sterling for a time lost half its value, Britain adopted the Gold Standard; that is to say, the currency was based entirely on gold, and silver ceased to be legal tender for sums over forty shillings. In 1817, a new coinage was issued, and the twenty-shilling sovereign replaced the twenty-one-shilling guinea. The Bank Charter Act of 1844 forbade newly founded banks to issue notes, and ordered the Bank of England to stock bullion of equal value to any increase in its note issue, so that it could always pay gold in exchange for banknotes on demand. Up to 1914, in spite of crises and trade depressions, the British organization of capital and banking worked with marvellous smoothness. Not only did we finance the development of our own industries, but loans from Britain financed the early stages of similar industrial developments in many other parts of the world.

At the present time, the Bank of England (nationalized in 1946) still does the banking business of the government and normally holds the reserve funds of the other British banks, such as Barclays, Lloyds, the Midland and the National Westminster. Each of the four big banking companies just named is the result of the union of many smaller banks, and they also have offices or agencies overseas in the Commonwealth and in some foreign countries. But there are also a number of small banks still surviving, some of which (such as the Merchant Banks) have specialized in certain kinds of banking. The key part which the banks and the accumulation of the capital still play in industrial development today is a reminder of their important function when large-scale industry was first developed. By being able and ready, against sound security, to lend large sums of money, banks have enabled businessmen to borrow capital for new and increased production, backing their judgment, sharing their risk, and thereby in the long run assisting the growth of the national wealth and welfare.

7 The revolution in textiles

In 1760 Britain had four textile industries which wove four different materials—wool, silk, linen, and cotton. Wool was so much the largest industry of the four and had played such a great part in building up our national wealth that Daniel Defoe referred to it again and again as he visited the different districts in his famous *Tour through the Whole Island*. Thus he describes the prosperity of the Norwich 'stuff-weaving trade by which so many thousands of families are maintained'. He also states that in 1724 'there was not in all the eastern or middle part of Norfolk any hand unemployed if they would work; and that the very children after four or five years of age could every one earn their own bread'. The West Riding of Yorkshire is described by Defoe as a 'noble scene of industry and application'. In one of the larger establishments Defoe saw 'a house full of lusty fellows, some at the dye-vat, some dressing the cloths, some at the loom ... all hard at work'. In the smaller cottages, he saw the women and children all busy carding and spinning. He also visited the great cloth market at Leeds. Then there were the West of England weavers, who produced serges and other cloth, especially broad cloth. Exeter had a serge market to which came the produce of the looms of Tiverton, Crediton, Ashburton, and the other towns. Defoe states that the serges sold at a single market were worth from £60 000 to £100 000.

An attempt to establish a woollen industry in northern Ireland during the seventeenth (or Stuart) century was indignantly opposed by the English cloth-workers, and an Irish linen industry was set up instead. After a slow start this became the staple trade of Belfast and Londonderry. But the manufacture of cotton goods, of which Britain was to become a world supplier, was still at the early stages of its development in the first part of the eighteenth century. Cotton materials were originally imported from India, as we have already noticed, and it was the ban on these imports which gave home-produced cottons their first chance: but even then what was produced was mostly mixtures of cotton and wool or linen. From 1736 to 1774 there was still a law against the use of any goods made entirely of cotton, it being presumed that they must have been imported from the East.

Defoe in the 1720s had little to say of East Lancashire—soon to be a region of busy cotton mills—beyond describing the marshy condition of its extension towards the sea. He speaks of Manchester as 'the greatest mere village in England ... neither a walled town, city or corporation; they send no member to Parliament; the highest magistrate is a constable'. But he noted that the population of Manchester was increasing and that it was making a cotton material called 'dimity' (for bedroom hangings) as well as coarse 'fustians' of cotton and wool. The Lancashire Defoe visited was mainly a county of poor farmers and cottagers, many of whom helped out their scanty earnings from the not very fertile soil by spinning and weaving the wool of the moorland sheep. But its textile workers were enterprising rather than conservative; they were already using and mixing together such varied raw materials as linen, silk, worsted, cotton, and mohair. The capital which would be needed for any big development was also accumulating fast through the expanding trade of the neighbouring port of Liverpool; and Liverpool could bring cotton in quantity from the West Indies and elsewhere. In these circumstances the jealousy with which the older woollen and silk industries regarded the growth of cotton could not prevent the last-named from seizing any chance for expansion that came along.

Spinning and Weaving

Accordingly, it was in the new, and at first somewhat despised, cotton industry that the inventions which began the revolution in the textile industries were first widely used. Ingenious men experimented and improvised in the older woollen manufacture; the inventions were taken up and widely applied in the new cotton industry, bringing about radical changes in production by the use of machinery; and, more gradually, machine methods of production were adopted in the woollen industry also. It is a complicated story, and before mentioning any of the particular inventions, it will probably help to say a few words about the basic processes in the textile industry as a whole.

The word textile comes from the Latin *textilis*, which means 'woven'. To weave the weaver must first have yarn, which is prepared by spinning. Spinning and weaving are among the oldest of handicrafts, and have been developed in most parts of the world, so that various kinds of cloth have taken their names from places where they were originally developed, e.g., fustian from Fustat, the old name for Cairo, calico from Calicut in India, and muslin from Mosul in Iraq. The word cotton comes from Arabic and again reminds us of the eastern origin of cotton cloth.

The revolution in spinning: from the cottage hand wheel and single spindle to multi-spindle machines driven by steam.

First, the spinning of yarn. The raw material has first to be cleansed and prepared: both cotton and wool have to be carded (from *carduus*, a thistle)—or the wool combed to make long-fibred worsted—these processes being different ways of separating and preparing the fibres for spinning. Then the fibre is spun. This was originally done by a hand spindle—a stick with a weight on the end is dangled by an attached fibre and rotated (i.e., spun) while other fibres are drawn out from the carded or combed bunch of raw material and attached by twisting until a continuous thread or yarn is formed. By the eighteenth century this process was carried out by a simple machine—the spinning-wheel. In this the spindle was mounted horizontally and turned by a wheel worked by hand or with a treadle.

Next, weaving. There are various forms of loom. But the basic process consists of the inter-crossing of two sets of parallel lines of yarn. The warp is a set of threads fixed to a frame, but fixed in such a way that alternate threads can all be raised together by means of attached cords, so as to create a gap or 'shed' in the warp. Through this shed is passed the shuttle carrying the weft, and the shuttle is passed backwards and forwards, as the threads of the warp are raised and lowered, until a length of cloth is woven. There are further processes, such as the bleaching of cotton and fulling or felting and dressing of wool, and in many cases the material is also dyed; but spinning and weaving are the foundation of all the textile industries. The weaver was literally a manufacturer—a worker by hand. The inventions brought machines which would work much faster and greatly multiply output.

The Flying Shuttle

First came the 'Flying Shuttle', patented by John Kay in 1733, while working in his father's woollen business at Colchester. By pulling a cord, the weaver could send the shuttle carrying the weft to and fro through the gap or 'shed' in the warp. This enabled a weaver, working alone, to weave broad cloth that had previously required two men at the loom; it also speeded up the work. Kay also made other improvements in textile machinery. New methods are often unpopular. Some weavers, fearing the new machines would throw men out of work, broke into Kay's house, in his native town of Bury in Lancashire, destroyed his machines, and burned and looted his property. Kay fled to France. He had suffered financial loss and may have been helped by the French Court, but very little is known about the end of his life.

His invention, intended primarily for the woollen industry, was taken up after some twenty years by the cotton weavers; sheds were built to house the larger loom which was needed with the new shuttle; and the immediate result was to create a famine in cotton yarn. A weaver now used up yarn faster than the spinners could supply it, and he often had to tramp three or four miles before starting his day's work, calling at the cottages of his spinners to collect enough yarn to keep his loom working. Men began to wish for a spinning-wheel which would spin more than one thread at a time.

Improvements in Spinning

It was not until thirty years after the invention of the flying shuttle that a Blackburn weaver, James Hargreaves, found a way to speed up spinning. His wife's spinning-wheel was accidentally overturned, and he noticed that the wheel continued to revolve while he held the thread in his hand. This gave him an idea and, being a carpenter as well as a weaver, he was able to work out a device for spinning several threads simultaneously. A number of spindles set up in a row are rotated by a wheel, which also moves a travelling carriage to and fro. As it moves to the right, threads are drawn out from the rovings of cotton attached to the carriage; as it moves back again, the twisted threads are wound on to the spindles. His first machine, invented in 1767 (patented in 1770), was a small one but even this could twist eight threads at once. It perhaps got the name 'spinning jenny' because it did the job commonly done by women, or it may have been so called after Hargreaves's wife. For a time Hargreaves kept his invention a secret, but other spinners noticed that his family produced great quantities of yarn, and they broke into the house and smashed the machines. Hargreaves then moved to Nottingham, where there was a cotton-stocking industry. There he set up a small spinning factory, and made machines which would spin 16, 20, and then 30 threads, and in due course 120 threads: but the 'jenny' was a small and compact machine which, like the spinning-wheel which it replaced, was normally used in cottages.

Hargreaves's invention practically coincided with Arkwright's spinning frame. Richard Arkwright was a barber and wig-maker of Preston, who became interested in spinning machinery as a money-making proposition and very probably 'pirated' the work of an earlier inventor, Lewis Paul. Be that as it may, after some experiments he completed his spinning frame, bigger and heavier than the 'jenny' and not capable of being worked by hand in a cottage room. This was able to produce thread strong enough for use as warp—which Hargreaves's machine had been unable to supply. Arkwright patented his famous machine in 1769 and set up a spinning factory in Nottingham.

Water-frame used at Arkwright's mill at Cromford to spin thread for cotton stockings.

Two years later he entered into partnership with a firm of Nottingham stocking-knitters, and together they built a spinning-mill at Cromford in Derbyshire. Because the new machine was worked by water-power it became known as the 'water-frame'. A letter written thirty years after its first erection describes Arkwright's cotton mill as 'a palace of enormous size, having at least a score of windows in a row, and five or six storeys in height'. Like other inventors, he had his difficulties. One of his mills was completely sacked by rioters, others were attacked by mobs. But on the whole, Arkwright was the most successful of the early inventors. He became a millionaire and a baronet, and ranks in history as the founder of the modern factory system.

Although it was now possible to make textiles entirely of cotton without a linen or woollen warp, English cotton goods remained coarser than those imported from the East until another invention was made. This was a machine designed by Samuel Crompton of Bolton, who is said to have looked like a combination between the youthful Napoleon Bonaparte and one of the early Methodist preachers. After years of hard work and poverty, he made a machine in 1775 that spun finer and stronger thread than either Hargreaves's spinning jenny or Arkwright's water-frame—and as it was a cross between the two machines it was called the 'mule'. This machine enabled even fine muslins to be made in England instead of importing them from the East. Crompton was, however, very unfortunate. Jealous spinners broke into his house and tried to wreck his machine. Manufacturers took up his invention but avoided recompensing him; he died penniless. But with his 'mule', spinning moved from cottage to factory and from village to town; the change was completed early in the nineteenth century, and an improved version of Crompton's invention, the self-acting mule, is still the basis of Lancashire's cotton industry today.

These inventions speeded up spinning. Spinning-mills were built beside streams, where the machines could be worked by water-wheels such as were used to grind corn; these were known as 'beck-side' mills. But the looms were still worked by hand, with the result that yarn was now being prepared faster that the looms could use it. Then Edmund Cartwright, a clergyman, became interested in the new machines. He visited the new spinning-mills, and suggested that weaving might also be done by a power-driven machine. His suggestion was laughed at, but he set to work, and made the first power-loom; it was a clumsy affair driven by a bull. About this time James Watt's steam-engine,[1] which had been used for pumping water from mines and blowing bellows in blast furnaces, was being adapted for driving machinery. In 1789—the year of the French Revolution—Cartwright's factory at Doncaster was fitted with a steam-engine. Two years later, a Manchester firm contracted to make a number of power-looms. Other inventors improved on Cartwright's work; and by the time of Napoleon's defeat at Waterloo in 1815 power-looms were beginning to come into wider use.

Steam now began to take the place of water-power, and some of the beck-side mills were deserted. Factories were set up near coal-mines and new towns sprang up to house the factory workers, who moved in from surrounding country districts. Meanwhile, some more inventions streamlined the production of cotton goods. The most important was the cotton gin for extracting the seeds from the cotton; this was introduced by the American, Eli Whitney, in 1793. Up to this time three-quarters of the raw cotton was imported from the British West Indies, the rest from Brazil, India, or the Levant: the American cotton plant had very little commercial value because its seeds were too

[1] See page 76.

tightly embedded in the fibres. The new machine, by replacing the costly hand-picking, made the southern states of the newly established USA a land of cotton: thirty years later they were supplying three-quarters of the total British demand, which in the meantime had multiplied itself eight times over.

Another important improvement was the use of bleaching powder to replace the older bleaching processes which took months to complete. Chloride of lime began to be manufactured for this purpose in Glasgow, where cotton was the main industry, in 1789. The production of calico was further helped by the invention of Bell's colour-printing cylinder, with which one man could do more work in a day than could be done by a hundred hand-printers. Our engraving of an early calico-printing establishment, even though the machines look clumsy and are tended by men in tailcoats and knee breeches, shows clearly a forerunner of the factory of today. Lastly, we may mention the lace-making machine, which did work that had been thought too complicated for anything but a skilful human hand. When artisans in 1816 attacked the factory in Nottingham, the inventor, Heathcoat, removed to Tiverton in Devon; there he was able to invent a process enabling the frames to be be driven either by water-power or by steam, and he set up a lace factory which is still at work.

Results of the Inventions

The cotton industry of south-east Lancashire and neighbouring districts, and of Glasgow and Lanarkshire farther north, was the first to benefit from the new methods of manufacture. These areas had local advantages for this particular industry in their humid climate, which facilitates spinning, and pure water available for bleaching and cleaning processes. An almost unlimited supply of raw material came readily to hand from overseas. The market for the finished goods, consisting chiefly of calico and others of the simpler and cheaper forms of cotton cloth, was likewise virtually inexhaustible.

It is no wonder that in the early nineteenth century cotton became firmly established as the first and greatest machine industry. Thereafter, for over a hundred years, it dominated all other export activities. By 1880 it had made Lancashire the most populous and most productive county in Britain, with two-thirds of the cotton trade of the world passing through its bleak but busy streets.

For a time the woollen industry largely despised the new machines, but gradually the wool-workers also introduced machines adapted to their special needs. Machinery driven by water-power could readily be installed by Yorkshire cloth-workers, for there were many streams in

Calico-printing.

the hilly districts of the West Riding. But in Norfolk, with its flat countryside, this was not possible; by the end of the eighteenth century, all that remained of the East Anglian woollen industry was the preparation of wool. However, Cartwright invented a combing machine on the same lines as his power-loom, by imitating the movements of the hand. Actually it was not until 1850 that the combing machine ('Big Ben') became efficient enough to oust entirely the hand industry over which their patron saint ('Bishop Blaize') had long presided. But already the Norfolk wool-combers were singing this dirge:

> *Come, all ye Master Combers, and hear of new Big Ben,*
> *He'll comb more wool in one day than fifty of your men*
> *With their hand-combs and comb-pots and such old-fashioned ways;*
> *There'll be no more occasion for old Bishop Blaize.*

When steam-power took the place of the water-wheel, Yorkshire again had the advantage of coal-mines close at hand, while Norfolk had to bring coal by sea. So the centuries-old East Anglian cloth trade came to an end just at a time when the distress which followed the Napoleonic Wars was most acute. Many families, unable to make a living, moved to the new industrial towns on the Yorkshire coal-field. Others emigrated to Canada or the United States to find employment in the new lands.

As we have seen, the introduction of new methods in textiles was unpopular, chiefly because of the dread of being out of work. One writer complained that 'the employment of machinery was one of the greatest evils that ever befell the country'. The setting-up of new machines often led to riots by bands of machine-breakers. The best known are those who in 1811–16 called themselves Luddites—perhaps after Ned Ludd, a half-witted lad of Leicestershire, who, being unable to catch someone who had been tormenting him, destroyed some stocking-frames in a fit of rage. The Luddites in various districts vented their rage on the particular kind of machinery which seemed to threaten their employment. In Nottingham, they attacked the stocking-frames because the master hosiers began to reduce wages and make stockings on wider machines. In Lancashire, the Luddites were hand-loom weavers; they succeeded at the third attempt in burning a steam-loom factory at Westhoughton, in April 1812. In Yorkshire, it was the 'croppers' who were Luddites—these were skilled workmen who cropped the nap on the cloth to give it a smooth surface; they objected to the use of a shearing-frame, which replaced their work. As a result, some rioters were hanged and others transported to Botany Bay in Australia. But their demonstrations and violent acts of protest against the changes, though bound to fail, were not altogether unreasonable, and we may be glad that the Luddites won the sympathy of the poet, Lord Byron: for it was true that people were being thrown out of work by the machines and were not at once re-employed elsewhere. This caused terrible suffering. But it is also true that in the end the use of machinery increased the demand for labour: the machine-produced goods were much cheaper and were sold in much larger quantities, so their manufacture *in the long run* found work for far more people than could ever have been employed under the old system.

8 The revolution in transport: roads and canals

Increase in trade made it essential for traders to have better means of transporting their goods. Coastal shipping had long flourished and it continued to expand: until the close of the nineteenth century it carried a greater weight of cargo than made up all our exports. But for many centuries the English roads had been in a very bad condition, and it was not until the latter half of the eighteenth century that any great progress began to be made.

Arthur Young, an agricultural expert who made tours at that time through nearly all parts of England, tells us that the roads were often little more than bridle-paths, quite unfit for any kind of wheeled vehicles. He advised travellers to avoid the roads around Newcastle, which 'must either dislocate their bones with broken pavements or bury them in muddy sand'. The Norfolk roads he described as 'ponds of liquid dirt', while the Essex roads were 'so narrow that a mouse cannot pass any carriage'. In winter, the road between Kensington and London was an 'impassable gulf of mud'. King George II and his Queen once spent a whole night on the road travelling the eight miles from Kew Palace to St James's Palace, and once the coach overturned in a ditch. It is little wonder that highwaymen found easy prey on such roads. Though the four horses were changed at every town, it took four days for a coach from London to reach Manchester or York, while the journey from London to Edinburgh took ten to fourteen days.

Turnpike Trusts

The great obstacle to improvement lay in the fact that the upkeep of the roads was a parish responsibility: they were renewed, improved, and repaired to the extent and by the methods which suited the needs of the people who lived there. The needs of long-distance travel and transport—except for horse riders and trains of pack-horses, which

Turnpike at Hyde Park Corner, by Rowlandson.

could get round the holes and unsafe stretches of highway—were simply ignored. The solution was the Turnpike Trust; we hear of them occasionally as early as the reign of Charles II, but it was the difficulty of moving the army northward to meet the Jacobites in 1745 which caused the need for them to be generally recognized, and 1773 is the date of a law which made it easy to administer them. Each Trust consisted of local people who were willing to invest their money in improving a stretch of main road in their own locality. Having improved it and arranged for its upkeep, they were empowered to recover their expenditure by a toll on every vehicle or beast driven along their road. Soon the turnpike gates on the high roads were almost universal: on leaving London, for instance, the traveller bound for Oxford would pass through one near the modern Marble Arch and a second at what is still called Notting Hill Gate. If the caricaturist Rowlandson is to be believed, such a gate was a very lively place and its corpulent keeper had a busy time enforcing his placarded list of tolls on coaches, carriages, and horse- and donkey-riders. The erection of turnpike gates and the vast improvements with which they were associated, ushered in the age of the flying coach and the private post-chaise, racing to Bath or Brighton or Gretna Green at nearly twelve miles per hour. For humbler purposes, too, pack-horses began to disappear when covered wagons could move more easily.

Roads and Bridges

But the Turnpike Trust itself was merely a way to raise money for the roads: its importance was that it gave scope for inventive minds to introduce better gradients and drainage and more durable and smoother surfaces. Towards the end of the eighteenth century three great road-makers were at work—John Metcalf ('Blind Jack of Knaresborough'), Telford, and MacAdam. For nearly thirty years Metcalf—blind through smallpox since the age of six—was at work superintending the making of roads in Yorkshire, Lancashire, and Derbyshire. He invented a smooth, durable road surface, made by pounding small stones together, and he tested the surface and slope of a road by walking to and fro, tapping the road with his hollow stick. The second famous eighteenth-century road-maker and engineer, Thomas Telford, became road surveyor in Shropshire. He advocated solid foundations, with a firm, moderately cambered surface. His chief work was in Scotland, where, between 1803 and 1821, he constructed 920 miles of road and more than 1200 bridges. As a result of his work traders and travellers were enabled to move freely between England and Scotland; this helped to bring a new era of prosperity to North Britain. In southern Britain, Telford's best-known work was the great London to Holyhead road, along the line of the old Roman Watling Street, which he furnished with new bridges and extended from Shrewsbury through the Welsh mountains to the Menai Straits and beyond.

An even more famous road-maker was John Loudon MacAdam (1756–1836), a Scotsman, who found a way of making roads as good as, but less expensive than, those of Telford. Even when a boy at school, MacAdam made a model section of a road. As a youth he went to New York, and there became a successful merchant. Later, back in this country, he experimented at Falmouth, and was able to put his ideas into practice, first as surveyor-general of the Bristol roads (1815) and finally, in 1827, as general surveyor of roads for the government. He realized, like Metcalf, the need for well-drained subsoil. If the subsoil were well drained and the road raised above the general level, then the subsoil would be strong enough, without the solid foundations of Telford, to bear the weight of the road surface and the traffic passing over it. His method was to make the top layer of the road of small broken stones, which the pressure of the traffic would crush and weld together into a hard smooth surface. To ensure that the stones for the road surface were not too large, he used to tell the stone-breakers: no stone should be larger than can go comfortably in the mouth. On one occasion MacAdam is said to have expostulated with an old man who was breaking the stone into too large pieces, only to have the old man pop a piece easily into his mouth. But the mouth was large and toothless!

In various parts of England he helped to plan, repair and build a great network of roads, on many of which the mail coaches[1] could travel at an average rate of eleven or twelve miles an hour, a speed that would have been thought impossible thirty years earlier. Visitors to this country from Germany and France were highly impressed by British roads. Whereas in 1754 the coach from Newcastle to London took six days, on the good roads of 1820 the journey could be made in forty hours. The coaches had been immensely speeded up. But this was true only of the best and most rapid passenger transport. To send heavy goods might take weeks; normally they would go by sea where possible. It was this slowness of goods transport which stimulated the construction of canals and, later on, of railways.

MacAdam's plan for road-making is still in use, though in these days of motor traffic what were once called 'macadamized roads' are reinforced with tar, and the surface is now known as 'tarmac'.

The construction of bridges was a problem which had to be faced by some road-makers. The old method of building a bridge was to sink either large boulders, or baskets filled with stones, into the bed of the river as foundations to support the arches. The old London Bridge was built in this way, stood for centuries, and supported rows of houses. But the art of bridge-making did not make much headway until the late eighteenth and early nineteenth centuries. Then progress was rapid, owing to the work of famous bridge-builders and engineers, such as Smeaton, Telford and Rennie. John Smeaton (1724–92), who attended Leeds Grammar School as a boy and became a Fellow of the Royal Society before he was thirty, had studied the canals and bridges of the Netherlands. His most famous bridge, 900 feet in length, was built across the River Tay, in Scotland. Telford's Menai Suspension Bridge, which carried his Holyhead road across to Anglesey, had the central portion supported by chains, so as not to interfere with the navigation along the Straits below. Rennie built the first Waterloo Bridge in 1817, and his son built a new London Bridge in 1831. When

[1] See p. 170.

The Duke of Bridgewater, who was only twenty-five when the Worsley Canal was opened, pointing to Barton Bridge, the 40-foot aqueduct over the River Irwell, and a line of coal-barges bound for Manchester. An appropriate inscription—Perrupit Acheronta Herculeus labor ('Herculean toil has burst through the underworld')—marks the mouth of the tunnel in the background, by which the canal emerges from the underground workings of the mines at Worsley.

The Most Noble *Francis Egerton*. Duke of Bridgewater
and Marquis of Brackley.
Seu Navis Brittanniæ Magister.
Magnificum pretiosus emptor.

bridges for railway traffic were built, even greater strength was
required; but the main problems had been solved by these great
pioneers in civil engineering. Smeaton founded the first society for the
profession, from which the Institution of Civil Engineers was
developed in 1818, with Telford as president.

NORTHERN ENTRANCE OF HARECASTLE TUNNELS.[1]

Tunnels on the Grand Trunk Canal, built by Brindley and Telford respectively.

Canals

The bad roads of the eighteenth century made the carriage of heavy
goods—such as coal, iron, clay, pottery, and machinery—very
difficult and sometimes impossible. River traffic was important, as we
have seen, but the course of rivers is often irregular, and they may
suffer from droughts and floods. In the second half of the eighteenth
century, canals or artificial waterways were made. The first English
canal-maker was James Brindley, a Derbyshire cottager's son.
Brindley was largely illiterate, but possessed high ability. He became a

wheelwright by trade. From 1759 he was employed by the Duke of Bridgewater to construct a canal from the Duke's colliery at Worsley to Manchester, eleven miles away.

Brindley began by cutting a tunnel (or adit) straight from the coal workings. He devised watertight embankments to carry the canal through bogs; and finally brought it across the River Irwell by an aqueduct at Barton Bridge which was regarded as a great triumph of ingenuity. Brindley trained his workmen or navvies, and fitted up special boats as forges and carpenters' shops, which were floated along each section of the canal as it was made. The canal proved a great success, and the cost of coal in Manchester was halved. The Duke then had the canal extended to Runcorn, thus connecting Manchester with the Mersey estuary and so with Liverpool. When the whole canal was completed, it was so much used in preference to the bad roads, both for goods and passengers, that the tolls paid for its use brought the Duke a large fortune.

Brindley also commenced a greater piece of work, the Grand Trunk Canal, which eventually extended southwards from Runcorn through the salt and pottery districts to join the Trent at Wilden Ferry. The first sod of this canal was cut by Josiah Wedgwood, the potter, one of the chief promoters, in 1762.[1] The canal, with all its branches, had a total length of 139 miles, and brought great benefit to the important pottery industry. Large quantities of clay, lime and coal had to be fetched from some distance; and the finished goods were bulky, brittle, and difficult to carry by road. The Grand Trunk Canal reduced the cost of carriage on clay and other materials from 30s. a ton to 13s. 4d. It also made bread cheaper by reducing the carriage on a quarter of wheat from 20s. to 5s. for a hundred miles.

During the four years from 1790 to 1794, no fewer than eighty-one Acts of Parliament granted permission to cut canals. Among the other famous canal-makers was John Smeaton, who constructed the Forth and Clyde Canal in Scotland. Another Scottish canal, the Caledonian Canal through the Great Glen, was the work of Telford but financially a failure; his best work in this field was the Ellesmere Canal, famous for its two aqueducts, which forms part of the Shropshire network linking the Mersey, Dee, and Severn. In general the canal was a perfect example of a labour-saving device. A *General History of Inland Navigation*, published in 1792, described canals as 'roads of a certain kind on which one horse will draw as much as thirty horses on an ordinary turnpike road, or on which one man alone will transport as many goods as three men and eighteen horses usually do on common roads'.

[1] See illustration, p. 88.

Canals had their defects: they were a rather slow means of transportation at best, and there were often delays at the locks; through-traffic was also seriously impeded by the absence of any standard width of water-way. But the development of England during the Industrial Revolution of the late eighteenth century and the early nineteenth century owed much to the canals. The pottery towns of Staffordshire, for example, trebled in size within a generation of their coming into use. Ports also benefited enormously by being brought into direct communication with the industrial districts. Lastly, canal transport helped farmers, who were provided with a wider market for their crops as well as a cheaper means of obtaining manure and other bulk supplies. Thus the canals are one factor which is common to the industrial and agrarian revolutions.

Most important of all, however, were the railways, which became the characteristic form of transport in the reign of Queen Victoria (see p. 121).

9 The revolution in farming

The deepe and dirtiest lothsome soyle
Yeldes golden grayne to careful toyle.
(Norden, in Elizabeth I's reign.)

While the invention of new machines was bringing about an Industrial Revolution, important changes were taking place in the eighteenth century in agriculture—both through the development of better methods and through the enclosure of the open fields to form compact farms, where these better methods could be practised.

Clover and deep-rooted lucerne for cattle food had been introduced in the seventeenth century, but their value for improving the soil and breaking it up with their long roots was not at first understood. The horse-drill for sowing seeds, and the horse-hoe for weeding, had been invented by Jethro Tull in the very early years of the eighteenth century; his method of sowing seeds in rows some distance apart actually produced a strike of labourers who believed the right way must be to scatter broadcast as in Biblical days! Nevertheless, Tull persevered, and eventually produced a book, *Horse-hoeing Husbandry*, with diagrams showing how easily his machine could be made.

Among other pioneers of eighteenth-century farming was the 2nd Viscount Townshend, who began farming in 1730, and by his constant praise of turnips as a crop earned the nickname of 'Turnip Townshend'. At his estate of Raynham in Norfolk, he introduced a new rotation of crops known as the Norfolk system, comprising four courses—turnips, barley or oats, clover, wheat. Thus he was able to keep all his land in use instead of letting a third of it lie fallow (or uncropped) each year, as under the old system of the Middle Ages. His new rotation of crops not only improved the land itself, but root crops and clover meant winter food for cattle—and therefore fresh meat for people during the winter. His soil at Raynham was light and sandy, and in earlier days 'two rabbits had fought for every blade of grass', but under the new cultivation it was greatly improved.

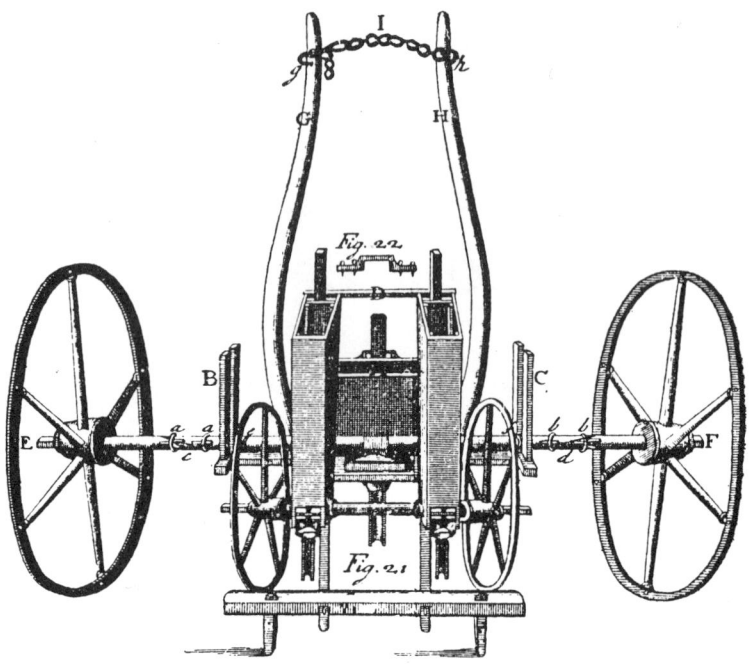

Jethro Tull's seed-drill.

New Techniques

Another Norfolk farmer, Squire Coke of Holkham, inherited in 1776 a badly cultivated, unproductive estate. He applied new techniques, often with more care than their original inventors had shown, and at the end of a long life—he died as Earl of Leicester in 1842—had multiplied his rent-roll by ten, while his tenant farmers prospered with him. By draining and manuring the light soil, Coke succeeded, to everyone's surprise, in growing corn. He also did much to improve the breeds of cattle and sheep; he studied grasses to find out which kinds were best for the animals. Every year, beginning in 1778, Squire Coke had a meeting at sheep-shearing time to which he invited farmers—sometimes 7000—from all parts of the country to discuss agriculture. 'Everybody made use of expressions towards Coke which affectionate children used towards their parents'—wrote Cobbett, a farmer and journalist who did not, as a rule, have much to say in favour of the landlord class.

Meanwhile another farmer, Robert Bakewell, of Dishley, Leicestershire, experimented in scientific cattle-breeding. Taking advantage of

Ploughing—preparing the soil for sowing.

the improved feeding provided by root crops and clover, he produced a breed of sheep, 'New Leicesters', nearly three times the weight of the long-legged, bony creatures previously reared. He then turned to cattle with equal success, and provided such good beasts that other farmers began to take more interest in cattle-breeding and so improved the meat supply. His work was continued by the Colling brothers, who after a visit to Dishley began to develop the modern breed of shorthorn cattle on their own farms near Darlington.

King George III—'Farmer George'—set up a model farm at Windsor, and even wrote articles for the *Annals of Agriculture*, a monthly publication which was continued for twenty-five years (1784–1809) by Arthur Young. Young's *Tours* of agricultural investigation have already been mentioned; in 1793 he became secretary of the newly founded Board of Agriculture. This was not the direct ancestor of the government department concerned with this subject nowadays, but a national society for collecting facts and figures and reports about new methods; it also offered prizes for essays on farming and for inventions of benefit to agriculture. This propaganda, as we should call it, was very necessary because farmers were slow to change, having always provided for themselves and for a local market in traditional ways and without being exposed to much competition. The result was a series of further improvements, which came slowly into use. New methods of draining the land were preached in Warwickshire and perfected in Perthshire. In 1813 Sir Humphry Davy published his *Elements of Agricultural Chemistry*, from which the modern use of artificial fertilizers eventually grew. A Scotsman (Meikle) invented a threshing machine as early as 1786, which came quickly into use in the Lothians: but in 1830 this machine, through which the steam-engine was harnessed to perform an agricultural task, was still a novelty in most parts of England.

These new methods brought prosperity to wealthy landowners, able to spend money on experiments, on machinery, and on new

Coke of Holkham.

breeds of cattle to improve their stock. For example, in the background of the scene in which Thomas Coke is proudly inspecting his Southdown sheep, Holkham Hall appears—the magnificent mansion he built with his farming profits.

The Need for Enclosure; the Enclosure Acts

It was, however, clearly impossible to practise this new farming on the old large 'open' or unfenced fields divided into 'strips'. At the beginning of the eighteenth century, as we have seen, much of the land was cultivated in the old style, as it had been throughout the Middle Ages. But as long as his land was not fenced off, a farmer could not grow turnips or clover on his strips—they would be eaten and trampled on by other men's cattle when they were given the run of the common fields after harvest. A man might see that his land could be improved by drainage, but where could he carry the water without making a neighbour's land sodden? If a man tried to produce a better breed of cattle, as Bakewell was doing, the beasts had to mingle with the ill-kept village herds, usually infected with footrot, scab and other disease. Again, it was difficult to keep one's own crops free from weeds when a careless neighbour's strips were overrun by thistles. Further, much time was wasted in going from strip to strip; and the land itself was wasted in the balks and pathways separating the strips.

In his tours over England, Arthur Young saw that if agriculture was to prosper it must make use of new methods. He also realized that as these methods could not be used on the old open fields, the latter must go, and the land of the unenclosed villages be redistributed. While some enclosures were carried out by general agreement among all concerned, the usual method was for each village to obtain its special Act of Parliament. A few such Acts had been obtained under Queen Anne and George I, and over 200 during George II's reign; but even at the accession of George III in 1760, the open-field system still existed in about half the counties of England—in a roughly triangular area on the east side of the country, bounded by the East Riding of Yorkshire, Norfolk and Wiltshire.

From about 1760 onwards it became more evident that efforts must be made to increase the food supply of the country. The population of England and Wales was seen by many to be growing rapidly in the later decades of the eighteenth century; this growth was very marked in the towns. Another reason for increasing the agricultural output was the series of wars with France, which made it impossible to import much corn from abroad. With bigger demand came bigger prices; and this made many farmers anxious to make better use of their land, and if possible to acquire a greater acreage. The number of enclosures therefore increased. During George III's reign some 3200 Enclosure Acts were obtained, including in 1801 a General Enclosure Act which simplified the procedure.

The actual process of enclosure, after an Act of Parliament had been passed, was carried out by Commissioners. They were generally named in the original petition asking for the Act, and their appointment was ratified by the Act. They were often three in number, and might be peers, gentlemen, clergymen or farmers; sometimes they acted without fee, but usually fees and travelling expenses had to be paid. The Commissioners generally held a public meeting in the district, and then appointed a valuer and surveyor. Each holding of land had to be valued and measured—and this was no light task. The Commissioners had to allow for the roads, either public thoroughfares or private roads leading to individual farms, and they could make regulations as to drainage. But the main task was the redistribution of the land in the district: the claims of the lord of the manor and all owners of land in the common fields, and of all who had legal claim to meadow, pasture, or use of the common had to be considered. It was a most intricate and complicated business. At the end, when the reallotment of land was finished, each landlord or farmer would have, instead of his former scattered strips and his right to a share in the common, a compact allotment of land, a farm or farms, where he could work and carry out improvements unhampered by his neighbours. Next came the expensive task of fencing or hedging the newly allotted farms. Boundary fences for each total share had to be put up, and payment for them was exacted from each farmer in proportion to the size of his allotment of land. The interior fencing of fields was left to the farmer as he chose. The whole business was most costly, from the beginning, when the petition had to be drawn up and presented to Parliament, until the final work of the Commissioners. Lawyers had to be paid, there were visits to London with travelling expenses and delays which also cost dear. Between the passing of the Act and the completion of the Commissioners' work of reallotment five or six years might pass. During that time there was uncertainty and confusion, and the land might be badly farmed in consequence until the changeover was settled.

Social Consequences

On the face of it, the system was a fair one. Parliament did not pass the Bill unless the owners of four-fifths of the area of property to be enclosed were in favour; it sent, as we have seen, Commissioners to settle the redistribution; and every strip belonging to the old open fields was replaced by an equivalent area. But the small man was nevertheless at a great disadvantage, because the compact piece of land which he received had not only to replace his arable strips but also the use he had formerly had from the common—the untilled land where he (like his neighbours) had kept his horse and cows and a few sheep and geese and hens, to say nothing of the free timber and firewood on which he had always relied. And the poorest class, the cottagers, who had no arable strips but picked up a living from the common, did not—at least if they were newcomers to the village—necessarily receive any compensation at all. Sometimes the freemen of an ancient town still share an unfenced common, such as the Port Meadow at Oxford; more often it is a little village green which survives to remind us of what was lost when the compact modern farms with their hedged fields came into existence.

The hedges or fences, too, cost money and, together with the proportion of the cost of the award which had to be paid by each person who benefited, were another thing which made it harder for the small farmer to keep his farm. Many peasants sold their bit of land to a more fortunate neighbour. They became landless men and worked as whole-time agricultural labourers: the big new farms were mainly arable and would need more men. But the fact that their families no longer had any 'stake in the country' was one strong reason

Air view of open fields under strip cultivation at Laxton, Notts, a few miles west of the Great North Road.

for a movement of 'surplus' population away from rural areas into the new industrial towns or overseas, which continued all through the following century. In this way the cultivation of the land passed mainly into the hands of men with capital. Small freeholders, who had been the most independent type of yeomen (because, being actual owners of their land they need obey no squire), kept their farms as long as prices were high. But at the end of the French Wars many of these had to sell up their possessions and go to the towns. In the end nothing was left of the ancient system of agriculture but the one or two unenclosed villages, such as Laxton (Notts), which still stand out, as seen from the air, in strange contrast to their neighbours.

Even Arthur Young, who had for years advocated enclosure, was forced to acknowledge the 'knavery of commissioners and attorneys' acting under the Enclosure Acts, and owned that 'by nineteen out of twenty Enclosure Acts the poor are injured, and most grossly'. Oliver Goldsmith in his poem, *The Deserted Village*, lamented that

> . . . *a bold peasantry, their country's pride,*
> *When once destroyed can never be supplied.*

The hardships of the villagers were increased during the Industrial Revolution by the gradual loss of their other means of livelihood, hand-spinning and part-time weaving. The spinning-wheel, in particular, had been a regular source of income, for under old conditions it required six or eight pairs of hands to prepare and spin the yarn needed by one weaver. But by the end of the century wool was being spun in factories, so the women and children of the countryside lost their small earnings. The menfolk also found that, when the power loom began to spread, the hand loom could no longer be brought out to supplement the profits of a small-holding. Then there were the incredibly harsh Game Laws—seven years' transportation was the penalty for being found by night on open land in possession of nets for rabbiting. But the most unbearable thing of all was the knowledge that the great agricultural changes, which enormously increased the nation's stock of wheat and meat, had brought no improvement at all to the lot of the landless rural worker, who eked out a miserable existence on inferior bread, potatoes, and cheese, washed down with weak beer or weaker unsugared tea.

Nevertheless, the future lay with the large compact farms, where the farmer had capital for purchasing machinery and stock for improving the land. One of the reasons which led to a great increase of enclosures was the desire of men who had made a fortune in trade or industry to become landowners. As early as 1724, Daniel Defoe had noted that on estates near London families of local gentry were being displaced by families enriched in business; and Cobbett, the writer who admired Squire Coke of Holkham, felt very differently about the people from London whom he termed 'the Squires of Change Alley'. The possession of land had political and social as well as economic value. Until the reform of Parliament in 1832, nobody but landowners was entitled to vote in county elections, and even later every candidate was supposed to prove himself a substantial landowner; the landed interest was the basis of political power. Parliament was controlled by landowners. The possession of land also conferred social distinction, for the lord of the manor or squire was the local magistrate or Justice of the Peace. But beside political and social distinction, the keen businessman who invested money in land would expect profitable returns. He wanted to bring as much as possible of the open fields and the 'common' under his control to farm according to modern methods for profit; or he might let the land after enclosure to tenant farmers at a high rental.

It is now clear that, though much distress was caused by enclosures, they were essential to work the improved methods of agriculture and without them it would have been impossible to feed the growing population in the factory areas. It is possible, too, that the hardships of the poor have been exaggerated by some writers: Goldsmith is said by Lord Macaulay to have introduced into his English 'Deserted Village' conditions characteristic only of Ireland. For it must be remembered that waste land also was enclosed, particularly during the Napoleonic war, and this bringing of new land into cultivation to meet the increased demand for food meant *more*, not less, agricultural employment. During the wars, too, tenants often took advantage of high profits to buy their holdings. During the years 1800–50 no English county, however rural, showed an actual decline in population, though London and the counties containing the new industrial areas showed by far the greatest increase.

The Highland Clearances

Changes in land use brought more acute and more prolonged distress to the inhabitants of many parts of the Scottish Highlands, but their plight attracted little attention at the far-off seat of government in London. Even today the English visitor to the far north is surprised when he finds that such a district as the wild and empty Strathnaver was once cleared of over 1000 people and their homes burnt down, allegedly with some loss of life. This was in 1807–21, when evictions by the noble House of Sutherland, owning almost the entire county of that name, reached a total which may have been as high as 10 000. The substitution of large sheep-grazing farms for tiny self-sufficient crofts dated back, however, to the failure of the rebellion of 1745, when the former Highland chieftains ceased to think of themselves as clan leaders and learnt that there was much more money to be gained from sheep than from a crofter's rent.

The soil being barren and the families large, a part of the population of these districts would in any case have moved to the industrialized Lowlands, to the new United States, or to the colonies. The more enlightened landowners helped to organize and finance the move, and they also promoted resettlement in the coastal districts of the Highlands, where crofters might earn more from weaving and, especially, fishing. Roads, bridges, and harbours were built to provide a further stimulus. Nevertheless, it was an inhuman though entirely legal practice under which families were driven off the land, where their forebears had lived poorly but securely as members of the clan. In the second half of the nineteenth century, feeling became still more bitter, as the fall in wool prices caused many sheep farms in their turn to be suppressed in favour of deer forests, entirely deserted except for a few autumn weeks when the Flying Scotsman express brought the fashionable sportsman and his servants to the north. It was not until 1886 that the Crofters' Holdings Act promised security to the remaining tenants.

10 Our heritage of coal

For centuries wood had been the principal fuel for household use—except in the districts where outcrop or surface coal was easily obtainable. Wood had also been used in great quantities (in the form of charcoal) for smelting iron-ore. Two loads of wood were required to make one load of charcoal, and two loads of charcoal were needed to smelt a ton of iron-ore. In the seventeenth century, the forests and woodlands of England were dwindling, and Parliament began to fear that ship-builders would be short of timber at a time when there was an increasing demand for new ships for trade and defence.

One result of the shortage of wood was to increase the mining of coal to provide fuel for domestic and industrial purposes. This led to a rapid opening of coal seams in Northumberland and Durham. Coal was sent from Newcastle to London by sea, and so it was known as sea-coal. At the time of the Civil War in Charles I's reign, the coal-pits of Northumberland and Durham were so valuable that some people suspected the Scottish army of planning to gain permanent possession of them. Corn apart, it was already the chief article of internal trade.

Transport of coal otherwise than by water was difficult on account of bad roads. Until the cutting of Brindley's canal from Worsley to Manchester in 1759–61, coal was carried in baskets on pack-horses. The usual load was 280 pounds, and the cost of carriage doubled the price of coal. The digging of canals not only assisted the development of the Lancashire coal-field, which up to the middle of the nineteenth century was second only to north-east England in importance; it also started the coal industry of the South Wales valleys, with iron-ore close at hand and convenient sea communications from Cardiff.

Owing to the increased demand for coal, the surface outcrops were used up, and miners had to dig down. At first they made pits thirty or forty feet deep, and worked within a small radius from the bottom of the shaft leaving more than half the coal in the form of huge pillars to support the rocks above. Lower seams had been reached by 1776, and pits as much as 600 feet in depth were being worked. These deep pits presented great difficulties—drainage, raising the coal to the surface, ventilation, and the hazard of explosive gas. As the mines went deeper the danger of flooding increased, and pumps were set up, worked by various contrivances such as tread-mills and water-wheels.

Power provided by wind and water is unreliable, and this led to the introduction of Savery's primitive steam pump, which had been patented in 1698 as 'an engine to raise water by fire'. Newcomen improved on Savery's engine, and Newcomen's engine was in use in many coal-mines during the earlier part of the eighteenth century. The way in which this was developed into the modern steam-engine, which could raise the coal as well as pump up the water, will be described in the next chapter.

Raising the coal to the surface was another problem which had to be faced as mines became deeper. In most collieries some kind of mechanical apparatus came into use, either a simple windlass or horse-gin[1] or crane. The winding tackle served also to lower and raise the miners; but some pits had no mechanical gear, so the coal was carried to the surface by means of ladders, in baskets slung over the shoulders of women and children, the distance climbed being equal, in at least one case, to the height of St Paul's Cathedral. Even after the steam-engine came to be used for haulage, there was still the difficulty of finding a rope strong enough to take the strain; the wire cable was not invented until 1839.

Prevention of Mining Accidents

The problem of ventilation was equally difficult. Most coal-mines contain harmful gases, and are only made fit to work in by having pure air forced through. The first method adopted was the provision of two shafts on different levels, the air rising in one and being drawn down the other. The air from the shaft was conducted through the mine-workings by a system of trap doors, which were opened and closed by boys and girls. This method was not sufficient for deep mines, and about the end of the eighteenth century a mining engineer, John Buddle of Wallsend, invented an exhaust pump. This drew the foul air out of one shaft by suction, which caused a current of fresh air to be drawn down the second shaft.

Upon the ventilation of the pit depended the miners' safety from dangerous gases. In the smaller pits 'choke-damp', or carbon dioxide, was the chief danger; but in the larger and deeper pits there was sometimes 'fire-damp', or methane. Fire-damp was the more dangerous, for the flame of the miner's candle caused it to explode without

[1] See illustration of token coin, p. 37.

THE DAVY AND CLANNY SAFETY LAMPS

VENTILATING FURNACE

A TRAP-DOOR

Section of the shafts and workings of a coal mine. Note the furnace, to ventilate by means of rising hot air at the foot of a shaft, and the Clanny safety lamp, sometimes in local competition with the Davy lamp.

warning, while choke-damp usually put the candle out before its suffocating fumes took effect on the miner himself, thus giving him time to escape.

Fire-damp made the lighting of mines a serious problem. The usual method was by the naked flame of a candle or by a lantern. Explosions were frequent, and caused great loss of life. A clergyman, the Rev. John Hodgson, who once lost over ninety of his parishioners in a colliery disaster, became the pioneer of a movement to establish societies for the prevention of mining accidents. The first of these societies was started in Sunderland in 1815. At about the same time the old North of England practice, by which mining disasters were exempt from coroners' inquests, was at last abandoned; it had taken two laws (1775 and 1799) to abolish the still more shameful Scottish custom of compelling miners to serve for life in the same pit as 'bondsmen', punishable if they ran away.

Thus public attention was directed to the need for greater safety in mines, and by 1815 an important step forward was made. After careful experiments, Sir Humphry Davy (1778–1829), one of the leading scientists of the time and a pioneer in chemistry, invented a safety lamp in which the flame is shielded by a cylinder of metal gauze fine enough to let the light through. But the conductivity of the gauze disperses the heat of the flame throughout the cylinder, so that the temperature is not high enough to ignite any gas outside, as the naked flame would have done. The lamp proved very useful. When told by a friend that he ought to patent the lamp as it would bring him a small fortune, Davy nobly replied: 'I never thought of such a thing. I am only too happy to have been able to help our miners. That is my reward.' In more recent years electric lighting has been introduced into the main galleries of the mines, and portable electric lamps are used in other parts; but as late as 1926 half a million British miners still carried Davy lamps, in which the 'cap' of burning gas within the gauze would give warning of the presence of fire-damp.

As the Industrial Revolution progressed, coal became more and more important to feed the ever-increasing steam-engines, for the iron manufacture, and for millions of new domestic hearths. In the first seventy years of the eighteenth century the output may have doubled to reach an estimated total of 6 million tons. Between 1770 and 1816 the 6 million became 16 million, which in turn was nearly doubled by 1836, and the 1836 figure more than doubled by 1854, the date when accurate statistics began.

Deeper shafts were sunk to reach lower seams of coal. By the end of the eighteenth century, wooden props were being used to support the roofs of the galleries in the mines, instead of leaving pillars of

Sketch by sub-commissioner, reproduced from 1st Report of the Children's Employment Commissioners: Mines and Collieries (Cmd., 21 April 1842): 'Hurriers at Elland Colliery (near Halifax) being drawn up crosslapped upon the clatch-iron. As soon as they arrived at the top the handle was made fast by a bolt drawn from the upright post; the woman then grasped a hand of both at the same time, and by main force brought them to land. The corve (coal-container which the children 'hurried' along the underground workings) on these occasions is detached from the hooks to render the load lighter'.

Hauling up child workers from a coal-mine.

unworked coal. But, because of the cheapness of child labour, boys and girls were still employed in coal-mines: some dragging the trucks of coal through the low narrow tunnels, others crouching for hours in the dark by the side of the trap doors which they had to open and shut as the trucks passed. It was not until many years later that reformers denounced the hardships endured by these children, and steps were taken (in 1842) to forbid work underground for females of any age and boys under ten.

Modern Developments

Since then governments have ceaselessly tried to improve safety and working conditions in the mines. An important law in 1850 established the principle of control, by officially listing coal-mining as a dangerous trade and requiring all mines to be inspected. Miners' earnings were next safeguarded against fraud by an Act of 1860 which gave them the right 'at their own cost to station a person (being one of the persons for the time being employed) to take account of the weight measure or gauge of coal', and the position of check-weighman, as he is called, was strengthened by two later laws. An Act of 1872 raised the age at which boys might be employed to twelve years; it was again raised in 1900 to thirteen years; in 1911 to fourteen years; in 1944 to fifteen; and in 1957 it was raised to sixteen. An Act of 1881 gave the Home Secretary the right to hold inquiries into the causes of accidents in mines, while another Act in 1896 regulated the use of explosives in blasting. The record of beneficial legislation is almost endless. But even at the present day, though it is no longer ill-paid or unregulated, the work of the miner at the coal face continues to be hard, cramped, dirty and, above all, dangerous.

Up to the First World War our output of coal grew continuously, though as early as 1865 a well-known economist (Professor Stanley Jevons) had written a gloomy book on *The Coal Question*, i.e., what was to happen when it was all used up. But in the first ten years of the twentieth century the annual total was 242 million tons, about four times the figure for the 1850s, and this was sufficient to provide both for all our own needs and for three-quarters of the total weight of British exports to all destinations. Well might Kipling write as he did in 1911:

> *Oh where are you going to, all you Big Steamers,*
> *With England's own coal, up and down the salt seas?*
> *We are going to fetch you your bread and your butter,*
> *Your beef, pork and mutton, eggs, apples, and cheese.*

11 The story of the steam-engine

The steam-engine was the key invention which made the Industrial Revolution possible, and for more than a hundred years it had the foremost place as a prime-mover for industry and transport; even in the days of jet aircraft the steam locomotive still has its devotees. Let us trace the story from the beginning—a long story, since the wet, white cloud we wrongly call 'steam' must have attracted attention as soon as early man placed the first pot of water on the first fire. What is popularly called 'steam' is really the little drops of water condensed from steam by the cooler air surrounding it, steam itself being an invisible gaseous substance which is formed when water changes into vapour. Steam expands, that is, it takes up more room than water. When the water in a kettle boils and turns into steam, the lid of the kettle begins to shake and rattle—because the steam is expanding. It is this expanding power of steam that has made it so useful to mankind.

Nearly 2000 years ago a Greek, named Hero, who lived in Alexandria, had invented a number of curious machines and experimented in the use of steam. He placed water in a globe with an opening at the top; in the jar were two tubes. When the water was heated, the steam passed out through the tubes and kept a ball turning round and round on two pivots. This apparatus was just a curious toy, but it showed that steam might be made to do work.

Through the centuries men continued to experiment with steam, trying to make it useful. In the seventeenth century an Italian physician, named Branca, and a French scientist, named Papin, made useful experiments. Papin discovered a way of using steam in a cylinder, so that none of its power was lost. But it was not until 1698 that an English military engineer, named Thomas Savery, made use of steam for an important practical purpose.

At that time the coal-miners (as stated in the last chapter), having worked out many of the seams of coal near the surface, were trying to reach lower seams. As they dug deeper into the earth water collected in the pits and there was danger of flooding. Savery invented what he called a 'fire engine' for pumping water out of mines by filling a cylinder with steam, condensing the steam by means of cold water so that there was a vacuum, or space, in the cylinder, and then allowing the cylinder to fill with water by means of the pressure of the air. This engine was called the 'Miners' Friend' because it drained the pit without the hard work of pumping by hand and baling with buckets. Several of Savery's engines were set up in mines, and enabled miners to work at a greater depth; and although his engines were slow and used a lot of coal, he claimed a share in the profits of a later, better-known patent.

Perfected in 1711, this appears to have been a wholly separate invention by Thomas Newcomen of Dartmouth, who was an iron-monger with an extensive business in tools. His first engine was used in a coal-mine, where they were most needed; they were also used in the Cornish tin-mines. They had many faults, and were wasteful of fuel, but remained in use for over seventy years—especially in coal-mines, where fuel consumption was of no importance—and during that time doubled the depth to which miners could go. A Newcomen engine developed $5\frac{1}{2}$ h.p., and it could raise 50 gallons of water a minute from a depth of 156 feet, which seemed no small achievement —until Watt set to work on it.

The model of Newcomen's engine which was given to James Watt for repair in 1764. It had recently been put in order by a London instrument-maker; Watt saw that, given the existing wasteful method of generating steam, the boiler was too small for the cylinder.

James Watt

James Watt (1736–1819) was a largely self-educated young Scotsman who was employed as mathematical instrument-maker to the University of Glasgow. He had already interested himself in the subject of the steam-engine when, in 1764, he was given a model of a Newcomen engine to repair. He became absorbed in its improvement, and after many failures he succeeded in making a model for an engine which would be greatly superior to Newcomen's.

But Watt had neither the money, nor the materials, nor the workmen to make a full-size engine which he could show to mine-owners and others, and no one in Glasgow took any interest in the scheme. At last Watt found a patron in Dr John Roebuck, who in 1759 had opened the first big Scottish iron works at Carron in Stirlingshire, where the famous guns called carronades were later produced. An engine was built at Carron, but at that time there were no tools accurate enough for such work. The result was disappointing, and as Roebuck was now suffering heavy losses in his own business, he could not afford further interest in Watt and his engine. Watt was in despair. He decided to give up engines, and take a job as a surveyor of a new canal that was being made. His work brought him to Birmingham, where he met Matthew Boulton, the head of the prosperous Soho Engineering Works housed in a fine new building at Handsworth, which was later (1802) to be the first large building ever lit by gas. Boulton was a keen businessman, and he agreed to take Watt into partnership. The engine, which had been first patented in 1769, was brought to the Soho works, where the workmen were more skilful than those at Carron, and it was soon functioning well.

The Boulton–Watt partnership, which began to operate in 1775, was indeed an event of great importance in the development of the steam-engine. For behind the inventive genius of Watt it put the solid business ability and established position of Boulton. Matthew Boulton (1728–1809) was himself an outstanding man. He had succeeded to his father's business of silver-stamping, but he had gone on to build up a considerable engineering works with 600 workmen, making metal articles of various kinds—perhaps the largest hardware business of the time. He was quick to realize the possibilities of development in Watt's early engine, for even in 1776, when the biographer Boswell visited the Soho works, Boulton declared: 'I sell here, Sir, what all the world desires to have—Power.' Later Boulton used steam-power in coining, and produced coins for the East India Company and a copper coinage for Great Britain. He took an interest in scientific and literary matters, and was a Fellow of the Royal

Society. When Boulton and Watt eventually retired, in 1800, they handed over the business to their sons, whom they had taken care to have well educated—and so the partnership went on in the names of Boulton and Watt.

Watt's engine was from the outset a great improvement on Newcomen's, because it had a separate condenser: when steam was generated in a cylinder which could be kept continuously hot, and condensed in a condenser which could be kept continuously cool, the result was a machine of greater power and lower fuel costs. Late in 1775, the first Watt engine to be sold was at work in a colliery near Birmingham, and a second was on order for John Wilkinson's blast furnaces at Broseley in Shropshire. Soon they were being sent to the Cornish tin-mines, where within ten years they had replaced all but one of the old, wasteful Newcomen engines. But these engines were only an improved form of pump: in flat country they were sometimes used as part of a water mill, pumping back the water that had turned the wheel. The next step was to make an engine with a rotary motion which would drive machinery for all purposes. With the help of his foreman, William Murdock, Watt solved this problem. Moreover in the next year, 1782, he patented 'a double-action expansive working engine', in which the piston was worked up *and down* by steam, a great improvement on the earlier engines in which the piston fell by its own weight.

One of Watt's first engines, photographed still in use in 1862.

Steam engines used for driving spinning-machinery in a Lancashire cotton mill.

The engine could now be adopted for general use in iron works, for forge-engines and bellows in blast furnaces, and for use in the sheet-iron rolling mills. In these mills, water-power had been used, but steam proved a great advantage, especially in severe winters, as a letter from Boulton to Watt shows: 'they are all frozen up, and were it not for Wilkinson's steam-mill, the poor nailers must have perished; but his mill goes on rolling and splitting ten tons of iron a day, which is carried away as fast as it can be bundled up; and thus the employment and subsistence of these poor people are secured.' The new engines were also adopted in some potteries, breweries, flour-mills, and—from 1785 onwards—in spinning factories. 'The people of Manchester are steam-mill mad,' wrote Boulton to Watt. Steam-power began to take the place of water-power, and mills and factories built on the banks of streams were deserted in favour of new premises in towns where coal was cheap.

But we must not be tempted to exaggerate. By 1800 Boulton and Watt's Soho works had produced about 500 steam-engines and the steady growth of the coal and iron industries made it easy to provide the material to make and work more of them. Nevertheless, in 1830 the go-ahead cotton factories still used 30 per cent of water-power, and all the industries of Birmingham, where steam-engines were first built, required only a dozen new ones a year—in 1826, for instance, thirteen, averaging 12½ h.p. For the early steam-engine was a hand-made, individual machine: there were no standard spare parts to be had; and when it developed a fault (a fairly frequent occurrence), the men to repair it must be sent for from the original makers. These men who understood steam-engines—successors to the millwrights who used to mend the old water-driven corn-mills—were not numerous: not till the middle of the nineteenth century did they come to form a regular trade of skilled engineers. In the meantime the manufacture of standard steam-engines had gradually become possible through the development of machine tools (see page 82).

The Earliest Steamboats

The next chapter in the story of the steam-engine was to make it useful on the water. Boats were rowed by oars; ships were moved by the power of the wind in their sails. Rowing was hard work; sails were useless if there was no wind, or if the wind was blowing in a completely contrary direction. In some parts of the world at certain seasons there was hardly a breath of wind, and ships might lie becalmed, unable to move for days, even weeks. When a steam-engine could be made to move a boat or a ship, that would be a great advantage.

The earliest experiments culminated in a paddle-wheel steamboat which was used to tow barges on the Forth and Clyde Canal in 1801–2. This was seen by the American, Robert Fulton, who took one of Watt's engines home with him to America, and in 1807 was steaming up the Hudson River at nearly 5 m.p.h. The first successful British steamboat was the *Comet*,[1] which was built on the River Clyde in 1812, and made regular trips between Glasgow and Greenock. When the first steamboat appeared on the Thames many people disliked it—'It is strange to hear and see it hissing and roaring, foaming and spouting like an angry whale'—but there were already four by 1814. The early steamships were small and coal took up too much space; they were preferred to sailing-ships chiefly in river navigation and ferry services, such as that maintained by the Dover–Calais steam packets, which began to run in 1821. As late as 1847 sailing-ships made up 96 per cent of the British mercantile marine, and iron was still a novelty in shipbuilding (as we shall see) long after it had set its stamp upon the whole life of the age.

[1] See illustration p. 91.

12 The new Iron Age

It has been claimed that iron comes second only to the air we breathe and the water we drink in the list of substances essential to the life of modern men. Iron is so plentiful—about 1 cwt of it, we are told, to every ton of the earth's crust—that we easily forget our dependency upon its use for nearly every kind of building and machinery, cutting-tool and magnet. But when we look back to early history, we readily divide the Ages of Stone and Bronze from the Iron Age when men first used implements and weapons of iron. It would be just as reasonable to make a further division at the time of the Industrial Revolution, when iron first became adaptable to its innumerable modern uses, and to say that after about 1800 civilized man was living in a New Iron Age.

The smelting of iron was carried on in Roman Britain, and throughout the Middle Ages. For smelting the iron-ore, charcoal continued to be used till the middle of the eighteenth century. Smelting was a local industry to be found in various wooded districts, because it was easier to carry the ore to the forests than to carry timber to the iron-fields. The most important iron-smelting districts were the Weald (or 'Wood') of Kent and Sussex, the Forest of Dean, and the Wrekin district of Shropshire. As Kipling sings:

> Out of the Weald, the secret Weald,
> Men sent in ancient years
> The horse-shoes red at Flodden Field,
> The arrows of Poitiers.

During the Tudor period and afterwards, when timber was needed for shipbuilding, several Acts of Parliament were passed to check the cutting down of trees for iron-making and these Acts greatly reduced iron production. A cheap and effective substitute was now obviously needed for the use of charcoal in smelting the ore. In 1619 an iron-master named Dud Dudley began experiments, but for various reasons he was not successful; his iron works were attacked and wrecked by jealous charcoal burners. The iron industry was in fact hampered by lack of cheap fuel until the middle of the eighteenth century. Abraham Darby of Coalbrookdale in Shropshire discovered about the year 1709 that, if coal was first turned into coke, it could replace charcoal in the high-temperature furnace used for smelting. But for various reasons his discovery did not become widely known in the trade before the middle of the century, when further improvements were made by his son, Abraham Darby II. By that time the coking process could be worked under more favourable conditions, because engines, driven first by water-power and then by steam, were becoming available to produce a strong blast in the furnaces.

The production of iron and steel involves many processes. First, the metal must be extracted from the ore, which comprises other substances. This is done by smelting in a furnace; in order to obtain the great heat necessary, a blast of air is forced through coke, ore and limestone; hence the name 'blast furnace'. Iron-ore smelted in a blast furnace with coke and limestone becomes pig iron, the raw material from which cast iron, wrought iron and steel are made. The use to which the iron is to be put determines its subsequent treatment. If cast iron is required, the 'pigs' are re-melted in a foundry, and poured into moulds. To make malleable or wrought iron, the 'pigs' must be heated and elaborately hammered in a forge. For steel, a still more elaborate process of reheating is needed to get rid of impurities and a proportion of carbon must be added, making true steel very costly. Cast iron is hard but brittle; wrought iron is soft but holds together; steel is strong and tough.

Abraham Darby's process applied only to the first stage of the iron industry, the smelting of the ore into pig iron. But there was greater demand for wrought iron, and this required refining—a process which used more charcoal than smelting had done until Henry Cort, a Lancashire man, discovered a cheaper method. In 1783 Cort planned a method of rolling out the iron by passing it between a series of rollers, instead of beating it with heavy hammers while still in a molten condition. The next year he perfected the use of the reverberatory furnace, invented twenty years earlier, in which the only contact between the fuel and the metal was the flame beating down on the pig iron, which was held in a basin-like container at the bottom of the furnace. Workmen used long poles to stir or 'puddle' the molten iron to drive out impurities. The metal was then taken to the rolling mills in large balls weighing about eighty pounds each. The use of the reverberatory furnace at last enabled coal to be used instead of charcoal.

One of the difficulties of the eighteenth-century ironmasters was to obtain an effective blast to maintain the heat in the furnaces. At Coalbrookdale and other early iron works a water-wheel was used to strengthen the draught. Then Smeaton attempted to solve the problem with the help of blowing-cylinders, which were introduced at Carron about 1768. Next Watt's steam-engine was employed by

Wilkinson in 1776 for working the bellows in a blast furnace; this, as we have seen, was a few years before it was adapted for working forge-hammers and to provide power for the rolling and slitting mills. Finally, James Neilson, the foreman of the Glasgow gasworks, suggested heating the blast before it entered the furnace. The 'hot blast' (patented in 1828) proved a great success; it cut down the consumption of coal by one-quarter, thus further reducing the cost of production.

When the use of coal was possible for all processes of the iron industry, the ironworks ceased to be located in the woodlands, and were established on coal-fields, as in Yorkshire, South Wales, South Staffordshire, and the valley of the Clyde. The last charcoal smelting furnace was extinguished in 1827. The cost of manufacture was lessened, and Britain was able to produce all the iron needed for her own use and a surplus for export, instead of having to import pig iron from as far afield as the Urals, which had been her position earlier. Between 1788 and 1830 the total output of pig iron, the raw material of the iron manufactures, was multiplied tenfold.

New Uses of Iron

The use of iron for various purposes rapidly increased. Iron rails were laid down for the tramways at the collieries as early as 1767, and in 1779 Abraham Darby III (the pioneer's grandson) built the first iron bridge. This elegant Coalbrookdale structure, with a 100–foot span, was well suited to figure in an engraving 'by permission most respectfully inscribed' to King George III. Iron was needed for the machinery in the new mills, and later for steam-engines. The perfecting of cast-iron production also enabled iron to be employed for additional domestic purposes; it was cheaper than copper, bronze, brass, or pewter; it was more easily handled than stone or wood. But these developments, and the kind of enterprise which made them possible, can perhaps be illustrated best from the career of the greatest of all the eighteenth-century ironmasters.

John Wilkinson, born in 1728, the son of a labourer in a Cumberland village, is said to have founded the family fortunes while still a boy by inventing a box-iron for laundry work, which his father patented. Next he developed the first accurate metal-cutting tool for large-scale work—a hollow, cylindrical boring-bar, mounted on bearings. This was valuable for cannon and also to give precision to the steam-engines with which Watt was then experimenting. At Broseley in Shropshire in 1776–80 he equipped himself for the large-scale manufacture of iron by introducing four of Boulton and Watt's engines to

The Cast Iron Bridge over the River Severn. Plate dedicated to King George III by the Coalbrookdale Company, 1782.

blow the bellows. This helped to make the fortunes of both firms, for Wilkinson became a regular supplier of cylinders for the engines of which Boulton and Watt became 'designers and erectors'. He also made 32–pounder cannon and howitzers for the government and sent his munitions down the Severn in the first iron barge. He cast all the ironwork for the Paris waterworks and erected the first steam-engine in France; he built a Methodist chapel of iron. His nickname, 'Iron-mad Wilkinson', is usually associated with his wish to be buried in an iron coffin; but a better illustration of his enthusiasm and single-mindedness (qualities which shaped the careers of many of his fellow-industrialists as well) is the tradition that Wilkinson never wrote a letter without mentioning iron.

Steel

Fine steel, used mainly for weapons, cutting implements, and small fittings, such as watch-springs, was not made in England before the seventeenth century, when Sheffield began the manufacture of shear-steel, chiefly from very pure Swedish iron. The first step towards the improvement of English steel production was taken by Benjamin Huntsman in the middle of the eighteenth century. Huntsman was a Sheffield clock-maker, who had difficulty in obtaining steel of a suitable quality for his work. In 1740 he succeeded in producing steel of a uniform quality by remelting the shear-steel in clay pots, known as crucibles, subjecting it and a small admixture of carbon to a great heat, and so freeing it from slag. The best steel is still made in crucibles, but the process was too costly for general use, and a century passed before steel production was developed by further invention. The new Iron Age was then succeeded by the age of cheap steel, in which we are still living.

Engineering

With the revolution in textiles and the invention of machinery, with the development of the steam-engine and the growth of the iron industry, there went the development of engineering. It is rather difficult to say exactly what an engineer is. In America he is the driver of a train; in this country he may be anything from the man who repairs the family car, radio, or TV to a highly trained scientist who has specialized in engineering. In the early days of machinery three trades supplied the men who undertook engineering jobs: clock-makers and instrument-makers; millwrights, who set up and repaired the machines in the textile factories, driven at first by water-power; and military engineers, who understood cannon, siege works and to some extent roads and canals.

Basic to the development of engineering was the machine-tool industry. The machine-tool is a mechanically driven tool which is employed to make the parts of other machines, and since these parts are machine-made they can be standardized. A skilled workman using a machine tool can make any number of parts of the same size. Except for the boring-machine mentioned above, Boulton and Watt had no such tools; they had to depend on hand tools, though they improved on some of these.

Joseph Bramah (1748–1814), working in London, devised some machine tools to use in making his patent locks, and he also invented an hydraulic press. He trained Henry Maudslay, who about 1800 perfected a self-acting lathe. Whereas previously a worker had to hold the cutting or shaping tool against the work, now the tool was fixed in a rest and adjusted to the work. Maudslay also made a very accurate measuring machine, which led to yet finer work on the lathe. Such machine-tools came into common use in the 1820s and enabled precise work to be done. Indeed, they were essential to the development of engines. 'How,' asked Nasmyth later, 'how could we have good steam-engines, if we had no means of boring a true cylinder or of turning a true piston-rod, or of planeing a valve face?'

Nasmyth's steam hammer in operation (from a painting by the inventor).

James Nasmyth was trained by Maudslay, and set up for himself in Manchester in 1834. Five years later he invented his steam-hammer, which cheapened the production of wrought iron and made it possible to forge larger machine parts, such as the paddle-wheel shafts which were beginning to be required for steamships. His contemporary, John Whitworth, also worked as a machine-tool maker in Manchester. He devised various standard sizes for machine parts, for example, for screws. Thus parts became interchangeable, and the supply of spare parts was made possible.

So it was that the making of tools became an industry in itself—the machine-tool industry. 'Tools', it was said in 1841, 'have introduced a revolution in machinery and tool-making has become a distinct branch of mechanics and a very important trade, although twenty years ago it was scarcely known.' And with the machine tools, the machine-makers were able to provide the machines and the engines required in ever-increasing numbers as the industrialization of the country went on. Machine-making also became more specialized. In the early days mill-owners had had to make their own textile machines before they could start to manufacture. But with the provision of machine tools, firms were established in the textile districts which specialized in making textile machinery.

Thus by about 1841 it was possible to distinguish various types of engineers. There were the makers of heavy machinery, steam-engines, mill gearing, and hydraulic presses; the makers of the machine tools; and the makers of the textile machines. Engineers were employed by railway and steamship companies to construct the locomotives and the marine engines, and engineers of some kind worked also for contractors, and in the mills and mines to look after and repair machinery. In a country with growing industry engineering was a growing profession, and as industry developed in foreign countries there were also many opportunities for British engineers abroad.

13 Changes in other industries: pottery and ships

We have now seen the big changes which transformed the textile industries, transport, agriculture, and the manufactures based on coal and iron. But the same period witnessed similar, if less dramatic, changes in other branches of industry. Let us examine one or two of these before we pass on to consider, in the next section of our book, the new ways of living to which all these changes led.

The Potteries, that is the six north Staffordshire towns which have been united in recent times to form the city of Stoke-on-Trent, owe the rise of their speciality very largely to the coming of the canals to that part of the country, as already mentioned. For it was the clay industry of Cornwall which supplied the material for the potters. In old days, drinking mugs and plates for ordinary use were sometimes made of horn, or of wood, or of pewter (the grey alloy of tin and lead) which has lately come back into fashion. Cups and saucers were not needed until coffee and tea first came to be drunk in England in Stuart times, and they were then imported from China by the East India Company. But coarse earthenware pots and jars were already being made in north Staffordshire, where there were supplies of black clay and terracotta which baked into a buff or reddish-brown colour. There was also plenty of brushwood there for fuel.

Like spinning and weaving, pottery was at first a cottage industry. Nearly every garden in the Potteries had its oven made of turf with a roof of boughs, and heated with charcoal, where they could bake such things as the large jars, in which at that time butter was sent from farms to shops in London and other cities. Packmen came round the Staffordshire villages each week to collect the jars and pots to be sold elsewhere.

At Bow and Chelsea there were potteries which tried to imitate the porcelain which came from China. The potters of Germany had already discovered that the secret of this fine ware lay in the material used for its manufacture: and in time they found deposits of the right

The potter's wheel—working by hand at Etruria.

kind of clay in Saxony. English potters at first used a mixture of pipe clay, sand from the Isle of Wight, and glass. But a great discovery was made about 1768 by William Cookworthy, a Plymouth druggist, when he showed that Cornish clay (kaolin) and china-stone were the materials the English potters needed to enable them to produce the fine kind of earthenware or 'china' known as porcelain. Cookworthy took out a patent and set up a china factory, but it was not a great success, and in 1777 his porcelain rights were bought by a Staffordshire firm with works at Stoke-on-Trent.

The discovery of the china clay opened up a new industry for Cornwall, and in time the quarrying gave employment to many former tin-miners; but the absence of coal in Cornwall prevented the setting-up of Cornish potteries on a large scale. The clay was therefore sent by sea to Chester, and later to Liverpool, and then conveyed laboriously overland to Staffordshire. The quarrying and preparation of china clay is still one of the great industries of Cornwall. It is not only sent to Staffordshire, but is exported to America and elsewhere from Falmouth and other west-country ports. Cornish clay is now also used in some other manufactures besides pottery.

In Staffordshire, in the latter half of the eighteenth century, many changes took place. New methods of glazing were introduced. The white Cornish clay was used to make a thin layer over the local clay, so that the ware came out of the ovens smooth and white. The increase in the use of tea and coffee, and in the number of coffee-houses opened in London and elsewhere, had led to a great demand for cups and saucers, and Staffordshire potters began making these in quantity. More ovens were built, but the supply of brushwood was not sufficient. Fortunately there were coal seams at hand, and the potters were able to fetch sacks of coal to feed their ovens. But as time went on, machinery and new methods made the old ways of working out-of-date, though the potter's wheel was still worked by hand—in fact, there is still some hand-decoration of the more expensive products, even in the twentieth century. Instead of working in their own little sheds, the men had now to work for a master-potter for a weekly wage. The industry kept the coal-miners busy, and attracted to north Staffordshire various craftsmen, who made crates, sieves, and other things needed in the potteries.

Transport was the most difficult problem the early master-potters had to face. The Cornish clay brought by sea to Chester or Liverpool had in the early days to be carried across country by pack-horses to Stoke-on-Trent and Burslem, and the finished goods were carried by pot-wagons along the roads to the River Trent or the River Severn and thence distributed to other parts of the country. But Brindley's Grand Trunk canal, begun in 1762, joined the Cheshire town of Runcorn on the Mersey to the Trent, and thus solved the problem of transport. We can now see how it came about that the first sod was cut by Josiah Wedgwood, the greatest master-potter of the eighteenth century, as one of the main investors in the canal scheme.

Wedgwood

Josiah Wedgwood (1730–95) was the son of a Burslem potter and himself started work at ten. He became highly skilled at shaping the pots on the wheel, and it was he who perfected the fine art of English pottery. In the course of a most successful career, he built a large earthenware factory together with a village for the work-people at a place near Burslem, which he named Etruria because of his special interest in the reproductions of classical designs recovered from graves in Italy. Wedgwood discovered and invented many improvements and machines for mixing clay, and for modelling and glazing china. He engaged clever artists, such as the famous Flaxman, to decorate his fine wares; but he also insisted on careful work in the manufacture of ordinary domestic earthenware, so that the simplest articles were well shaped and finished. One of the improvements was to give a clean white finish instead of a dirty yellow. Wedgwood was not without

rivals—Spode, for instance, who, like Wedgwood, became potter to
King George III—and famous wares were established outside the
Potteries area at Derby and Worcester. But from his Etruria works
came a vast variety of goods. As a result, the use of earthenware—'common Wedgwood'—became general in English homes,
while large quantities were exported to European countries and to
America.

*Wedgwood's Etruria factory, opened on 13 June 1769 and sited so as to adjoin the projected
Grand Trunk Canal. Typical pot kilns can be seen on both sides of the main buildings.*

Wedgwood himself was a real character. It was said that he used to
stump around his works, and smash any article which did not satisfy
him. On the bench alongside he would chalk: 'This won't do for Josiah
Wedgwood.' He worked tirelessly to raise standards, both by experiment in new methods and by trying to turn workmen who were
sometimes drunken and lazy into skilled hands. He was very active in
promoting turnpike roads as well as canals, and by these means he
helped to reduce costs of transport and also loss by breakage. He also
tried to raise social standards by starting and encouraging schools and
chapels, and took much interest in public affairs. He was a man of
cultural and intellectual interests, and a Fellow of the Royal Society;
members of his family have been well known in public life down to
our own time. His name indeed became a household word, as his

pottery and that of other English potters went all over the world. A traveller in the early nineteenth century reported that, all over Europe, 'one is served at every inn upon British ware'.

New Types of Ships

Shipbuilding was another of the industries for which inventive minds (such as 'Iron-mad Wilkinson's) suggested improvements, and it was another of the cases in which there was an obvious need for new development at this time. For under the Navigation Laws, which dated back to the time of Oliver Cromwell and partly even to the Middle Ages, it was in the main compulsory for British trade to be carried on by ships which were built, owned, and manned in British territory. There was also an expansion of the Royal Navy as a result of the wars against the French, especially the Revolutionary and Napoleonic Wars of 1793–1815, and the need for a special kind of ship in the growing trade with India—one that could carry the maximum of cargo on that long, expensive voyage and yet defend itself, if necessary, from attack in distant oceans.

By the end of the eighteenth century the oak-built ship had reached its greatest size. The ships of the East India Company, the finest merchant vessels afloat, were about 1000 tons, while Nelson's flagship, the *Victory*, was just over 2000 tons—one-fortieth of the size of the largest modern Atlantic liners. About 1760 it had been found an advantage to fasten sheets of copper to the outside of ships below the water-line to give them greater speed. The copper did not become fouled by crusts of seaweed and shell-fish, nor was it eaten by the Toredo worm as was the case with the wooden hulls of earlier ships; thus the vessels could move more easily through the water. Copper was expensive, but it did not need periodic scrapings. Moreover, the supply of timber for shipbuilding (like the wood for producing charcoal) was rapidly becoming used up, so shipbuilders began to experiment with the use of iron fittings to replace certain natural shapes of timber.

This was the beginning of a great change. The mixture of wood and metal was followed in due course by the all-iron hull which made it possible to build much larger ships. As early as 1787 iron boats were built in north Lancashire for use on canals, and a small iron ship was built near Glasgow in 1818. Many people thought iron ships would never be possible. How could iron be expected to float? Yet, strange as it may seem, an iron vessel did not weigh as much as a wooden one. Strong iron frames were only one-third the thickness of wooden ones—only four inches thick, while those of a wooden vessel had to be twelve inches thick. This gave the ship more room for stowing cargo and shipbuilders were therefore encouraged to use iron, though the Royal Navy (because of the deadly effects when iron plates were splintered in action) used only wood as late as the Crimean War.

Early in the nineteenth century, as we noticed in an earlier chapter, experiments were being made with steamships. But these first steamships were wide and clumsily shaped. They were driven by paddle-wheels, one on either side, but if the vessel rolled in rough weather, one wheel might be wasting energy by beating the air. In 1823 the General Steam Navigation Company was founded at Deptford, and other passenger lines followed; but steamship-building continued to be a small and uncertain business. For, while the early experiments in steam navigation were being made, shipbuilders were working on a newer and faster type of sailing ship, the clipper. Clippers, with fine lines almost like those of yachts, were first built in America, and when they appeared in British waters, notably the Thames and Mersey, British ship-owners were aroused to compete against these American rivals for the carrying-trade. The first British tea-clipper was built in 1850, and until 1870 this remained the fastest type of vessel afloat. Sailing-ships of all kinds, making their voyages from London and the Clyde and Liverpool to every port in the world, were still the standard cargo vessels of the mid-nineteenth century.

The Shipyards

Shipbuilding on a small scale was carried on all round the coast in any convenient port or estuary, but the main centres in the eighteenth century were on the banks of the Thames and on Tyneside. On the Tyne, for instance, the work had originated in a very small way with the construction of shallow-draught boats, called 'keels' (as in the famous song), which were used to carry coal down the river to sea-going vessels off the coast. Later, coastal colliers were built, and finally still larger and more ambitious types of vessel, the iron and steel of the modern shipyard being readily available there. Plymouth, Portsmouth, and Chatham, on the other hand, were concerned only with the construction or repair of the ships of the Royal Navy.

For the first new developments we must turn to the Clyde, where the first British steamship, the *Comet*, Henry Bell built in 1812. This was the start of an enterprise, based on the accessibility of coal and iron, which in time made shipbuilding rather than the cotton manufacture the premier industry of Glasgow; the manufacture of iron steamers was established there as early as 1841. Another new centre was Birkenhead, which made the first iron paddle-steamer ever seen in

The steamship Comet *(1812), which in favourable weather conveyed passengers between Glasgow and Greenock rather faster than the coach.*

America, and in shipbuilding rapidly out-distanced Liverpool. As for London, it was not until 1835 that iron shipbuilding was started by William Fairbairn (1789–1874), a brilliant Scottish engineer who migrated from Manchester. His yard was at Millwall, in between the West and East India docks. But Fairbairn had to face much conservative opposition, and although he built about a hundred iron ships of different sizes, in the end he turned his attention to bridge- and boiler-making instead. Thus shipbuilding is an interesting example of an industry where the new inventions were applicable but, for a long time at least, were only slowly and fitfully applied.

In conclusion, we may notice two special features. Shipbuilding was a business which required much capital, to buy the raw material and pay for the long and elaborate processes of construction. It therefore had, almost from the first, big employers of labour, such as Sir John Laird (1805–74), who in the first half of the nineteenth century practically created modern Birkenhead. On the other hand, as soon as the ships came to be of any considerable size, a large number of workers were necessarily employed together in building them, with the result that shipwrights, as they were called, were one of the first crafts to form strong trade unions. The clash between big employers and the trade unions, beginning in the shipyards as early as 1825, will be noticed in a later chapter.

Ports and Docks

The expansion of British shipping called for an expansion of port and dock facilities. The modern port systems, with their channels of approach, docks and landing quays, were a nineteenth-century creation.

By 1800 London badly needed docks. During the eighteenth century about three-quarters of imports into England passed through London, so that the Thames became congested with the fleets of merchant ships, and much of their cargo used to lie on the wharves out in the open. The first modern dock was the West India Dock, which was opened in 1802. Within five years this was followed by the opening of two more docks—the London and the East India—on the north bank of the Thames, and the Surrey Commercial Docks on the south bank. The last-named occupied the site of the old Greenland Dock, used in earlier centuries by whalers. Further evidence of the pressure of trade demands is given by the fact that within two decades Telford was at work constructing St Katherine's Docks, immediately below the modern Tower Bridge. The docks were built by joint stock companies, which charged dues for their use and for the use of the adjoining warehouses.

Each of the leading provincial ports developed a similar system. Hull built its first dock on the site of its ancient fortifications in 1774. Liverpool, as we might expect from what we already know of its rapid commercial growth in the eighteenth century, began early, its first dock being opened in 1715, a second in 1753. In the case of Bristol, on the other hand, where the Dock Company was incorporated in 1803, high dock charges are regarded as an important cause for its loss of trade to Liverpool.

Safety Measures

Danger had never been far away on the seas, and therefore measures were sought to safeguard both the cargoes and the lives of the crews. At the end of the seventeenth century London merchants had the habit of meeting at Lloyd's coffee-house. Here they developed methods of insuring ships and cargoes. At first informal, the meetings of merchants led to an association, which eventually became the world-famous insurance organization of today. By the end of the eighteenth century Lloyd's had a general form of insurance policy, and was issuing information on the movements of ships; about that time, or a little later, Lloyd's was keeping a classified register of shipping— a valuable indication to shippers of the seaworthiness of merchant vessels.

From an early date the need had been realized for lights to warn ships at night of danger spots. The exact origin of Trinity House is unknown, but a religious guild for mariners existed in the Middle Ages, and received a charter from Henry VIII; it was soon responsible for various maritime duties concerning lights and buoys. Later on, the Corporation of Trinity House gradually took over control of privately owned lighthouses and built some new ones. Between 1800 and 1830 it was busily engaged in setting up new lights round the English coast, in active competition with a newly established authority for Scotland, the poetically named Commissioners of the Northern Lights. In 1836 an Act of Parliament empowered it to purchase rights over coastal lights from private owners. Trinity House recovered the cost of building and working lighthouses from the tolls levied on the ships, but control over these dues was transferred in 1853 to the Board of Trade. The courageous efforts of lighthouse-builders are well illustrated by the story of the successive Eddystone lighthouses, built on the Eddystone rocks fourteen miles from Plymouth. The first, built in 1698, was destroyed a few years later in a storm, its builder being drowned; the second, built in 1709, was destroyed by a fire; the third was built by Smeaton in 1759, but with foundations which showed signs of weakening later on in the nineteenth century. Trinity House then decided on yet another new structure, and the present lighthouse was completed in 1882.

From time to time some fearful wreck on the coasts would arouse public feeling for the seamen. Lieut.-Col. Sir William Hillary, who lived in the Isle of Man and had seen many a wreck on its shores, put forward a plan which resulted in the foundation in 1824 of the Royal National Lifeboat Institution. This has proved a grand example of a voluntary charitable organization. It soon began to place life-boats at danger spots on the coast, as did also some private individuals and other societies. Experiments were made with different types of life-boat, and a policy was developed for rewarding the life-boatmen for their dangerous services and paying pensions to the families bereaved by accident. The RNLI has grown into a large organization, but is still maintained by voluntary contributions.

EARLY SOCIAL EFFECTS

14 The factory towns

In the next three chapters we shall look at some of the social changes at the end of the eighteenth and beginning of the nineteenth centuries. These were, of course, largely the result of the developments in industry and agriculture which have already been described. But in order properly to understand what happened it is important to bear in mind two other main factors governing this period.

One is that it was an age of great wars. In 1775–83 Britain had been fighting, first the American colonists, and then the big European alliance which was formed to help the rebels in America and to win back, if possible, what Britain had gained by her victories in the Seven Years War (1756–63). After the American war had ended in our defeat, there was an interval of barely ten years before the outbreak of the last and greatest of our struggles against France, which lasted with two short intervals for twenty-two years—up to the final overthrow of Napoleon. About the middle of this period it was officially estimated that more than 10 per cent of the male population of military age were under arms; probably one other war-worker would be required for every two fighting-men. Such a situation could not fail to impose a heavy strain both on family life and on industrial organization.

Moreover, the Duke of Wellington's victory at Waterloo marks, not only the climax to a series of great military exploits, but the end also of a great commercial struggle between Britain and France. Napoleon had called England 'a nation of shop-keepers', which prompted Pitt's retort that it was also a nation which never lost its martial spirit. Napoleon realized that trade was the life-blood of his main enemy, and he did his best to ruin British commerce by a blockade of British ports. But even Napoleon could not manage without British goods, and British coats, caps and boots for the French army were smuggled into France by way of Hamburg. On the other hand, when the British harvest failed in 1810, and famine was near, Napoleon, anxious to

Wellington at Waterloo.

obtain British gold, allowed the export of corn to Britain on payment of an export duty. Thanks to this action, famine was averted. And thanks to the courage and initiative of Nelson and to other British sailors and soldiers, Britain was able to hold her title of 'Mistress of the Seas' and to keep her trade routes secure. As our industrial output rose, merchants were able to find markets for their products throughout the world, and although some of the war years had been years of deep depression in trade, others had seen our exports mount to greater heights than ever before in our history.

But a time of war is always a time of hardship for many people: in 1800–13 there were no fewer than five years in which the average price of wheat exceeded 100s. a quarter. This fact encouraged acceptance of the gloomy forecasts made by the Rev. Thomas Robert Malthus in his *Essay on Population*, first published in 1798. He taught that, apart from such special measures as deferment of the age of marriage, the growth of population always tends to outrun the growth of the food supply. Therefore permanent improvement in the standard of living of the masses, however desirable, was quite unfeasible.

This dismal conclusion, widely accepted by the classes to which it was not deemed to apply, connects with the second main fact which governs this period. Britain was fighting against the greatest of revolutionary movements, and this had the effect, from 1793 onwards, of making proposals for any kind of reform very unpopular because they could be denounced as unpatriotic, 'the kind of thing we were fighting against'. Accordingly, the policy of our government in this period was to refuse to listen to the grievances of the workers (or those who could find no work); to assume that the employer would manage his business best without government interference; and to concentrate on avoiding any possibility of a revolution in Britain by firm measures to check disorder.[1] The panic outlived the war and the downfall of Napoleon. As late as December 1819 repression culminated in the Six Acts. One of these required public meetings to be sanctioned by magistrates; another extended the heavy Stamp Duties imposed on newspapers, so as to put any kind of political periodical out of the workers' reach.

The Factory System

We can now see how it was that the government welcomed the new factories, because they produced the wealth which helped us to beat the French, while it turned a deaf ear to complaints about the new conditions of work and life which factory employment brought with it. There had been attempts at introducing a factory system long before the Industrial Revolution. As early as the reign of Henry VIII, John Winchcombe—'Jack of Newbury'—is said to have employed 600 workers, men, women and children, in various branches of the cloth manufacture; and other clothiers of that time also set up houses full of looms. But workmen complained bitterly of exploitation by wealthy clothiers; in most rural areas a special Weavers' Act (1555) forbade one man to own many looms; public opinion in general favoured the older system of work done at home. And so the development of the factory system was delayed until the eighteenth century, when conditions favoured important changes in the textile industry. A silk-throwing factory was set up at Derby in 1719, but it was the invention of the water frame fifty years later which (as we have already seen) made factories essential to the rapid development of cotton spinning.

By 1769 our population, for reasons previously outlined, was almost certainly expanding more rapidly than at any earlier period in modern history. Britain had a growing market for textile goods in

---

[1] In addition, rebellion in Ireland led to the Act of Union (1801), which made the island for more than a century a part of the United Kingdom, ruled by one parliament.

foreign countries and colonies overseas; prosperity had resulted in an increased demand at home also, and at the same time clothing was needed for our soldiers and sailors engaged in the recurrent wars in Europe and beyond. This increased demand was more readily met by a system of mass production, and this encouraged the building of mills or factories to house the new machines, and to collect under one roof a large number of workers employed by a single capitalist master or by a partnership or company of capitalists.

The growth of the factory system brought with it two important changes in the capitalist system as it had worked previously, in what is often called the 'domestic' stage of industry. In the domestic stage, the capitalist provided the raw material, but not the spinning-wheels or, in most cases, the looms for weaving; he was concerned with the purchase of the raw material and the sale of the finished product rather than with the actual processes of manufacture, which were carried on mainly in the workers' homes. But under the factory system the capitalist employer owned the machines as well as the raw materials; the work was done on his premises; and it became part of his business to study and improve the process of manufacture. This change clearly made the workers more dependent on the employer than they had been before, and one of the most hated features of factory life was its discipline—the need to start punctually, to work regular hours and to do the job systematically, things which people did not need to bother about when they worked in the privacy of their own homes.

But at the same time the mustering of so many workers under a factory roof gave opportunity for forming trade unions, and these unions enabled the workers in due course to bargain successfully for better wages and better conditions of employment. Other results of the coming of factories and of new capital into industry, and of increased production, were a cheapening of goods and in the long run a higher standard of living for all. But these advantages lay far in the future. The factory system first grew up, as we have seen, during a period when England was engaged in a series of wars. One consequence was fluctuations in trade and employment from year to year: another was a financial crisis, resulting in the suspension of cash payments by the Bank of England (26 February 1797) and the first introduction of income tax. Yet a third was a panic measure, following upon a whole series of Acts of political repression aimed at 'revolutionaries', by which the younger Pitt's government forbade the existence of trade unions. These Combination Acts of 1799 and 1800 will be considered later, as they were the starting-point of the history of the modern trade union movement.

The Village Poor

But the actions of the authorities to meet the emergency of the French wars were not all of them repressive. The Berkshire magistrates when they met at Speenhamland, near Newbury, in 1795, intended at first to establish a minimum wage system for the county under the obsolete Elizabethan Statute of Apprentices. Even the alternative course which they adopted in deference to farming opinion—the 'Speenhamland system'—was well-intentioned. Berkshire, followed by most of the other counties in southern and eastern England, decided to make up the wages of 'every poor and industrious man' to a total sum fixed by the size of his family and the varying cost of a loaf of bread. The dearer the bread, the higher the wage—that was reasonable; what was not reasonable was the undertaking to make up wages, which meant that farmers had no reason to pay a living wage since the smaller wage got a larger addition from the rates. The result was that the rates became a terrible burden on the country, while a great number of farm labourers, though kept from starving, were made to feel that they were a class of paupers, because they were unable to keep themselves and their families by the wages they actually earned. Some of the big farmers began at this time to employ regular gangs of women for hoeing and weeding. This tended to reduce the rates, since the women came from the labourers' families, at the expense of home life and probably of health. The practice was not abolished by law until 1867.

Moreover, the new farming robbed many villagers of the strips of land which had provided much of the family's food supply, and at the same time the money earned by the wife and children at wool-cleaning, carding, and spinning rapidly decreased. The hand-loom weavers, some of whom were also small-scale farmers, did not suffer appreciably by the competition of power-looms before 1815, but their weekly earnings then fell fast, until in the 1830s and 1840s a whole-time weaver did not earn as much as 10s. (50p) a week. Under these new conditions it was difficult to maintain a family, and many villagers drifted reluctantly and by slow stages (in days when there were no railways) to the new factories and mines. It was made easier for them to go because the Law of Settlement had been modified. After 1795 it was illegal to remove a new arrival from a parish until he actually asked for poor relief.

Movement of Population

One of the most striking features of the rise of the factory system was the shifting of population towards the factories of the north and the Midlands. The new industrial areas increased their inhabitants very fast.[1] At the first census in 1801 London, with more than a million inhabitants, was the only town in Great Britain whose population exceeded 100000. In the next forty years, however, four thriving provincial trade centres reached 200000—namely, Liverpool, Glasgow, Manchester, and Birmingham (in that order). Glasgow, for instance, grew twice as fast as Edinburgh, which had been ahead of it as recently as 1801. The very first factories, because they were dependent on water-power, had often been placed at lonely spots in the upper valleys of Pennine streams where the current flowed fastest. But from 1785 onwards the steam-engine had been installed in many spinning-mills, replacing water-driven machinery, and by 1815 it was also beginning to be used for the new power looms. This led to a grouping of factories in large centres where coal was locally mined or otherwise obtainable. At the same time there was an increase in iron production to meet the demands for new machinery, which was now almost entirely of iron to stand the strain of steam-power.

Isolated villages on the coal-fields or near the iron furnaces in the north and Midlands rapidly expanded into towns. These districts had been poor and thinly populated and now became rich and crowded, whereas towns in East Anglia and parts of the West of England—which had prospered under the old domestic system and were far from coal-fields—gradually declined and superfluous villagers moved from many districts. Few people moved long distances—many families went on foot and took their belongings with them. What usually happened was that they ventured to the nearest town or the next county, and it was the districts closest to each of the industrial areas which contributed most largely to its new industrial population. The Irish travelled farthest but they travelled most easily, crossing the sea for as little as 4d. a head to fill the great ports like Liverpool and Glasgow, and bringing with them from their native land an appallingly low standard of life and civilization. The effect was to prolong slum conditions—or even to create them.

The New Towns

This rapid movement of population led to acute overcrowding. New towns were built without proper supervision. There was in those days no planning of housing development to hinder this expansion; there were no building regulations, no sanitary inspectors, no government control, and indeed very few accepted standards of decency, to prevent people from living where they chose or how they chose. A man who

[1] See Appendix II, Table 2.

Scene on Thames-side between Lambeth and Vauxhall (Pictorial Times, October 1846): *'The open sewers are one chief cause of the filth and disease of this locality.'*

lost his job or his land in one place had no council house, no unemployment insurance or national assistance to enable him to go on living there. When he found a job in a new place he would welcome the enterprise of builders who ran up jerry-built cottages, for otherwise he would have had literally nowhere to live. And thus there soon arose a very grievous housing problem—as our reformers learned fifty years later on, when they began to tidy up the towns which the early nineteenth century had left for later generations.

Men who bought building sites put up as many houses as possible on those sites. The rows of houses were crowded close together; they were even built back to back, in which case through ventilation was impossible and half the rooms had no direct light. There was little attention to drainage, sanitation or water supplies. The building materials were usually of the cheapest quality, and there were special shortages which caused building-work to be scamped during the long war period. Lack of a good water supply was another of the evils of the new towns. Often water was sold; for example, at Hyde near Manchester, the poor people had to pay a shilling a week to water-carriers. 'Many of the poor beg water, many steal it,' said a witness to a Royal Commission on sanitary conditions in 1842. With this scarcity of water, even for drinking, impure water from stagnant ditches was used for cooking. It must be remembered that many houses—then as again after the two world wars—had to accommodate several families. And in those days of the early factory system, even undrained cellars were often let as separate dwellings.

Two other essentials to health—fresh air and light—were also lacking. The old window-tax, increased in 1784, amounted at one time during the Napoleonic war to 8s. for houses with six windows or less; £1 for seven windows; £1 13s. for eight windows, and so on. To save expense windows in older buildings were blocked up—as we can still see today in some old houses—and when new houses were built the number of windows was reduced as much as possible. Stairways were often without any windows and were pitch dark at noon. Moreover the windows in many houses did not open, and there was no inlet for fresh air. Factories, also, were built entirely to suit the work and not the workers. Until 1833 there was no State interference and no factory inspectorate.

The streets of many towns were badly drained and were full of holes. After rain the gutters were flooded with filthy water; and at other times were full of all kinds of decaying refuse. There were no regular scavenging services. Proper sewers did not exist: the drains from the best houses emptied into underground cesspools. It is little wonder that typhus, cholera and other fevers were prevalent, though the arrival of the first great cholera epidemic from Russia in 1831 caused the first local boards of health to be established by Parliament. But as soon as the scare was over they were allowed to lapse. To sum up, between 1815 and 1832 the death-rate, which had been falling for about a century, was again on the increase.

How the workers lived was not then regarded as the business of the factory owner or capitalist; in the early years of the factory system, when all was experiment and change, he certainly had enough to do in organizing the output and sale of the factory's products. As the supreme head, he of course decided the hours of work and the rate of wages, though the larger factories had overseers for engaging and dismissing employees, and for keeping the factory hands at work. Again, the factory buildings and equipment were also the concern of the employer: but he normally regarded them from the standpoint of their cheapness and handiness without much consideration for health and safety.

However, while the conditions under which men, women and children of the labouring class worked and lived were in many cases worse than similar families had experienced before the Industrial Revolution, the value of the wages was not. Except for those who were unemployed and special groups like the hand-loom weavers, workers after the immediate post-war period—which may be said to have ended with a fall of prices in 1820–1—were on the average better off than the generations before 1793. As for the more limited group of workers employed in the new factories, a Government Commissioner declared in 1832 that their wages were 'so large as to appear almost incredible to those accustomed to regard the scanty earnings of the agricultural labourers'.

15 Women and children; the Factory Acts

In this chapter we are going to consider how women and children fared in this age of change, taking the children first, because the early Industrial Revolution brought some of them, the very poorest of the poor, into a prominence they had never had before. As we saw in the last chapter, the first factories were placed in the hills, where quick-flowing streams and rivers would turn the mill-wheel. But there were very few people living up in the hills of Derbyshire, Lancashire, and Yorkshire, so the difficulty of finding workers was solved by sending for children. One of the most terrible things about eighteenth-century life, as Captain Coram had shown, was the treatment of orphaned and deserted children, of whom London and the larger towns had great numbers for which to provide. The parish in which they were born used to apprentice them almost as soon as they could walk, to any master who was willing to employ them and pay for their keep. Whether they really learnt a trade, as apprentices were supposed to do, or were just used as cheap labour and, when they came of age, turned loose on the world without any special skill, depended on the sort of master they happened to get. These pauper apprentices were sent off in large numbers to the factories, where buildings of a rough-and-ready kind were put up for the children to live in during the long period, seven or ten or more years, of their legal apprenticeship. They had few rights of any kind, and no right to leave their employer's service.

This was so hard on the children that in 1802 a law was passed to improve the conditions in which they lived when not at work and to forbid the factory-owners from making them work for more than twelve hours a day; they were also forbidden to make them work at night. From this we can imagine the sort of life these children had been leading. But this particular form of employment for children was already coming to an end by 1802, because the newer and larger factories were built near the coal-fields and towns quickly grew up around them. The people living in those towns sent their sons and

Scene from Michael Armstrong the Factory Boy *by Frances Trollope, published in 1840.*

daughters to work in the factories, not as apprentices but as wage-earners, just as naturally as in earlier days they would have found work for them to do at home. The children did not earn more than a few pence a week, but it paid for their keep. The employer, on the other hand, wanted the children not only as cheap labour but for two special reasons: their fingers were more sensitive than those of adults, so that they quickly learnt the work of 'piecers', who join the broken ends of thread, and it was easier for small bodies to worm their way under or through the machinery for cleaning it. There was also, alas! the advantage of their comparative docility. Adults, as we have previously noticed, resented the regular hours and controlled activities of factory work and were less in awe of the foreman or manager. Children, on the other hand, as they had never worked under any other conditions, would accept factory rules without much audible protest, and if they broke them could easily be punished.

The work was not always exacting. *Michael Armstrong the Factory Boy* and his friends are not pictured in a scene of unending labour, and in real life we know how, in the Lanarkshire of the 1820s, young David Livingstone learnt his Latin grammar for college from a book propped up against the machines. But the hours were very long—often twelve hours a day and frequently more—and the conditions (heat, noise, dust, and unfenced machinery) often led to children becoming sickly and their bodies stunted. It is not a proud memory that the wealth of early nineteenth-century Britain was built on such a foundation; but before we condemn the factory-owners too sweepingly we should remember that child labour was nothing new—it was, for instance, a prominent feature of the woollen industry when Defoe was on his tour, long before the factories began. We ought also to take into account the sort of life which was led by other children in the time of the early factories.

Education

Only a minority of children attended school at all regularly, even if they were not otherwise employed. There was often a primitive Dame's School, to which the very small ones were sent at a trifling fee, to be kept quiet rather than to learn, and since 1782 Sunday Schools (popularized by Robert Raikes of Gloucester) had been available. These concentrated on teaching their pupils how to read the Bible and were supported by the churches for that purpose; diligent pupils of course acquired the ability to read in general, but at the rate of one lesson a week progress was extremely slow. In some fortunate neighbourhoods there was a Charity School, probably dating from the reign of Queen Anne, or there might be one of the new National Schools attached to the parish church—the National Society had been founded in 1811 to promote education in Church principles—or a school belonging to the rival Nonconformist British and Foreign School Society, which dated from 1808. These schools would teach the three Rs after a fashion, but attendance at them did not often lead on to the Grammar School, which commonly required the payment of fees and was in practice reserved for the sons of the middle and upper classes. For girls there were no grammar schools and very little education of any kind.

A school using the Monitorial System.

To complete our list, we must mention the half-dozen great Public Schools, like Eton, Westminster, and Harrow, though they were far out of reach of the ordinary people we are thinking of. But even there the life was hard, the teaching harsh, and the curriculum narrow—six hours of Latin and Greek six days a week, with the Greek Testament for a change on the seventh—from which we can judge what it was like at less favoured schools.

The latest method of teaching for the masses, thought to be a labour-saving device as valuable as the spinning inventions, was styled the 'Monitorial System'. Each lesson was to be taught by the master to a select group of older pupils; when they knew it by heart, the school was to be divided into classes, each of which would learn the same lesson from one of the older pupils or 'Monitors'; in this way a single master, it was claimed, could teach a school of almost unlimited size. We can only guess at the means employed to keep order and secure results by this system!

Most children worked, as a matter of course, if their parents could hear of any work that they could do. Parents as a whole did not resist the employment of their children in factories, not only because they needed the additional earnings but because factory work was not necessarily the worst work. Apprentices in shops and handicrafts might have a kind master; on the other hand, they might be treated more inhumanly than by an overseer in a factory, whose activities were in public. Life on the farm, which often gave employment in bird-scaring to children who were only just old enough to walk, might be healthier but was often much lonelier than the bustle of the factory.

Worst of all, perhaps, was the work in the galleries of the coal-mines, where the smallest children sat alone in the dark to open and shut the ventilation doors, while bigger ones dragged the trucks of coal with bent backs or even on all fours along the low passages.

Work Done by Women

Women were also employed to haul or carry coal between the face, where the miner worked with his pick, and the more or less distant pithead of the primitive collieries; they were employed in far greater numbers in the cotton-spinning mills. It was not a new thing, though a bad thing, for them to do heavy industrial work: we have referred before to the nail-and chain-making of the Black Country, in which women had for centuries been prominent. Indeed, it is a remarkable fact that in the case of the well-to-do merchant class the Industrial Revolution had the opposite effect. In the old days, when the master-craftsman or shopkeeper usually had his home above his place of business, his women-folk naturally took some part in the work that was going on; many a widow ran a business with success until her sons were old enough to take over. But with the growth of factories and factory towns, it became usual for the successful factory-owner to live in some select residential quarter remote from the factory, and it became a mark of his success that his wife and daughters lived in ignorance of his business or of any other business; their idleness advertised his wealth. The more energetic and adventurous women of this class looked with secret envy upon the comparative freedom of the mill-lassie in shawl and clogs.

The Industrial Revolution gave two benefits to working women. Firstly, by transferring the place of work from the home to the factory it made it possible for the home to be kept tidier, healthier and more private. How encumbered a cottage must have been in the old days when it contained spinning-wheel, weaver's loom, wool that was being prepared for use, unspun rovings, unwoven yarn, raw material just arrived from the clothier, and parcels of yarn or cloth due for return to him! Secondly, the regular if small wage, earned in the factory and paid direct to the person who earned it, gave women their first chance to be independent of father or husband. Of course, the wage of the unmarried daughter or the wife who kept on at the factory (the usual practice in the cotton towns) might all be needed to support the home, but what was earned was indisputably hers.

There might have been a third benefit. In theory, the factory system gave women workers the same chance as men now had of securing better wages and conditions by forming trade unions, when they had become legal again in 1824–5 after a quarter of a century of suppression. But women, it must be confessed showed little readiness to give time or money or interest to organizing in their own defence, even where—as in the coal-mines—they were given degrading work to do, of a kind unsuitable to their sex.

Shaftesbury, the Children's Friend

However, it was not so much the efforts of the early trade unions as the devoted work of a great Tory nobleman and Evangelical religious leader, the 7th Earl of Shaftesbury (1801–85), which ended the gravest

A child sweep of 1853, ringing the area bell for admittance to a town house. Earlier in the year a proposal by Lord Shaftesbury to make sixteen the minimum age for entering the trade had been successfully denounced by a fellow-peer as 'a pitiful cant of pseudo-philanthropy'.

evils. As Lord Ashley he sat in the House of Commons for a quarter of
a century (1826–51), and it was during this period chiefly that his
campaigns on behalf of women and child-workers established a higher
standard than had existed before the Industrial Revolution. This last
fact is clearly shown in his much longer struggle on behalf of the
'climbing boys', exposed to death or injury inside the twisting chim-
neys of the big houses they were sent to clean, for this terrible practice
dated from the earlier part of the eighteenth century. Not only did it
arise before the worst evils of the new industrialism; it also outlasted
them. Public sympathy was first claimed for these hapless children,
who were employed as small, and therefore as young, as possible, by
the eighteenth-century philanthropist, Hanway, and in William
Blake's *Songs of Innocence*, published in 1789:

> *When my mother died I was very young,*
> *And my father sold me, while yet my tongue*
> *Could scarcely cry"Weep!'Weep!'Weep!'*
> *So your chimneys I sweep and in soot I sleep.*

Yet the system went on almost unchecked until the time of Dickens
—Oliver Twist, it will be remembered, narrowly escaped being
bound apprentice to a sweep—and figures prominently in Charles
Kingsley's *Water Babies* in 1863. Not until 1875 did Lord Shaftesbury
finally triumph over custom and supposed convenience.

Nearly all the philanthropic works, which still cause Shaftesbury's
portrait (here reproduced) to be among the select few that mean
something to the average visitor when he sees them at the National

Portrait Gallery, belong to a period a little later than that which we are now considering. But it seems appropriate to end this chapter with his great reforms; for the struggle for the Factory Acts marks the transition to the less inhumane Victorian era.

The Struggle for the Factory Acts

There was a long, painful struggle to bring about improved conditions in the factories, and the method was by getting Parliament to pass Acts which would prohibit the worst practices. To us today it seems obvious that such regulations should exist, but at the time people did not look at things in the same way. To begin with, very often the facts were not known, at least until government commissions were appointed to investigate and report. Many of the manufacturers held that Factory Acts would be an interference with private property and free enterprise. They argued also that they would increase their costs. And to increase costs would lead to a fall in sales and profits which would bring unemployment and so, instead of helping the workers, would do them harm. The manufacturers, without being deliberately cruel, wished to get their labour as cheaply as possible. At the same time, where self-interest is involved, people are easily led to ignore suffering and cruelty.

From time to time there was a demand for reform. In 1802 the Health and Morals of Apprentices Act was passed, following on some recommendations made by the better Lancashire mill-owners, including the elder Sir Robert Peel. The Act, as has been noticed already, fixed the maximum day for pauper apprentices at twelve hours, and forbade their working at night. In addition, factories were to be properly ventilated and whitewashed. Apprentices were to have better clothes and sleeping accommodation, and were to be given a little elementary education. The JPs were to enforce the provisions of the Act, and to send visitors to the factories.

But the Act had little practical effect. The JPs were often friends of the local manufacturers, and did not enforce the law properly. It was possible also to evade the Act, which applied only to apprentices, by engaging unapprenticed paupers for a term of years—and other children were now readily available. Meanwhile one important factory-owner, Robert Owen, had shown in his New Lanark mills that it was possible to improve factory conditions and make the mills pay at the same time, and he tried to convince other mill-owners of this and to bring about the State reform of the factory system. Another Act was passed in 1819, applying to cotton factories only, which forbade the employment of a child under nine. Once more, however, there was little result; there was still no adequate inspection, and the age of children employed might be unknown or concealed.

But in 1832 the reform of Parliament made other changes more feasible,[1] and by this time factory reform in particular mustered a number of energetic supporters. Though Robert Owen had sold his factories and was engrossed in trade unionism, his place as leader was taken by Ashley (the future Lord Shaftesbury), and he acted in association with men who represented many different political, religious and social groupings. The best-remembered, perhaps, is John Fielden, Quaker and Radical MP, whose spinning factories at Todmorden, Yorkshire, were among the largest works in the world. To him fell the honour of carrying the Ten Hours Bill in 1847, when Lord Ashley had temporarily vacated his seat in the Commons. Others were John Doherty, a trade union organizer; Richard Oastler, a Tory land agent, who stirred men's consciences by letters headed 'Yorkshire Slavery', which he wrote to the *Leeds Mercury* in 1830; and Michael Sadler, an importer of Irish linen and Fellow of the Royal Society. There was a strong agitation in favour of reform, inside Parliament and outside. Parliament set up a committee to make inquiries, and Ashley pressed for real reform. As a result the Factory Act of 1833 was passed, the first **really** effective Factory Act, often known as Althorp's Act from the name of the leader of the House of Commons who sponsored it in its final form. It applied to all textile factories—not only to cotton, like the Act of 1819. No child under nine was to work in a mill; children under thirteen were restricted to a nine-hour day; and young persons of thirteen to eighteen were restricted to a twelve-hour day. The most important feature of the Act was that it was to be enforced by the first salaried inspectors. These were men whose full-time job it was to see that the law was obeyed in the factories, and they largely succeeded. The Act also provided for two hours' schooling a day for each child-worker under thirteen—though what the sense of this was it is difficult to see. The children were at work while the schools were open, even if there were schools near by; the factory-owners were not likely to be helpful in providing specially for schools or teachers; and nine hours' work plus two hours' schooling would leave the children with almost as heavy a burden as 'young persons'.

Further Factory Legislation

Nothing had been done so far to limit directly the hours of adult-workers, and therefore the struggle had still to go on for a shorter

[1] See below, p. 162.

working-day and also for greater safety and better conditions in both factories and mines. Lord Ashley carried on his noble work of pressing for reform.

A Royal Commission brought to light some of the horrors of the mines, and in 1842 Parliament passed the Mines Act. This prohibited the employment underground of women and girls, and of boys under ten—Lord Ashley would have preferred to make it 'under thirteen'. Fifteen was at the same time made the minimum age for the highly responsible work of an engineman in charge of the winding apparatus on the surface. It required another Act in 1850 properly to establish inspectors of mines; they had been included in Ashley's Bill in 1842, but their powers were whittled away by the House of Lords.

The Factory Act of 1844 made an important step forward. Women were classed as 'young persons', and so their working-day was restricted to twelve hours. Children's hours were reduced to six-and-a-half and more practical provision made for education. The same Act required the fencing-in of machinery. Unfenced machinery, and also the practice of cleaning machinery while in motion, had caused many accidents. Women's hair and clothing were particularly liable to catch in the machines, causing serious injury. Inasmuch as it made the fencing of machinery compulsory, the new law also protected adult men; in addition, the Act prohibited women, young persons or children from cleaning and shifting machinery while it was in motion.

Three years later the Factory Act of 1847 was passed. At last the provision of a ten-hour day for women and young persons became law. Ashley had worked long for this, and had hoped that it might also restrict the hours of men, because it was difficult to keep the factories working with the labour of men only. But some employers still found means, by working women and young persons in shorter shifts, to work the men for as long as fifteen hours a day, and two more laws were required, in 1850 and 1853, to establish the principle that factories might only be open to women and young persons for twelve hours daily (8 on Saturdays), within which they might work a 10½-hour day (7½ on Saturdays). The extra half-hour remained until 1874, but adult male-workers were more interested in the fact that their own hours were now indirectly but effectively restricted—a change which marks the beginning of the transition away from the bleak age of the earlier nineteenth century in which Lord Shaftesbury performed his heroic labours.

16 Britain after Waterloo—the new society

The growth and misgrowth of industrial towns and the hardships, slowly surmounted, of the industrial life of women and children are characteristic features of the first half of the nineteenth century in its entirety. But the period just after the close of the Napoleonic Wars in 1815 was also darkened for contemporaries by special problems, which we can now appreciate more easily in the light of two later post-war eras. War in this case had given an intermittent stimulus to industry—the 'false and bloated prosperity', as the journalist William Cobbett called it; there had been heavy demand for arms, cloth and leather for the armies. Now slump followed. Factories and plants were found too big for peace-time needs; capital could not be used, profits fell, and employment fell also. Iron-workers, gunmakers, clothiers and food contractors all suffered. At the same time men came back from the Army and Navy; half a million men were looking for work in an economic system which was contracting.

War had helped British farmers. British agriculture had had a virtual monopoly, for war had shut out supplies of foreign corn. As population was increasing at the same time, there was a greatly increased demand for bread which led to high prices for wheat. As a result new land was ploughed, marsh and waste were reclaimed, enclosure was pressed on. When peace came, foreign corn was again available, and prices fell. Tenants could not pay their rents, poorer land went out of use, agricultural wages and employment were reduced. It was to give landlords and farmers a measure of protection that the Corn Law was passed in 1815. But this, by raising the price of bread, hit at the factory workers and the unemployed. Apart from a protective measure of this kind, governments at the time had little understanding of economics, and had no plans for dealing with the economic problems facing the country. The general policy was to let things alone, a policy to which French economists had given the name of *Laissez-faire*.

A contemporary impression of the charge of the 15th Hussars at Peterloo, on which the Prime Minister (Lord Liverpool) commented that 'the magistrates were substantially right' in giving the troops the order to 'disperse the crowd'.

Post-war Distress

Consequently, there was unrest and disturbance. We have already mentioned the machine-breaking activities of the Luddites in 1811–12; these were revived in 1815–16. Other rather similar outbursts of popular discontent occurred in places as widely separated as London (Spa Fields riot) and Scotland (the so-called Battle of Bonnymuir), though the most dramatic episode, the one which created most stir at the time and is best remembered now, was the 'Peterloo massacre' in August 1819 at Manchester. On that occasion a squadron of Hussars, riding in to break up a huge but peaceful demonstration of workers, caused eleven deaths and about 500 injuries to the panic-stricken crowd. These casualties, which deeply impressed the public mind, were at least inflicted in hot blood. When the farm labourers of southern England demonstrated in the winter of 1830–1 against threshing machines and starvation wages (between which they saw a connection), His Majesty's judges sent three to the gallows and 420 to the penal settlements in Australia.

The discontent had many causes—unemployment, low wages, the high price of bread, unfair taxation, the need for parliamentary reform—to which we might add the underlying resentment against the whole nature of factory work and all the miseries of life in the industrial town. Hand-loom weavers vainly struggling to compete with machinery; workers who found themselves 'stood off' by some sudden slump in an export trade; and to a lesser extent everyone who was trying to fit into the new industries and the life of the new towns—all these were the victims of that change from the old to the new. But we may pause here to remind ourselves by a brief survey that this was also an age of energy and progress.

Agriculture and Industry

First, the methods of agriculture were greatly improved. George III, 'Farmer George', and the great landowners had been united in their zeal for agriculture. The enthusiasm which animated members of the Board of Agriculture and others was voiced by Sir John Sinclair in 1803. 'We have begun', he said, 'another campaign against a foreign country (France) . . . let us not be satisfied with the liberation of Egypt, or the subjugation of Malta, but let us subdue Finchley Common; let us conquer Hounslow Heath; let us compel Epping Forest to submit to the yoke of Improvement.' In 1815 there were two centres of progress in agriculture. First, there was 'old England', the eastern counties—Essex, Suffolk and Norfolk, with Hertfordshire and Leicestershire. The second centre of successful farming was in the Lowlands of Scotland. The farms of East Lothian were among the best managed in Britain, and on them new methods of breeding and cultivation had been quickly adopted or in some cases invented.

In 1815 some people were already viewing with concern the growth in the number of persons employed in industry and commerce. Accurate measurement of change was now for the first time possible, as the first census taken in 1801 was to be repeated at ten-year intervals. In 1811, 6 129 000 persons were dependent on agriculture and mining as against 7 071 000 persons on commerce, navigation and manufacture. Agriculture and mining produced to a value of £107 246 000; commerce, navigation and manufacture produced £183 908 000. Was it wise, men asked, to sacrifice agriculture to industry, for England to become like Tyre of old and Venice in the Middle Ages, a purely commercial and industrial state dependent on other countries for her bread and meat?

The coal-mines grew in importance year by year. Gas-lighting, for instance, started about the end of the war in London and other large

Gas lighting in the streets. The lamps were lit each night by a lamplighter.

towns, and by 1837 an ancient export trade in coal had risen to a million tons a year. On account of the demands of the Army and the Navy, the iron industry had been prosperous during the quarter of a century before 1815. The price of iron had been rising, and wages had also been increased. The restoration of peace in 1815 caused a sudden drop in demand, but soon iron exports, particularly to America, were rising more rapidly than any others. Many small masters shared in the profits during the good times, for Sheffield and Birmingham were then towns of small workshops rather than large factories, Sheffield dealing in cutlery, Birmingham in machinery, hardware, and a great number of small articles. The largest factories in Birmingham represented a capital of £6000 to £8000, but the majority had a capital of less than £1000.

In the textile industry, the woollen trade, which had long been the chief source of England's industrial wealth, now occupied second place, having been overtaken by cotton. In 1815 it was estimated that the profits from the cotton manufacture amounted to £23 million, while those of the woollen industry were only £18 million. Machinery driven by water-power or steam was coming into general use in the cotton factories for spinning the yarn, and for finishing processes. All this pointed to future prosperity.

Hand-loom Weavers

But power-looms made slow progress; in 1823 the number of steam-looms in the whole country was apparently not much above 10 000. This was enough, however, to force down the earnings of the hand-loom weavers, who long continued to be one of the largest and poorest classes of the industrial population. They were at least half a million in number, and perhaps considerably more. They included some who were reluctant to change from a job which had at one time given them good earnings and an independent way of life; but very many were simply unable to find another job. It should be noted that these hand-weavers no longer included any large proportion of part-time farmers, for the loss of their 'strips' had driven many of these to move to the industrial districts, where the women and children could find work in the mills while the men worked at home. The hand-weavers were to be found in the silk industry of Spitalfields and Macclesfield, and in all the woollen-weaving districts from Glasgow to Norfolk, and from the West Riding of Yorkshire to the south-western counties of Gloucester, Somerset, and Wiltshire. Their desperate struggle to stave off the introduction of the machine by cutting the price of handwork continued in out-of-the-way places until some time in the second half of the nineteenth century.

Improvements in Transport

By 1815 the means of transport had been improved. With better roads, there was great rivalry between various coach services. Newspapers viewed with concern the racing between drivers of stage coaches. In 1815 Edinburgh was only sixty hours coach journey from London; in the middle of the eighteenth century, the journey had taken from ten to fourteen days.

Steam-power had already been applied, as we know, to navigation in river estuaries and canals. The Calais packets began to ply in 1821, and in 1824 the holiday-steamers which made the fortunes of Margate and Ramsgate; regular Atlantic crossings by steamer date from the 1840s. A start had also been made with the application of steam-power to the work of propelling a locomotive. The first 'iron-horse' or steam

Cumberland Terrace, Regent's Park, with its seven huge porticoes, built in 1827.

carriage was made in 1801 by Richard Trevithick, a Cornishman; in 1804 his road locomotive ran adventurously through the London streets to Paddington and Islington. A number of steam coaches made a brief appearance on the roads during the next twenty or thirty years; but the future lay with George Stephenson, a colliery engine-man, who in 1814 had made an engine, named *Blücher* after the famous Prussian general who was shortly to fight at the side of the British against Napoleon. This engine drew coal trucks, not passengers—but the coming of the railways brings us to the Victorian Age.

Enough has been said to show that the era of Waterloo, marked by economic distress, is also marked by economic progress. Similarly, while this was a period in which appalling slums were being created, so that the horrors of Manchester, Liverpool, Birmingham, and Glasgow rivalled the horrors which had existed in East London for a century or more, it was also a period of important social advances.

Social Progress

London, for instance, was beautified by the great building schemes of the Prince Regent's architect, John Nash; he designed the processional way from his master's residence at Carlton House (where Carlton

House Terrace stands now) up Regent Street and Portland Place to the great terraces at Regent's Park. This is also the period of the development of Belgravia as a sumptuous new aristocratic quarter for the world's wealthiest capital. The middle class, on the other hand, both in London and the provinces, were housed in villas of little or no architectural merit, which arouse no interest today; but it was a most important aspect of the change from old to new that this class was increasing rapidly in numbers and influence. Merchants and bankers; the new factory-owners; the old profession of the law and the new profession of engineering—all these were beginning to have a new sense of their own importance, even in comparison with the landed magnates who had ruled Britain for five generations, unchallenged since 1688. After 1815 the men of influence in politics included Peel, the son of a successful cotton-spinner; Canning and Huskisson, men of middle-class origins who represented commercial interests as successive Members of Parliament for Liverpool; and Brougham, a self-made Scottish lawyer with a special interest in the reform of education. In 1828 Brougham helped to found London University; the improvements in curricula and teaching, which began about the same time at Oxford and Cambridge, are another mark of the rise of the middle class.

As for the workers, it is impossible to generalize. It is not enough to say that the purchasing-power of their wages was on the whole greater than before the French Wars, though this fact is sufficiently important to bear repeating. For we cannot estimate with any accuracy what proportion of individuals or families gained less by the better wage rates than they lost through periods of unemployment. Nor is it satisfactory to point to the increased chances of self-improvement which the industrial towns offered, though it was obviously easier than before to change one's job for the better. By 1825 all the bigger towns had Mechanics' Institutes, with lectures and library; in the next year a Society for the Diffusion of Useful Knowledge was set up to provide cheap books for the ambitious worker—all this by voluntary effort. But we have to admit that there may have been very many workers whose only ambition was to be allowed to return from the rush and din and ugliness of the new town to the simpler, slower life they had left behind for ever in the country.

The champion of this last type was William Cobbett (1762–1835), the self-educated son of a poor farm-labourer, who became soldier, farmer, politician, and journalist—but it is as a journalist that he is still remembered. In his *Rural Rides*, which were written in the 1820s as a series of diary items for his paper, the *Political Register*, Cobbett is never tired of praising country life in the good old days, before

London became the 'Great Wen' and the nation fell into the power of bankers, stock jobbers, and all the many new types which he heartily disliked and denounced.

Cobbett wrote so well that his opinions still colour our picture of the age. But perhaps we get a truer picture from the career of a man like Robert Owen (1771–1858), a penniless shop assistant from Newtown in far-off Montgomeryshire, who became one of the chief factory-owners of the day. Having made a fortune in a few years at his New Lanark mills (near Glasgow), he went on to be the pioneer, not only of improved conditions for his work-people and their families, but of the co-operative movement, national trade unions, socialism, and other new ideas which grew out of the industrial changes. And, finally, Cobbett's outlook is certainly less representative than that of George Stephenson, the wholly uneducated son of a colliery fireman—he was seventeen before he learnt to read—to whom the Industrial Revolution gave the chance to develop the locomotive engine and plan the railways. The Stockton and Darlington railway, with which so much of our modern civilization begins, was being opened at the very time when Cobbett was riding through the country and saying that every change *he* saw was a change for the worse.[1]

---

[1] Cobbett's point of view had been largely shared by the poet Shelley, who died in the heyday of political repression under Lord Liverpool. (See Appendix I, No. 3.)

THE GREAT
VICTORIAN AGE

17 The coming of the railways

Queen Victoria had been on the throne for rather more than a year when the first of the main line railways existing today was opened from London to Birmingham in September 1838. In the course of her reign, and chiefly in the first half of it, the network spread throughout Britain, so that the railway became the standard form of transport for passengers and goods alike—much quicker than the canal, much cheaper and easier and quicker than travel by road. Not only so, but the building of railways in foreign countries, in the Empire, and in India, became one of our most valuable export industries: the rails, the engines and carriages, and the skilled operatives to start the new system—all these came from Britain and were an advertisement of our industrial leadership.

By the time of the great Queen's death in 1901, railways had spread to most civilized countries, but the British railway system was so complete, well built, and efficient that we still retained an advantage over our rivals in the ease with which raw materials, coal, foodstuffs, and finished goods could be moved about the country. Even today the railway viaducts and bridges and some of the big railway stations, like Euston (before its reconstruction) or the huge vault of St Pancras, are regarded by many as the best architecture of all that was inherited from the Victorian period. So we may well make the railway the starting-point for our study of the period of Britain's greatest power and prosperity and self-satisfaction, which we call 'Victorian'.

The railway resulted from a combination of two ideas—the mounting of a steam-engine on a carriage so as to use its power to propel that and other attached carriages; and the propulsion of the carriages along a track made of parallel lines. We have already mentioned Trevithick's

Puffing Billy *(still to be seen in the Science Museum, South Kensington) has two cylinders, rocking beams derived from Watt's engines, and a cog wheel linking each pair of driving wheels: coupling rods were introduced on* Blücher.

locomotive, which ran along the road in Cornwall and in London. Primitive railways, made at first of wooden planks, were then already a fairly common device for moving heavy material in mines and quarries, and on Tyneside and in South Wales iron railways often ran from the collieries down to the canal or river; the standard gauge of British Rail today reproduces what was found to be a convenient width for these early coal-trucks. It was in South Wales in 1804 that Trevithick's locomotive was put on a railway, and in Northumberland in 1813 that William Hedley produced *Puffing Billy*. This engine, as we can see, is a very clumsy machine, but it is evidently intended to draw other wagons along an iron railway, though the smallness of the flange on the inner edge of the wheels suggests that its speed would be extremely slow. *Puffing Billy* attracted the attention of George Stephenson, the engine-wright at Killingworth, a neighbouring colliery, and in 1814 he built his *Blücher* on the same general plan; but it was so much better that it could draw no fewer than eight trucks containing thirty tons of coal along the level, and even up slight slopes, at a speed of about nine miles an hour.

The Stockton–Darlington Railway

Eight years later, a railway for goods traffic was being planned between the towns of Darlington and Stockton-on-Tees. It was first intended to use horse-drawn trucks, but Stephenson suggested that steam locomotives should be used, and he was appointed to carry out the work. He built another engine, the *Locomotion*, and this drew a train of trucks at a speed of twelve miles an hour when the railway was opened for goods traffic in 1825. At first many people thought it would be unsafe to travel in a train drawn by a steam-engine—the engine might blow up, or the train catch fire. But before long, the merchants of Liverpool and Manchester decided to have a railway between their towns, and Stephenson carried out the work. The directors' prize for the best locomotive was won by Stephenson's famous *Rocket*, which travelled at the rate of twenty-nine miles an hour.

The Liverpool and Manchester Railway, opened in 1830, ran passenger trains as well as goods trains. In 1831, over 256 000 people travelled by train in six months, although the total length of the railways was only sixty-nine miles. In 1836–7 there was a short-lived 'boom' in railway construction, which provided more capital for two big schemes already under way for lines connecting London with Birmingham and Bristol, and the first of the big London stations was opened, Euston.

Of course, railway travel to begin with was by no means comfortable. There was much jolting and shaking. But in 1837 the diarist Charles Greville, when travelling from Birmingham to Liverpool in four-and-a-half hours, found nothing disagreeable about it except the whiffs of stinking air. 'Town after town, one park and country house after another, are left behind with the rapid variety of a panorama. The most surprising feature of all, apart from the speed, was the wonderful punctuality. It gave to man something of the precision of a machine.' Greville also notes that 'one engineer', on that journey in the first year of Victoria's reign, reached the astonishing speed of forty-five miles an hour, and that he was promptly dismissed by a prudent company running no risks. In a leaflet, *Rules for Railway Travelling*, some helpful advice is given: 'If a second-class carriage, as sometimes happens, has no door, passengers should take care not to put out their legs.' 'Beware of yielding to the sudden impulse to spring from the carriage to recover your hat which has blown off, or a parcel that has been dropped.'

At first some of the older and more select towns petitioned Parliament to keep the 'new-fangled notion outside their boundaries'. Other

Liverpool–Manchester Railway. Early train made up of four-wheel rolling stock and drawn by Jupiter (manufactured by Robert Stephenson and Co. in 1831 for £800). Ten years later,

people asked what would become of coach-makers, harness-makers, coach-masters and coachmen, inn-keepers, horse-breeders, and horse-dealers if the railways were allowed to take the place of travel by coach. Many landowners tried to prevent railways being built through their estates, and when they had to sell the land to the railway companies, they made them pay very high prices. But the early fears of the new means of travel died down, and the rapid development of passenger traffic proved even more important than the carriage of goods.

Construction of Main Lines

Then came the great 'railway mania', following nearly ten years after the first boom and marked by great schemes for amalgamations as well as for new lines, with huge investments by the general public, sensational profits, and sensational losses. The leading spirit was George Hudson (1800–71), the 'Railway King', a York draper who organized the Midland Railway Company, with its headquarters at Derby, and other shorter-lived combinations. In 1847 the bubble burst; Hudson and many other people were ruined; and he was accused (but not convicted) of fraud.

But railways, like the habit of Stock Exchange speculation, had come to stay, and between 1848 and 1870 the railway mileage in Britain increased from 4600 to 13 600 miles. The chief lines in this country were constructed between 1833 and 1862, and most of them were planned by George Stephenson (1781–1848) or his son Robert Stephenson (1803–59). The latter was engineer for the London to Birmingham line, which was built by 20 000 men in five years. His other achievements included the high-level bridge over the Tyne at Newcastle and the Britannia tubular bridge at the Menai Straits. Another of the famous railway pioneers was Isambard Kingdom Brunel (1806–59), the son of an exiled Frenchman. In 1838–41 he built the main line from London to Bristol, with its tunnels and bridges.

The long Box Tunnel on the section between Chippenham and Bath set a particularly hard problem for him to solve, as water gushed freely through crevices in the rock. Brunel was also prominent as the chief advocate of the seven-foot 'broad gauge', which the Great Western Railway did not finally abandon until 1892. His last great railway undertaking was the Royal Albert Bridge at Saltash, to carry the first lines into Cornwall.

The Brunels, father and son, were outstanding practical engineers and their careers illustrate how in those days able men learnt their jobs by doing them, that is by practical experience rather than by specific training in a technical college. Their careers also show that jobs were less specialized than they are today, and consequently a clever man might turn his hand to several different occupations in one lifetime. The father, Marc I. Brunel, served in the French navy but fled during the Revolution. He worked as an architect and civil engineer in New York. Then he came to England and was active as inventor and engineer. He invented certain machine tools, machinery for sawmills, and a stocking frame, and he drew plans for bridges in this country and abroad, and constructed the first tunnel under the Thames.

His son, after going to school in Paris, learnt his job as an engineer in his father's office and in working on the Thames tunnel. Apart from his achievements as a railway engineer, he designed Clifton suspension bridge at the age of twenty-five. Later he designed three famous ships. The *Great Western* was the first steamship built for the Atlantic crossing; the *Great Britain* was the first large ship with a screw-propeller; the *Great Eastern* held the world record for size—and, alas! uselessness—for nearly half a century. Brunel also designed a number of docks, piers and buildings. And he was a strong supporter of the Great Exhibition of 1851. Such men were the planners and pioneers of the railway age.

The work of the railway navvies, however, should also be remembered. It demanded great physical strength and powers of endurance. It was sometimes dangerous, especially when tunnels had to be blasted, often with insufficient safety devices. But it was comparatively well paid and attracted labourers from country places, especially districts where main lines were being constructed, of whom a large proportion eventually settled in the towns. A great many navvies came also from Ireland.

Railway building, 1836—a cutting excavated largely by hand labour.

Although the express services between principal towns soon reached high speeds, comparable with some twentieth-century services, it took years of practice before local trains ran to time as often as they do now. Another problem for the early railway companies was the method of signalling. The electric telegraph, first patented in 1837, did more than any other device to ensure safety, railway companies being the first organizations to make practical use of this great invention; by 1848, 1300 miles of telegraph wires had been set up along railway tracks. The telegraph could be used to send messages to advise station-masters of the approach of a train, to give notice of delays, and so on. But a better method of signalling to engine-drivers was needed. In due course the system of 'distant' and 'near' signals, operated by wires from a signal-box, was worked out, the intervening space being sufficient for the train to come to a halt at the second signal.

Further Development of Railways

In the second half of the nineteenth century more spectacular works were undertaken than had yet been known. Two of the greatest were the Severn Tunnel and the Forth Bridge, both of which took several years to build. They were under construction at the same time. The Severn Tunnel, $4\frac{1}{2}$ miles in length, by taking the railway under the river greatly shortened travel between South Wales and the West of England. In 1886 the first train ran through the tunnel, with a load of steam coal from Aberdare to Southampton. The Forth Bridge, with piers nearly as high as St Paul's Cathedral, was formally opened in 1890. It provided a direct route for the railway from Edinburgh to Dundee, Perth, and Aberdeen, and thereby facilitated travel between London and the north of Scotland. Gladstone, when he visited the bridge, was strong in his admiration of the work. It did indeed mark a great advance in science, engineering and industry since his early days when, as he described it himself, he had 'crossed the Forth in a little bit of an open boat, tumbling about'.

At first the government had left the building of a railway to unrestricted private enterprise, once the railway company had received powers from Parliament to buy the land required and to make all the other complicated financial arrangements for the work. But it was soon found necessary to pass certain Acts regulating the management. The Railway Passengers Act of 1844 required every railway to run some trains carrying third-class passengers at the rate of a penny a mile. The companies found that the third-class 'parliamentary' trains, as they were called, paid best of all, and third-class carriages were placed on all trains. An Act of 1871 required companies to notify all accidents, and the Board of Trade was to hold an inquiry when an accident occurred. About this time great improvements took place in the building of carriages; padded third-class seats, restaurant cars, and sleeping-cars for night travel began to be introduced; steel rails took the place of iron ones; and a better braking system made travel both safer and more comfortable.

Among the many small local companies, which had built the railways by private enterprise, a process of amalgamation went on. The Great Western Railway, for example, which had built the line from Paddington to Bristol, later took over four smaller companies which had laid down sections of line as far as Penzance. Similar amalgamations went on in other parts of the country, so that before the First World War the main railway companies were seven or eight in number. After that war, in 1921, the number of companies was reduced to four, the GWR, the LMS, the LNER, and the SR. Since then the main event in the story of railway management has been the nationalization of the railways after the Second World War. National-ization had long been a controversial political measure, and its good and bad features are still debated.

The Advantages of Railways

In the early days, of course, there had been considerable opposition to the railways, as there generally is to anything new. All those interested in coach and road travel, and in canals, and also country gentlemen who wished to preserve parks and country houses in peace and quiet, did what they could to oppose the coming of lines of track and steam monsters which disturbed cattle and frightened horses. Some people scoffed at the possibilities opening out; they argued that a speed greater than that of the old stage-coach would be too dangerous, and that the new tunnels and bridges would collapse. In spite of such fears the railways grew rapidly. Fears, however, were not altogether with-out foundation, for there were numerous accidents and some awful disasters.

Among the worst were the accident at Abergele in North Wales in 1868, when thirty-three people perished by fire, and the collapse of the Tay Bridge in 1879, when, in a great storm, the bridge and a train with all its passengers were destroyed. Accidents, though frequent, did not prevent the gradual establishment of public confidence. A prominent businessman, who travelled much, declared: 'I have proved that rail-way travelling is safer than walking, riding, driving, than going up and down stairs, than watching agricultural machinery, and even safer than eating, because it is a fact that more people choke themselves in England than are killed on all the railways of the United Kingdom.'

The advantages of railways were indeed to become so obvious that they came to be accepted as a matter of course. The railways had effects, direct and indirect, on almost every sphere of life. Most impor-tant were the industrial and social effects.

The industrial effects of the extension of railways were far-reaching. They enabled factories, wherever they were situated, to receive coal, machinery, and raw materials at cheaper rates, and to have their manufactured goods carried to all parts of the country as well as to the ports for shipment abroad. They brought standardized brick and slate to replace the use of local building materials, which were often more picturesque; but they also enabled farmers and others to improve upon local prices for their products by sending to the big industrial towns. Again, the speed of railway transport enabled fruit, vegetables, and milk to be conveyed safely as well as cheaply, and there were special trains for bringing fish from the fishing ports to inland towns. The working classes benefited in many ways: in towns, food was cheaper and more plentiful; in the rural districts, increased production gave increased employment. There was also the speeding-up of the mails and—in the later part of the century—the institution of the newspaper train, which carried the London papers, for better or worse, far and wide into the provinces.

The social effects of the railways, their effects on the lives of the people, were also far-reaching. In the old days people had been tied by circumstances to their village; most were born, lived and worked, and died in the same place. The railways made it much easier to move. Men could leave the village and seek work elsewhere, and the rise of new centres of population, which the industrial changes stimulated at this time, was largely aided by travel on the railways. This mobility contributed much to our success as an industrial nation by enabling new manufactures to grow wherever development was easiest and most profitable.

In the new towns men escaped the old feudal influences of the countryside, the authority of the landlord and parson. The old class-structure was greatly weakened; in the towns men were largely free of the old influences, and new ideas were rife. Even today people in the towns are usually more open to new ideas in politics and economics than people in the country. Thus railways, with the freedom of travel, facilitated Victorian liberal and reforming ideas and contributed to the growth of democracy.

They also directly assisted the growth of active political life by enabling the leaders to speak at any centre of population—even from the train itself, as Gladstone did in 1879—and by carrying political material, in the form of newspapers, pamphlets, and books, to distant parts of the country.

The railways also made possible holidays by the sea or in- the country. The railways opened up the Highlands of Scotland to walker and tourist, and the deer forests and grouse moors to wealthy sports-men. A visit to 'the seaside' became the summer holiday of millions; places like Blackpool, Bournemouth, and Weston-super-Mare were largely created by the railways. To all this excursion trains and cheap tickets contributed, and with them came the chance of pleasures and experiences for the masses which before had only been open to a few.

18 The coming of Free Trade

If the rapid spread of the railways was the physical change which was most typical of the Victorian age, there was an equally characteristic change in people's ideas which showed itself in the success of the Free Trade movement. This had its roots in Adam Smith's *Wealth of Nations* (1776), which said that the prosperity of a nation was helped by every increase in its external trade. But most countries had an extensive tariff—a list of customs duties which restrict the importation of foreign goods by making them more expensive. Adam Smith argued that, if there were no tariffs (except purely for revenue) every country would be able to sell abroad the things it produced most cheaply, and buy in return the things that it could not cheaply produce for itself.

What Adam Smith advocated was the kind of policy which his first great disciple, the younger William Pitt, adopted when he became Prime Minister in 1783. He tried to reduce any duty which was heavy enough to encourage smuggling: that on tea, for example, was brought down from 119 to 12½ per cent. He made a commercial treaty with France (1786), by which each country reduced the duties levied on the principal imports coming from the other one. He also proposed, and struggled unsuccessfully for, complete free trade between the United Kingdom and Ireland. Thus Pitt's policy was leading Britain in the direction of free trade, when the French wars of 1793–1815 intervened. These ended for the time being not only the treaty with France, but every project for the reduction of tariffs in the spirit of Adam Smith.

The attack on the tariff was renewed by William Huskisson as President of the Board of Trade in the 1820s. But it was not until the reign of Queen Victoria that Britain put free-trade principles systematically into practice, allowing unrestricted admission to almost all of the world's products, and relying on the skilful manufacture and cheapness of our own products (together with other sources of wealth) to keep the total balance of trade regularly and substantially in our favour.[1] The few duties which remained—on tea

[1] See Appendix II, Table 5.

and tobacco, for instance—were not designed to restrict trade but as a convenient form of tax which nearly everybody would have to pay.

The great trial of strength on this matter concerned the importation into Britain of cheap corn. This would lower the price of home-grown corn, to the disadvantage of landowners and farmers, but it would make wages go further (cheap bread and more of it), to the advantage of town workers and farm labourers. It was a problem which had already arisen in the later eighteenth century, when Britain as the result of the growth of population and industry was ceasing to be in normal years an exporter rather than an importer of corn. There were already import duties in existence to protect the landowner and farmer against the possibility of very low prices for their crops. But they were lowered or suspended if prices rose to famine levels, as they did during the French Revolutionary and Napoleonic Wars. It was to meet the post-war situation, which we have already described, that a Parliament representing chiefly the landed interest passed the drastic Corn Law of 1815. This forbade the importation of foreign corn until British corn reached the price of 80s. a quarter, and thus the farmer was protected against foreign competition. But the law also had an adverse effect on the working population of the country. The price of the 4-lb. loaf now rose from 10d. to 1s. 2d., although the ordinary farm-labourer earned only 10–12 shillings a week in cash. It is not surprising that there were riots and discontent.

But it was unreasonable to blame the Corn Law for all the troubles of the time. It now seems, looking back, as if the agitation against the Corn Laws was exaggerated and as a result their evil effects were overdrawn. The price of corn at that time still depended much more on the harvest at home than on the import of corn from abroad. In years of good harvest the price was relatively low and, in spite of protection, agriculture might be distressed. In 1821, for example, Huskisson presided over a committee of inquiry on the 'depressed state of agriculture'. Huskisson himself concluded that the law failed to help the farmers, though it hampered the course of our foreign trade, whilst in bad times the prohibition of imports made it more difficult to help the poor. A quarter of a century later, as we shall shortly see, the repeal of the Corn Laws did not in fact lead to any immediate decisive fall in prices, such as its advocates had often confidently prophesied.

The Work of Huskisson

The teachings of Adam Smith, which had influenced the Younger Pitt to make a commercial treaty with France and generally to reduce the tariff, had rather been lost sight of in the stress of the great French Wars of 1793–1815. But interest in them now revived, and not only the Corn Laws but also the old Navigation Laws were bitterly attacked. It was the advisers of King Richard II in the fourteenth century who had laid the foundations of our Mercantile policy by Navigation Acts that forbade English merchants to import or export goods except in English ships; but the most stringent laws belong to the time of Cromwell and the Restoration. The various Navigation Acts still in force in the eighteenth and early nineteenth centuries required that goods imported from America, Asia and Africa into Great Britain, Ireland, or the colonies be carried in British-owned ships, and that goods imported from Europe be carried in British ships or in ships of the country from which the goods came. These Acts had encouraged and 'protected' British shipping, which aroused the resentment of foreigners. During the French Wars, indeed, British shipping had a practical monopoly; but when peace came, other nations imposed or reimposed restrictions similar to our own.

The first easing of British restrictions on shipping took place in 1814 in favour of the United States of America; and in 1824–5 a number of other treaties were made to give ships of a foreign power as good access to our ports as that particular foreign power gave for our ships to theirs. But another twenty-five years were to pass before the Navigation Acts were finally repealed.

William Huskisson (1770–1830), the author of the treaties of 1824–5, had helped in Parliament to pass the Corn Law of 1815, but since then he had gradually changed his views in the direction of freer trade. He was a man of great knowledge and experience. As a youth he had worked at the British Embassy in Paris, and this training was useful to him when he came to negotiate commercial treaties with foreign countries. He was a Member of Parliament from 1796 to 1830, and for the last seven years of that time he represented the commercial constituency of Liverpool. He was President of the Board of Trade from 1823 to 1827, and that was when his chief work was done. He was held in great respect by the business and financial sections of the country, but became more and more opposed to protection for agriculture. This disagreement with the strong agricultural interests in the government led him to resign in 1828; two years later he was fatally injured by a locomotive at the opening of the Liverpool and Manchester Railway.

Besides his revision and extensive easing of the Navigation Acts, Huskisson also strove hard after 1820 for reform of the Corn Laws— reform, for as yet there was no talk of total repeal. Huskisson aimed at a sliding scale of duties, so arranged that the duty on foreign corn would be gradually lowered as the price of corn grown in England rose. In 1828, after Huskisson had resigned, the government did make a law for a sliding scale, but it was not exactly what Huskisson wanted, and in practice aroused as much opposition as the original law of 1815.

In one respect, Huskisson followed a policy which would not have been approved by later free-traders. He maintained a policy of imperial preference. That is to say, he made the duties on colonial goods entering this country lower than those on foreign goods; and, since this country still dictated policy to the colonies, he fixed colonial tariffs in such a way as to give a preference to British as against foreign imports into the colonies.

During the years 1822–8, when trade was prosperous, the government under the influence of Huskisson and the Chancellor of the Exchequer (F. J. Robinson) followed a general policy of reducing tariffs and internal taxes. The Chancellor's optimistic budget speeches led people to speak of him as 'Prosperity Robinson'; various taxes were abolished or reduced, including the ancient window-tax, which Robinson halved, although this was not finally abolished until 1851. This was the sphere of the Chancellor of the Exchequer, but Huskisson at the Board of Trade gave his attention to a thorough revision of the tariff system.

The revision lay mainly in the reduction of import duties on raw materials and semi-finished goods. Huskisson swept away prohibitions of import and prohibitive duties, and put in their place moderate duties, setting 30 per cent of the value of the goods imported as an upper limit. Goods on which import duties were greatly reduced included copper, zinc, tin, wool, silk, and cotton. Huskisson fixed the moderate level of 30 per cent as an upper limit, because he thought that duties above that level would encourage smuggling. Previously, smuggling of goods had caused considerable losses to the revenue. When, for example, in 1823 the duties on Irish and Scotch spirits were reduced it was soon found that the revenue was greater than before, because, with the lower duty, the profit to be made from illicit manufacture was no longer worth the risk involved. A number of export prohibitions and bounties (i.e., sums paid by the government to encourage exports) were likewise abolished, thus leaving outward-bound trade as well to find its natural course.

Huskisson also repealed a law which forbade artisans to emigrate, and he would have permitted the free export of machinery, but this idea caused alarm in our manufacturing districts, so for the time being a licensing system was introduced. But in principle Huskisson made it possible for the foreigner to acquire both the machines and the skill for competing against British industry.

Huskisson was also responsible for a codification of the customs. Over a thousand separate Acts were repealed, and the remaining laws codified. By 1826 there was a consolidated tariff system for the United Kingdom (Great Britain and Ireland had previously had different customs duties). Free trade was coming about by stages. Huskisson was preparing the way for Peel, as Peel did for Gladstone.

Peel and the Tariff

Sir Robert Peel (1788–1850) was the son of a wealthy cotton manufacturer. The profits his father made gave him the best education of the time, at Harrow and Christ Church, Oxford, and he devoted his great intelligence and ability to public life. His main work, so far as free trade is concerned, was done while he was Prime Minister from 1841 to 1846.

Peel's principle was to carry on Huskisson's work of reducing the tariff. If trade expanded, sufficient revenue might still be obtainable from duties levied at much lower rates on a bigger turnover of goods. But as a temporary measure Peel revived a tax of the war period—which has grown and continued ever since; thus in 1842 an income tax at 7d. in the £ on all incomes over £150 was introduced. Peel then proceeded to the reduction of tariffs. He divided imports roughly into three classes: raw materials were to pay least, up to 5 per cent; partly manufactured goods were to pay more, up to 12 per cent; fully manufactured goods paid the highest rates, up to 20 per cent—although this compared well with Huskisson's 30 per cent. In 1843 the export of machinery was freed. In 1844 the remaining export and import duties on raw wool were abolished. In 1845 most raw materials were admitted free; in the next year this was virtually made complete, and many semi-manufactured goods were also admitted free. The year 1846 also saw the reduction of duties on sugar, cheese and butter, and the abolition of those on livestock, meat and potatoes.

The Anti-Corn Law League

But the last stronghold of protection—the Corn Laws—remained, in spite of many proposals made to the government for their repeal. In 1839 the Anti-Corn Law League was founded in Manchester. The agitation against the Corn Laws was essentially a movement of the new manufacturing interest, which the Industrial Revolution had created, against the older agricultural interest striving to maintain its privileged position. Thus the League attacked the landlords as sole beneficiaries from the Laws and maintained that they were standing in

Signing a petition for the repeal of the Corn Laws.

the way of industrial progress. It was argued that our export trade was hampered because we would not accept foreign corn in payment for our manufactured goods. It was also suggested that, if foreign countries were not able to use their surplus corn in this way, they would take to manufacturing for their own needs, to the detriment of our factories. These arguments appealed strongly to the industrial employing class. To the wage earners it was pointed out that the Corn Laws were there for the purpose of raising the price of corn, and that their repeal would mean cheaper bread, and this argument attracted numerous working men from the ranks of the Chartists.[1]

[1] See page 164.

Richard Cobden and John Bright were the chief supporters of the League. Richard Cobden (1804–65), the son of a poor Sussex farmer, started his business life as a clerk; he later set up on his own account in Manchester as a calico merchant and manufacturer. He found time to remedy the weaknesses in his education, studied economics, and became an advocate of free trade. John Bright (1811–89) was a Rochdale cotton manufacturer and a wonderful orator. The League sent out numerous speakers, including Bright and Cobden, to address meetings in the chief towns. The new railways, spreading over the country, were a great boon to the organizers, carrying the lecturers on their tours. At the same time the reduction of the Stamp Duty on newspapers from fourpence to one penny made them cheaper than before,[1] and helped the League to spread a strong Free Trade propaganda. 'Honest Hodge', it has been said, found tracts in his village inn and learned to spell the big word 'MONOPOLY'. Not less important was the introduction of the Penny Post in 1840, which helped the League to shower anti-Corn Law literature on the towns and villages of England.

Cobden entered Parliament as member for Stockport in 1841, and set to work to form a party of Anti-Corn Law Leaguers among MPs. Bright became MP for Durham three years later; he was a Quaker and he regarded his political activities as part of his religious duties. In spite of all this activity, however, a motion for free trade was defeated in Parliament.

Repeal

But in the autumn of 1845, an unexpected ally came to the aid of the Leaguers. After several good seasons, it was a year of exceptionally heavy rain. In England, the wheat crop was ruined; in Ireland, the potato crop, the peasants' chief food, failed, and the people were faced with famine. 'Famine, against which we have warred, joined us,' said John Bright. 'It was the rain,' writes John Morley in his *Life of Cobden*, 'that rained away the Corn Laws,' It was impossible to refuse help to the starving Irish peasantry; Britain also was short of food; only an abundance of the cheap corn from abroad could bring relief.

The Prime Minister, Sir Robert Peel, wished to open the ports to foreign corn, but his cabinet was divided in opinion, so he resigned. Lord John Russell, the leader of the Whig opposition, failed to form a new government to take his place, and Peel came back to office. He was now completely converted to free trade by the potato famine in Ireland, the threat of famine in Britain, and the outcry of public

[1] See page 188.

Scene at the Sessions House, Wakefield, when Lord Morpeth, a Whig Free Trader, was nominated as sole candidate for the West Riding. This by-election took place while the repeal of the Corn Laws was under discussion in the House of Commons: note banner depicting the rising sun of free trade (4 February 1846).

opinion led by the Anti-Corn Law League. 'It was the rotten potatoes that put Peel in his damned fright,' said the Duke of Wellington. But when Peel was convinced as to the right step to take, he took it, even though it practically ended his political career. In spite of bitter attacks, in June 1846, Peel succeeded in passing the Bill to repeal the Corn Laws. All that was left was a maximum tariff of 10s. a quarter for the first three years (1846–9).

The institution of free trade in corn did not at once have the disastrous effects which landowners and farmers had predicted. The average price of corn in the following twenty years was 52s. a quarter, which had also been the average for the five years before repeal. The difference in the situation, a difference which did no harm to farmers, was that the industrial workers were now prospering and had more money, so they bought more. Imports from abroad increased; but it was not until the 1870s that the United States and Canada began to grow and export corn in large quantities at a price with which our farms could not compete. Then came the result which Peel's opponents had prophesied—the fall of rents and profits, the ruin of farmers, and the depopulation of the countryside. As we shall see, it took two world wars to set British farming on its feet again.

On the very day on which the repeal of the Corn Laws was finally accepted by the House of Commons, Peel was outvoted on another matter, and his government came to an end. In his resignation speech, he said: 'It may be that I shall leave a name sometimes remembered with expressions of good will in the abodes of those whose lot it is to labour and earn their daily bread by the sweat of their brow, when they shall recruit their strength with abundant and untaxed food—the sweeter because it is no longer leavened by a sense of injustice.'

But the Act which removed a sense of injustice from the people of Britain had no such effect in the sister island, where the potato crop did not return to normal until the autumn of 1849. In spite of special imports of maize, a big apparatus of soup kitchens and public works, and private English charity to the extent of about £500 000, the Irish starved. The British government was reluctant to abandon its *laissez-faire* principles, and public opinion in Britain was not very sympathetic to the need and claims of Ireland—which is one reason for the unspeakable horrors of the famine years being rapidly forgotten. A recent estimate gives 1½ million as the approximate number of those who died of hunger, malnutrition, or fever.[1] In addition, by 1851 a million or more had emigrated, including some hundreds of thousands who settled in Glasgow, Liverpool, Cardiff, and other easily accessible parts of Britain. The census of 1841 gave the Irish population as 8 175 124, which is believed to be a serious under-estimate; by 1851 it had shrunk to 6 552 385. The emigration continued, and at the present time the Republic and Northern Ireland together have only about 4½ million inhabitants.

Triumph of Free Trade

In 1849, three years after the repeal of the Corn Laws , the Navigation Acts were also abolished after a long and bitter struggle in Parliament, and at last all our foreign trade was thrown open to the ships of all the world. The ship-owners declared this would be the ruin of British shipping; but the quarter of a century following the repeal of the Navigation Acts was one of the greatest periods of expansion in the history of British shipping. As freight charges were now necessarily competitive, this is another case where the withdrawal of protection proved to be an all-round advantage. Thus the Great Exhibition of 1851 was meant to demonstrate the merits of our free-trade system, as well as of our other freedoms, to the outside world. The scene at the opening ceremony is worth looking at. It gives something of the atmosphere of an aristocratic society long past; there is the group composed of the Queen, a regal figure in pink and gold brocade, her

[1] C. Woodham-Smith, *The Great Hunger*, p. 411.

Queen Victoria in the 'great transept', receiving the Commissioners for the Exhibition at its opening on May Day, 1851.

young children, and ladies of the Court; we see the marvel of the Hyde Park trees growing inside the Crystal Palace and providing the reason for its imposing height; but above all, this famous scene marks the moment when Victorian Britain emerged triumphantly from the difficulties of the long post-war period.

Peel had died from an accident in 1850, but the most brilliant of his followers, W. E. Gladstone (1809–98), took up his work, and as Chancellor of the Exchequer in a series of great budgets used all his skill to reduce import duties to the absolute minimum, that is, to what was needed for revenue. When Peel opened his attack on customs duties in 1842, some 1052 articles had been subject to duty; in 1853 Gladstone still found 466 taxed articles, and by his budget of that year reduced the number; in 1860 he found 419 and reduced them to 48. Only 15 of these were of importance, including the duties on spirits, sugar, tea, tobacco, coffee, wine and timber. Gladstone abolished the timber duty in 1866, and took the first steps with regard to sugar, that duty being abolished by his successor in 1874. When in 1860 Cobden had negotiated a commercial treaty with France, so that each country made certain tariff reductions to the advantage of the other, it began to look as if Adam Smith's views might prevail and all Europe, or even the whole world, exchange its goods freely on free-trade principles. The immediate effect of the treaty was to double the export of British manufactures to France, though the French silks which came in return hurt the trade of our own silk-weavers. Every system of trade probably injures the interests of some groups: but it is safe to say that to the average British worker free trade at that time spelt cheaper food, more employment, and the absence of any serious grievance about taxation.

The customs duties which Gladstone retained were used for revenue purposes only, that is to say, they were not protective of British producers by keeping foreign goods out but were used only to raise revenue. In levying duties for revenue he concentrated on a few major articles in general consumption. Hence the duties on tea, sugar, beer, spirits and tobacco. He avoided taxing raw materials and foodstuffs— hence he abolished the tax on timber as soon as the revenue could afford it, and moved towards the abolition of the sugar duties; for sugar, besides being a food, was also a raw material in the making of jam, sweets and confectionery. He aimed in all respects to free industry, and to help the wage earner by reducing the prices he had to pay and by giving him employment. These principles were the principles of free trade.

Free trade had come. The basic fact was that, before Huskisson, Peel and Gladstone, the country had suffered under an incredibly complicated and muddled system of taxes, both customs duties and internal excise duties, which had for the most part originated in an earlier age and under different conditions. A great army of collectors had been required and, so complicated were the laws, even the officials had difficulty in understanding and applying them. Now, after the industrial developments, British industry and commerce no longer needed protection. Britain was ahead of other nations, and our trade was expanding. What paid us best was not protection and restriction, but the vast expansion of trade all over the world—the export of more and more British goods, which could only be achieved if we were prepared to take foreign imports in return for our exports.

Many free traders believed also that free trade would make for international peace. Free exchange of goods would bring prosperity not only to this country but to other countries as well. And in exchanging their goods countries would become dependent upon each other. It would be foolish to make war on one's customers, and war would dislocate the intricate machinery of transport, exchange, and banking. Hence it was thought that, the more international trade developed, the more secure would be the peace of the world. This belief contributed to the feeling of security and comfort in mid-Victorian England.[1]

[1] The contrasted insecurity and discomfort of the preceding period, for which Free Traders later invented the name of the Hungry 'Forties, were movingly portrayed by Tom Hood. (See Appendix I, No. 4.)

19 The coming of trade unions and co-operative societies

The prosperity which came to Victorian Britain with the building of the railways and the establishment of free trade was shared by the workers in the form of higher wages, shorter hours, and more regular employment—but only to an extent which would nowadays seem very small and unfair. Their share in this prosperity would have been even smaller than it was if the workers had not made tremendous efforts to form special organizations to protect their interests, both against employers, who naturally wished to keep down the wages they had to pay, and also against unscrupulous shopkeepers, who often overcharged and swindled the poorer classes.

Trade unions came into existence early in the eighteenth century, particularly in the woollen industry, to keep up the level of wages either by striking for more money or by trying to exclude any worker who had not served a full seven-year apprenticeship; for the smaller the supply of workers in a trade, the easier it was for them to get their way about wages and other conditions. In some trades, unions were forbidden by special statutes, and they could also be proceeded against at common law, for 'conspiracy in restraint of trade'. But it was not until the great French wars that their activities, in the eyes of the law, came abruptly to an end, when Pitt in 1799 and 1800 passed the Combination Acts which banned trade unions as a revolutionary danger to the safety of the realm. We say 'in the eyes of the law', for some unions continued an underground existence throughout the period when they were illegal. Either they held their meetings in secret or, like the Greenock Coopers' Society in June 1811, went on issuing their regular membership cards and, if questioned, could doubtless pretend that they were merely a club or friendly society. Coopers might admit they were all interested in making the barrels for the salted herrings, but not that they ever combined to help each other over wage rates.

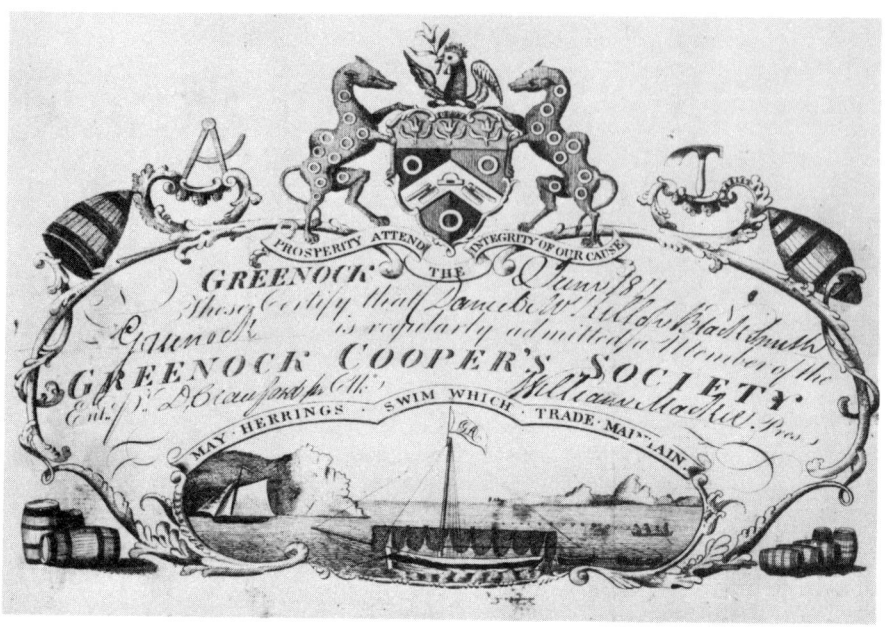

A Trade Union Membership Card of 1811.

Repeal of the Combination Laws; the GNCTU

The hero of the first period of trade unionism was Francis Place, a tailor, who had worked his way through hard times, from an apprentice to a master. He owned a very successful shop at Charing Cross, and his parlour there became a meeting-place for reformers. In this and other ways he gave publicity to the cause he had in hand—the repeal of the Combination Acts. His friend, Joseph Hume, a Radical MP, with Huskisson's help secured the appointment of a parliamentary committee. As a result of its inquiries, in 1824 all laws against trade unions were repealed. The immediate result, as might have been expected, was an outburst of strikes, culminating in one by the shipwrights which reduced the entire port of London to idleness. Employers were angry and alarmed, and another committee was appointed amid great excitement. But petitions from Manchester, Sheffield and other industrial towns poured in to Members of Parliament, and workmen even made their way to the House of Commons, demanding that their case should be heard. This determination on the part of the workers defeated attempts to reimpose the Combination Acts, but severe limits were set to the powers of the unions. They must confine their activities strictly to 'consulting upon and determining the rate of wages and prices'; special penalties were fixed for indulging in any form of 'molestation' or 'obstruction'.

Another man who influenced the early Trade Union movement was the Welshman, Robert Owen, whose experience in improving the conditions of labour in his own cotton-mills at New Lanark led him to try to extend his ideas of industrial organization over the rest of the country through the now legalized trade unions. He realized that the isolated strikes of small local unions would not avail. There must be co-ordinated, national action. He founded a Builders' Union, which he hoped would be strong enough to take over the whole of the building work in the country and run it without any employers. This was followed in 1834 by a Grand National Consolidated Trades Union, which was joined by half a million people.

There were at this time far-reaching, though often vague, plans in the minds of the union leaders. One plan was for a general strike or 'national holiday' (the Chartists later spoke of a 'Sacred Month'). This would be a means of breaking the capitalists' hold over industry, and giving the workers power. There were two ideas of how this would happen—either through a violent revolution or by a peaceful change-over from capitalism to socialism. 'The men may remain at leisure,' it was said, 'no law can compel them to work against their will. They may walk the streets with arms folded. . . . What happens in consequence? . . . Government falls into confusion, and every link in the chain which binds society together is broken in a moment by the inert conspiracy of the poor against the rich.' Thus, some of the workers thought, might come the social revolution which would give them power and redress their ills. The leaders of the GNCTU seem also to have pictured as the final development a scheme of workers' control over the whole industrial system, with local lodges as the base of a pyramid which might have at its apex a kind of trades parliament. In the early twentieth century these ideas reappeared as 'syndicalism', but the GNCTU is remembered chiefly in connection with a single famous episode in trade union history.

The Tolpuddle Martyrs

While workers in mines and the textile and other industries were forming unions, farm labourers had been doing the same. In 1830 starvation conditions existed in many rural districts of southern England, and there were demands for higher wages. Bands of farm labourers marched from village to village, appealing sometimes to the squire, sometimes to the local magistrates, sometimes to the farmers themselves. We have already mentioned the severe repression which followed this episode, sometimes known as the Last Labourers' Revolt. Another of its consequences was a brief flare-up of trade union activity in the countryside.

Owen's Grand National Union formed a special sub-division, the Friendly Society of Agricultural Labourers, and wages tended to rise. When the labourers in the Dorset village of Tolpuddle were threatened with a reduction, they wrote to the Grand National Union for advice. As a result two brothers, named Loveless, and four other men formed a branch of the Friendly Society of Agricultural Labourers, and many labourers joined it; the authorities became alarmed. Although farm and other workers could no longer be tried for 'combining' to obtain higher wages, it was known that members joining the Union went through a quaint ritual with masks and other curious things; so it was decided to charge them under another of Pitt's repressive laws made during the French wars—the Unlawful Oaths Act of 1797. The Loveless brothers and four other men were arrested, tried at Dorchester in 1834, and sentenced to seven years' transportation. It was a savage sentence to pass upon men of good character who had done no violence, and George Loveless was a Methodist lay preacher.

This fierce vengeance on the Tolpuddle Martyrs, as the men were sympathetically called, aroused great indignation. Nevertheless they were shipped off to Tasmania to work in chains; it took four years to get the remainder of the sentence remitted, and it was another two years before they returned to England. As for Owen's Grand National Union, it was wrecked by internal strife, and fell to pieces about the end of 1834. The Builders' Union also perished.

Trade Unions in the '40s and '50s

The Tolpuddle trial alarmed other unions. For fifteen years or so we hear less of their activities. The energies of the workers were devoted instead to the agitation for the People's Charter, a six-point political programme drafted by Francis Place, of which the main object was to demand the parliamentary vote for every man. If this movement had had any success, then no doubt Parliament would have been used to help the trade unions. But up to the time of the final failure of the Chartists in 1848, the chief benefit the trade unions brought to their members was through their eventually successful organization of support for the Ten Hours movement, which had begun in the factory districts as early as 1831. The bitterness of the hostility shown towards any interference with the power and authority of the employer, such as a trade union must necessarily seek to practise, may be judged from

Herkomer's picture 'On Strike', exhibited at the Royal Academy in 1891. The artist, whose father was a joiner and woodcarver in Bavaria, arouses strong feelings of sympathy.

The Economist's description of the Ten Hours Bill of 1847 as 'The Lords leagued with the Commons to prohibit industry'.

In the middle of the century, however, there was a revival of trade unionism, based on new aims and a better organization for the new Unions of better-paid workers. There was more thought of conciliation and of the closely related material interests of employer and workers. In many cases the strike was no longer regarded as the best weapon. In addition to such practical advantages as insurance of tools, the Unions offered Friendly Society benefits—payment in times of sickness or unemployment, and assistance to the family on the death of a member. They also helped members to emigrate so as to reduce competition for jobs, though this device was exploited by rogues who made the round voyage. But the important fact is that, when men paid a high weekly subscription in expectation of substantial benefits, they were not so willing to risk the Unions' funds in long disputes with employers. They settled disputes by arbitration rather than by strikes. In 1851, a number of Unions connected with the engineering trade united to form the Amalgamated Society of Engineers. It had a full-time paid secretary, and headquarters in London, and its organization was established on such sound principles as to become a 'New Model' for others to imitate. In course of time the Carpenters and Joiners and other trade unions, each composed of skilled artisans who were able to pay a fair-sized regular subscription, followed the same policy. Such unions were respected by employers because they had money in the bank and prudence as their first principle.

Growing Power of the Unions

But some of the smaller unions were less respectable: in 1866 at Sheffield, for instance, they put gunpowder in the grinding-trough of a cutlery worker if he did not conform with their requirements, or dropped a keg of gunpowder down his chimney. Sometimes injury or death resulted. Many employers became alarmed at the growth of trade unionism, and some of them hoped that the Combination Acts would again be brought into force. In 1868 the Unions began to meet together in an annual Trades Union Congress (TUC) to discuss matters of general welfare. Parliament, having in 1867 given the vote to working-class householders in towns, who included many trade unionists, decided that it would be wiser to give the unions more power rather than less, and this was done by the Trade Union Act of 1871. This measure for the first time provided full legal protection for their funds, and gave them the status of Friendly Societies. The Unions, however, were not satisfied with the Liberal government which passed the Act, for it did not allow picketing during a strike. They therefore looked in 1874 to the new Conservative government. Disraeli, who was anxious to win their support, gave the Unions what they wanted. His Act of 1875 legalized peaceful picketing during strikes, and also made it impossible to prosecute strikers under the common law of conspiracy.

At the 1874 election two working men had taken their seats in the House of Commons; they were the first MPs elected to represent specifically working-class interests. They were both miners: Thomas Burt, MP for Morpeth; and Alexander Macdonald, who was returned for Stafford. A dozen years later an Oxfordshire stonemason, named Broadhurst, who had been a trade-union leader, became an under-secretary in Gladstone's third Ministry.

A wave of trade unionism that swept the country in the early 1870s aroused farm workers to form the Agricultural Labourers' Union, led by Joseph Arch, a Warwickshire farm-hand and lay preacher. But in the later '70s, when agriculture suffered an acute depression owing to the importation of American wheat and there was widespread un-employment on the land, membership of this Union decreased. By 1894 it had ceased to exist, and the present National Union of Agricultural Workers was not formed until after the First World War. Trade Unionism also experienced great difficulty among railway workers, for the employing companies said that, to be safe and efficient, a railway ought to have the same sort of discipline as an army. The Amalgamated Society of Railway Servants, formed in 1872, was for a long time too weak for strike action, but in 1890 the first serious stoppage secured some government assistance against dangerously over-long hours of work. Even so, all but one of the principal com-panies refused recognition to the unions down to the First World War.

In the summer of 1889, however, a famous dock strike in London marked the beginning of the gradual rise to power of the mass of unskilled labour. The dockers' union had been started in the previous year by Ben Tillett, an Irish immigrant's son who had begun work in a brickyard at the age of eight. Oratory and publicity for the strikers were, indeed, provided mainly by two helpers from the skilled union of engineers, John Burns and Tom Mann; but after the winning of the 'Dockers' Tanner' (sixpence, i.e., $2\frac{1}{2}$p, per hour) and a minimum four-hour engagement, Tillett was installed for a whole generation as the successful leader of a union for a type of worker which had been thought incapable of the necessary self-restraint and cohesion. Other similar unions sprang into existence at the same time as the dockers'; and although two of the older unions lost some ground in 1893, when the Lancashire cotton-spinners and the coal-miners tried to resist wage reductions during a collapse of trade, by the last year of the century total membership had reached 2 million.

The Co-operative Shops

Robert Owen was the pioneer of co-operation as well as of nationwide trade unions. He set up a non profit-making store for the benefit of his employees at New Lanark, and later on gave much of his energies to schemes for co-operative production—that is, forming groups of craftsmen who would join together to sell the things they made, thus getting rid of the capitalist employer. Too many slackers flocked to the co-operative workshops, as they were called, for them to achieve any lasting success, but it was as a result of Owen's teaching that in 1844, during a trade depression, twenty-eight flannel weavers joined together to establish the first modern consumers' co-operative. The modest-looking shop which they opened in Toad Lane—Lancashire for 'the old lane'—Rochdale, was the home of one of the weavers, used to keep the stock which they bought with the original capital of £1 a head.

The system was as simple as the place where it was first practised. They bought at wholesale prices and sold at retail prices. The profit, after allowing for the cost of running the shop, was shared out among themselves in proportion to the amount of purchases each of them had made. This profit was the 'co-operative dividend'. Membership grew; the capital also grew, for each new member had to pay for a small share (on which he would get interest); and there was no limit to the number of similar societies which could be started anywhere. The idea spread fast—in Lancashire and Yorkshire, then into Scotland and the Midlands, last of all to London and the southern counties, where conservative prejudices were strongest.

In 1863 the first Co-operative Wholesale Society started business, in Manchester: this meant that the retail shops were now large and numerous enough to join together to form their own organization to make wholesale purchases on their behalf. This enabled them to buy more cheaply, as large concerns can usually do; and although the CWS made a slow start—after twenty years their annual profits were only about £20 000—they grew to have their own factories, bakeries, etc., and nowadays are among the largest trading organizations in the United Kingdom.

But what did all this do for the people, comparable to the steady pressure of the trade unions for higher wages, shorter hours, and better working conditions? The answer is threefold. First and foremost, the 'Co-op' helped people to a higher standard of living by giving good

The premises at Toad Lane, Rochdale, where the Society of Equitable Pioneers opened shop on 21 December 1844. The upper floors were occupied by a nonconformist congregation until 1849.

value for money, since the dividend was really a reduction in prices. It also played a part in the struggle against the adulteration of food, and helped the trade unions to get rid of the last 'truck' shops. The second main virtue, however, was that the movement encouraged thrift, because it was always made easy to leave the dividend to accumulate at a good rate of interest.

Third, the 'Co-op' was a real contribution towards the growth of democracy. Each store was managed by a committee elected by members and composed of members, working under the eyes of critics who had a direct interest in checking each mistake or extravagance. This makes it all the more creditable that the stores have also kept up the tradition, derived from Owen's teaching of a century ago, of devoting some part of their profits to educational and cultural objects. This mixture of hard-headed business with a genuine desire for self-improvement was one of the strongest features of the great Victorian age.[1]

[1] Compare Tennyson's description of a Mechanics' Institute outing (Appendix I, No. 5).

20 The workshop of the world

This proud title was in a sense held by Britain throughout the nineteenth century, but its third quarter was the time when our industries had become big enough to supply all demands. It was likewise the epoch when the rest of the world had reached the stage of making big demands for the goods we could supply, but had not yet gone on to the next stage of supplying the goods for themselves. At the 1851 census our population was shown to be one-half urban, one-half rural—perhaps the ideal mixture, but in any case one which indicates the great growth in our manufacturing towns since 1815.

About the same time the nations of Europe and the United States of America, which might have begun to overtake our industrial lead, entered upon a period of conflict and upheaval—the struggle for national unity in Germany and Italy, the rise and fall of the Second Empire in France, in America the slavery dispute and the war between the States—which in varying degrees distracted their attention in the next two decades from the peaceful development of manufactures. Our own Crimean War, on the other hand, in which such bitter and often needless hardships were suffered by the men in the field, brought little 'economic discomfort' to the trading community.[1]

British businessmen saw their chances and took them. Between 1850 and 1872 the value of our exports rose from £71 million to £256 million. In the same period the total quantities of coal, pig-iron, and cotton cloth produced in Britain—three staple commodities in which we already dealt largely—were approximately doubled.[2] The tonnage of shipping cleared from British ports multiplied itself two-and-a-half times in just over twenty years (1854–75), and in 1870 the volume of our external trade (i.e., goods coming into, and going out of, the country) was more than that of France, Germany and Italy put together and was between three and four times that of the United States of America. Gold discoveries in California and Australia helped to make this a period of rising prices, and in such periods profit-

---

[1] See J. H. Clapham, *Economic History of Modern Britain*, Vol. II, p. 365.
[2] See Appendix II, Table 4.

making is comparatively easy; what is more remarkable, wage-levels rose sufficiently for their purchasing power to go up a little, year by year. It was a period of tremendous optimism, in which Dr Samuel Smiles, the author of *Self-Help* (1859), *Thrift, The Lives of the Engineers*, etc., used the careers of the earlier industrial pioneers to point an attractive road to fortune to English and Scottish youth.[1]

Science and Self-Help

This worship of self-help perhaps does a little to explain one most extraordinary deficiency in the equipment of the Workshop of the World, namely the poor provision made for scientific and technical education. Several foreign countries outstripped us in this respect, although we were the wealthiest country and owed our wealth largely to scientific progress. An adequate training in science could only be obtained in a rather haphazard way, by private study and experiment, or by apprenticeship to industry or to some private researcher. Improved provision for medical training had been made early in the century; but it was not until its last decades that organized courses of study in chemistry, physics, engineering, and so on, began to be established in universities[2] and technical colleges and, in the case of chemistry and physics, in schools.

Thus the great Victorian scientists, the men who laid the foundations of modern science and opened the way to so many practical applications of the principles they discovered, usually 'picked up' their knowledge and training by following various paths very different from the broad highway now offered in the science courses of modern educational institutions. The scientists of those days, like the businessmen, were self-made men. Sir Humphry Davy, for example, who was responsible for 'discovering' Faraday, the central figure in the scientific advances of this period, had himself begun life as apprentice to a surgeon and apothecary. He studied chemistry on his own, and then assisted Dr Beddoes, who had set up at Clifton, Bristol, a Pneumatic Institution for treating disease by breathing. Davy became known by his own researches in chemistry; he was appointed a lecturer at the Royal Institution, which had been set up privately for scientific research and lectures and granted a royal charter in 1800. Gaining knowledge and training in these ways, Davy went on to his own great researches in chemistry, which make him one of the

---

[1] See Appendix I, No. 6, for the same optimism expressed in the language of a poet laureate.

[2] A significant exception was Manchester University where courses in both chemistry and engineering were introduced soon after its establishment (as Owen's College) in 1851.

Paddington Station in 1862, shortly before the replacement of iron by cheap steel in rails, rolling stock, and even station roofs. But the painter, Frith, who guaranteed that all his figures (including the two detectives) were drawn from life, gives a wonderful impression of the youthful vigour, enterprise, and opulence of Victorian England, the Workshop of the World.

pioneers of that subject. And, as we know, he invented the safety-lamp for miners.

Michael Faraday (1791–1867), another self-educated scientist, was a blacksmith's son. At twelve Faraday was an errand boy, and then he was apprenticed to a bookbinder and stationer. He read much and went to lectures. He went to hear Davy at the Royal Institution. Afterwards he bound a set of notes and sent them to the great man. Davy was so impressed that he took on Faraday as his assistant and thereby opened a scientific career to him. Faraday indeed went on to a lifetime of research. He made basic advances in chemistry, but is today best remembered for his work as a pioneer in physics and electricity. It is hardly too much to say that the whole development of electrical engineering, on which twentieth-century life is so dependent, can be traced back to Faraday's discovery of electro-magnetic induction in 1831.

Lord Kelvin (1824–1907), another great pioneer worker in the field of electricity and physics, had what seems today a rather more conventional scientific education. For his father happened to be a mathematics professor at Glasgow University, and Scotland was in many matters of education ahead of England. As a Glasgow student the young William Thomson, as he then was, was able to get a little laboratory training from the professor of astronomy. He proceeded to

Cambridge, distinguished himself as a mathematician there, and almost at once became professor of natural philosophy (science) at Glasgow, where he was the dominant scientific figure for over fifty years. Besides his achievements in pure science, Lord Kelvin was concerned with the laying of the Atlantic cables and the improvement of the mariner's compass. He also set up the first physics laboratory for students in Great Britain.

Yet, as late as the '70s and '80s, our most important inventors had no proper scientific training. Swan, whose incandescent electric lamp shone out in 1878—a year before Edison's—was a manufacturing chemist, who had left school at twelve and been an apprentice in a chemist's shop. Sidney Gilchrist Thomas, the inventor of the modern method of basic steel-making, had a classical education and a clerical post, though he studied metallurgy as a spare-time occupation at the Birkbeck Institute.

Cheap Steel

The outstanding invention of the mid-nineteenth century was cheap steel, the use of which brought to an end the age of universal iron associated with the name of Wilkinson. Hitherto, even after Neilson's hot blast had enabled a great new iron-making centre to develop on Clydeside, ousting cotton, the amount of iron processed into steel had remained small—in the early '50s the ratio of pig-iron to steel was more than 7:1. Then came the Crimean War, the need for efficient cannon, the consideration that they would be more efficient if they could be made of steel, and Henry Bessemer's discovery (in 1856) that steel could be produced cheaply by applying a powerful hot blast to molten pig-iron in a 'converter', carbon being added after the impurities had been expelled. The adoption of this method (which was further improved by the German Siemens, who used an open-hearth furnace instead of the converter) now provided cheap steel, with only one restriction—the iron-ore used must not contain phosphorus. Such ore was to be found in Cumberland and could be imported from Sweden or Spain; the result was to encourage the growth of the iron and steel industry (as we must now call it) at Barrow-in-Furness and still more in the Middlesbrough area and South Wales, to which ore could be cheaply shipped. Our steel trade therefore flourished on the restriction to one kind of ore. But it lost its advantage after 1879, when S. G. Thomas (as mentioned above) showed how to make steel from ore containing phosphorus by its absorption into basic slag. For Germany then began to expand her rival industry from the phosphoric ores of Lorraine.

By the '70s, therefore, cheap steel was replacing iron in most of its manufacturing uses, with the result that every kind of structure became more durable: railway lines, for instance, lasted three or four times as long as before. It helped also in the final triumph of the steamship, for steel plates were thinner than iron though equally strong, so the steel-built ship was lighter and rose higher out of the water. This enabled it to stow more cargo before being weighed down to the safety-line introduced by Samuel Plimsoll; and this was very important, because the great drawback to the steamship had been the difficulty of carrying cargo *and* coal in sufficient quantity.

The Age of Steamships

This problem was already being tackled from the other end by making the propulsion of the steamship more efficient and thus economizing in fuel. The screw had replaced the paddle-wheels of the earliest steamboats, and in 1854 John Elder of Glasgow invented the compound engine; this was followed by the triple and quadruple expansion engines, which reduced fuel consumption by 50 per cent in ten years. Even so, such beautifully designed sailing-craft as the tea-clippers of the China trade, built latterly of wood on an iron frame,

Railway communication leads to the development of a new port at Barrow-in-Furness, Lancashire.

might still have held their own in some cases against the iron steamer; but the opening of the Suez Canal in 1869—the year when the *Cutty Sark* was launched—provided a handicap on the route to the East which no sailing-ship could surmount.

Thus all through the second half of the nineteenth century the British iron and steel industry was building the most up-to-date vessels for our own mercantile marine, still easily supreme, and for many of our competitors. The shipbuilding industry flourished at Glasgow—where the Clyde, once fordable at low tide, had to be dredged to nineteen feet to serve the shipyards stretching along its banks for twenty miles. It was also well established on Tyneside and elsewhere on the north-east coast of England and on the west at Birkenhead; and was even carried across the Irish Sea to Belfast, where Harland and Wolff (a German immigrant) developed after 1860 ship-yards which grew to be the largest in the world. It was not until about 1900 that ships were equipped with the steam-turbine engine, which had been invented by Sir Charles Parsons in 1884, with the different purpose of generating electricity. But long before this Britain was deriving full benefit from all the changes. We built the ships; being faster and more efficient than before, they carried more goods at lower cost; every voyage in British service meant a profitable exchange of our cotton and other manufactures and coal for foreign raw materials and food; or else other profits were made by us from selling the ships to foreigners or from hiring them out in the carrying trade of foreign countries.

The construction of shipbuilding yards and of merchant ships was accompanied by the building or extension of docks. The work of the earlier part of the century was continued. New docks were added to the London system, including Tilbury (1882–6) some twenty miles down the river. Liverpool docks were extended and in 1894 Manchester opened its Ship Canal to the Mersey. Southampton, with its magnificent estuaries, revived after 1850; it became the headquarters of the P. and O. Line to the East, though the famous Ocean Dock which can take several of the world's largest liners at the same time was not constructed until 1912. During the second half of the nineteenth century, some ports, thanks to railway communication, sprang up almost out of nothing, like Barrow-in-Furness and Grimsby. Cardiff, which had fewer than 2000 inhabitants at the first census, and built its first dock in 1839, built further docks and came to pass Newcastle as the world's greatest coal exporter. Bristol, the second port in the kingdom in the Middle Ages, likewise enjoyed a great revival of trade and prosperity after 1884, when the corporation bought up the recently built docks at Avonmouth. These accommodate the larger vessels, which cannot be brought up the river into the heart of the ancient city.

As steamships gradually took the place of sailing-ships, steamships did on the ocean what railways did on the land. Just as the railways linked one part of the country or continent with another, so steamships linked up distant parts of the world and all its different continents by regular ocean lines, until it was no more expensive to bring many tons of corn from Canada than it had been to bring a few hundred quarters from Norfolk to London in the seventeenth century. There was also the effect on trade of the opening of the Suez Canal, already mentioned. This was the work of the French engineer, Ferdinand de Lesseps, and by linking the Mediterranean with the Red Sea, it provided a shorter route for ships bound for the East—India, China, Australia, New Zealand—which now avoided the long detour round the Cape of Good Hope. The East India Company had for many years tried to trade with China, though the Chinese disliked the intrusion of foreign 'barbarians' on to the soil of the Celestial Empire. But after our Chinese War of 1840–2, China was opened to British and other European trade, and our exports to China increased from £936 000 in 1850 to £6 138 000 in 1870. Hong Kong became a crown colony, whose prosperity rivalled that of Britain's entrepot market at Singapore.

Zenith and Decline of British Agriculture

As for agriculture, it was far from ruined by the repeal of the Corn Laws in 1846. On the contrary, the decade 1853–62 proved to be the golden age of English agriculture, and 'high farming' with plentiful capital expenditure continued to show good profits up to the '70s. The foundation of the Royal Agricultural Society in 1838 and of the Rothamsted Experimental Station in 1842 had prepared the way for an era of scientific progress.

Better methods of land drainage were now introduced. It was at a Royal Society Show in 1843 that a drainage engineer, Josiah Parkes, first saw some little clay pipes made by a gardener for heating his master's forcing frames. Parkes at once realized that such pipes could be used instead of ditches for draining fields. 'My lord,' he said to Earl Spencer, 'with this pipe I will drain the whole of England.' In order to encourage farmers to spend money on scientific drainage, Sir Robert Peel introduced the first Public Drainage Act, by which the government set aside £2 million for making loans to farmers for that purpose. The study of agricultural chemistry became more than guesswork, and fertilizers, such as guano, bone meal, and phosphates, were applied to the soil with good results. Swedes, mangel-wurzels, and other novel root crops were grown. Russian linseed and North American meals were imported for feeding cattle, and the improvement in the breeding of stock continued. Again, the railways played an important part by providing wider markets for the staple farm products, corn and cattle, while also making it easier and cheaper for the farmers to acquire such things as machinery, fertilizers and high-quality seed corn. These changes enabled high profits to be combined with economy in the use of labour. For agriculture, which had employed nearly 2 000 000 in 1851—it was then much the largest industry in Great Britain—employed less than 1 500 000 persons in 1871. Yet at the latter date the cultivated area had reached record size: as late as 1938 the acreage under farm crops was only two-thirds of what it had been then.

But the position of the farm-labourers of the '50s and '60s, who were not driven from the country though they might be attracted by the higher wage rates of the towns or better prospects overseas, was fortunate indeed in comparison with the lot of their fellows—and of the farmers who employed them—when the prosperity of the countryside came suddenly to an end.

Between 1875 and 1884 cold springs and wet summers resulted in poor harvests; the harvest of 1879 is said to have been the worst in the century. About the same time, the home market was suddenly flooded with the cheap corn from the great new cornfields of America, which were large enough to derive full benefit from machinery such as the McCormick combine harvester, then practically unknown in Britain. Their new railways enabled the corn to be brought eastward for shipping, and steamships brought it to Britain where it could be sold at a lower price than our own—and there were now no Corn Laws to protect the British farmer. The price of corn dropped. In 1876, wheat had fetched 44s. a quarter, in 1877 it rose to 50s., but by 1885 it had dropped to 32s. A second wave of agricultural depression followed in 1891–9: in 1894 the average price of wheat fell below 23s., a figure to which the records of 300 years afford no parallel. Many British farmers were faced with ruin, and there was great distress among labourers.

Farmers now turned much of their land into pasture for rearing cattle, which was fairly well worth while in spite of imported frozen meat. Stock farmers, if able to invest money in their farms, found the breeding of pedigree herds very profitable. The increasing population in towns demanded more milk, butter and eggs, so dairy farming became prosperous. Fruit-growing and market-gardening and, in some districts, potato-growing—all of which served town populations—increased. But all this amounted to very little in comparison with the good profits and plentiful, if ill-paid employment—a man to every twenty acres, or thereabouts—which the great corn-farming districts had formerly provided. Many of the younger men had to leave the countryside and look for work elsewhere.

The 'Great Depression' and the Growth of Imperialism

It was often hard for such newcomers to find work in the towns, for from the 1870s onwards there were recurrent phases of severe (though generally localized) unemployment. London, for instance, in the winters of 1886 and 1887 was the scene of two famous demonstrations of protest, addressed by the leaders of the reviving socialist movement[1] and held in check by deployment of the Guards in Trafalgar Square. Nevertheless, the long period of deflation from 1873 to 1896, during which wholesale commodity prices on the world market fell by nearly 40 per cent, was far from disastrous for the urban working class as a whole. Its dietary benefited from the cheap transatlantic grain, which was followed by an influx of cheap meat from the United States, Australia and New Zealand, and Argentina. Soon the modern methods of chilling and freezing, introduced in the 1880s, became applicable to fruit and dairy produce as well. The cost of food was only one—though then by far the biggest—item in a worker's household budget, nearly all of which was helped by falling prices, since cus-

[1] See p. 206.

tomary wage rates were hardly ever pressed down with the same rapidity.

Employers and investors viewed the situation differently, as these twenty-three years produced three distinct slumps in trade, involving a loss in profits and of interest. The principle of free trade was not seriously challenged, for a home-grown food supply did not seem to be essential for a 'workshop of the world': by 1890 agriculture contributed only one-thirteenth of the gross national income. But free-trade Britain had not envisaged a world which was ceasing to be an open market for the wares of its British Workshop. Large-scale rival manufactures were now being developed on both sides of the Atlantic, often under the shelter of a high tariff, reintroduced originally to safeguard a nation's agriculture. Furthermore, new industries were emerging in such fields as chemicals and electrical apparatus, where Britain had done much of the pioneer work[1] but was now falling behind, even in the home market. Hence the gloomy forebodings about the future of the British economy which characterize the period of the 'great depression', though they were very largely dispelled and forgotten during the mounting prosperity of the eighteen years preceding the First World War.

Present-day historians often look back to the 'great depression' as the turning-point in Britain's fortunes. They point to the vigour which our competitors showed in the creation of big units of industry and commerce (such as the American Trusts), in experimenting with mass production and 'scientific management', and especially in the field of scientific and technical education, where the new German Empire led the world. The British by comparison were undoubtedly inclined to be complacent, slow to improve upon machinery in which they had locked up much capital or to alter systems of production and exportation which had carried their goods all over the world. Yet it would be wrong to think of their reaction to the depression as purely negative, for these were the years in which the idea of empire reached its zenith.

Emigration was no new phenomenon. Altogether about 19 million people emigrated from Britain in the hundred years after Waterloo, inspired to move in good times by the hope of bettering themselves and making a good use of their savings, and in bad times by the belief that any change must be for the better. But the collapse of British agriculture meant that the new steamers at this time carried a particularly valuable cargo of emigrants in the dispossessed farmers and

---

[1] W. H. Perkins, for instance, discovered the first of the aniline dyes (mauve) in 1856, but by the end of the century the Germans were exporting them to all markets, including the British.

Emigrant ship embarking passengers at Waterloo Dock, Liverpool, in 1870.

farm-labourers and their stout-hearted wives. The majority went, indeed, to the United States as the obvious land of opportunity, but they also opened up the prairie provinces of Canada and helped Australia to become a great producer of wheat as well as wool.

The uprooting of thousands of families was inevitably a very painful business:

> *From the lone shieling of the misty island*
> *Mountains divide us, and the waste of seas—*
> *Yet still the blood is strong, the heart is Highland,*
> *And we in dreams behold the Hebrides!*

The Scots were perhaps readier to express their emotions than the exiled English, but all who went left much behind, though they gained much in the new homes they created. Great was the cost of empire-building, but it was one of the positive achievements of this period.

Another was the deliberately expansionist policy which we know as imperialism. The growth of tariff barriers abroad was combated by maximizing the area under British control, either by direct rule or by a degree of influence which kept it open—as in the case of China and much of South America—for the sale of British goods and the purchase of raw materials which we needed. This was partly a matter of the use made of Britain's accumulated capital: out of the large sums invested overseas, the share going to the Empire increased in fifteen years (1870–85) from one-third to one-half, and by 1889 private shareholders had financed four new Chartered Companies to develop North Borneo and the regions later known as Kenya, Nigeria, and Rhodesia. The first and third of these names point to areas of white settlement, such as already existed in Cape Colony and Natal. But the main expenditure of manpower in these imperialist ventures, which temporarily increased the British 'share' to one-quarter of the world, consisted in a rather small number of pioneers (including missionaries as well as explorers), administrators, traders, and technicians.[1] The only large garrison required w ᵃ ᵎ in India, which as the economic jewel of empire[2] also had the most highly qualified administration. To complete our brief sketch of imperial growth we may note that the decade of the 1890s, in which the European powers contended most eagerly for oversea possessions, was marked by a doubling of expenditure upon the Royal Navy, on whose invincibility the Empire rested secure.

Queen Victoria's Diamond Jubilee of 1897, in which representatives of a hundred native races paraded through the streets of her capital, was quickly followed by the early defeats and long-drawn-out humiliations of the South African War of 1899–1902, when imperialism lost much of its glamour. Today the British Empire which the Queen's subjects had built up is even more remote from our own lives and way of thinking than the Workshop of the World which had its heyday in the middle years of the long reign. Yet in so far as the history of Canada, Australia, and New Zealand—for which there is no space within the limits of this book—has continued to be entwined with that of Britain, the reason lies partly in that dream of empire which once brought one-fourth of the world's peoples under the same ultimately liberal traditions of government as had slowly made their way within the island.

[1] Cornish miners, for example, helped in the early exploitation of Malayan tin, Transvaal gold, and Zambian (North Rhodesian) copper.

[2] In 1897 India, with which Burma was included, was the biggest market in the world for British exports (£27 out of £293 million), and imports from India had a higher value than those from any other part of the Queen's dominions.

21 New trends in government

The reign of Queen Victoria (1837–1901) had begun soon after a series of reforms, passed by Parliament in the years 1832–5, which greatly affected the lives of all the Queen's subjects. These included the Factory Act of 1833, already described; a new poor law, designed chiefly to do away with the wasteful Speenhamland system; and a law which started the modern Town Councils. But the first and most important of all was the Parliamentary Reform Act, passed in June 1832, for this brought to Parliament the sort of MPs who were interested in passing other reforms; it also enabled people to argue that, since Parliament itself had been reformed once, it could be reformed again—until after a hundred years of change we arrived at the present democratic rules for choosing members.

The Great Reform Act, as it is often called, did two things, both of which are connected with the industrial changes which had been taking place. A number of small towns and villages which had returned Members of Parliament in earlier centuries lost their special representatives, and most of these seats, totalling 143, were redistributed to the big towns, like Manchester, Birmingham, and Leeds, which had expanded enormously through the Industrial Revolution. Others were allocated to the most populous counties, as an addition to the two MPs which each county had returned since the Middle Ages, or to the newer, outlying districts of London. In the second place, the Act recognized the fact that the middle class—small capitalists, tradesmen, shopkeepers, minor professional men, even clerks—had been made more important by the growth of industry. In towns the old and complicated system of voting, which often enabled one or two rich men to control the entire result, was swept away and the right to vote was given to every householder (male and over twenty-one) who owned or rented premises worth £10 a year.

An Era of Middle-Class Rule

For a generation, accordingly, the middle class, in so far as its members chose to study political questions and used their right to vote, decided the result of every General Election. But the skilled artisans and other urban workers in regular employment were gradually drawing closer to the middle class, both in their standard of respectability and in their comprehension of public affairs. One famous illustration of this was the self-discipline with which the Lancashire mill-workers faced the sudden fall in their standard of living on account of the cotton famine during the American Civil War of 1861–5. The opportunity was seized to attend adult schools or construct much-needed parks—two of the activities which qualified for public relief, and when private charity contributed £2 million for their needs, this huge sum was disbursed in such an orderly way that administration cost only 0.5 per cent. Whilst the people of Lancashire endured their misfortune without any resort to political extremism or social disorder, the prosperity of the nation as a whole was not seriously affected.

This helps to explain the fact that there was very much less fuss than in 1832 when Disraeli—a Tory Chancellor of the Exchequer—induced Parliament to pass the Reform Bill of 1867. The vote was now extended to all householders in towns, however small the value of the property, and to occupants of lodgings worth £10 a year unfurnished. In 1884 this system was applied also to the county seats, so that farm labourers and coal-miners (who often lived in villages straggling over the coal-field) might have the vote. In 1872 the Ballot Act had established secret voting, and in 1885 the Redistribution Act made single-member constituencies almost universal, so that each vote cast might be equally independent and equally important.

The franchise laws of 1867, 1884, and 1885 were not further altered until the end of the First World War.[1] It is often said that they established democracy in Britain: they certainly were important steps in that direction, but there was still a considerable way to go. Women were left out altogether. Of the men, the proportion who still had no right to vote, either because they were not householders or £10 lodgers, or because they did not remain in one place for a minimum period of twelve months, or because they received poor relief, was at least one in every three. Moreover, as MPs were not (until 1911) paid for their services, candidates for Parliament came from the families of the aristocracy and landed gentry, or—to an increasing extent, as time went on—from the middle classes; a working-class representative, for whom a trade union or other organization would have to find money, was still a rarity in Parliament right up to the death of Queen Victoria. Of course, there were many MPs who sympathized with the workers and helped to pass reforms for their benefit, but it was not the same as

[1] See Appendix II, Table 3.

if they had been free to elect men who understood their needs from their own experience.

Chartism and the New Poor Law

The history of the Chartist movement (1838–48) is really an illustration of this. It is usual to point out that, when payment of MPs was authorized in 1911, all the six political points of the Charter had been in principle conceded, except the not very sensible proposal for general elections to be held annually. But William Lovett and Feargus O'Connor, the two principal leaders—both of whom were sent to prison during the period of agitation—and the bulk of their followers wanted something more than manhood suffrage, vote by ballot, and other changes in electoral arrangements. They aimed at getting a different kind of MP, the sort of Member who had first-hand experience of the sufferings of the poor. The result would be the enactment of a policy of social reform. So far from being completed in 1911, the Chartist demands in this sense only began to be considered about 1906, the year in which (as we shall see in due course) Members of Parliament of a new social type first appeared in significant numbers.

The social reforms which the Chartists advocated were often vaguely described as impracticable or inconsistent with each other. But they were certainly united in their outcry against the new poor relief system of 1834. Joseph Rayner Stephens, a Wesleyan minister turned Chartist agitator, called it 'this damnable law, which violates all the laws of God'. Yet the law which bore most hardly upon the lives of the workers was left unaltered throughout the Queen's reign.

The new Poor Law of 1834 stopped the Speenhamland system of rates in aid of wages by trying to abolish outdoor relief. If the poor needed help, let them come to the workhouse for it. If they came to the workhouse, let them find that the help they got—food and shelter for themselves and their families in return for task-work—was administered in such a strict, mean, and humiliating fashion that people would rather die than become paupers. If they would not become paupers, then they must either find a job, however hard and poorly paid, or emigrate, or die. In spite of Dickens's *Oliver Twist* and in spite of the Chartist agitation, the grim new workhouses remained the typical public buildings of Victorian England.[1]

Outdoor relief was never wholly abolished, especially in the case of the aged, and after about 1870 the principle of abolition survived

---

[1] His admission to a London workhouse in 1891, when it still involved the separation of a six-year-old child from his mother, is vividly recalled by 'Charlie' Chaplin in *My Autobiography* (1964), p. 19.

Marylebone Workhouse in the West End of London: new ward to accommodate the 'houseless poor', designed in 1867.

chiefly in rural areas. In some localities the Board of Guardians, elected by the ratepayers to supervise the system, encouraged its salaried relieving officers and workhouse master to administer the law humanely, and the workhouse infirmary, where the sick lay, gradually took on more the character of a hospital than a place of punishment. But the fear of the workhouse remained one of the biggest factors in creating and maintaining the habits of hard work, thrift, and adaptability—whole families would move about the country, on foot if necessary, in search of employment—which made what the books call our 'Labour Force' (i.e., the workers) so efficient an instrument for creating wealth.

The supervision of the Poor Law, at first entrusted to commissioners, was the main task of a new government department set up in 1871. This was the Local Government Board, having as its other work the control of the town councils, which had been reformed and put on an entirely new basis in 1835. Local government was a second point at which the law affected the life of the workers, especially in the new industrial towns, for the law intervened to restrict within narrow limits the improvements which a council could provide for the town it served.

Local Government

As with the central government, so also with local government there was a need for reform. The corporate towns were in a deplorable state, and the reforming Parliament in 1833 set itself to this task also. First a commission of inquiry was appointed, and in its report it revealed how corrupt were the conditions prevailing. The town government or corporation was, in many cases, elected by only a handful of residents, those who claimed an ancient right to be 'freemen', and the majority of residents were excluded thereby from any share in control. When elected, the corporations were often neglectful of their duties. Funds, which had been placed in their hands for charitable purposes, were not properly used, or were even used for private purposes. Charities for schools, when in the hands of the corporation, were often abused; salaries would be paid to masters where there were perhaps only one or two pupils. To put an end to these abuses, the Municipal Corporations Act was passed in 1835 and it applied to about 200 corporate towns. In all cases, the town council was to be elected by all the male ratepayers. The councillors in turn were to elect their mayor, who held office for one year, and a number of aldermen as additional members of the council, on which they served for six years—twice as long as an ordinary councillor. At regular intervals there was to be an audit of the town's accounts. This important Act, which marks the beginning of democratic government in local affairs, should be remembered along with the great Reform Act of 1832.

Further important local government legislation was passed late in Queen Victoria's reign. The Local Government Act of 1888 created new local government authorities—the county councils, whose members were to be elected by popular vote—and these took the place of the older administration of county affairs by the JPs. London was made a separate county.[1] The larger boroughs, with a population of over 50 000, were given a position of equal importance with the counties; they were made County Boroughs. These new authorities, the County and County Borough Councils, became the most

[1] This consisted of the built-up metropolitan area, taken from the neighbouring counties, but did not include the ancient City; the LCC had larger powers than other councils and often led the way in social reforms.

important local government authorities. They were given by Parliament powers to look after bridges and roads, public health and housing, and by subsequent Acts (e.g., the Education Act of 1902 and the Local Government Act of 1929) powers over other matters, including education and the maintenance of the poor.

In 1894 another Act was passed, setting up a number of lesser elective authorities—Urban District Councils, Rural District Councils, Parish Councils, and, for the smallest parishes, a Parish Meeting.

These various local government laws prescribed in detail how the ratepayers were to elect councillors, how aldermen, mayors, chairmen, etc., were to be appointed, and what salaried officials (town clerk, borough treasurer, etc.) were to be provided. These laws also indicated certain jobs for each council to do—preservation of good order, street lighting and cleansing, and so forth—to which other laws from time to time made additions. But in Britain, unlike many other countries in Europe, a local council, however enthusiastically it may be supported by local opinion, had (and has) no power to engage in any activity, however praiseworthy, which the law has not declared to be a proper activity for local councils. It was the business of the Local Government Board to watch for, and check, any attempt to expand. When Birmingham, for example, wanted to collect the savings of its citizens and have its own municipal bank, it required a special Act of Parliament, secured by the influence of Joseph Chamberlain; less influential towns have asked to follow Birmingham's example, but their requests have always been refused.

Growth of Municipal Services

If we ask what local councils did with the rates they collected for the benefit of the ratepayers they were collected from, the answer is that until well into the second half of the century they did very little but keep up the streets—and keep down the rates. The Improvement Commissioners, remaining from an earlier epoch in about half the boroughs, were only one of the many vested interests which fought against a forward policy. One advance, however, was in the work of the police. A force had been established for London under the control of the Home Secretary in 1829, and each borough was required by the Act of 1835 to appoint a special watch committee for organizing a salaried body of police. The counties were allowed in 1839, and in 1856 compelled, to do the same; but until county councils were set up these police were placed under county magistrates, who in 1888 combined with the new county councils to share control by means of a Standing Joint Committee, comparable to the present-day police authorities.

A well-known London policeman, about 1850.

The respectable poor no doubt profited from the institution of the police, though the richer classes gained most.

The faint beginnings of what we may call a more generous type of service may be dated from a clause in the Public Health Act of 1848, permitting the establishment of municipal parks, and the Libraries Act of 1850, which allowed the use of a rate of $\frac{1}{2}$d. in the £ for library purposes, provided the money was not used for the actual purchase of the books! But it was Joseph Chamberlain's mayoralty in Birmingham in 1873–6 that set the example of municipal enterprise, which our towns have imitated and improved upon ever since. To acquire ownership of the town's water supply was often the first step towards a careful study of public health. A municipal gas company paved the way for municipal control of the use of later innovations—trams, electricity, buses, etc. Parks—or at least a recreation ground—and a public library were now to be found in many towns, but Birmingham led the way with a municipal School of Art. To all this, Chamberlain added a famous housing scheme, which cleared more than forty acres and developed the main shopping street of Birmingham, Corporation Street, on a system of short-term leases from which the Corporation (and hence the ratepayers) derive great benefit as owners of the sites.[1]

Such schemes, requiring the sanction of Parliament either through general Acts, such as Disraeli's Artisans' Dwellings Act of 1875, or through the private Acts by which a particular town gets special powers for its own development, were numerous from the '70s onwards, and they acquired additional impetus from the Local Government Acts of 1888 and 1894. The new county councils gave rural England, broadly speaking, the services which were already meeting many of the needs of the urban population. The new county borough councils helped matters on by providing the larger towns with more powers and greater dignity than heretofore. The lesser councils also organized certain services in their smaller spheres, especially the Urban District Councils, which tried to meet the needs of town life in large suburban areas and the straggling streets of the coal-fields. Rural districts and parishes, on the other hand, being sub-divisions of rural parts of counties, were kept more closely under the financial supervision of the county councils.

Growth of Government Departments

The needs of the age likewise produced some growth in the central government and its scale of activities. In 1900 the Civil Service was still, in comparison with today, numerically small and very sparing in its expenditure. Its modern development really only begins with the decision taken by Gladstone's government in 1870, which caused higher officials, forming the administrative grade—the level at which the most responsible work was done—to be recruited exclusively by a

[1] See ilustration, p. 175.

competitive entrance examination from highly qualified university graduates. But the number of departments was slowly growing. Those which had most dealings with the public were the Home Office for police and prisons, the factory inspection system, and the maintenance of good order generally; the Board of Trade; and the newer Local Government Board. In 1885 some of the services for Scotland were assigned to a separate Scottish Office; four years later a Board of Agriculture was set up to deal with the pressing problems of the great depression. The Board of Education, created out of a committee of the Privy Council, was newer still (1899) and shared with such minor departments as the Office of Works (controlling Crown property) and the Post Office the unenviable position that the Minister in charge of the Department was not necessarily a member of the Cabinet.

The Post Office

The multifarious activities at the post-office counter of today—pensions alongside parcels, licences jostling letters, and a special queue for the Savings Bank—are a natural development from the fact that in Victorian times the Post Office was the only centrally administered government service with which people in every class of society had any regular dealings. When Queen Victoria came to the throne in 1837 the public post had already been in existence for 200 years, but was about to be transformed as regards both speed and scope and cost.

Until the end of the eighteenth century, mails were carried by post-boys on horseback. Then a certain John Palmer, who had charge of the mails at Bath, suggested to the Prime Minister, William Pitt, a scheme for running fast mail coaches which could carry letters cheaply because the passengers paid well for extra speed. The first of these coaches started from Bristol for London on 2 August 1784, and services soon multiplied throughout the country. Each coach was accompanied by an armed guard in case of attack by highwaymen. At the end of the eighteenth century, most large towns had a daily delivery of letters, and small ones two or three a week. By 1829, the date of the opening of the General Post Office at St Martin's-le-Grand, on the north side of St Paul's Cathedral, the mail coaches had long been the standard means of fast travel between London and the provinces. But the railways, even in their earliest days, transformed the speed at which letters were conveyed. The first travelling post office began to ply between Birmingham and Liverpool in 1838, and soon the wayside stations on all main lines were being serviced by special sorting wagons and contrivances for picking up and setting down mailbags at speed.

The early steamships, too, though lacking space for bulkier cargo, were well suited to speeding-up the overseas mail. When in 1840 the British Admiralty invited tenders for carrying American and other mails, Samuel Cunard, a Canadian ship-owner, obtained a contract and a subsidy for carrying the mails from Liverpool to Halifax, Nova Scotia, and Boston, Massachusetts. He was a pioneer in the use of steamships for long journeys, and his example was followed by the Peninsular and Oriental Line, which undertook mail services to India, Ceylon and China. By 1874, when the Universal Postal Union was founded to regulate charges and conditions for postage between countries, it was possible to send a letter almost anywhere in the civilized world at a cheap uniform rate, prepaid by an adhesive stamp.

It was the distinctive achievement of the British Post Office that it led the way in bringing the postal service within the reach of the masses. In January, 1840, a penny post for the whole of Britain was introduced by Rowland Hill (1795–1879) in place of the old system of charges which varied according to distance and weight and were paid by the recipient—a very complicated business. Hill, who had been a schoolmaster, had long advocated postal reforms. He was specially attached to the Treasury in order to carry them out. Postage stamps came into use in May of the same year, being defined by Hill as 'a bit of paper just large enough to bear the stamp, and covered at the back with a glutinous wash which, by applying a little moisture, might be attached to the back of the letter'. A few years later, in 1855, the first street letter-boxes were set up in London to save people going to the Post Office with their stamped letters. The penny post led to a great increase in the number of letters—the quantity had already multiplied ten times by 1870.

Post cards (an Austrian invention) came into use in Britain in 1870. But it was not until 1883 that the Post Office undertook to carry parcels, though it is evidence of Victorian earnestness that the book post had been instituted in 1848. One other landmark in postal history was the extension of penny postage to all correspondence within the British Empire. This principle—of enormous value to imperial good feeling—was first brought into limited practice on Christmas Day 1898.

New Functions; The Savings Bank

Besides organizing the transmission of letters and parcels, the Post Office acquired the telegraph and telephone systems. The first experiments in electric telegraphy were made in 1837. But it was not till 1868 that the government decided to take over all the private telegraph companies, excepting the systems used by the railways for their own business. The transfer took place in 1870; the government paid a total of £11 million to the companies, and from that time telegrams had to be sent through the Post Office. Submarine cables enabled the telegraphic system to be extended to other countries. In 1851, the first successful cable was laid between Dover and Calais, and from that time businessmen on the Stock Exchanges of London and Paris could keep each other informed as to prices of stocks and shares during the day's work. In 1866, the first regular telegraphic service between Britain and America was established, and there was soon a network of cables, the joint property of British and foreign governments, which gave direct and instant communication with most parts of the world.

The telephone, which was invented in 1876, was also taken over by the Post Office for development in 1896. But it was not until the twentieth century that the habit of telephoning made letter-writing in some circles appear old-fashioned. It is more important for us to refer now to one completely non-postal activity which dates back to 1861 and is very characteristic of the Victorian age about which we are thinking, namely the Post Office Savings Bank.

Gladstone, who as Chancellor of the Exchequer was responsible for its foundation, regarded it as one of the greatest achievements of his career. On the opening day there were 435 deposits of an average amount of £2; these had grown by December 1960, to 21 500 000 accounts, averaging about £78 each—a remarkable growth, even when we make full allowance for the fall in the value of money. But the great thing about the Savings Bank was the idea that it stood for—to encourage the saving of small sums by enabling the depositor of a shilling or two to earn interest on his money and to feel that his deposit, being guaranteed by the state, was at least as secure as the investments of the richest man in the land.

Gladstone and other chancellors of his period kept taxes low by rigid economy and a stern refusal of social services. National expenditure per head of the population remained stationary for thirty years (1857–87). The money was left, as Gladstone once said, 'to fructify in the pocket of the tax-payer'. A system of government which kept things cheap (including for example the cost of postage) and did all it could to encourage the habit of thrift was, in his view, helping the people in the best possible way by enabling them to help themselves. If they failed to struggle upwards, then in the Victorian view the poor might have a claim to private charity but not to any generous assistance from the State.

22 Town life and health

One of the problems which the Victorians were very slow to tackle (and which to some extent is still a problem for us today) was the effect on people's health when more and more of them were packed together to live and die in the streets of ever-growing towns. The health conditions of London and other ancient urban centres had been very bad, though mitigated towards the end of the eighteenth century by the work done under the Improvement Acts. The quality of the new industrial towns was worse, with a great mass of shoddy building (dating often from a period of maximum growth in the 1820s) which deteriorated as it grew older. Meanwhile the population was still increasing fast: the Queen's subjects in the United Kingdom numbered 26 million at the beginning of her reign, 42 million at the end of it. If we exclude Ireland, where the population after the famine of 1846 had declined at every census, the increase is still more remarkable: England, Wales, and Scotland—in spite of the millions who emigrated—had two inhabitants in 1901 for every one they had had in 1837. In 1851 the division between town and country was almost exactly even, but by the end of the century three-quarters of the people lived in the towns.

It was therefore a very important fact that the conditions of town life, which up to the '60s were getting worse rather than better, did at last begin to improve, so that the '70s brought a decisive fall in the death-rate. The horrors of the earlier years had been eloquently described, not only in several of the widely read novels of Dickens, but by Disraeli in a story called *Sybil or The Two Nations* (the widely separated nations of the rich and the poor) and by an earnest German, Friedrich Engels, the friend and associate of Karl Marx, the founder of Communism. His account of *The Condition of the Working Class in England in 1844* gives an unforgettable picture of Manchester—grim factories overshadowing dark streets and lanes, the undrained, uncared-for rows of poorly built cottages, the clouds of black smoke, the malodorous River Irwell swirling underneath the narrow bridges. Twice there had been a big scare, in 1832 and 1848, when epidemics of cholera in London and the provinces ravaged the homes of rich as well as poor, with the result that Boards of Health were set up by Parliament to see to matters of water supply, drainage, etc. But each time that the epidemic subsided, health measures were allowed to fall into neglect, even though they were championed by one of the first great civil servants in our history. This was a social reformer as determined as Lord Shaftesbury, but, unfortunately, greatly inferior to the 'Children's Friend' in social influence, sympathy, and tact.

Edwin Chadwick

Edwin Chadwick (1800–90) was a native of Manchester, who had much to do with the making of the Poor Law in 1834 and became Secretary to the Poor Law Commission established to carry out the new system. In that connection he visited the worst slums to see for himself how the poor lived. His experiences led him to press for a government inquiry on public health and housing; a rise in the number of deaths from typhus made an examination of conditions in London urgent, and the Bishop (Blomfield) suggested that it should cover the whole country. So in 1842, Chadwick published his famous *Report on the Sanitary Conditions of the Labouring Population*, which revealed the startling fact that owing to insanitary conditions the number of deaths in one year from typhus fever alone was double that of the lives lost by the Allies in the battle of Waterloo.

Besides the lack of sanitation there was the evil of overcrowding. In 1840 there were 15 000 persons in Manchester living in cellars. In Liverpool the number was twice as great. To find a parallel Chadwick harked back to gaol conditions in the eighteenth century before they were reformed by John Howard, declaring that 'more filth, worse physical suffering and moral disorder than Howard described as affecting the prisoners, are to be found among the cellar population of the working people of Liverpool, Manchester or Leeds'. Nevertheless, the Board of Health scheme which he succeeded in establishing in 1848 did not include London in its sphere of action; in other towns it could recommend but not, usually, compel the appointment of a local Health Board; and for want of support it came entirely to an end in 1854. Chadwick then turned his attention to more hopeful projects—omnibuses, post-office telegraphs, and London University all benefited by his many-sided activities.

The reasons for the long delay in tackling the needs of the towns are many and various. We may put first the strength of *laissez-faire* opinion, that is, the widespread belief (to which the economic writers of the day contributed) in leaving things alone. Any government measure was bound to interfere with people's liberty of doing what they liked with their own property, and would probably result in a muddle; whereas if there was no measure taken, the situation might

IMPROVEMENTS UNDER THE ARTISANS' AND LABOURERS' DWELLINGS' IMPROVEMENT ACT, 1875

displaced 21,000 persons from unwholesome houses, and have erected within the municipal boundaries healthy dwellings for about 150,000 persons. In 1875 an Act entitled the "Artisans and Labourers' Dwellings Improvement Act" received the assent of Parliament. This Act confers on the sanitary authorities of all towns of more than 25,000 inhabitants very extensive powers of dealing with unwholesome and dilapidated houses, especially as regards compulsory power to buy land or other property, as formerly any owner who chose to be cantankerous or greedy could paralyse any contemplated municipal improvement which touched his property.

Mr. Cross's Act has recently been taken up in good earnest by the authorities of Birmingham—a town which, though exceptionally salubrious among great cities as far as advantages of site are concerned, yet has, in its central districts, a miserable region of damp, dilapidation, and decay; where the deaths are twice as numerous as in the suburb of Edgbaston—young children die especially fast, as one of the tenants pithily put it, "There's more bugs than babies"—where perfect health is unknown and decent habits almost impossible. Those who have read Mr. Councillor White's graphic description of the condition of St. Mary's Ward will not deem the above expressions a whit too strong. A plan of improvement, drawn up in accordance with the representations of the Medical Officer of Health, has been brought forward by Mr. White and carried before the Council, and it is gratifying to add that it was unanimously accepted, although a few aldermen and councillors abstained from voting owing to motives of delicacy, because they owned property on the line of intended demolition. It will be perceived, on reference to our map, that the proposed scheme is one of an extensive character; it is intended to combine the advantage of new and improved dwellings for the poorer classes with convenient thoroughfares. Those who know Birmingham are aware how much a route for vehicular traffic is needed between New Street and Bull Street. In the proposed improvements a new thoroughfare will commence in New Street, opposite the Exchange, and will be carried right through, across Legge Street and Bagot Street, into the Aston Road. New subsidiary side streets will also be made, and the

'A miserable region of damp, dilapidation, and decay'—an area in central Birmingham as depicted by The Graphic *before reconstruction under the Act of 1875.*

get better of its own accord or through some private and voluntary work of benevolence. This view was very popular among the well-to-do classes: *Punch*, for example, saw fit to caricature the public health movement in the guise of a severe nurse trying to scrub a reluctant Master John Bull, with whose reluctance the reader was clearly expected to sympathize. There were also powerful vested interests— jerry-builders; landlords of old, deteriorated, but profitable property; water companies whose affairs (and water) would not bear looking into, and so forth—which made it difficult for town councils and even for MPs to inquire into the housing conditions of the poor.

There was also much genuine ignorance, for the expansion of the towns had been accompanied by the removal of the better-class homes into 'eligible residential areas', situated usually in the outskirts and distant from the homes of the workers. As late as the 1880s, it was a great novelty when the first university settlements brought even a handful of university graduates to reside in the poor quarters of London and other large towns. To find out how the workers lived therefore required an effort and a deliberate venturing into strange and disagreeable scenes, for which the hard-worked head of a business or a professional man had no time, while for his women-folk it would be thought unladylike and unsuitable. Many people genuinely believed accounts of slum conditions to be hopelessly exaggerated or, alternatively, accepted them with resignation as originating in the drunkenness, laziness, and folly of the poor. There were many besides his own horse that seemed to agree with Tennyson's 'Northern Farmer', when he said: 'Take my word for it, Sammy! The poor in a loomp is bad.'

But the biggest difficulty of all lay in the physical facts of the situation. In days when surgeons used to operate in dirty overalls, it is obvious that the connection between dirt and infection was understood but dimly if at all; and without the modern microscope the influence of a tainted water supply was easily ignored. Mass-produced drainpipes, water-closets, and hot-water systems were eventually among the greatest gifts of the Industrial Revolution to man, but these objects and others like them were still neither cheap nor plentiful in Early Victorian England. In 1832 a bath with a hot-water supply was the latest novelty at the London Mansion House, and we may surely suppose the City Fathers to have budgeted a little more lavishly for the honour of the Lord Mayoralty than for their personal requirements. Therefore, as the crowds poured into the towns it seemed sufficient to subdivide old houses and build new ones, at top speed, without considering that there was any need to improve on the standards of accommodation which had been found adequate by the immigrants before they left their original home, no doubt small and overcrowded, or perhaps a mere hovel on the edge of an Irish peat-bog. A typical village had had no drainage system or artificial water supply: it took time for men to face up to the fact that, when the equivalents of fifty villages were laid side by side to form some raw new town, a new problem of building and planning had been created, for which our new industrial methods must somehow find a solution.

Reforms of the 1870s

Health of towns, fortunately, was not made a party issue. A Royal Commission, the report of which laid down a list of requirements 'necessary for civilized social life', was appointed by Disraeli, completed its work under Gladstone, and had its recommendations carried partly by the Liberals, chiefly by the Conservatives. The requirements included: good water, proper drainage, removal of nuisances (such as excessive noise, smells, and smoke caused by industrial processes), healthy streets and houses, measures to prevent the spread of disease. The first step, taken in 1871, was to establish the Local Government Board to supervise all 'local government'. The novelty of its work is shown by the fact that the phrase itself had only been coined a dozen years before. Then in 1875 a Public Health Act laid down rules for sanitation which all owners of houses had to obey. Every local council had to appoint a medical officer of health, a surveyor, and a sanitary inspector, and it might provide a water supply for its area unless this was already provided efficiently by a private company. Sewers must be maintained in good condition; the making, paving, cleaning and lighting of the streets must be attended to; and scavengers must be employed to collect refuse regularly. Other duties of the sanitary authorities included the supervision of markets and slaughter-houses; and their inspectors had the right to seize and destroy unsound food. They might, if necessary, provide public baths and wash-houses. The medical officers must take proper measures to prevent the spread of infectious diseases. Later, the inspectors were also empowered to examine the sanitary conditions of workshops.

Some cities had already taken the initiative in these matters. Liverpool had appointed a medical officer as early as 1847. London got its first medical officer in 1848; Manchester came next in 1869; Birmingham also had its first medical officer already at work in 1875. But the whole basis of the law was the past experience that the areas which were most reluctant to adopt health measures were often those where they were most needed.

In the same year as the Health Act, the Artisans' Dwellings Act gave local authorities power to condemn, clear, and redevelop slum areas. Mention has already been made of the great work undertaken at this time in Birmingham, though this required the help of a special Act of Parliament. But Birmingham did not stand alone. Manchester had a similar big clearance scheme in Deansgate under another private Act of 1869. Liverpool in the '80s was prominent in getting rid of cellar residences; Leeds, rather later, tackled the back-to-back houses for which it was specially notorious. In London the Metropolitan Board of Works, soon to be superseded by the London County Council, in eight years secured the rehousing of 28 352 persons—less than 1 per cent of the population, but a beginning. Established in 1855, this now long-forgotten local authority had already provided London with its main drainage system and the Victoria Embankment, under which one of the principal sewers lies gracefully concealed.

A third law of 1875 was the Sale of Food and Drugs Act. This tackled the problem, not peculiar to towns, of articles prepared from injurious and falsely described ingredients; the law made arrangements for inspection and analysis of samples and was not greatly altered until 1928. In this connection it must not be forgotten that the Education Act of 1870[1] played a great part by making people less ignorant and on the whole less gullible. Universal elementary education also stimulated the activities of the town councils: people could understand more readily what was being done for their benefit and therefore co-operate—they could also understand what was *not* being done, and therefore agitate. The provision of parks and recreation grounds, for instance, the so-called 'lungs of the great cities', now went ahead without much prompting by Parliament, and the growth of education certainly encouraged the growth of municipal art galleries, museums, and libraries, and—in some enlightened neighbourhoods—the use of local government powers to make towns less ugly. Not all the new town halls, for example, were hideous; the erection of municipal buildings on the grand scale often marked the moment when a town began to take a new pride in its appearance.

Medicine

Although the provision of a complete public health service in the modern sense was utterly beyond the imaginations of the contemporaries of Gladstone and Disraeli, the 'shilling doctor' of the poorer quarters of the town, no less than the up-to-date physician visiting the rich in his brougham, had an important cumulative effect

[1] See page 199.

on public health. It has already been mentioned that medical training provides an exception to the general rule of indifference to the need for scientific education. Between 1818 and 1831 medical schools were established in Bristol, Manchester, Sheffield and Leeds, and interest in the subject also revived at Oxford and Cambridge. By the end of the century every industrial area had its quota of qualified medical practitioners; the type is described for us from first-hand knowledge in the novels of Francis Brett Young and A. J. Cronin.

Meanwhile surgeons were still faced with two old but formidable problems. One was the pain caused to the patient who was operated on without anaesthetic, the other was the blood-poisoning which so often set in after an operation, wound or accident. Various experiments in the use of gases to limit pain had been made, including some by Davy and Faraday. Eventually Professor J. Y. Simpson of Edinburgh himself inhaled a number of vapours, and in 1847 he found that chloroform was the most useful. It soon came into general use as the first anaesthetic.

The other problem was made worse by the crowding of patients into hospital wards, especially when the hospitals were old and dirty. The connection between dirt and disease was scarcely suspected, and so infection spread easily on the hands of doctors and nurses and from patient to patient. Blood-poisoning, or hospital gangrene as it was called, was so deadly that it was safer to be treated at home than go to hospital. In the 1840s Semmelweiss in Austria and Oliver Wendell Holmes (doctor as well as writer) in America practised and advocated the use of antiseptic materials in hospitals. But they were opposed by conservative medical men, and made no impression at the time. Later the French scientist, Pasteur (1822–95), working on fermentation and decomposition in connection with brewing and wine-making, discovered that these processes were caused by living organisms or germs, and that these germs came from the air. Joseph Lister (1827–1912), who was professor of surgery at Glasgow and Edinburgh, realized in 1865 that such germs must also be the cause of blood-poisoning. By using antiseptics to destroy germs—by sterilizing hospital equipment and treating wounds—he revolutionized surgery and, though his methods are now outmoded, he first made it comparatively safe. His great work was recognized when he was made Lord Lister in 1897.

Every improvement in hospital practice was powerfully assisted by the long-maintained influence of Florence Nightingale (1820–1910). By her work during the Crimean War, and afterwards in England, she made a revolution in hospital administration and in nursing. She raised the standard of cleanliness in hospitals and she did much to make nursing a regular and respected profession, with training standards of its own.

From 1880 onwards a number of germs, or bacteria, causing diseases were isolated and studied, and means of counteracting them discovered. The use of soap and water to secure household and personal cleanliness, new methods of avoiding contamination of food, and the process of pasteurization of milk to destroy bacteria have all furthered improvement in health. To attack bacteria directly in the human body is, however, difficult by means of antiseptics; they destroy the bacteria but may also destroy or harm the patient. But the old method of inoculation was further developed by Pasteur, who treated hydrophobia by inoculation with a weakened form of the rabies virus. Another method is to inject a blood-serum from an infected animal, and not the living organism of the disease. Thus in 1890 a German doctor discovered a serum which could be injected against tetanus, and in 1892 a serum or anti-toxin was prepared for immunization against diphtheria. As a result tetanus was very greatly reduced in war wounds, and diphtheria, once the scourge of childhood, in the long run almost disappeared. In 1954 for the first time the County of London recorded not a single death from this cause.

Below the Poverty-line

Improvements in medicine and higher standards of sanitation, hygiene, and building practice must all have contributed (though in unknown proportions) to the fall in the death-rate, which was approximately halved in fifty years. The decline was slower in the first half of the period (1875–1900), but even then it was commonly believed that reasonably healthy conditions of town life were at last assured. That this, alas! was not so, was shown, to the general surprise, by a remarkable book on *The Life and Labour of the People of London*, of which the first volume was published in 1889. The author, Charles Booth, a retired Liverpool shipowner, collected full details, by door-to-door inquiry in carefully chosen 'sample' areas, of how people lived—wages, rent, size of family, regularity of employment, etc. What he discovered was that no less than 30 per cent of the population of the world's richest city lived below the poverty-line: that is to say, the food, clothing, and shelter which they could buy with their earnings were not sufficient to keep them in proper physical condition. Clearly, for those 1 200 000 souls the metropolis must be a place of ill-health and misery or dumb despair; the legislation for the betterment of town life completely passed them by. It was thought and hoped that these dreadful statistics applied to London alone, but a dozen years later a similar inquiry at York, a city which was neither particularly large nor particularly poor, gave a corresponding figure of 28 per cent—and this was believed to have been calculated more exactly than Booth's. This established the fact that all our industrial towns must contain, chiefly in the families of the unskilled workers, a mass of people who never had a chance to live even physically satisfactory lives. The problem was perhaps at its worst in the large ports, crowded with Irish immigrants and destitute foreigners, such as the Jews fleeing from persecution in Russian Poland. But another class of people who were conspicuously poor in material goods at least were the farm labourers. Their pay was about half that of a factory hand; their hours of work were unlimited; and their whole life was passed under the often tyrannical eye of the farmer by whom they were employed.

The efforts of Parliament and local authorities had largely got rid of the squalor and disease, if not of the drabness and boredom, which had made the early Victorian town a wretched place, even for the craftsman and factory worker in steady employment. Rising wages had helped them on, so that in the '90s this class was sure that progress had been made; for them Victorian comfort was no illusion. But it was left for the twentieth century to begin the task of pulling up the 'submerged tenth', now found to be nearer three-tenths, for which the Victorian world planned no benefits—except casual employment, some casual charity, the Poor Law, and the police.

Voluntary Action

Meanwhile, however, something was also being done by voluntary action. A strong point in the progress of English society has always been the part played by individuals and organized groups. People have not been content to wait for the State to do things for them; they have agitated, planned, and worked to help themselves and others. Thus while economists and social theorists might argue for *laissez-faire* and individualists feared that State action would be destructive of liberty, there were always some people to whom evil social and spiritual conditions called urgently for redress, and such people thought out their own ways of bettering those conditions. Charity was often privately organized, collections made of money and goods, and aid distributed to the sick and aged. Two notable examples of private initiative which developed organizations on a national scale are to be found in Dr Barnardo's Homes and the Salvation Army.

Thomas John Barnardo, half Spanish and born in Dublin in 1845, was a medical student in London training to become a missionary,

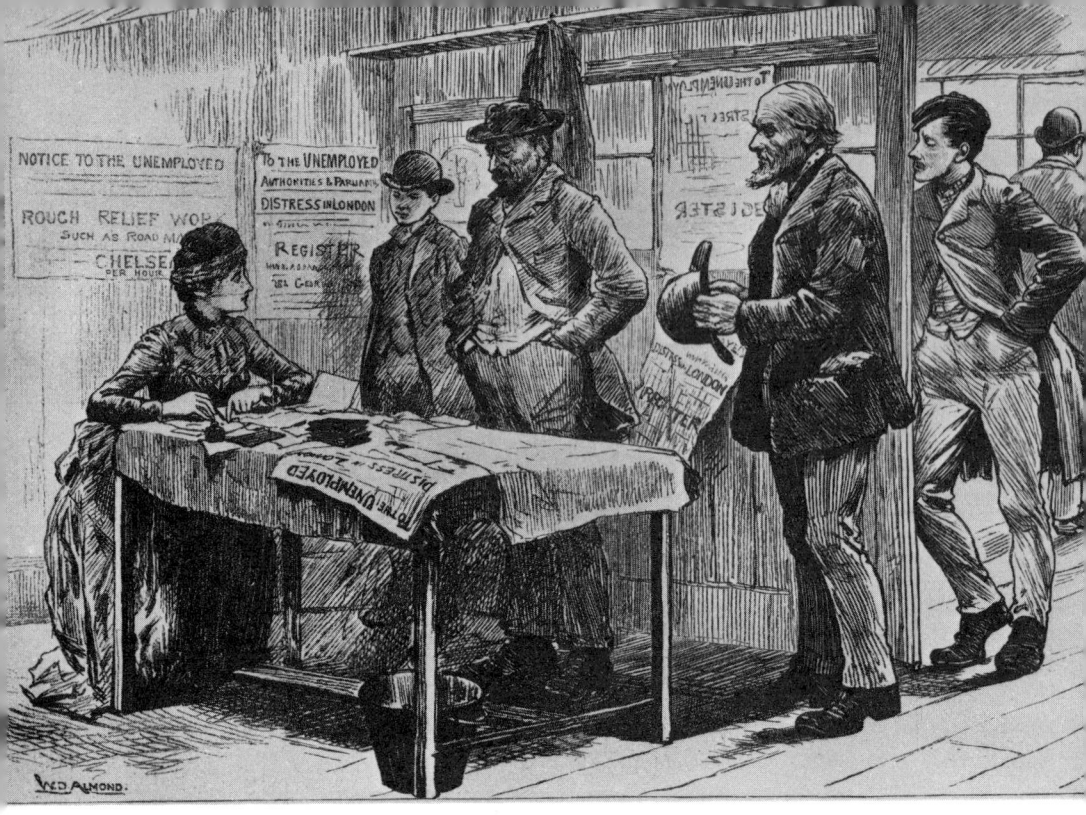

Registering the unemployed—an attempt to organize help by voluntary action.

when his experience of the East End during a cholera epidemic in 1865 drew his attention to the multitude of homeless children. He began to devote himself to their care. The first Dr Barnardo's Home was opened in the heart of the East End in 1870, and by the time of the founder's death in 1905 there were 112 of them in all parts of the country—a huge organization devoted to finding, feeding, clothing, housing and educating homeless children. Industrial training for the Navy and the mercantile marine, and arrangements for emigration to Canada all played an important part in a system which by 1905 had already given about 60 000 children a completely new start in life. The religious principles which found expression in all Barnado's work were equally strong in the parallel organizations developed during the same period by the Methodist and Anglican Churches, as the lack of a Christian upbringing was felt to be the worst part of any destitute child's predicament.

The creation of the Salvation Army was the work of William Booth (1829–1912). Booth was born in Nottingham. For a time he was a Methodist minister, and he showed from the first his passion for open-air meetings and forceful evangelism. Later he worked at a mission in the East End of London, and what he saw there convinced him of the need for some organized, disciplined effort to improve the spiritual state of the people. He therefore formed the Salvation Army in 1878. He directed it himself as 'General' and built it up into a large organization on semi-military lines. His book *In Darkest England, and the Way Out* (1890) told something of its story. From its small beginnings in the East End of London, the Salvation Army has become a vast international organization. Its religious teaching is at one with that of other Protestant faiths, but it believes in realistic and popular methods. A large place is given to music and song—the brass band and street-corner meeting mark the Salvation Army everywhere. The Salvation Army is also active in social work—night shelters, homes for the destitute, and training and emigration schemes. Its work has been most valuable socially and spiritually in helping the poor and distressed. Thus the history of the Salvation Army shows how, amid the general indifference to squalor and poverty in the great Victorian age, individual consciences nevertheless were roused, with results from which we are still benefiting today.[1]

[1] See Appendix I, No. 7, for a description of London as seen through the eyes of a down-and-out who was also a poet.

23 Victorian aspirations

In Victorian times the view held was that, if you worked hard enough, you deserved to get on and very probably would get on, and that, if you got on in the world, you would be able to buy everything you or your family needed in order to lead a happy and healthy life. Good food and good shoes, good schools and good holidays—money would buy them all, without any difficulties of scarcity or over-crowding, so the great Victorian motto was Self-Help.

For all who could follow this motto there was a standard of comfort to be attained, which centred upon the home. A parlour, overcrowded with furniture and knick-knacks, was a thing which the middle class had always had. Now the thrifty artisan in regular employment was also getting one, as the long rows of respectable brick houses spread to right and left of the tramway lines, which, from the '70s onwards, made residence in the congested central area of the town avoidable. Outside amusements were few; hence the frequency with which the piano figured in the home. Furniture was solid and heavy, designed to last a lifetime, during which perhaps the only visible changes would be the accumulation of family photographs, from the '70s onwards, as the camera and its products became cheaper and more efficient. In an upper middle-class home the *objets d'art*, displayed on stands significantly known as what-nots, would be more expensive but not necessarily less crowded or more artistic than those on view else-where. But the drawing-room in which they stood would look more lived in than the parlour of the less leisured classes, used chiefly on Sundays or to impress an unfamiliar visitor.

The quality and still more the quantity of the food was a dis-tinguishing feature of the way of life to which self-help might lead—otherwise there was the unskilled labourer's unwholesome and unvaried diet of white bread, margarine, cheap jam, tea, and potatoes. The skilled artisan and the shopkeeper ate meat (including breakfast bacon) to an extent which astonished the thrifty foreigner; they favoured rich, often indigestible puddings and cakes; and 'something tasty' would commonly be cooked for supper. On Sundays and other festive occasions hospitality was often the excuse for what we should nowadays regard as gluttony, all the more so if the household had been caught up in the growing teetotal movement, so that there was no

Victorian Interior.

additional expenditure to be allowed for on bottled beer or something stronger. The price of food fell rapidly in the last quarter of the nineteenth century, so wages went further, and the imports from overseas which (as we have seen) spelt ruin to the farmer, spelt the cheap loaf, Empire meat, tinned salmon and tinned fruit for the tables of many wage-earning families.

Then, as now, the standard of life depended a good deal upon the number of members of the family or household actually at work. This often tended to put the middle and working classes more nearly on a level, so far as money was concerned, than either side would have supposed. For workers' children usually left school as soon as possible—at some point between the eleventh and thirteenth birthday; those who had reached the top Standard (or class level) were allowed to leave early, and the factories could take on any child as a half-timer at eleven (up to 1893, at ten). They therefore contributed something to the family budget at an age when the perhaps more fortunate children of the middle class were only about half-way through their education and training.

The Position of Women

The same thing was true of the women-folk of the family. Working-class girls were employed in large numbers in the mills of Lancashire and Yorkshire and, indeed, in the lighter jobs throughout industry. They also provided the vanished Victorian army of domestic servants, well over a million strong, which cleaned and cooked and looked after the children in the three- and even four-storied houses of the suburbs. The daughters of the middle class might become shop assistants in the better trades; if they had acquired a reasonable education (rather a big 'if') they might aspire to the rank of governess in wealthier homes. But the typewriter, and consequently the typist, was still a novelty, and the City office, until very near the end of the Victorian era, had usually an all-male staff. In the well-to-do Victorian family a woman's place was emphatically the home, with Mrs Beeton's *Household Management* (1861) as an appropriate guide to duties as well as menus.

Nevertheless, it would be wrong to ignore the efforts which were being made to alter the position of women, for there was perhaps no social movement of the time which had in the long run such important consequences. Florence Nightingale and her band of nurses in the horrors of the Crimean winter 1854–5 gave the first impetus to the demand that women of the upper classes should be allowed to play a part in the world outside the home. The advance was on three fronts.

By a series of laws beginning in 1870 an end was slowly made of the monstrous legal position by which the property of a married woman—land, a share in a business, or money in the bank—used to become the property of her husband to do as he liked with. In fact as well as in fiction, an heiress could be reduced to penury through marrying an adventurer.

Then there were educational developments. The first modern girls' schools, such as Queen's College, Harley Street, and Cheltenham Ladies' College, dating from 1848 and 1850, had great difficulty in recruiting suitable staff, and the old practice of employing an untrained governess for the daughters of the family died hard; it was firmly rooted not only in a Victorian parent's notions of feminine modesty but often also in the desire to make up for the heavy public-school fees expended on the sons. However, the whole level of education of girls at school was gradually raised. Moreover, from 1869

A portrait of Queen Victoria by W. W. Alais after a photograph taken in 1861.

onwards the foundation of women's colleges at Cambridge and Oxford made it possible for pioneers to enter the professions. But the way was often barred by male prejudice, even in the case of the profession where feminine participation was most obviously needed, namely medicine. The pioneer, Elizabeth Garrett Anderson, was obliged to take her own medical degree in Paris; but she secured the opening of London medical degrees to her sex in 1877. The modern hospital in Euston Road, which is called by her name and was the first to be staffed exclusively by women, has grown out of the dispensary for women started by her in the same poor London neighbourhood in 1866.

Lastly, women began to be allowed to figure in public affairs—a natural development, we might suppose, of the great Queen's reign, though she herself did nothing to help it on. In 1867 a proposal was made that they should have the Parliamentary vote—eighty members of the House of Commons were in favour, though nothing came of that until half a century later on. But women ratepayers were allowed to vote in the municipal elections in 1869, and in county council elections from the start in 1888; and when the century closed women could also serve on (not merely vote for) district councils and the boards which managed poor relief and schools. A late-Victorian cartoonist, however, could still make an uproarious cartoon on what he took to be the utterly ludicrous idea that some day there might be women police.

Interests and Amusements

Another factor which made the old saying 'An Englishman's home is his castle' less true was the appearance in the '90s of a new style of newspaper. Hitherto the papers had been serious, informative, and largely local in their circulation: *The Times* and *Telegraph* might reach the north of England, but local organs of opinion—not merely the *Manchester Guardian*, the *Yorkshire Post*, or the Welshman's *Western Mail*, but papers published independently in every one of the larger towns—were more usually read in their particular areas. When the Victorian age began there were heavy duties levied on each copy sold, on the advertisements it contained, and on the paper which had been used for printing it. These were denounced by radical reformers as 'taxes on knowledge', designed to keep the poor in ignorance. But even when the last duty—that on paper—was abolished by Gladstone in 1861, so that 1d. (2.4p) became the standard price (except for *The Times*), the regular readers belonged mainly to the middle class. Parliamentary debates, reported in great detail, filled the unattractive columns of small print; there were no big headlines, no photographs to catch the eye; no 'stunt' articles to encourage family arguments.

The *Daily Mail*, first published in 1896, changed all this. Within three years it had a circulation of more than half a million, far greater than that of any other newspaper; the others were therefore forced to adapt themselves to the new pattern of journalism. A paper was now expected to be entertaining, exciting, full of new ideas (both good and bad), and always giving people something to talk about. For the first time it became common for an artisan family to take a daily paper, and it was no longer possible for strict fathers to pull up the drawbridge of the home, as it were, against new thoughts of which they disapproved.

Not all Victorian homes were strict, of course. They might even be divided into types, according to their outside interests. There were those whose members found society and entertainment, as well as deeper things, in the affairs of church or chapel—the Bethels, for instance, which filled the Welsh mining valleys with song. And there was also the society of the private bar and the music hall—the East End of Albert Chevalier's Cockney songs. The former was probably the more representative type, since respectability of appearance, habit, and behaviour commonly distinguished the skilled from the unskilled worker; and drunkenness, against which the temperance movement, inspired by the churches, was leading a slowly victorious campaign, was thought of as the great cause—though it was equally often the consequence—of failure in the struggle for a livelihood. Saturday-night drunkards sprawling in the gutter, Sunday-morning families marching primly through the streets to church—we must admit that both belong to the true picture of Victorian Britain.

Indeed the Victorian age was an age of contrasts. We still talk of the Victorians as puritanical, prudish, hypocritical, and tasteless, but we know that there was Victorian energy and optimism, and Victorian achievement. To many people the word 'Victorian' carries the feeling of stuffiness—of over-filled and over-decorated rooms with curtains shutting out the view and windows tightly closed, of people in dark, sombre and formal clothes, men with uncomfortable-looking, high, stiff collars and women in garments of great length and complexity. It is true that the solid domestic comfort, with large meals laid before large families, depended on domestic servants, sometimes household drudges, who slaved in the basement kitchens, who carried endless trays, coal and hot water upstairs, in the tall Victorian houses, and who carried the slops down. But it is also true that the general material progress of that age had never been surpassed in earlier history, and that the average standard of life in Victorian England was higher than almost anywhere

Daily Mail report (11 April 1898) of a battle during the Anglo-Egyptian reconquest of the Sudan.

THE GREAT BATTLE.

STIRRING STORY OF THE SOUDAN VICTORY.

HEROIC DEEDS.

HAIR-BREADTH ESCAPES OF BRITISH OFFICERS.

TERRIBLE CARNAGE.

LIST OF OUR KILLED AND WOUNDED.

SPECIAL TELEGRAMS.

From the fuller details of the Soudan battle, furnished to-day by our war correspondent, one may now gather a just estimate of its value to British arms.

The blow to the dervishes is even more crushing than was at first thought. Twelve emirs, including Wad-el-Bishara, former Emir of Dongola, were slain, 3,000 to 4,000 dervishes killed, and 4,000 prisoners are the fruits of the victory.

The battle, too, was rich in those incidents which show the mettle of the British race, its stubborn valour and cool intrepidity.

THE DERVISH ROUT.

HOW THE BRITISH WON NAKEILA

(From Our War Correspondent.)

UMDABIA, April 8.

The details I have already despatched give but a meagre idea of the brilliancy of the attack on Mahmud's position. I therefore supplement them by the following :—

The force left here at six o'clock on Thursday evening, and halted from seven till one a.m., but the troops slept little, being told off to water.

They then marched till dawn.

Sunrise revealed the four brigades in position, the guiding—as, in fact, all the staff work throughout the whole battle—being wonderfully accurate.

The dust raised by our army had dimmed the sun, but presently the light also revealed the enemy's position. It appeared a line of bushy dom palms—a grey streak in front with flags of yellow, white, pale brown, and blue indicating the zariba; undulating gravel, tufted with coarse grass, stretched out in front.

The whole army advanced

IN A MAJESTIC LINE

till within 600 yards, when they halted, and watched the artillery bombardment begun.

Sunday church-going at the end of Victoria's reign.

else in the Europe of those days, not to mention those many parts of the world which we still call underdeveloped.

The Religious Background

The progress and prosperity of Victorian days had a religious basis. As one leading English historian[1] has said: 'No one will ever understand Victorian England who does not appreciate that among highly civilized, in contradistinction to more primitive, countries it was one of the most religious that the world has known. Moreover, its particular type of Christianity laid a peculiarly direct emphasis upon conduct. ... If one asks how nineteenth-century English merchants earned the reputation of being the most honest in the world (a very real factor in the nineteenth-century primacy of English trade), the answer is: because hell and heaven seemed as certain to them as tomorrow's sunrise, and the Last Judgment as real as the week's balance-sheet. ... Evangelicalism made other-worldliness an everyday conviction and, as we say, a business proposition; and thus induced a highly civilized people to put pleasure in the background, and what it conceived to be duty in the foreground, to a quite exceptional degree.' The Victorians put duty before pleasure—that means they worked hard, and, as England's position was at that time highly favourable, they worked to good effect; they therefore made money and prospered. And as they shrank from spending money on amusement and seldom wasted any,

[1] Sir R. C. K. Ensor, *England, 1870–1914*, pp. 137–8.

they saved. A part of those savings passed by gift or bequest to the churches and chapels which were springing up in their thousands and to the great charitable organizations of the day. But most of it went back into industry and made more money. Thrift, like honesty, was manifestly the best policy.

The outstanding popular heroes—heroes whose great qualities are still admired—were religious men and men of serious purpose in life. Such were Shaftesbury, Bright, and Gladstone; David Livingstone, the missionary and explorer of darkest Africa; and General Gordon, the admired soldier who fell facing the spears of the heathen dervishes in lonely splendour at Khartoum. It is true that this was also the age of Charles Darwin, whose *Origin of Species* in 1859 first confronted the educated public with a picture of a world of slowly evolving creatures in marked contrast to the traditional notion of a single act by the Divine Creator. A highly simplified idea of evolution as meaning 'man descended from a monkey' then produced a vigorous controversy between some scientists and the Churches. A few free-thinkers and agnostics became conspicuous in high places, and there was a more numerous class of those who kept silence about their religious doubts. But the general tone of the national life was scarcely affected. Up to the last years of the reign, the English—still more the Scots and the Welsh—continued to be a sabbath-keeping, God-fearing race, who christened their children 'Gordon' and flocked to Hawarden Church to hear Gladstone, 'the People's William', read the lessons for the day.

Holidays

Let us end this brief survey on a lighter note. The coming of the machine meant the spread of the holiday habit. Both the Saturday half-holiday—known on the Continent as 'the English week-end'—and the Bank holidays, the first of which was celebrated in August 1871, were innovations characteristic of the new industrial Britain. Indeed, by the '70s so many people had the leisure and the means to seek recreation in the country that the great enclosure movement, which had been slowly eating up what was still left of the commons, came at last to an end. The saving of Epping Forest for the Londoners (it was opened by Queen Victoria in 1882) was only the most spectacular of the triumphs of the Commons Preservation Society, an early precursor of the National Trust.

The Lancashire Wakes weeks, which took the cotton workers in their thousands to pack the sea-front at Blackpool (the first mere holiday resort to reach borough status, in 1876), are a reminder that 'going away' for something more than a day or half-day trip out of

Victorian Street Scene—The King's Road, Brighton, in December 1879.

town was an activity in which a considerable part of the masses could now afford to share. These were not 'holidays with pay', but holidays for which families saved up, in order to enjoy once in the year the benefits of living on an island. The pier and the front at Brighton spelt London by the sea to the millions of the great city; Bath in its great days had had no such meaning. As for the middle-class family, the fortnight or so in seaside lodgings was so inevitable a part of the yearly round that a host of fishing villages grew into resorts as fast as the railway could reach them.

Brighton, as depicted for the readers of *The Graphic* on a fine winter afternoon in 1879, has a more fashionable public than in summer. The dresses of the women would obviously prevent any athletic activity except riding, for which the side-saddle provides a rather dangerous

facility. The girls' school 'crocodile' reminds us of some of the other restraints of Victorian education. The variety of conveyance—from bath-chair and goat-carriage to victoria and landau—lends interest to the scene and reminds us of the dependence upon servants: notice that some of the carriages have two men on the box. But if one should ask, how this particular scene would be changed, say twenty years later, the answer will remind us that Victorian society, which we have been trying to picture, was the creation of the new machinery. For the newest social influence—cheapening travel, emancipating women, loosening home ties, adding enormously to the enjoyment of life, and providing Britain with yet another export trade—was the coming of the bicycle, which in the course of the 1890s had reached its modern form.

AN EVENTFUL HALF-CENTURY

24 The Edwardian era

When Queen Victoria died at Osborne House on 22 January 1901, she had reigned so long that most people felt it to be the passing of an epoch in British life. Looking back, however, we can see that what followed her death was a kind of interlude. Changes were beginning then which became much more marked after August 1914, when the outbreak of the First World War finally rang down the curtain upon the slow-moving, domestic drama of Victorian life. The term 'Edwardian' is therefore used nowadays to cover the short reign of Victoria's pleasure-loving, genial son, Edward VII, together with the first years of King George V, a more dutiful but at first a less popular figurehead, who succeeded his father in 1910.

For the upper classes this was indeed a Golden Age, when money was spent more lavishly and ostentatiously than the prudent Victorians would have thought proper; the great country mansions teemed with obsequious servants and the surrounding woodlands with carefully preserved game. Edward VII is remembered as a gourmand and philanderer on whose entertainment huge sums were expended by owners of these lordly estates, his son as a crack shot who made record bags of high-flying pheasants. What was more important, this was an age in which wealth acquired on the stock exchange or in wholesale trade for the first time enabled its possessors to mix on equal terms with the old landed aristocracy. Their patronage stimulated technical developments, such as electric lighting, the telephone, and fitted bathrooms, all of which penetrated downwards through society. The private motor car remained the plaything of the rich, but by 1914 London had a service of motor omnibuses competing against the tubes and electric tramways, which were themselves a product of the age of electricity.

For the middle classes, too, this was something of a Golden Age. Their numbers increased rapidly with the growth of large-scale

Motoring in the summer of 1905—an Edwardian idyll.

commerce and of banking and insurance, all of which employed much salaried staff. If the upper classes are reckoned at approximately 5 per cent of the population, those in the middle were about four times as numerous, and with income tax seldom exceeding a shilling (5p) in the pound their position was more comfortable and less insecure than that of the wage-earner, who paid no direct taxation. It was the middle class which then populated what are now the inner suburbs of the big towns. Except for such special cases as the 'garden cities' on the outskirts of London and one or two provincial towns, their homes would be judged by modern standards to be spacious rather than convenient. But no normal middle-class family would be without a resident maid-of-all-work, whilst one in three employed two or more servants who, in the case of professional people such as doctors and lawyers, would probably include a man.

For the workers and their dependants, on the other hand, this was an era of hope rather than achievement. Some valuable social reforms were introduced, a Labour Party began to figure in Parliament, and the trade unions became more powerful. But by 1911 fifteen years of rising prices had brought about a situation in which—for the first time for two whole generations—the level of real wages was evidently falling.[1] Moreover, Britain was slowly losing its position as 'workshop of the world', and even its possession of the world's largest empire was beginning to look insecure. These trends threatened the superior standard of living which the skilled artisans in Britain had enjoyed whilst other countries were struggling to establish their industries and markets.

International Rivalries

Until the end of the nineteenth century, Britain possessed a great and growing export trade and could afford to admit imports freely. In 1891, for instance, we spent upon imports a sum equal to one-quarter of the entire national income. But other countries, especially the United States and Germany, were rapidly developing their industries and becoming competitors in the race for world trade. The type of goods being manufactured elsewhere included the very goods on which Britain's earlier trade had been based, notably textiles. In the 1820s, textiles had constituted one-third of British exports, and in 1860 one-half; but by 1913 they had fallen back again to one-third. On the other hand, metal and engineering products, which in earlier years had been relatively small, had increased by 1913 to form nearly one-quarter of our total exports; clearly, the future of Britain depended upon adaptation to a changing world.

In 1903–5 the fact that the world was changing, and changing to our disadvantage, provided the basis for a 'Tariff Reform' campaign, conducted by the enterprising Birmingham businessman and imperialist politician, Joseph Chamberlain. He carried a large part of the Conservative Party with him in his twofold claim. He showed by numerous illustrations that British industrialists were being swamped in the home market by cheap goods, made in Germany or other foreign countries, which could be kept out by a tariff. He also claimed that it would be advantageous to combine the reintroduction of a tariff with a system of imperial preferences. This would strengthen the bonds of empire by giving Britain an assured market for its manufactures in the self-governing Dominions, which would in return receive an assured market for their raw materials, including foodstuffs. This last item proved fatal to the project. At the election of 1906 working-class voters rallied to the Liberal slogan of 'Dear Bread!'.

[1] See Appendix II, Table 7.

Chamberlain had spoken, if not wrongly, then certainly too soon.

Imports per head of population were increasing faster than exports, but this was largely ignored at that time because of our other compensating advantages. As our mercantile marine was then four times the size of any other, large sums were earned in the carrying trade. As the City of London held the world leadership in all matters of finance, large sums were likewise earned by British banks and insurance companies which assisted foreign firms in the conduct of their trade and industry. As much wealth accumulated year by year in British hands, openings were found for investing it abroad, where the risk was likely to be greater but so was the rate of profit. By 1912 the total of overseas investments was some £3500 million, nearly half of it being placed inside the Empire, and the amount invested annually had reached £180 million. The yield was therefore a further very large item in the invisible exports, which enabled Britain to import much more than the visible exports could have balanced. Thus the position up to 1914 was that big reserves were still available to meet the shock of increased competition in the world markets, and that investors, who included a large section of the upper and middle classes, did not fully share the disquiet of the workers regarding the rise in prices.

Members of the former classes were, however, seriously disturbed by the decline in Britain's political security. The last two Victorian decades had witnessed the rapid expansion of the Empire, particularly in Africa, where it had resulted in a clash with the Dutch or 'Boer' settlers in the Transvaal and Orange Free State. Although the South African War of 1899–1902 ended in the annexation of these territories, with their gold-mines and other resources worked by much oppressed African natives, the defeats which the British forces suffered in the opening phase of the war had revealed the readiness of other powers to intervene against them, if British naval supremacy had not rendered this impracticable. Hence a novel feeling of insecurity arose, which had two important results.

One was a search for allies and supporters. In 1902 a treaty was signed with Japan, and in 1904 an *entente cordiale* with France, a friendly understanding which was extended three years later to include Tsarist Russia. The other result was a fixed determination to keep a safe margin of superiority over the German Navy, which had begun to expand at the turn of the century and grew more rapidly after Britain formed its links with Germany's two European rivals. Though still much smaller than the British, the German Navy had a strong technical basis in a steel-making capacity which exceeded that of the British, and a strategic advantage in the fact that, whereas the British Navy needed to control the seaways of a world-wide empire, the Germans

HMS Dreadnought.

had only to gain control of the waters surrounding the British Isles to win a decisive victory by invasion or blockade. In 1906 the competition became more acute after the British launched the *Dreadnought*, whose guns could destroy any existing warship without coming into torpedo range. Each side then concentrated upon dreadnoughts, which by 1914 had their turbine engines driven by oil. But for the present purpose it is sufficient to notice that by 1908 so much public interest had been aroused that, when Liberal ministers proposed to reduce expenditure on vessels which already cost more than £1 million apiece, they were met with the music-hall refrain, 'We want eight, And we won't wait.'

Impact of Educational Reform

One reason for an increasingly alert public opinion was some improvement in the educational standards of the masses; by 1900 it could for the first time be assumed that anyone under forty years of age had been taught the three Rs—reading, writing, and arithmetic—in a regularly organized school. This was a sphere in which Victorian England had lagged behind the Germans and some other continental peoples, the provision of schooling for the poorer classes having been left to the Churches. Thus the Church of England maintained 'National Schools', the Nonconformists 'British Schools', and the Roman Catholics yet others. Since the 1830s these Voluntary Schools had, indeed, been both subsidized and inspected by the State, but as late as the 1860s the 1 300 000 children in voluntary schools are believed to have been outnumbered by those who did not go to school at all. It was not until the Reform Act of 1867 had enfranchised the working-class householders of the towns that schooling was made available to every child under a law drafted by one of Gladstone's ministers, W. E. Forster; a wealthy Quaker, he had married the daughter of Dr Thomas Arnold, who in 1829–42 had been the famous reforming headmaster of Rugby School.

Forster's Education Act of 1870 laid the foundation of a national network of schools: 'Our object', he said, 'is to complete the present voluntary system and to fill in the gaps.' Wherever the voluntary schools could not provide enough school places for all local children, a School Board was to be elected by the ratepayers to provide school premises, and enforce attendance if it thought fit. Then in 1880 education was made compulsory for all children under twelve, and in 1891 it was made free—previously there had been a maximum fee of a few pence a week.

The system was very complicated in administration. There were over 2500 school boards, supporting their schools from the rates as well as from government grants, and school managers for each voluntary school, supported from the government grant and Church subscriptions. But down to the end of the nineteenth century England made no state provision for secondary education. This was all the more surprising because in Scotland the parish and town schools had for several generations made it possible for the 'lad o' pairts' to make his way through to the university, however poor his home, whilst in Wales the opening of its first university college in 1872 was followed by the institution of intermediate schools in 1889, so that university opportunities might be linked with the elementary schools already provided.

One reason for this lamentable deficiency was the strong Victorian belief in freedom of enterprise, which had led to the proliferation of private schools, ranging from highly respected proprietary establishments to the type described in some of Dickens's best-remembered pages. Another reason was the existence of many ancient grammar schools, such as the various foundations of King Edward VI, which expanded to meet the wishes of the urban middle class—so long as what it wanted was a mainly classical curriculum. And, still more important, the social strata which dominated the Victorian House of

Commons had found the form of secondary education which fitted their own needs. The landed upper class, and the wealthier professional and business families who wished their sons to receive a similar training in the ideology of the gentleman, were catered for by a rapid increase in the number of 'public schools'. Only seven ancient foundations were included under this name in a statute of the 1860s, but by then the methods adopted by Arnold at Rugby (which was one of the seven) were being copied by other boarding schools, which were likewise public in the sense that they were not run for private profit. Some of these were converted grammar schools, such as Sherborne, Uppingham, or Repton; others were wholly new institutions—often styled 'Colleges—such as Wellington College, set up under royal auspices for the sons of Army officers, or the High Church Woodard foundations. The same expensive type of boarding school was also developed for girls, but much more slowly, as a resident governess continued to be regarded as the ideal preceptress as long as 'a woman's place was in the home'.

In 1899–1901, however, the problem of secondary education on a much humbler basis suddenly became acute, because the law courts disallowed the practice of the more enlightened elementary schools, which had been offering more advanced courses for their senior pupils. The result was the Education Act of 1902, passed by A. J. Balfour, Conservative Prime Minister in succession to his uncle, Lord Salisbury from that year until 1905, when his government resigned shortly before an election. The new law abolished school boards, whose powers were transferred to the local authorities, some of which (as we have seen, p. 166) had not existed in 1870. Another feature was that in future the local rates could be used to support the voluntary schools as well as those of the local authority. This pleased Conservative Anglicans and incensed Liberal Nonconformists, because the latter were satisfied with the simple Bible religion taught in Board Schools and had looked forward to the gradual extinction of the Anglican National Schools, which were far more numerous than their own sectarian schools but chronically short of money. Yet the most important feature, especially in the long run, was the wholly new provision made for secondary education.

County and county borough concils were empowered to build their own county or municipal secondary schools or to take over existing 'voluntary' secondary schools, whose financial situation often made them welcome the intervention of a local authority. Supported largely from the rates, these schools offered a good education to all who could afford a small fee. Defined as 'a general education, physical, mental, and moral', it tended to place less emphasis upon the traditional classical subjects and more upon modern studies, including science. In addition, there were always some scholarships which provided exemption from fee-paying, and in 1906 the new Liberal government gave an additional grant to those schools where the 'free places' were not less than 25 per cent of all admissions. By 1914 about 200 000 children were being taught in secondary schools which belonged to the national system, and it was possible to speak of an 'educational ladder', by which a child of poor parents might climb from the public elementary school all the way to the university.

The Social Policies of Liberalism, 1906–14

When the Edwardian era began, the Liberal Party had been for many years in eclipse, after Gladstone's proposal in 1886 to give Home Rule to Ireland had been rejected, not only by the aristocratic landowners among his former supporters, but also by a democrat with great ambitions—namely Joseph Chamberlain. Besides his unsuccessful campaign for tariff reform, he was responsible for the one important social reform made during the long period of Conservative rule which followed. This was the Workmen's Compensation Act of 1897, which threw the cost of compensation for the loss of life or limb upon the employer in a large number of dangerous trades.

Apart from the readiness of the voters to rally to the traditional cause of free trade, the Liberals probably owed their triumph at the election of January 1906—which produced the biggest turnover of votes since 1833—chiefly to a widespread feeling that social reform was now overdue. The findings of Charles Booth (see p. 180) had recently been confirmed by Seebohm Rowntree's analysis of conditions in York in *Poverty, a Study of Town Life*. Social problems were being highlighted by novelists, such as H. G. Wells, and by the brilliant dramatist Bernard Shaw. Attention had been drawn to the poor physique of urban youth by the examination of recruits for the South African War, and out of that generally barren conflict an idealistic youth movement was about to be born, with the publication in 1908 of *Scouting for Boys* by Lt-General Baden-Powell, the hero of the siege of Mafeking.

Confirmed in office by the election, the new Prime Minister, Sir Henry Campbell-Bannerman, was prompt to conciliate his allies of the Labour Party by passing a Trade Disputes Act (see p. 202), and he extended workmen's compensation to much bigger categories of employees, ranging from seamen and fishermen to postmen and domestic servants. An attempt to satisfy Nonconformist grievances over the Education Act was blocked by the House of Lords, but its

Slum children.

general objects were furthered by the introduction of school meals for the necessitous and of school medical inspection, while shortly after the death of 'C–B' in April 1908 the Children's Act set up the first Juvenile Courts. But even bigger changes followed the promotion of Asquith to the premiership, and of Lloyd George from the Board of Trade to be his successor at the Exchequer.

In 1908 the Liberals showed clearly that they regarded themselves as having been elected with a special mission to help the very poor, who had shared so little in Victorian prosperity. For it was the very poor—persons with a total income of less than 10s. (50p) a week—who benefited by the Old Age Pensions Act, under which the State gave 5s. (25p) a week (reduced to 7s. 6d. or 37p for a married couple) to support them after the age of seventy. In favourable circumstances, such as a married daughter having a room to spare, this was enough to banish the fear of ending one's days in the workhouse which had haunted the lives of so many.

Younger people of the same distressed class were the chief gainers from two new institutions of the following year—Trade Boards and Labour Exchanges. The Trade Boards, composed of employers' and employees' representatives meeting under a neutral chairman, had power to fix wage rates for 'sweated industries'. These were occupations such as cheap tailoring, in which the crowd of destitute applicants for a job—including at this time an influx of Jewish refugees from pogroms in Russia—kept wages at starvation level. It was no new evil. Thomas Hood's famous description of the 'sweated' sempstress:

> With fingers weary and worn,
> With eyelids heavy and red,
> A woman sat in unwomanly rags,
> Plying her needle and thread—
> Stitch! Stitch! Stitch!
> In poverty, hunger, and dirt—

had appeared in *Punch* at Christmas 1843. What was new was the attempt to remedy the evil otherwise than by occasional acts of charity. Labour Exchanges had a parallel object—to reduce unemployment, especially among casual, unskilled workers, by providing centres at which information about jobs would be freely available.

Lloyd George's special achievement was the introduction of compulsory State-aided insurance. Part I of his Insurance Act of 1911 insured the entire wage-earning population against sickness by means of a fund, made up of weekly contributions from the employee, the employer, and the State in the proportions of four, three, two. This provided the sick worker with doctoring, medicine, and maintenance. Though a direct imitation of what had been done in Germany since 1883, the scheme caused a loud but ineffectual outcry, especially among housewives who resented any interference in their relations with their servants. The Insurance Act Part II was experimental in character. It created a fund much in the same way as the sickness insurance to provide against unemployment, but its operations were restricted to a few trades—building, engineering, shipbuilding and ironfounding—where the amount of employment available fluctuated violently. The benefit was also restricted to a maximum of fifteen weeks in any one year.

In other respects too, the Liberals set the nation's feet upon a path which it has continued to tread. One example is the softening of the criminal law by introducing probation for others besides first offenders, and Borstal training in lieu of imprisonment for young persons. Another is the recognition given to the particularly arduous calling of the coal-miner, who in 1908 secured an eight-hour day and in 1913 a minimum wage. It may be claimed that both these statutory concessions were made under strong pressure from the trade union, but the shop-assistant's legal half-holiday was conceded to a type of worker who (as in the case of Wells's *Kipps*) was not apt for organization. The list might be much further prolonged, but it is more important to notice two big limitations to the Liberal achievement.

One was the failure to reorganize the Poor Law, in spite of the work done by a Royal Commission, appointed by the Conservatives just before they left office in 1905. The majority of the members wanted to transfer to the ordinary local councils the supervision of the poor, which ever since 1834 had been entrusted to specially elected Boards of Guardians, whose methods of administration were traditionally harsh. This obvious reform was prevented by John Burns, the former trade union leader; he was now the responsible minister, but was so much at the mercy of reactionary civil servants that even his own Town Planning Act was used to prevent any plans from being carried out. The Guardians lingered on until 1929, whilst the more thorough-going changes in the Poor Law, proposed by a minority of the Commission including Beatrice Webb (p. 206), were in some cases delayed until after the Second World War.

The other self-imposed limit upon the Liberal social reforms was their hesitation in using taxation as it is used nowadays, as a means of reducing inequalities of income. This was the more surprising because the previous Liberal administration had introduced heavy death duties in 1894. Lloyd George did, indeed, propose some increase of taxation in his 'People's Budget' of 1909, which so horrified the House of Lords that it refused to let it become law until a general election showed that it had popular support. Even so, the sequel was a further bitter struggle, involving a second election in the same year (1910) before the Lords eventually passed the Parliament Bill, which deprived them of any control of finance and restricted their veto on other legislation to a two-year period. Yet the People's Budget amounted to no more than a rise in income tax to 6p in the pound, a new super-tax on incomes over £5000, and a 20 per cent duty on the enhanced value of land, if the seller had not himself brought about the enhancement. As to the result, in 1913 the working man was still making a larger contribution to the revenue, chiefly through indirect taxes on beer and tobacco, than the amount he received from it in social services. Socialists had long intended, and were ultimately destined, to change this.

Origins of Socialism; Marx and Other Influences

Socialism was a direct result of the big industrial changes, showing itself as modern industry grew up in Britain and, later, in France, Germany and elsewhere. The new machines produced great wealth for those who owned and controlled them, and economists taught that the efforts of private businessmen in competition with one another were essential to the smooth working of the economic system—in that way *laissez-faire* would provide what was best for everybody. But it was soon apparent that modern industry also brought with it many abuses, such as the ruthless exploitation of women and children, the herding together of the population in slums, the desperate poverty of displaced handicraftsmen, and the incidence of widespread unemployment. The socialists therefore argued that industry should be taken out of private hands, and that land and capital should be brought under State control, so that the whole economy would be organized and redeveloped for the common good.

Robert Owen—the successful mill-owner who, soon after the Napoleonic wars, pioneered in trade unionism, the co-operative movement and other new ideas—has often been called 'the father of English socialism', but (as we have seen in earlier chapters) he had little lasting influence except upon consumers' co-operatives (pp.148–9). A much greater effect was produced upon the world at large—and eventually upon Britain—by a German Jew, Karl Marx, who came to live in London soon after the publication of his *Communist Manifesto* in 1848. Though an impoverished exile, he had at his disposal the resources of the British Museum Reading Room, where he found much of the material for his long (and long-winded) *Das Kapital*, of which the first part was printed in 1867.

Marx argued that capitalism was characterized by a class war, in which the rich grew richer and the poor poorer, because the greed for expansion and more profit drove the owners of capital to aim at its concentration in fewer and fewer hands. Small businesses would be swallowed up by great monopolies, and in this process the fate of the workers would be increasingly miserable. Ultimately, this misery must lead to a violent revolution, by which the workers would overthrow the capitalist structure of society and take all power into their own hands—the dictatorship of the proletariat, to be followed in due course by a classless, fully Communist society. Marx dismissed Owen and other early English socialists as mere Utopians, but his own theory of violence made little immediate appeal to English people. For one thing, the limited liability laws of 1855 and 1862 rendered it possible to invest money in a business in such a way that, if it failed, the investor could not be held liable for anything beyond what he had invested. This encouraged the growth of a large number of small shareholders—so there were more capitalists than before and not fewer, as Marx had confidently expected. And already, while he was writing in London, some improvements were being made to the workers' lot—and many more followed in the new century. Thus Marxism gained more numerous converts abroad, though it returned to Britain with new force after Lenin's adaptation of it had triumphed in the Russian Revolution.

In 1881, however, a group of intellectuals was influenced by the progress which Marx's ideas were already making in Germany to form a Democratic Federation, which three years later became the Social Democratic Federation. Its leaders were H. M. Hyndman, who had travelled widely on the continent and in the United States, and—for the first year—William Morris, the well-known artist, craftsman, and poet. Its supporters included such men as John Burns and George Lansbury, and it expounded Marxist views at meetings in Trafalgar Square and elsewhere. But Hyndman had such a propensity for quarrelling with his associates that the SDF remained small and ineffective until its demise in 1911.

A much more influential and longer-lived organization was the Fabian Society, founded in 1884 to introduce socialism through a 'policy of permeation'—very different from the methods advocated by Marx. The policy was to educate public opinion by publishing *Fabian Tracts* to prove the need for big social reforms, and then to get them carried out almost unnoticed in the field of local government. In Edwardian times the 500 members of the Fabian Society included a number of prominent people, like the indefatigable researchers into economic problems, Sidney and Beatrice Webb, and Bernard Shaw, the impact of whose plays has already been mentioned. Finally, two other writers may be named who had an independent influence on socialist thought at this time. One was the American, Henry George, whose *Progress and Poverty* (1879), proposing a Single Tax on land values, stimulated a demand for the land to be nationalized. The other was an ex-soldier, Robert Blatchford, who since 1891 had championed the interests of the underdog in his weekly paper, *The Clarion*, which presented vaguely socialist proposals in a style which attracted popular attention.

The Labour Party Formed

Two miners had been elected to Parliament as early as 1874, and by 1886 there were ten working-class MPs. But they sat with the Liberals, and were sometimes designated 'Lib–Lab'. In 1893, however, an Independent Labour Party was founded under the chairmanship of James Keir Hardie, intending to pursue socialist policies, though they thought the name of 'Socialist' was un-British and might prove unpopular. Hardie was a Scotsman of humble birth, who had worked

*Keir
Hardie.*

in the mines at the age of ten and first became known as a miners'
organizer. When elected to the House of Commons for South West
Ham in 1892, he arrived in a cap and workman's clothes, determined
to steer clear of the older parties. But at the next election, in 1895, all of
the twenty-eight candidates put up by the new ILP were defeated—even Hardie himself. A wider basis was clearly needed, for
which purpose Hardie set out to win the support of the trade unions.

Accordingly, a meeting was held in London in 1900, at which
delegates from the three political bodies (SDF, Fabian Society, and
ILP) with about 70 000 members met the representatives of about
500 000 trade unionists—the minor part of the trade union movement
which was interested. A Labour Representation Committee was then
appointed, which secured the election of Hardie and one other

candidate to Parliament the same year.[1] But by 1906 the situation was transformed, because the trade unions—for reasons to be examined later—were anxious to obtain new legislation which their own body of MPs might win for them. The consequence was that twenty-nine LRC candidates were returned at the polls, including Ramsay MacDonald, who was destined to become the first Labour Prime Minister; and later in the same year (1906) the name of Labour Party was formally adopted.

In addition to the twenty-nine, the new party had the general support of twenty-four other MPs, more than half of whom owed their seats to the power of the miners' union in colliery districts. In 1909 these all adhered to the party, which after the two elections of the following year still had a strength of more than forty in the House of Commons, where men like Hardie, MacDonald, and Arthur Henderson were weighty spokesmen for the interests of the workers.

The Growing Power of Trade Unions

During the Edwardian era Parliament twice took action to meet direct challenges to the power of the trade unions. The first challenge came in the Taff Vale case, when the Amalgamated Society of Railway Servants was sued by a railway company in South Wales which had suffered loss by a strike. In 1901 the courts decided that the union was liable for heavy damages, which meant that trade union funds were deprived of the security gained (as members had believed) by the Acts of 1871 and 1875. Every trade unionist could see that it would be impossible to strike, if one result would be the forfeiture of their entire funds in legal compensation for the civil losses which a strike invariably inflicted on employers. The newly formed Labour Party therefore pressed the Liberal government to pass the Trade Disputes Act of 1906. This gave the unions a privileged position by exempting their funds from any liability for losses caused by trade disputes; and at the same time the right to picket during a strike—which had also been reduced in 1901, in the case of *Quinn v. Leathem*—was more clearly recognized than before.

The second challenge came in the Osborne case. Many trade unions contributed to the Labour Party from their funds, especially after the passing of the Trade Disputes Act had increased the number of unions which thought it was worth while to be affiliated to it. Was this legal—or ought union funds to be restricted to trade union objects and

---

[1] Hardie's change of constituency to the Merthyr Burghs, for which he sat until his death in 1915, is a reminder that the South Wales coal-field now rivalled the Scottish as a centre of working-class militancy.

benefit payments for members? It was an awkward point, especially as many trade unionists were Liberals or Conservatives. In 1908, W. V. Osborne, a branch secretary in a railway union, started a legal action to stop the use of the union's funds to finance the Labour Party, and the following year the courts finally ruled in his favour. The link between the Party and the unions was automatically weakened and sixteen MPs were deprived of a salary.

The Liberals again came to the rescue. In 1911 they provided all MPs with a salary of £400 a year, which was a great boon to the working-class member. Two years later, in response to Labour pressure, they passed the Trade Unions Act. This authorized trade unions to take part in and to pay for political activities, subject to two conditions: a majority of members must express their approval by ballot, and any who disapproved must be allowed to contract out of payments for such purposes. Contracting-out was a system which suited the Labour Party, since its opponents in a trade union commonly failed to fill in the special form which was required, either because it was simpler to let the matter slip or because they did not wish to disclose political opinions which might make them unpopular with their fellow-workers.

Trade Unions were growing, both in size and determination. As to their size, attempts were being made to form unions for an entire industry rather than separately for each craft. There was already the Miners' Federation of Great Britain, founded in 1888. In 1910 Tom Mann and Ben Tillett formed the National Transport Workers' Federation, to include dockers, carters, and all other transport employees except railwaymen. And in 1913 several existing unions amalgamated in the National Union of Railwaymen, though the more highly skilled and better paid footplate workers held aloof. As to their outlook, this was a time when trade unionists emulated the socialists in their discussion of big ideas. One of these was Guild Socialism, which envisaged the placing of each industry under a guild of producers. But the most effective were Syndicalism, which came from France and aimed at militant action on a local basis, and Industrial Unionism, which was equally militant but came from America, where the emphasis was laid upon the need for big centralized organizations to match the strength of the employers.

These new ideas helped to produce a series of big strikes—by railwaymen, seamen and ship's firemen, dockers, and coal-miners—which came in 1910–12 in quick succession, much to the dismay of the general public. They were in each case the largest strikes the particular industry had experienced; about 850 000 mine-workers were out early in 1912. They were also marked by unusual acts of violence, especially in Liverpool and South Wales. Tonypandy in Glamorgan, for example, earned special fame, both as the scene of a riot, in which the troops intervened with fixed bayonets to protect the colliery buildings, and as the place of publication of a syndicalist pamphlet, entitled *The Miners' Next Step*. After a further big strike in the summer of 1913 had been defeated by the dock employers under the chairman of the Port of London Authority, the formation of a 'triple alliance' of miners, railwaymen, and transport workers suggested that the next trial of strength would take the shape of a synchronized strike by all three. In the background there already lay the threat of a General Strike, which was one of several indications that Parliament was ceasing to be regarded as the supreme arbiter, to which every sectional interest in the community owed unqualified obedience.

Crisis at Home and Abroad

Looking back on the domestic crises of 1911–14, the historian is tempted to overdramatize the situation. When a junior Liberal minister recalled 'those far-off days' in a book written almost immediately after the war which was then impending, the emphasis was different.

> The common abundant life of the people (wrote C. F. G. Masterman[1]) flowed on in tranquillity. Suffragettes were breaking windows and burning houses; and Sir Edward Carson, with the assistance of all the country houses, was organizing rebellion in Ulster. But few took these minor upheavals seriously. And for the most part the belief of a steady progress of Society, eliminating the bitterness between rich and poor, was dominant.

Nevertheless, even a Liberal minister, whose account sees elimination of bitterness in a period of increasing strikes, points to two ways in which the constitution was being set at defiance.

Since women—as well as nearly two-thirds of the male population—had then no say in elections to Parliament, it is hardly surprising that the long postponement of their enfranchisement, for which the philosopher, Mill, had pleaded during the enactment of the 1867 Reform Bill, should have provoked a section of them to direct action. This had begun in 1905 under the leadership of Mrs Emmeline Pankhurst, the diminutive but resolute widow of a medical practitioner in Manchester, who claimed that the best political argument was a broken window pane. The destruction of property by the militant suffragettes, whom she organized as the Women's Social and Political Union, rapidly escalated to the destruction of valuable public property, such as paintings in the National Gallery, and the contents of

[1] *England After War* (London 1922), p.xi.

humble pillar-boxes as well as country mansions. When imprisoned, suffragettes went on hunger strike and in some cases suffered serious injuries from forcible feeding; one achieved martyrdom by throwing herself under the King's horse at the 1913 Derby. The so-called Cat and Mouse Act was passed, so that prospective hunger strikers could be released from prison but brought back if they caused further trouble. On the whole, however, the resort to violence seems to have alienated male opinion, for none of the series of measures for female enfranchisement, which were brought before Parliament in various forms almost every year from 1908 to 1914, succeeded in reaching the statute book.

The women's resort to violence differed very much from the movement among the workers in that its leadership and the most active of the rank and file members were drawn from the middle and even from the upper classes; the Lancashire mill-girl, Annie Kenney, who was a protégé of Mrs Pankhurst and her daughters, was the most notable exception. This was still more true of the much more dangerous crisis of confidence which arose in 1912–14 over the affairs of Ireland. The Parliament Act prevented the House of Lords from holding up Irish home rule beyond August 1914, when it would have been approved by the Commons in three successive sessions. Thereupon English Conservative politicians, with the backing of some senior Army officers and imperialist writers such as Rudyard Kipling, urged Protestant Ulstermen to resist the law by force of arms and supplied funds for the purpose.

The formidable preparations of the Ulster Volunteers under Sir Edward Carson, a Protestant barrister from Dublin, caused the Liberal government to offer a temporary exemption to Northern Ireland. But they also caused the Catholics of southern Ireland to organize the Irish Volunteers in reply. In their case there was, exceptionally, some link with the direct-action policies of the trade unions, for the Volunteers took over the nucleus of a socialist Citizen Army, which had been formed in Dublin during an attempted revolutionary strike of transport workers under syndicalist leadership in the autumn of 1913. At the end of July 1914 the situation over Home Rule was still deadlocked, after a Buckingham Palace conference under royal auspices had found both sides unyielding in their claim to two counties (Tyrone and Fermanagh), which adjoined Northern Ireland but had a slight majority of Catholics in their population.

Thus the Edwardian era might have ended in a collapse of the old habits of political compromise, had not an international crisis supervened to restore at least a superficial unity. In 1905, 1908 and 1911 Britain had been involved in European troubles, when her new international commitments obliged her to support France against Germany in the affairs of Morocco, and Russia against Germany's dependent ally, Austria–Hungary, in the affairs of the Balkan Peninsula. But in 1913 peace-loving Liberal ministers had heaved a sigh of relief when the small powers of the Balkans fought two wars over Turkey—wrongly believed to be quite moribund—without any of the great powers being directly involved. The assassination of the heir to the Austro-Hungarian thrones at Serajevo on 28 June 1914, was therefore regarded at first as an outrage which would have serious consequences only for the unruly peoples of the Peninsula.

As late as 26 July the only warlike measure taken in Britain was the decision to hold the fleet together after a trial mobilization, and for another week a strong element in the Cabinet and in the Liberal press urged that the *Entente* with France and Russia should not be treated as the equivalent of a military alliance. Asquith and his closest associates in the Cabinet, on the other hand, felt that Britain's world position would suffer if she left her friends in the lurch, and they knew that this was also the attitude of the Conservative leaders. But it was the German invasion of Belgium, which was a breach of a treaty of 1839 as well as of more vaguely accepted standards of international behaviour, that occasioned the British ultimatum of 4 August. By then Lloyd George and other influential waverers in the Cabinet were convinced that this would be a war for democracy. As for the general public, which in those days had no clear picture of international relations, one large element responded to the thrill of the naval rivalry with Germany at last coming to a head, whilst another felt a moral obligation to defend 'brave little Belgium'. In the absence of Gallup polls, no one can claim to know which was the larger.

25 Disappointments of war and peace, 1914–39

The war which began on 4 August, 1914, was generally expected to end by Christmas, when the small but highly trained British Expeditionary Force of Regulars (about 100 000 strong) would enter Berlin, accompanying their much more numerous French allies and supported by 'the Russian steam-roller' pressing into Germany from the east. It turned out instead to be the 'Great War', in which the United Kingdom lost three-quarters of a million men—9 per cent of all who were of age to serve—whilst twice as many suffered wounds which might handicap them for the rest of their lives. To these must be added the 200 000 killed and more than 400 000 wounded from the volunteer armies raised by the Dominions, from India, and from other parts of the Empire. And these huge losses were sustained in four-and-a-quarter years of incessant conflict, during which all but the last four months brought more disappointments than foretastes of final victory.

This is clearly illustrated by the course of events on the western front, where both sides concentrated their main forces. In the first few weeks of the war the German armies wheeling across Belgium came almost within sight of Paris before they were checked at the Marne. For the next three years the enemy trench-line ran from the Belgian coast to the Swiss border with little variation, in spite of great onslaughts such as are associated with the names of Ypres, the Somme, and Passchendaele. Even in the spring of 1918 the Germans were able to bring reinforcements from the eastern front to threaten Paris again, and place the Channel ports in jeopardy, before the tide of battle finally turned. And the overwhelming triumphs of Foch and Haig in the last months of the war—achieved with the help of tanks and superiority in the air—were still won on French and Belgian, not on German, soil.

The eastern front moved more rapidly, but mainly to the disadvantage of the Allies. An initial Russian incursion into eastern Germany was crushed at Tannenberg, where Hindenburg and Ludendorff made

Canadian machine-gunners at Passchendaele.

their names, and although the numerous and intensely patriotic but
ill-armed Russians proved more than a match for the multi-racial
armies of Austria–Hungary, the Germans were generally able to
relieve the pressure on their weaker ally. By 1917 they had occupied
Russian Poland and other border provinces of the Tsarist Empire, and
in that year the two revolutions in Russia put the country at their
mercy, the result being the armistice and (later) the treaty of Brest-
Litovsk, under which much Russian territory passed for the time
being into German hands. Moreover, the need to help the Russians
had, at an earlier stage, involved Britain in what was felt to be the
biggest disaster of the war—an attempt to knock out Germany's other
main ally, the Turkish Empire, by capturing Constantinople (Istan-
bul). This failed, first as a naval attack and then as an amphibious
operation, in which both the British and the 'Anzacs' (Australian and
New Zealand Army Corps) suffered huge casualties in their efforts to
capture the heights of Gallipoli from a toehold on the shore.

Although the failure of this enterprise caused the youthful First Lord
of the Admiralty, Winston Churchill, to lose office, the Navy which
he had prepared for war succeeded in its principal task of blockading

Germany, so that she was in fact subjected to a remorseless, four-year siege. Yet the man in the street was gravely disappointed when the Battle of Jutland (31 May–1 June 1916) ended in the escape of the enemy fleet from its much more powerful opponents after an engagement in which we had lost more ships and men. Public opinion was also disturbed by the initial success of the ruthless German submarine campaign in the early months of the following year, before the Admiralty could be brought to accept the proposition—which could be demonstrated mathematically—that merchant vessels were less vulnerable to torpedo attack if they sailed in convoy; but the risk of starvation was not taken at its face value, because the German action had brought the Americans into the war with all their enormous potential resources.

Nevertheless, when these various vicissitudes gave place to the final victory, Britain for a moment—a moment which is now too easily forgotten—seemed to stand on a veritable pinnacle of power. Her Empire had stood the strain. In South Africa the rebellion of an irreconcilable minority of Boers had been put down under the leadership of General Smuts, Britain's enemy in the war of 1899–1902, who proceeded to organize the conquest of Germany's African colonies. In Ireland the Easter Week rising of 1916 in Dublin had been suppressed without difficulty, albeit that the execution of fifteen ring-leaders after trial by court-martial provided the republican cause with martyrs who have never been forgotten. Britain had sent far larger armies to the continent than in any earlier war, and they had played a larger part in the final campaign than either the French, who had borne the brunt of the first campaigns, or the Americans, who were not yet ready to deploy their full strength. At the same time Britain had all along been the predominant partner in the naval blockade, which had eventually sapped the enemy's morale.

Thus in the winter of 1918–19 it seemed remotely improbable that the new German Republic, struggling painfully into existence under the eyes of an Allied Army of occupation, would within the measurable future constitute any serious threat to British interests, whether in politics or commerce. As for our other enemies, Austria–Hungary had dissolved into its component nationalities, to the advantage of Italy and other, minor Allies, such as Serbia (the nucleus of Yugoslavia), Romania, and Greece. The Turkish Empire in Asia, from Iraq to Palestine, had been conquered after hard fighting in 1917 and 1918, largely by British forces, so that there was even a proposal in military circles for placing the Middle East with its wealth of oil under a third vice-royalty, side by side with India and Ireland. Lastly, there was the change of regime in Russia, where the fall of the Tsardom in March

1917 had been followed by the fall of the Parliamentary republic in November. At the time of the Armistice Lenin and the Bolsheviks (Communists) had been in power for twelve months. The provinces which they had surrendered to Germany were now at the disposal of the Allies; the rest of Russia was in the throes of a civil war, which the counter-revolutionaries or 'Whites' were confidently expected to win; and Bolshevism was regarded, not as a creed with greater binding-force than the Tsardom had ever possessed, but as a disease which would soon die out if it was prevented from spreading westwards into Germany and other temporarily troubled areas of Europe.

Enough has perhaps been said to indicate that the sequel to victory was to be a period of frustration and disappointment—even before the events of 1939 made tragic nonsense of the belief, long cherished by liberals in Britain and elsewhere, that the Great War had been a war to end war.

The War and the People

The campaigns of the war and the changes in the map which were their most obvious end-product are not the only ways in which those eventful four years set their mark upon British history. For the first time in our recorded history a clear majority of all able-bodied men were called upon to fight abroad, whilst the population at home was also closely affected by its wartime experiences.

Three kinds of soldiers were sent into the field to man the trenches. First, those of the Regular Army, including the BEF and regiments recalled from India; their losses in the first year were so great that the survivors were to be found mainly in the higher levels of command and as a stiffening of NCOs in new formations. Second, there were the 2½ million volunteers (including peace-time Territorials), who responded to the appeal, 'Your King and Country needs *you*'. And third, from 1916 onwards there were conscripts, who eventually included all men between eighteen and fifty not required for munition-making or other essential work at home. Though composed of three different categories, the Army—and still more the Navy—retained the stamp of class distinction, as the great majority of officers continued to be recruited and trained separately from other ranks. Indeed, the upper and middle classes are said to have suffered more than their share of casualties, because it was the duty of in-experienced young subalterns to lead the endless attacks, in which men stumbled forward across a shell-pitted no-man's-land against heavily defended enemy trenches.

Yet the old social order did suffer two heavy blows. The appalling

In the trenches.

conditions of life in the trenches—extremes of discomfort, dirt, and danger to be endured in the front line, perhaps for a week at a time—formed a tie, not easily forgotten by the survivors, among men of utterly different social, intellectual, and religious backgrounds. At the same time the sheer wastefulness of trench warfare, which until the final months never produced any result commensurate with the casualty lists, created a profound distrust of the higher command, from General Haig downwards. Since discipline never broke down, it is evident that this discontent waited to find expression later—in the anti-war literature which influenced public opinion in the 1930s. But it can still be traced half a century after the event, when a distinguished Oxford historian, looking back upon his years in the field, wrote: 'What alarmed me was the lowness of professional competence among the higher ranks ... these commanders just did not know how to set about their task of winning the war.'[1] And even in 1918 another junior

---

[1] L. Woodward: *Great Britain and the War of 1914–1918* (1967), p. xviii.

officer had ventured to pen lines in which we can see some faint stirrings of democracy.

> '*Good morning; good morning!*' *the General said*
>   *When we met him last week on the way to the line.*
> *Now the soldiers he smiled at are most of 'em dead,*
>   *And we're cursing his staff for incompetent swine.*
> '*He's a cheery old card,*' *grunted Harry to Jack*
> *As they slogged up to Arras with rifle and pack.*
> *But he did for them both by his plan of attack.*[1]

In the nature of things, democracy in wartime stirred less faintly among civilians. Thus in December 1916 popular dissatisfaction with the conduct of the war provided the essential basis for the intrigues by which the Conservatives, who had entered Asquith's Cabinet the previous year, dislodged him in favour of Lloyd George. Not only was he the first man of the people to become Prime Minister of the United Kingdom, but his achievements as 'the architect of victory' depended in large measure upon his ability to captivate mass audiences with his Welsh rhetoric and to charm individuals of any class by his personal magnetism. There were, indeed, some limits to his authority: he proved unable to remove Haig from his post as Commander-in-Chief, in which he enjoyed the support of King George V, and he soon quarrelled with Henderson, who represented the Labour Party in the small War Cabinet through which he controlled affairs. But throughout the war years Lloyd George was the minister who did most to keep the workers loyal to the national cause.

Their power in the community was rising rapidly. The membership of the trade unions increased from 4 to 6½ million, and the needs of munitions industries brought into existence a new type of local trade union official, the Shop Steward. His primary business was to watch over the process of 'dilution'—the introduction of unskilled and semi-skilled workers, many of them women, who enormously expanded output by performing routine machine-minding jobs which the skilled artisans in peacetime kept strictly for themselves. Introduced first in the shipyards of the Clyde, from which some of them were deported to other areas as enemies to the war effort, the shop stewards formed the spearhead of a movement to raise wages and insist on improved working conditions—such as the provision of canteens, hitherto a rarity—to which the government generally gave way.

---

[1] S. Sassoon: *Counterattack and Other Poems* (1918), p. 26.

A parallel change was a remodelling of the Labour Party, whose position was challenged by Lloyd George in the summer of 1917, when he contemptuously dismissed Henderson from the War Cabinet and put a weaker representative of Labour in his place, because the Party had made an unwelcome demand for Henderson's attendance at a projected socialist conference in Stockholm. Accordingly, in January 1918 a new and much stronger constitution was adopted, as drafted by the Fabian, Sidney Webb, aiming 'To secure for the producers by hand and by brain the full fruits of their industry, and the most equitable distribution thereof . . . upon the basis of the common ownership of the means of production and . . . popular administration and control.' This definitely socialist programme had little prospect of immediate success, but at the same time the vital practical step was taken of organizing the party on the basis of local groups of individual members, such as had hitherto existed only in the ILP. These local Labour Party groups were to be directly represented (as were also the women adherents) on the National Executive Committee, which provided guidance for the Party's representatives in Parliament. The majority in the NEC was still, however, made up from the affiliated trade unions, which continued to subscribe the bulk of the party funds.

January 1918 was likewise the month in which three great advances towards democracy completed their relatively smooth passage through the wartime Parliament. One of these required that all children without exception should receive full-time education from five to fourteen. In introducing the law which bears his name, H. A. L. Fisher, an historian and university teacher whom Lloyd George had brought into the Cabinet, stated that about 600 000 children had been allowed to leave school prematurely for munitions and other war-work—whilst the textile factories even in peacetime employed 'half-timers' from the age of eleven. Both the other advances were embodied in the Representation of the People Act. All men were now enfranchised at the age of twenty-one, subject to six months' residence in the constituency (which disqualified about 5 per cent). The enfranchisement of women, now acceptable to seven-eighths of the House of Commons (as shown by voting in Committee), was likewise enacted, subject to two limitations designed to prevent any immediate outnumbering of the male electorate; there was to be a minimum age of thirty and a minimum requirement of the payment of rates, either directly or through a husband.

The war had witnessed a rise in the number of women employed in commerce and industry by rather more than one-half, from 3.2 to nearly 5 million; their help to the war effort as a whole had constituted a silent but unanswerable argument for giving them the vote.

London bus-conductress—a novelty of the First World War. The omnibus has solid tyres and the minimum of weather protection.

The following year the cumbrously named Sex Disqualification (Removal) Act threw open in principle 'any public function, office or post' and 'any civil profession or vocation', and a special Act (passed just before the election) enabled the first woman to take her seat in the House of Commons. In 1928 the Equal Franchise Act gave women the majority position which they may be expected to retain in any fully democratic electorate, whilst in the following year a woman trade union official, Margaret Bondfield, entered the Labour Cabinet. The House of Lords for the time being remained closed to them, and down to the Second World War the number of women MPs never exceeded fifteen or the number of their Parliamentary candidates sixty-nine. Nevertheless, the war had brought about a lasting trend towards equality of the sexes. Working-class women, having earned good wages in munitions, were less willing to accept without protest an inferior economic status, whilst those of the well-to-do classes, for whom war-work had been a purely voluntary activity, were unlikely to instil in their daughters the old class prejudice which identified 'ladies' by their abstention from paid employment. The feminine invasion of the business world, which had begun at the turn of the century as typewriters came into general use, now gathered speed. Nearly all the professions likewise welcomed a minority of women members, though the Civil Service required resignation on marriage, as did most employers of teachers—at least until the London County Council removed the ban in 1935. The clergy of most denominations lagged (and still lag) behind, albeit the Congregationalists of the City Temple had appointed their first woman preacher in 1917.

A return may now be made to the situation at the time of the Armistice. There was a general election the following month, which Lloyd George fought as leader of the coalition; although all serving men were entitled to vote, irrespective of their age, the election came so quickly that few were able to take part. The Labour Party, which believed it would have received their votes, won fifty-nine seats; this made them the official Opposition, as the Asquithian Liberals were reduced to twenty-six. Power rested indubitably with Lloyd George, 'the man who won the war', who was returned at the head of a very large, mainly Conservative coalition. Time would show the value of his promises to the returning soldiers, such as the provision of 'homes fit for heroes to live in'.

The Onset of Mass Unemployment

During the first four post-war years Lloyd George remained the most prominent of European statesmen. Britain emerged from the peace conference at Paris with the lion's share of the German and Turkish colonial possessions. At the end of 1919 the first serious start was made on the complicated task of introducing self-government to India, where Gandhi was already the idol of the people; but the only direct threat to the power of victorious Britain was a miniature civil war in Ireland. Auxiliary forces which were recruited to restore order, known from their uniforms as 'Black and Tans', vied with the Irish Republican Army in the brutality of their reprisals. However, in 1922 Lloyd George succeeded in negotiating a treaty which set up the Irish Free State in the south, linked with the United Kingdom by the same ties as Canada; this left six counties of predominantly Protestant Ulster as part of the United Kingdom, with a provincial legislature in Belfast which had already begun to function under the Government of Ireland Act of 1920. Although the IRA continued to promote an all-Ireland republic by acts of terrorism on both sides of the new border, whilst the Protestant Ulstermen repressed the Catholic minority in the North, it seemed for a time that the Welsh Wizard had solved the problems with which the British people had been vainly grappling ever since the days of Gladstone. Nevertheless, in the autumn of 1922 the majority of the Conservatives broke away from the coalition, so that Lloyd George lost office—as it turned out, for ever. The occasion for the breach was a crisis over foreign policy, when Lloyd George risked a war (in which Britain would not have had the backing of the Dominions) by championing the Greeks against the Turks in Asia Minor. But the Conservatives also believed that the time had come for them to take an independent line over the domestic situation, which in their view demanded a policy of 'Drastic Economy'. For already the decline of trade was leading to the onset of mass unemployment.

The war had been followed by a trade boom, during which wartime deficiencies of all kinds were made good at high prices. Money was then readily invested in the expectation of increasing exports of Britain's traditional products; two-fifths of the Lancashire cotton mills, for example, changed hands at seven times their original capital value. But as early as April 1920 trade began to decline, so that by the close of 1921 there were more than 2 million insured workers who were without employment. In 1922–39 (both years inclusive) the full total seems never to have fallen below 1¼ million.[1]

Unemployment insurance had been extended in 1920–1 to cover nearly all manual workers except farm labourers, domestic servants, and the less-skilled categories of railway employees; and also to provide separate support for dependants. But although the Dole, as it was disparagingly called, was made available for two additional periods beyond the fifteen weeks covered by the payments into the insurance fund (see p. 203), the amount received meant an immediate reduction in the standard of living for the recipient and his dependent family, whilst in the long run he would be thrown back upon poor relief, administered by the Board of Guardians. At Poplar in east London the Guardians went to prison in September 1921 sooner than keep to the low level of relief approved by the government, and a year later the first of many Hunger Marches converged on the capital to demonstrate the extent of the distress in South Wales, the North of England, and the industrial Lowlands of Scotland. These were the seats of our former staple industries—iron and steel, coal, shipbuilding, and textiles—to which prosperity failed to return even in the later 1920s, when a boom of record dimensions in the United States stimulated trade in many parts of Europe.

---

[1] The lowest figure for insured unemployed was 1 059 000 in May 1927, but the uninsured (for whom there were no official totals) represent an addition of up to 25 per cent. See Appendix II, Table 6.

Some of the causes of this decline lay further back, in the long period when the lack of competition from our less industrialized neighbours had encouraged British firms to neglect technological improvements and up-to-date methods of salesmanship. But Britain's economic decline was greatly accentuated by the war. The sale of part of our foreign assets and investments to pay for munitions from abroad had temporarily diminished our 'invisible' income, whilst a rise in world prices reduced the purchasing power of the income that remained. A much more serious factor, however, was the increased competition from other industrialized powers, not only the United States, but also small but efficient European rivals like Sweden, Switzerland, the new Czechoslovakia and newly independent Poland. There arose, too, an enterprising Far Eastern competitor in Japan, the one Asiatic country which had modernized itself in the later nineteenth century.

By 1928 we were paying out 50 per cent more than before the war for the imports we bought, and getting in only 33 per cent more for exports sold. Cotton goods, now produced on a large scale in Indian as well as Japanese factories, made up only one-fifth of British exports; Poland and Germany, using more machinery, had taken over much of the coal trade; and throughout the decade the volume of iron and steel exports from Britain stayed below the level of 1913. Some trans-oceanic markets, which had been lost during the war, proved difficult to regain, and the new or newly enlarged states of post-war Europe were in many cases building up their own heavy industries with patriotic fervour behind a high tariff wall. Moreover, two of Britain's major European markets were restricted for special reasons: Soviet Russia aimed at self-sufficiency through a remarkable system of state planning, whilst trade with the German Republic was hampered by reparations. These were the payments in money and in kind, with which the Germans undertook in the peace treaty to compensate the Allies for war damage. Their only means of paying was to increase their exports and reduce their imports—which was disadvantageous to British trade—and when they in any case proved obdurate, the French and Belgians in January 1923 temporarily occupied the Ruhr, to the further disadvantage of international trade and relations in general.

We may now turn to consider briefly how the governments of the 1920s sought to handle the economic difficulties. In 1923 the Conservative Prime Minister, Stanley Baldwin, a Midlands ironmaster with a strong social conscience, proposed to fight unemployment by a tariff, which was rejected at an election. The sequel was the first, short-lived Labour government, dependent upon Liberal votes for survival and in fact having fewer seats in the Commons than the

Conservative Opposition. Its chief importance was to show that Ramsay MacDonald and his colleagues were not revolutionaries but loyal supporters of Parliamentary institutions. Their only substantial social reform was a Housing Act (p. 241), but the Prime Minister, who was also Foreign Secretary, worked hard to secure the peaceful conditions in Europe which would benefit British trade. He promoted the Dawes Plan, under which the Germans (helped by an American loan) undertook scaled-down payments of reparations. MacDonald also gave official recognition to Soviet Russia, hoping to negotiate a trade treaty there. But he was defeated in 1924's second general election. Charges against a Communist journalist named Campbell, who urged soldiers never to fire on fellow-workers, had been dropped on government orders, and just before polling-day Moscow's direct control over British Communism was 'revealed' in the alleged Zinoviev Letter.

The reaction of the voters is a reminder that the unexpected survival of the Communist regime in Russia made public opinion at all times apprehensive of Communist activities in Britain. As early as 1920 the British Socialist Party, a little group which had preserved the Marxist doctrines of the extinct SDF, had joined forces with some left-wing shop stewards to set up the Communist Party of Great Britain. Its membership was undisclosed but certainly small; although it put forward as many as twenty-six candidates for Parliament, no more than two were ever elected. But it was the prime mover in the hunger marches (already mentioned) and other demonstrations by the unemployed, which it organized through the NUWM (National Unemployed Workers' Movement), and in 1924 it began its efforts to infiltrate the trade unions through the so-called 'minority movement', headed by Tom Mann. In addition, the public was aware that the Party was linked with the Third International, based on Moscow, of which Zinoviev in 1924 was President.

Accordingly, Baldwin was in power from 1924 to 1929 with a strong Conservative government, including Churchill as Chancellor of the Exchequer, in which capacity he sought to bring back the golden age of British commercial predominance by the return to the gold standard at pre-war parity. This may have helped the world-wide financial activities of the City of London, but it hampered exports, which our customers now had to pay for in terms of a gold-based pound sterling. Only a year later, this precipitated the General Strike of 1926, which must be considered in the context of trade union activities during this period. But first we may notice that the decade closed with an election which returned Labour as the largest single party in the Commons, though it again required Liberal support to achieve a majority. This was the more readily forthcoming because the Liberals, no less than the Labour Party, had gone to the polls with the conquest of unemployment as their main political objective. Lloyd George, in particular, fought the 1929 election with a bold policy—backed by the economist J. M. Keynes—of public works to deal with unemployment. This policy was set out in the Liberal Orange Book—'We Can Conquer Unemployment'. But the Liberals did not win, and Labour proved ineffective.

Trade Unionism and the General Strike

The trade unions had expected that their increasing authority in the community would lead to very different results. They had emerged from the war with larger numbers and a more aggressive spirit. In Glasgow, for instance, the period of demobilization was marked by a general strike in support of a forty-hour week, so as to spread employment to the returning Servicemen. The leaders, who included ILP Members of Parliament as well as militant shop stewards, were overawed by the deployment of tanks and machine-guns in the city; but although these particular efforts failed, hours in industry as a whole soon fell from the pre-war figures of fifty-four or more to forty-eight and in some cases even less. By 1920 union membership had reached 8.3 million,[1] which was more than half the total of manual workers, and next year the Trade Union Congress, to which about three trade unionists in four were affiliated, instituted a General Council 'to co-ordinate industrial action'. What this might mean had been demonstrated in August 1920, when the threat of a general strike was used to prevent Lloyd George's more bellicose colleagues, such as Churchill, from making the defence of Poland an excuse for hostilities against Soviet Russia.

Another very significant development was the revival of the pre-war 'Triple Alliance'. In 1919 one component, the railwaymen, fought off a wage reduction by a strike which lasted less than a week. Another, namely the dockers, secured an official inquiry into their conditions of work, at which their grievances were stated to great effect by Ernest Bevin, their pugnacious secretary, who became known as 'the dockers' KC'. But the key position was held by the Miners' Federation, which cast 615 000 out of 720 000 votes in favour of a strike. This induced the government to appoint a Statutory Commission under Mr Justice Sankey to investigate the chaotic conditions of an industry in which 3000 mines of very varying yield were

---

[1] See Appendix II, Table 6.

operated by 1500 separate managements. The miners gained a reduction of hours to seven a day and an increase in pay, but not the implementation of a majority recommendation that both the royalty to landowners and the mines themselves should be nationalized. They were naturally aggrieved, and when the decline in coal exports and in the consumption by our own heavy industries caused the mine-owners to demand a wage-cut they were prompt to strike, under the impression that the other members of the Triple Alliance would call out their members in sympathy. But on 'Black Friday' (15 April 1921) they made a last-minute withdrawal, on the ground that the miners ought to have accepted a temporary compromise. The miners held out alone for more than three months; their surrender was followed by a fall in wages for other industries as well.

Although a concomitant fall in prices meant that most workers—and especially the unskilled—continued to be better off than before the war, it was natural for the trade unions to compare the position with the higher level of earnings in the short post-war boom. In the summer of 1925 matters were brought to a head by the return to the gold standard, which led the coal-owners to demand a further wage reduction and an increase in hours in order to make their export prices competitive again. An immediate clash was avoided by a nine months' subsidy, which enabled the government to make preparations for an eventual major conflict, whilst a second Commission under a leading Liberal politician, Sir Herbert Samuel, reported in favour of a thorough reorganization of the industry, to be preceded, however, by a 'temporary sacrifice' of wages. The miners replied uncompromisingly, 'Not a penny off the pay, not a minute on the day', and this time they had the backing, not merely of the Triple Alliance, but of the General Council of the TUC.

A nationwide General Strike began accordingly on 2 May 1926, with the calling-out of a 'first line' of workers. In all the chosen industries, which included transport, printing, iron and steel, chemicals, and building, the response was overwhelming: altogether, about 3 million workers stood resolutely idle. But the response of the middle class to the cry of the constitution in danger was likewise overwhelming, as about one-third of a million volunteers registered for duty as special constables, dockers, or—what was perhaps the most important group—motor-transport drivers. The government also made play with a widely distributed propaganda organ, *The British Gazette* (which had an enthusiastic editor in Churchill), and a propaganda statement in Parliament that the strike was illegal and that trade union funds were therefore liable to confiscation. Although the government succeeded in maintaining food supplies, after a week tempers were clearly rising, especially where the police intervened in force to safeguard the passage of lorries, buses, and other 'black' transport. In Glasgow, for instance, a hundred men arrested for offences in this connection were later sent to prison, as were eighty-four in the mining town of Doncaster, whilst anxiety about Communist influences became so acute that two Welshmen were imprisoned for having Communist literature in their possession.

What would have happened if the TUC had gone ahead to call out its 'second line'—which would have cut off electric light from the streets, for example—can only be surmised, for in practice it had not intended to do more than shock the government into a compromise with the miners. Accordingly, the leading members of the Council welcomed informal proposals from Samuel for a reorganization of the mining industry and its wages structure, and when the miners turned them down, asserted that they 'were not aware of the general industrial situation ... They lived in villages, and they thought in the mass.' The TUC then felt justified in abdicating from responsibility for a situation which by the ninth day looked as if it might get out of hand, even though the government's terms were unconditional surrender. They believed, indeed, that Baldwin's personal influence would prevent any victimization of strike leaders, but although the disregard of the Prime Minister's wishes by the more vindictive element among the employers provoked a spontaneous revival of strike action in the next few days, the surrender of 12 May was decisive.

Looking back from the standpoint of the 1970s, the peaceful termination of what was potentially the most dangerous conflict in modern British history seems to have been due primarily to the reluctance of the trade union leaders, and still more of their allies in the Labour Party in the House of Commons, to offer any challenge to the constitutional supremacy of Parliament. But foreigners noted with envy that compromise was still a part of the British way of life among all classes, as epitomized in Baldwin's claim in a broadcast during the strike that he was 'longing and working and praying for peace'—or in King George's behind-the-scenes deprecation of the suggested attack on trade union funds.

The conflict left scars. The miners stayed out until the winter, when hunger compelled them to accept the owners' terms. The Conservative Party flouted Baldwin's wishes by passing the Trade Disputes Act of 1927. Besides outlawing any strike 'designed to coerce the government', this measure made picketing more difficult, forbade civil servants to join any union affiliated to the TUC, and reversed the 'contracting-out' clause of the Act of 1913. Trade union membership, which had already fallen heavily since the peak year of 1920, fell year by year until 1934 and did not reach a new and higher peak until after the Second World War. But the General Strike also had some more constructive results. The Labour Party dissociated itself more firmly from the doctrine of the class war, which became the distinctive tenet of the Communists and the ILP; in 1935 the latter became a separate party, which won only four seats in Parliament. A readiness to collaborate with the more enlightened capitalists likewise found expression in the Mond–Turner Talks between Sir Alfred Mond of the giant chemicals combine, ICI,[1] and trade union representatives, including Bevin. The theme was the need to increase productivity as the surest means of raising wages—and reducing unemployment.

World Crisis and 'National' Government

The second Labour government's plans for relieving unemployment proved ineffective from the onset, in spite of the appointment of a special Minister for Employment, one of whose assistants was a young and aristocratic recruit to the Labour Party, Sir Oswald Mosley (6th Baronet). When he proposed bold measures to increase purchasing power and to finance industrial development, including tariffs, MacDonald preferred to accept his resignation, so by 1931 Mosley was organizing a party of his own, soon to become the British Union of Fascists. The new premier experimented with marketing boards, to enable farmers to sell at fixed prices, and a quota system for the coal industry, so that collieries should not compete against each other for markets. He also increased expenditure on the insurance fund, so that the unemployed should not be reduced so quickly to poor relief, and removed a bitterly resented obligation that they must continually prove that they were 'genuinely seeking work'. But the number of insured unemployed, which was over $1\frac{1}{2}$ million in January 1930, had risen by the end of the year to an unprecedented total of $2\frac{1}{2}$ million, as the result of a world crisis which no British prime minister could have brought under control.

October 1929 witnessed the beginning of the greatest economic depression which the modern world had ever experienced, in the collapse of a prolonged boom in shares on the New York stock exchange—a much-enlarged version of the South Sea Bubble—when 'millionaires became beggars in a day'. Soon there were 12 million Americans out of work, whilst the repercussions spread far and wide across Europe. In Germany, for instance, the inability of the parliamentary republic to cope with the problem of 7 million un-

---

[1] See page 238.

Queuing for the dole—note the white-collar workers as well as the labourers in cloth caps.

employed led to the rise of Hitler to power in January 1933. For Britain too, the 'economic blizzard' had important though less tragic consequences.

As the head of a minority ministry, MacDonald was obliged to accept a demand for a Committee on National Expenditure under an insurance company chairman (Sir George May), whose report was published at the end of July 1931; by then the international financial and commercial situation had further deteriorated through the wide repercussions following the collapse of the principal bank in Vienna. The May Report called for the Budget to be brought into balance by such radical measures as a 20 per cent cut in unemployment benefit. Drastic action seemed all the more urgent because another report, published earlier in the month, had called for a different balance to be remedied—namely the very unfavourable balance in Britain's world trade after nearly two years of crisis. Within a fortnight a run on the pound began, as nervous foreign investors called back their short-term deposits from London, and American and French help was made conditional upon the balancing of the Budget. Nine members out of a Cabinet of twenty-one, supported by the TUC Council, refused to cut unemployment benefit by 10 per cent, which was said to be the irreducible minimum if confidence was to be restored abroad. The government therefore broke up, but to the surprise and indignation of most of his colleagues, MacDonald accepted the King's commission to form a new government 'to deal with the national emergency'.

The new 'National' ministry comprised four Conservatives, two Liberals (one of them in place of Lloyd George, who was incapacitated by illness), and four of the former Labour ministers. These last were bitterly attacked by the Labour Party in general and by the TUC, but MacDonald had a clear majority in Parliament for additions to income tax and reductions in the payment of all public employees (including teachers), in principle on the same scale of 10 per cent as was to be applied to the unemployed. However, the run on sterling was only temporarily halted by the foreign credits which were now forthcoming, and in mid-September the run became a stampede when news spread of a mutiny at the Invergordon naval base in the north of Scotland. This was in fact a strike with no undertones of sedition, the crews of the Atlantic fleet refusing to put to sea when it was learnt that some young sailors might find their take-home pay cut by as much as 25 per cent. Redress was quickly promised, but it was too late: on 21 September the National government was compelled to abandon the Gold Standard which it had been formed to defend.

This situation was held to justify the prolongation of the coalition by holding an election, in which the appeal to patriotism won it a huge majority and a 'doctor's mandate' to do whatever might be necessary to restore the health of the economy; only fifty-two Labour members retained their seats. Since nine-tenths of the 'National' majority was made up of Conservatives, MacDonald was virtually their prisoner. Although he held on to the premiership in spite of failing health until the summer of 1935, the real power rested with Baldwin and Neville Chamberlain, the younger son of Joseph. As MacDonald's successor, Baldwin won a second election for the National government in November 1935, when the Labour Party rose to 154. He also showed his unfailing skill as a manager of public opinion during the well-remembered week at the close of the following year, when King Edward VIII chose to abdicate rather than abandon the idea of marrying an American divorcee, Mrs Wallis Simpson. The government which Chamberlain formed on Baldwin's retirement in May 1937 is less happily remembered for its handling of the international issues which now dominated the scene (see p. 251); but we may note that, at the outbreak of war in September 1939, the ministry still contained vestiges of Liberal National and National Labour participation.

The most important economic measure of the National government was the Import Duties Act of 1932, imposing a general 10 per cent duty,[1] with an exception for most foodstuffs and many raw materials—about one-quarter of the full range of commodities. But Neville Chamberlain as Chancellor of the Exchequer found it more difficult to move towards the empire free trade, which had been the second aim of his father's tariff reform programme. An Imperial Economic Conference was duly held at Ottawa later in the same year, at which the Dominions proved to be hard bargainers, so that the biggest economic change within the Empire was a 4 per cent increase in the proportion of United Kingdom imports which came from India and the dependent colonies. The new tariff wall was, however, a help to the 'rationalization' of the export industries by closing down redundant units in accordance with a general plan, as in the case of the Lancashire cotton-mills and the shipyards of the north-east coast. Meanwhile, the agriculture of the United Kingdom was encouraged both by subjecting foreign imports to a quota system and by subsidizing crops in cases where public opinion might resent outright protection of the farmer. It was the dawn of planning by government. Even the blow which the City of London had suffered when Britain went off gold was mitigated by setting up an Exchange Equalization Fund, to smooth out fluctuations in the value of the currency and encourage the formation of a Sterling Area—the countries which still based their finances on balances held in London.

Although the World Economic Conference, which met in London in June 1933, came to nothing after President F. D. Roosevelt had made it clear that the value of the American dollar would be determined with reference exclusively to American interests, that year saw the start of a gradual revival of world trade. British light industries, such as the making of motor cars and the electrical manufactures, recovered their foreign markets, and there was a remarkable boom in private housing construction, which showed that, thanks to falling price-levels, the middle class and skilled workers in uninterrupted employment had suffered no irreparable losses during the crisis. Furthermore, in the later 1930s Britain's belated plans for rearmament competed for a share in the supply of skilled labour, especially for the building of military aircraft. But almost up to the outbreak of war Chamberlain's private correspondence bears witness to his anxiety to avoid any step which might imperil the recovery of Britain's regular industries.

---

[1] Imports of a few luxury manufactures, notably motor-cars, clocks and watches, had been taxed by the McKenna Duties of 1915, which had been maintained by all later Chancellors of the Exchequer with the exception of Snowden in the Labour Government of 1924.

The Plight of the Long-Term Unemployed

Unemployment was at its worst from August 1931 to January 1933, when the percentage of insured workers without employment reached 23 per cent (2 995 000); but in the later months of that year the total fell for a time below 2 million, and after considerable fluctuations it sank in August 1939 to 1¼ million, which was the lowest figure for ten years. To blame the government for the slowness of the recovery is perhaps rash, since the same problem has proved equally intractable in a later generation. What the National government can be blamed for is the insensitiveness to human need shown in its administration of relief.

The cuts imposed in September 1931 were brought to an end in the summer of 1934, and in 1939 the purchasing power of the benefit paid to an unemployed man with a wife and two dependent children was roughly the same as it had been before the cut. This, however, amounted to only one-half of what the National Assistance Board deemed adequate for the support of the same size of family thirty years later on. Moreover, from 1931 onwards these meagre payments were made conditional upon a household Means Test, to ascertain whether unemployed persons could derive some part of their support from savings, pensions, or the earnings of any member of the household, down to a child who might be serving out of school hours as an errand boy. This was resented as an injustice in itself; as a humiliation, since it meant the probing of officials into private affairs; and as a disrupting influence on family life, because sons and daughters who left home had no further legal responsibility for unemployed parents.

Many young people left home for another reason, namely the fact that the renewed prosperity of the new light industries already mentioned was not accompanied by any appreciable revival of the staple trades, which had been depressed since 1921–2. Whilst the more enterprising of the younger generation moved to the new workplaces springing up in outer London, the home counties, or the Birmingham–Coventry area, the older generation and the more apathetic of the young stayed put, even in such tombs of industry as Merthyr Tydfil, which had once boasted the biggest ironworks in the world and in 1935 had an unemployment percentage of 63·6, or Jarrow, where the shipyard was rationalized out of existence, so that it became 'the town that was murdered'. Thus the unemployed, and particularly the long-term unemployed, were concentrated mainly in areas of early industrial development: South Wales, Tyneside, West Cumberland, the industrialized Lowlands of Scotland, Northern Ireland, and Lancashire.

In 1934 the first four of these were allotted commissioners to administer grants for the 'economic development and social improvement of the depressed areas', which the House of Lords renamed 'Special Areas'. Lloyd George pointed out more purposefully that an award of £2 million compared very unfavourably with the scale of the New Deal, by which President Roosevelt was fighting unemployment across the Atlantic. A number of small Trading Estates were set up, but although more money was made available—some of it going to the various clubs and voluntary activities which tried to boost the morale of the unemployed—it proved very difficult to get new enterprises established in areas which were already run down and in some cases semi-derelict.

In 1937, 27 per cent of the unemployed had been out of work for a year or more, which for the older men made the position virtually hopeless. It was this wastage of human life which became a folk-memory outlasting the many brighter features of Britain as it was before the Second World War. Thus the man with nothing better to do than stand on the street corner still confronts us in a novel of that era, written from personal experience:

> He was standing there as motionless as a statue, cap neb pulled over his eyes, gaze fixed on pavement, hands in pockets, shoulders hunched, the bitter wind blowing his thin trousers tightly against his legs. Waste paper and dust blew about him in spirals, the papers making harsh sounds as they slid on the pavement.[1]

[1] Walter Greenwood: *Love on the Dole* (1933), p. 255.

26 The changing pattern of life and work

Despite the disappointments on which we dwelt in the last chapter, the quarter-century which separates the outbreak of the First World War from that of its successor was a period of improved material conditions for that large majority of the population which was not directly affected by the blight of unemployment. After the war with its great increase in government activities of all kinds, the salaried middle class was found to have grown from 12 to 22 per cent, a fraction which nearly always kept its standard of living well above that of the workers. The position of the latter can be judged fairly accurately from statistics, which show that the average of real-wage rates fell in 1920–2, but never to the 1914 level; rose again in the later 1920s; and rose still further in the 1930s, when 1932 was the only year in which they fell. In 1935–6, when Rowntree renewed his study of York (p. 201), he found that, in the course of a generation, the number of its citizens living in stringently defined 'primary poverty' had declined from 15·5 to 6·8 per cent. The history of housing, of leisure activities, and—to some extent—of education bears out the general impression of betterment, having its starting-point in the democratic reforms of the war years, which have already been noted, and also in the contemporary advance of technology.

The Wartime Stimulus to Technology

In time of war a modern government can harness the national resources to any required extent for the development at top speed of inventions which may have war-winning capabilities. Such was the tank, which in the last phase of the First World War gave the British Army a decisive advantage over the enemy. More commonly, the same technology is competitively exploited by both sides, as in the case of the air weapon, which in 1914 was still in its infancy. Count Zeppelin's airships created considerable alarm as they cruised over southern England, and the German Fokker aircraft were the earliest efficiently armed fighters; but by the Armistice Britain had achieved air supremacy with a hundred times as many aircraft as in 1914, flying nearly twice as fast and climbing five times as high. In April 1915 the Germans made the first use of asphyxiating gases, which was contrary to the spirit, though not to the letter, of the Hague Conventions, but the products of British and American chemists later outdid them in frightfulness. The two sides likewise vied in the improvement of high explosive for their heavy artillery, which the British also employed in depth-charges against submarines. Or we may cite a more humane example in the advances made in medicine and surgery, far exceeding those of any earlier war; in Britain research was directed, for instance, towards such diseases as dysentery and typhus and to the development of new antiseptics for the military hospitals.

All these technologies had of course an earlier history. Even the tank requires as its driving-force the internal combustion engine, which had been gradually perfected, mainly by German and French engineers, since the 1880s. Zeppelins were an adaptation of the balloon, which antedates the French Revolution, and the first successful heavier-than-air flight had been made by the Wright brothers in North Carolina in 1903. Modern explosives began with Nobel's invention of dynamite in 1867—and the list of peacetime origins could easily be continued. But the war gave an impetus to new technologies, which enterprising firms afterwards carried further: returns available for 1930–8 show that both the manpower and the finance devoted to research and development were approximately trebled in those years in spite of the world depression. And the intense government activities of wartime, mentioned above, left a permanent mark in the formation in 1916 of the Department of Scientific and Industrial Research, which leads on to the present-day provision of a Chief Scientific Adviser to the government and a Science Branch under the Secretary of State for Education and Science.

The Speeding-up of Transport

In post-war Britain the motor-bus, already a prominent feature of the London scene, developed into what is still the most ubiquitous form of short-distance public transport; in Birmingham, for instance, in 1926–37 the proportion of passengers carried on the tramways fell from 83 to 40 per cent. The ease with which bus-routes could be set up made them the indispensable link between city centres and the new outer suburbs, and they were even more important for village life, giving ready access for the first time to the attractions of the nearest town. The public also benefited from the introduction of motor-coach services, and their competition obliged the railways to lower their long-distance fares. Since their freight charges likewise fell because of the rapid increases in road-haulage vehicles, the railway companies which had flourished for so long faced a very uncertain future; they had been under government management during the war, and on their return to private ownership were reduced from 120 to the four large regional companies named in an earlier chapter (see p. 127).

As for private transport, in the 1930s there were still 10 million pedal cycles on the roads, but the previous decade had seen the heyday of the motorcycle, often equipped with a sidecar. By 1931 these were being overtaken—in all except the most literal sense—by the mass-produced motor car, made by William Morris at Oxford and Herbert Austin at Birmingham by techniques copied from the American, Henry Ford. This, however, was merely the beginning of a major social change, for a total of 1 million private cars meant that they were the envied possession of only one family in every ten.

An assembly-line for the mass-produced motor car.

Alcock and Brown with their converted Vickers-Vimy bomber aircraft.

Travel by air, though still wildly beyond the means of everyman, was the subject of widespread interest. In June 1919 two British airmen, Alcock and Brown, made the first Atlantic crossing in just over sixteen hours, flying a converted bomber, and in the same year a daily passenger service was started between London and Paris. Imperial Airways was founded with a government subsidy in 1924, and within ten years there were regular flights as far as India. The use of dirigibles was discredited after the burning-up of the R 101 on its maiden voyage in 1930 with the Minister for Air on board, and many of the longer routes were still operated by flying-boats. To complete the picture, in 1938 British aircraft carried fewer than 70 000 passengers between the United Kingdom and the Continent, and about twice as many on internal air routes.

Developments in Industry

The four railway companies and the two manufacturers of popular motor-cars are two examples of a tendency to form very big industrial units. The soap-making firm of Lever Brothers joined with its Dutch counterpart as Unilever, with a world-wide interest in fats and their products. The largest of all entirely British firms, Imperial Chemical Industries, was constituted in 1926 from existing enterprises in alkalis, explosives, and dyes. Two up-to-date steel works, set up at Corby (Northants) and Ebbw Vale in the 1930s to restore a heavy industry of vital importance, were likewise large-scale undertakings. But the lighter manufactures, which (as we have seen) were developing fastest in the inter-war period, were usually powered by electricity; this meant that their factories did not need to be large or near the coal-fields for the machinery to be economically run. They were therefore spread fairly widely, especially on the periphery of London, where there was access to a varied supply of labour, a good domestic market, and facilities for export.

Engineering was now very much to the fore, as the ramifications of the electrical industry made it almost as important as the new British staple manufacture of motor vehicles—aircraft and motor-cycles as well as cars, lorries, and buses. Applied chemistry, too, contributed in a big way, for ICI hoped to supply the whole Empire with artificial fertilizers, whilst plastics and synthetic fibres made a wholly new impact on consumer needs. Plastics provided the material for innumerable household articles, from telephone receivers to bathroom equipment, as well as for automobile bodies and aircraft turrets. Synthetic fibres, which in the early 1920s made the fair sex fairer by the sheen and colourfulness of artificial silk stockings, were by 1939 jointly responsible with improvements in the machine-cutting of garments for the revolution which has made mass-produced clothing of all kinds almost as attractive as exclusive models. Broadly speaking, these were the industries which grew consistently at rates above the national average and competed with reasonable success on the world market.

Though it had lost its position as a prime British export, coal was still used directly, or in the form of coal-gas, for heating, cooking, and (to a rapidly diminishing extent) for lighting; and indirectly, to fire the steam-engines which drove the machinery of the older factories, the locomotives of the railways, and the screws of very many ships. Moreover, small-scale hydro-electric developments (chiefly in the Scottish Highlands) scarcely detracted from the basic importance of coal to operate the electric power stations, which from 1927 onwards were being converted into a nationwide network by means of the high-voltage lines erected by a new public authority, the Central Electricity Board.

Nevertheless, the most important development as regards power was Britain's increasing dependence on the refined petroleum which drove all forms of motor-vehicle on the highway and the newer types of ship, from the tankers which carried the crude oil from the producing lands to the giant Cunard liner *Queen Mary*, built on Clydeside in the 1930s for the two national purposes of reducing unemployment and recapturing the speed record for the North Atlantic crossing. Only two centuries before, a traveller in Persia had described its oil resources as 'one of nature's ulcers. A strong, suffocating smell of naphtha,' he explained, 'announced something more than ordinarily foul in the neighbourhood.' But even before the war the adoption of oil fuel for the latest dreadnoughts had led the British government to acquire a controlling interest in the Anglo-Persian Oil Company, and after it the oil wells of the Middle East were the main reason for Britain's continuing interest in the affairs of the Arab world. Although the British Empire also controlled other sources of supply in Burma and Trinidad, ICI showed prescience in its persistent (but never commercially successful) attempts to produce oil by the hydrogenation process from coal, so that the United Kingdom might be self-sufficient in the event of another war. But no one appears to have foreseen the peacetime dangers from increasing dependence upon a diminishing world resource of which the producer countries could at any time create an artificial famine.

Agriculture

The word 'famine' suggests a return to the subject of agriculture, about which nothing has been said in our account of the half-century during which Britain relied confidently upon the cheap produce of distant continents (see p. 158). The First World War created anxieties about the food-supply—and in 1917 a threat of actual famine—which brought renewed prosperity to those who worked the land, some of the poorest soils being brought under the plough for the first time since the fall of Napoleon. Two permanent results were the establishment of the sugar-beet industry to provide an additional home-grown food and of the State Forests, which originated in a timber famine in the last war year. But in the 1920s prices fell again, much land reverted to rough pasture, and it again became almost impossible to make a decent living from the soil.

One consequence was the break-up of big estates, which no longer yielded any satisfactory financial return to the landowner, whilst the decline of the aristocracy meant they no longer compensated by their social glamour. Another was a further drop of about 14 per cent in agricultural employment; farm labour became less cheap with the passage of the Agricultural Wages Act by the Labour government in 1924, but twelve more years elapsed before it was brought into the unemployment insurance scheme. But the third consequence was the emergence of a new class of farmer-owners in possession of nearly half the agricultural land, who were well organized in the National Farmers' Union and whose interests won support from all who wished to stimulate the home-grown food supply in a time of increasing international tension.

Accordingly, the National government used the apparatus of quotas and bilateral trade treaties to cut down competition from such well-established imports as Danish bacon, eggs, and butter; they subsidized the production of milk and cereal crops, and eventually bacon, and set up Marketing Boards to raise the prices of four main products. Between 1931 and 1937 the volume of agricultural output was increased by one-sixth, and in the latter year the Agriculture Act offered official help in another direction—for the investigation of soil problems, including the need for additional drainage, and the problems of animal infections, such as the dreaded foot-and-mouth disease.

The application of science to agriculture in Britain went back at least as far as the start of the continuous field experiments at Rothamsted, near St Albans, in the 1840s; veterinary surgery had become a fully organized profession in the second half of the nineteenth century; and a closer study of the chemistry of the soil and the biology of plant life had accompanied the mounting interest in artificial fertilizers. But now the growth of agricultural science was paralleled by rapid advances in technology. The cooling, cleansing, and sterilizing apparatus of the modern dairy had its counterpart in the machinery of the 'milking parlour', which visited the fields. Tractors began to come into use in every season and for almost every laborious operation of the farming year, though they did not displace the horse as a typical feature of the rural scene until after the Second World War. Finally, there was the introduction to Britain of the American combine harvester, which reaps, threshes, and—in the later models—harvests the grain into bulk containers. The same quantity of wheat, which in 1830 was garnered by sickle and flail in 57·7 man-hours and in 1896 with a reaper-and-binder and stationary thresher in 8·8 man-hours, could now be completely processed in 3·3 man-hours. To work on a farm became for the first time a likely ambition for the machine-minded, town-bred boy.

Housing

The proper housing of the people was a social problem which had been accentuated by the war. Building had come to a standstill, so houses were in short supply and included some whose unchecked deterioration added to the number of slum premises. In addition, the Rent Act

Massey-Ferguson combine harvester at work.

of 1915, which restricted rents on existing small houses as a measure against war profiteering, made small capitalists chary of building houses for rent, which had hitherto been a favourite form of investment. In 1919 Lloyd George appointed as the first Minister of Health Dr Christopher Addison, who established the new principle that housing was a social service which was the proper concern of local authorities.

The Addison Act agreed to cover whatever loss might be incurred by a local council when it built houses for rent at the level fixed in 1915 for older property, but this proved too expensive. Addison was dropped by Lloyd George, and the 170 000 houses built by councils under his scheme were followed by the building of twice as many, mainly for sale to owner-occupiers, on the basis of a subsidy for 'non-parlour' houses; this was introduced by Neville Chamberlain in 1923 as an incentive to private enterprise. The day of the large-scale municipal housing estate dawned, however, with the first Labour government, when Wheatley, a left-winger from the Clyde, offered larger subsidies for houses which the local authorities were to provide for renting. The Clydesider, however, was also shrewd enough to secure the co-operation of both sides in the building industry by planning for a term of fifteen years. Wheatley's houses had slightly larger dimensions than Chamberlain's, and they were the first to be equipped compulsorily with a bathroom instead of a bath in the scullery; more than half a million were built before the National government changed the policy in 1932. Henceforth there were no subsidies to meet ordinary housing needs, but Building Society mortgages facilitated the erection before the end of the decade of another 2½ million houses, half of them selling at less than £600 and requiring a down-payment of as little as 5 per cent.

Local authorities were still responsible for carrying out slum clearance, but slum dwellings and overcrowding continued to be the lot of the very poor: in Scotland—which is not included in the figures so far given—rather more than 300 000 working-class houses were provided (mainly by local authorities) between the wars, but 200 000 more were needed to end overcrowding, which was seven times as widespread as in England and Wales. In general, however, public and private enterprise between them had provided homes of an improved standard for all families of ordinary size and with regular earnings. Big estates had been opened up on the perimeter of London and all the more prosperous southern and midland towns, whilst the cluster of new houses on the edge of a picturesque village might have even greater local significance, since they meant not only a leap forward from the sanitary conditions of the middle ages but also, in many cases, the emancipation of the rural labourer from the 'tied cottage' which had kept him at the mercy of his employer.

Albeit some ill-natured observers of the contemporary scene alleged that the novel bathroom was used for coal storage, there is no doubt that much care and expense were lavished upon the new homes. It may help to account for the decline of drunkenness, which never returned to its old dimensions after the stringent licensing regulations of wartime. The upkeep of house and garden was, however, a private concern which we must take for granted as we turn to consider how people now employed their leisure hours.

The Uses of Increased Leisure

The general introduction of the eight-hour day in the first post-war years was followed in 1934 and 1937 by laws which made it compulsory for two significant groups—young shop assistants, and women and youths in factory employment. In 1938 a further major advance was recorded in the Holidays with Pay Act, which gave official encouragement to the provision of one such week; in a single year the number of wage-earners who received it rose from 3 to 11 million. Meanwhile, the turn-over from heavy to light industry and the reduction of physical effort almost everywhere by new machine-processes meant that work, though it might be more monotonous or require closer attention than before, was seldom so exhausting to the body. Leisure time, no longer needed for mere physical recuperation, could have a more positive content.

The war had accelerated an existing trend away from the churches, whose activities had filled the weekday evenings as well as the Sundays of many Victorian families; for it required more than a conventional faith to withstand the uprooting from familiar surroundings and the seemingly wanton havoc of life in the trenches. To some extent the gap was filled by clubs and societies of many kinds. In addition, the young were attracted by the public dance hall, which spread to Britain from the Continent. It was also significant that horse races, on which the Nonconformist churches at least had always frowned, were now supplemented by greyhound racing in the evening, which was more convenient for the worker. The three-day matches of Test and county cricket continued to attract mainly middle-class spectators, but there was a mounting interest in professional football, now that supporters had time and money to travel to away matches. In 1923 a crowd of 200 000 tried to make its way into the Wembley Stadium, when the Cup Final was played there for the first time and the Cup—also for the first time—was presented by the King. By 1938 this interest had been consolidated by the football pools, on which about 10 million people were believed to be spending an average sum of £4 a year.[1]

Both cricket and football were ancient popular pastimes, to which the professional element added a specially high standard of skill. Both games were now catered for by a large variety of amateur private clubs, as were also such games as bowls (well known to Shakespeare); golf, which was played by James VI and I; Rugby football, which takes its name from the school where it began in 1823; and the late Victorian innovation of lawn tennis. There has never been a census of participants, but two trends show that much of the new leisure was used in this way. The schools attended by working-class children more often included the playing of organized games among their regular activities; and local authorities spent much larger sums on the provision of games facilities of all kinds—even an occasional nine-hole golf course—in the parks and recreation grounds which they managed on behalf of the ratepayers.

Another feature of the age was the revived interest in the countryside among the urban population, which did not always prefer a seaside town for an annual holiday and was also tempted to spend half-days or weekends in nearby rural areas, made accessible by the

[1] Professor E. J. Hobsbawm observes in *Industry and Empire*, p. 137, that the spread of the game to the rest of the world began with the works teams established by expatriate British employers and employees.

new bus routes or the hiring of a motor-coach. High hopes for the future were roused by the foundation of the Youth Hostels Association—for England and Wales in 1930, for Scotland in 1931; by 1939 the former had a membership of 83 000. In 1937 the Physical Training Act began the expenditure of public money on summer camps and recreation centres. Mention must also be made of the growing activities of the National Trust, founded in 1895. Besides saving hills and viewpoints, woods and commons from being built on, this body also preserved from destruction historic manor houses and clusters of ancient cottages, making it easier for the imagination of the visitor to recapture something of our island's vanished past.

The imagination was of course fed in other ways. The demand for newspapers, which had increased greatly in all classes during the anxious years of the war, was afterwards stimulated by the rivalry among several wealthy proprietors, who eventually competed for readers by offering free life insurance, a set of Dickens, or household goods in return for a period subscription. This would in theory be recovered from advertisers, induced by the large readership to pay more per column-inch of space. In the end the *Daily Express*, shaped by the genius of Lord Beaverbrook to furnish men, women, and children of every class with a varied diet of light entertainment, got ahead of the *Daily Mail*, which catered for a rather narrower, bourgeois outlook. The *Daily Telegraph*, *The Times*, and the *Manchester Guardian* could console themselves for their very much smaller circulations by reflecting (to quote a later *Times* advertisement) that their clientèle were 'top people'. But it is worthy of note that in the 1930s mammoth circulations were also being achieved by two London papers which are now extinct—the *Daily Herald*, which was politically under the control of the trade unions, and the mainly Liberal *News Chronicle*.

In pre-paperback days, books were regarded as a luxury purchase. The middle class had always patronized subscription libraries, but until 1919 the public lending libraries, authorized by Act of Parliament in 1850, could not spend more than the yield of a penny rate. The modern library system, able to supply every kind of need in town and country alike, dates therefore from the immediate post-war era, whereas the first cheap but well-produced paperbacks—'Penguins', followed by non-fiction 'Pelicans'—did not appear until 1935. Although their sales were not at first enormous, a rival publisher was inspired to start a parallel venture, namely the Left Book Club, which supplied its members with a specially written, limp-cloth volume every month. Some of the authors represented the Communist tendencies which now had a hold in university circles; all were hostile to the National government. The membership, which reached 50 000 in the first year, was an important factor in the remoulding of public opinion between 1936 and 1940.

Whilst the printed word appealed above all to the intelligentsia, this was the era of other, more popular appeals to eye and ear. It was the golden age of the cinema, when the social attractions of the 'Picture Palace' often eclipsed those of the public-house. In the 1920s the film was still silent, but an English genius, Charlie Chaplin, was enabled by Hollywood's resources to produce great works of art. Lesser comedians also flourished; newsreels stimulated an interest in distant events; and the earliest documentaries showed the possibilities of genuine instruction. The 1930s brought the sound-track, with historical and other long and immensely costly feature films, making the best acting-talent of the day accessible in some degree to all.

Except in London, the cinema largely extinguished the interest in the theatre, but it had an important competitor inside the home in radio broadcasts—a development from the morse-code wireless signals, which Marconi had sent across the Atlantic at the turn of the century. In 1922 the British Broadcasting Company began daily transmissions of one hour's duration from Savoy Hill, London. The decisive year, however, was 1926, when the suppression of newspapers during the General Strike gave a special importance to news on the wireless and, in December, the Company became the British Broadcasting Corporation, with very extensive powers for organizing a nationwide service of news, entertainment, and enlightenment. Sir John Reith, a Presbyterian minister's son who was Director-General for the first twelve years, used the monopoly to great effect. He kept the news free from government control, the entertainment eminently wholesome, and the programmes for enlightenment barely distinguishable from formal education. From 1936 onwards Reith also controlled programmes of television, first demonstrated by a fellow-Scotsman, J. L. Baird, ten years earlier. But these were only in their infancy when the outbreak of war caused their cessation, whereas in September 1939 great importance attached to the fact that the BBC already possessed an Overseas Service, addressed both to the Empire and to certain foreign audiences which it was desired to influence.

Education—The Narrow Ladder

Despite the high hopes which had been raised by the Fisher Act of 1918, the education of the masses did not keep pace with the increase of leisure, which a better educated people might have used to greater advantage. To begin with, most children stayed all the time in the same elementary school in which they had first learnt to read and write, with little or no special account taken of their needs during the final years from which there was no longer any possibility of exemption. In 1926 pressure from the Labour Party resulted in the Hadow Report, which called for a clean break between primary and secondary education; the latter to be provided for all children between eleven and fourteen or preferably fifteen. This meant in practice the provision of a senior school or separate senior department with a 'modern' bias; by 1931 one-third of the eleven to fourteen age-group in the elementary schools was provided for in this way, by 1939 two-thirds. The Fisher Act had also intended that there should be compulsory Continuation Schools for all who started work at fourteen, but this proposal was abandoned in the campaign for reducing public expenditure at the collapse of the trade boom in the early 1920s, when there was even a temporary halt to the attempt to reduce the maximum size of class from sixty to fifty pupils. In 1930, indeed, a Labour Bill advanced the school-leaving age to fifteen, but the Party accepted its rejection by the House of Lords after much amendment in the Commons, because the Roman Catholic schools feared the additional building costs. In 1936 the National government solved this problem by providing the voluntary schools with building grants, but fixed the start of the new leaving age at 1 September 1939, which in the event meant a further and considerably longer postponement.

The Act of 1918 had aimed furthermore at widening the ladder from free primary to free secondary education by increasing the proportion of 'free places' in the secondary grammar schools maintained or aided by local authorities. In 1920 this reached one-third, and by 1939 it was nearly one-half, although 'free places' had been replaced by 'special places', which required the passing of a means test as well as a competitive entrance examination. But even with the addition of the fee-payers, who came mainly from middle-class homes, these schools provided only one-seventh of the nation's children—and predominantly boys—with the five-year course which culminated at sixteen in the School Certificate. This was the passport to most salaried jobs and forms of professional training.

The second stage of the educational ladder was narrower still, in spite of Fisher's institution of State scholarships and the power given to local authorities to institute others of their own. One reason was the scarcity of adequate Sixth Form courses, except in the Direct Grant schools; these were a number of the more prestigious grammar schools, which from 1926 onwards received grants directly from the government whilst admitting only a modest proportion of non-fee-paying pupils in return. Another reason was the very slow growth of the English universities. After the foundation of London University (p. 119), the big provincial cities were for the most part content to finance 'university colleges', whose students took examinations set by London. A big change came in 1900, when five new universities were chartered in one decade, but these were all of small dimensions. The total for England and Wales was still no more than ten, to which the inter-war period added only one university (Reading) and new university colleges at Leicester, Hull, and Swansea. Yet a third reason for the narrowness of the ladder was the policy adopted by the two ancient universities of Oxford and Cambridge, which accepted a share in the government grant to universities but continued to favour the admission of students from well-to-do homes, who would play a full part in the social and athletic activities for which their colleges had long been famous. Even their scholarship awards, though open to all comers, tended to favour classics and other subjects which flourished mainly in the public schools and direct grant grammar schools.

To sum up, in 1939 Great Britain had only about 50 000 full-time university students, and to that total the four ancient but highly democratic universities of Scotland contributed three times their share; Wales too, with a single university established by nationalist pressure in 1893, had a substantially higher percentage of students than England. Of all those who were then pursuing their university studies, approximately one in five had climbed the educational ladder by moving up from a public elementary or primary school with the help of a free place, and moving up again from secondary school to university by competing in further examinations for entrance and/or scholarship awards.

The Classes and the Masses

The educational system was perhaps the most significant of the influences which kept social distinctions alive in Britain at a time when they were dying a natural death in many otherwise comparable communities, such as those of the United States and the Dominions. For not only were Oxford and Cambridge dominated by the public-school element, but those universities continued to be the principal source of recruitment for the higher echelons of the Civil Service, the professions, and the biggest concerns in industry and finance. As for politics, even Labour Cabinets found a quota of public-school men indispensable, and trade unionists still felt that their homely accents struck a discordant note in the club-like atmosphere of the House of Commons.

The upper classes were helped to maintain their position by the moderate level of taxation; except for the death duties imposed since 1894, the inroads it made on accumulated capital or high earnings were as yet far from catastrophic. In the later 1920s, for example, when the gold-based pound bought five or six times as much as ours today,[1] the full standard rate of income tax was 4s. (20p) in the pound, plus a graduated super-tax or surtax on anything above £2000. But allowances reduced what was actually paid on the then substantial middle-class income of £700, if its earner was married and supported three children, to the modest sum of £23. The wage-earner, who paid no income tax, in many cases contributed almost as much to the revenue through indirect taxes, such as the excise of tobacco and beer.

The workers were, on the other hand, the principal beneficiaries of the expanded social services, from which they now received much more than what they paid in taxes and insurance contributions. Those services had, however, a tendency to reinforce older social cleavages. The choice made between residing on a municipal housing estate or in a suburb of houses built privately for sale often had this effect; so did that between sending children to a municipal or a privately owned school and the use or non-use of other facilities, good or bad, which were designed for families of restricted means. In the case of unemployment insurance, benefits earned by contributions became, as we have seen, entangled with others which bore the stamp of poor relief. Health insurance claims were met by general practitioners who normally had a waiting-room for 'panel patients' quite separate from that for private fee-payers, who were also more readily visited in their own homes. The distinction was even sharper as regards hospital treatment, which was not covered by the health insurance scheme; those who could not pay fees either obtained admission to a voluntary hospital as an act of charity or were relegated to municipal institutions which had grown out of the old poor-law infirmaries. In 1925 some of the deficiencies of the health insurance scheme were indeed remedied by Neville Chamberlain in the Widows', Orphans' and Old Age Contributory Pensions Act; this gave some protection for dependants in the event of early death and pensioned contributors at sixty-five—five years before they would receive the statutory old age pension, which had been raised in 1919 to 10s. (50p). But the benefits were

[1] See Appendix II, Table 7.

still restricted to weekly wage-earners—a concession to the masses, not a national provision to include all classes.

The survival of the class structure of society did not, however, prevent the continued growth of the desire to promote social betterment by a personal contribution, which had shown itself in the Edwardian era. In 1919 the National Council of Social Service was set up, to co-ordinate the work of branch councils in the towns and of the Women's Institutes and other pioneer activities in the villages. The 1920s and 1930s witnessed a great expansion in the Scout movement and youth clubs, in nursery schools and adult education classes, in Hospital Flag Days and other fund-raising devices, all of which depended very largely upon the readiness of the classes to serve the masses. In the last years before the outbreak of the Second World War the inability of the government to relieve the plight of the unemployed caused deep stirrings of the social conscience, especially perhaps among the younger intelligentsia. Thus, when war came, the ground was prepared for the classes and the masses, which the Victorians had always contrasted as part of the natural scheme of things, to be merged through a rising spirit of egalitarianism.

27 The Second World War: dividing–line for Britain

From the Norman Conquest onwards, our historical record is scored with dividing-lines. Within the time-span of the present book, such events as the introduction of steam-power, the first Parliamentary Reform Act, and the outbreak of the war in 1914 all rank as such. But the mark made by the total war which Britain had to wage in 1939–45 is deeper than most, setting its stamp upon almost every side of the nation's life. To some extent this was realized at the time. The expulsion of the British Army from the Continent after only nine months of the war; invasion for a short while more imminent than it had been since the sailing of the Spanish Armada;[1] the havoc created by the big bomber-raids of 1940–1 and by the new German air weapons in 1944; the varying fortunes of war in the Middle East; the collapse of empire in the Far East; and the acute anxieties attending upon the successful re-entry to the Continent, first through Italy and then across the Normandy beaches—each of these created some underlying uncertainty about Britain's future role. Whilst final victory swept away many doubts, it was difficult to ignore the fact that the biggest quantitative contribution to the overthrow of Hitler's Germany had been made by Russian man-power and American machine-power, and the latter was still more clearly seen to be responsible for the termination of Japanese resistance by the effects of the atomic bomb.

Accordingly, when the six long war years came to an end, it was generally expected that economic difficulties lay ahead, but that these might be easier to cope with because of the many forms of social progress which the war had stimulated. Few people, however, expected the bonds of empire to be relaxed so rapidly and so completely as they have been, fewer still that Britain, the only country that had fought the war unflinchingly from start to finish, would find it so

---

[1] Since the role played by Churchill's speeches at this critical time is well known, it may be of interest to recall that the Minister of Information found it appropriate to add his contribution by broadcasting all seventy-four lines of Macaulay's poem on this theme.

hard to grapple with the problems of its reduced status in the new world of the post-war generation.

Causes of War

The causes of the Second World War are often traced back to the settlement which followed the First, to injustices in the Treaty of Versailles and the failure of the United States to join the new League of Nations, which might then have been strong enough to redress them. Yet the 1920s were an era of optimism, crowned by the Locarno treaties (guaranteeing the Franco-German frontier) and the Kellogg Pact (renouncing war); indeed, it was not until 1932 that the British Cabinet abandoned its Ten-Year Rule, which based defence upon the supposition that war against any major power lay at least so far ahead, and in that year further hopes of a prolonged period of peace were roused by the opening of the World Disarmament Conference with Arthur Henderson as its very earnest president. Viewed as a whole, however, the 1930s were a time of lengthening shadows, in which realists and idealists alike were reluctantly brought to admit that another great war was brewing in Europe, from which Britain would be unable to stand aside.

The reluctance was very great. In 1931 Japanese aggression in China was left unchecked, because both Britain and America would not risk becoming embroiled with what was now the third-strongest naval power. In 1935–6 the Italian dictator Mussolini was able to conquer Abyssinia (Ethiopia) because Britain and France shrank from a direct confrontation in the Mediterranean. In both these cases the united support of the many small powers in the League of Nations was judged by the British government to have little practical value, and in a third case—the Spanish Civil War of 1936–9—the League was not even appealed to when Germany and Italy intervened under various subterfuges to ensure General Franco's victory over the legally established republic. About 2000 British volunteers fought for the republican cause in Spain, of whom more than half were killed or wounded. These were nearly all adventurous young idealists of the Left; public opinion in general was more clearly revealed by the so-called 'Peace Ballot' of 1935 (organized by the League of Nations Union and other bodies), in which 11 million votes were cast in favour of continued membership of the League, but fewer than two-thirds of that number favoured military measures if necessary, to enforce the will of the League against an aggressor nation. And for most of the decade Churchill—who had been out of office since 1929—found little response in any political party to his eloquent appeals for a strong foreign policy based on strong and necessarily expensive armaments.

Britain's difficulty was Germany's opportunity. In January 1933 a series of political crises, brought on chiefly by mass unemployment, had enabled Hitler to secure the Chancellorship. Whilst crushing internal opposition with extreme ruthlessness, he won the favour of nationalists, industrialists, the military caste and many of the jobless, by re-arming Germany in defiance of the peace treaty. Then followed the four well-known stages in German aggrandizement: in March 1936 the remilitarization of the Rhineland, forbidden by the peace treaty and at Locarno in order that the French frontier might never again be exposed to attack; two years later, the annexation of Austria; in September 1938 the Munich agreement, by which Britain accepted the severance of the German-speaking areas of the Sudetenland from Czechoslovakia, the ally of France; and in March 1939 the absorption of the rest of Czechoslovakia, in defiance of the promises made at Munich.

At each of the first three stages it would have been possible for Britain and France to call Hitler's bluff, for it is now known that even the *Luftwaffe* was less fully developed than he pretended and that his generals were quite unready for a major war. Baldwin and Chamberlain have therefore been blamed by posterity for Appeasement—their willingness to accept Hitler's many specious promises at their face value and their unwillingness to speed up rearmament, on which Britain, as late as 1936, spent less than half as much as Germany. Yet even the Munich agreement, abjectly placing a friendly democratic people at Hitler's mercy, received strong popular support, as shown for example in the majority approval of Chamberlain as premier recorded in the Gallup Polls, which began the following month. A war postponed might be a war avoided. Almost anything appeared preferable to the carnage of the trenches, as experienced in 1914–18, or the still greater carnage of indiscriminate bombing attacks, such as the Germans had demonstrated in 1937 on the hapless Spanish town of Guernica.

But by March 1939 Chamberlain had come to realize—belatedly, as it is easy to claim in retrospect—that bargaining with Hitler (or his confederate, Mussolini) would not give Britain any lasting immunity from direct aggression by 'Greater Germany'. He therefore gave the guarantee to Hitler's next prospective victim, namely Poland, which led directly to the outbreak of war in September. British rearmament had by now gathered momentum, and Chamberlain reassured our French allies by doubling the Territorial Army and even introducing peacetime conscription for twenty-year-olds. He failed lamentably, however, in reluctant and tentative efforts to make a military pact with Soviet Russia, which had joined the League of Nations in 1934 and was the only power in a geographical position to render the guarantee to Poland effective, if it chose to do so. Hitler, on the other hand, was much more ready to swallow—or appear to swallow—his hatred of Communism, so on 23 August the unexpected signature of the German–Soviet Non-Aggression Pact made war the only alternative to a dishonourable acceptance of a further advance of German power in Europe.

One very important result of the pacific policies pursued for so long by Baldwin and Chamberlain was the unity with which the declaration of war was now accepted as inevitable. In Britain itself support came from a strong majority in all political parties (except for the Fascists and Communists, who counted for little), whilst help from the Commonwealth and Empire was forthcoming on an even larger scale than in 1914, when formal ties were much closer. Nevertheless, three elements of disunity must be mentioned because of their influence on the post-war situation. The Irish Free State, which in 1937 had become the republic of Eire, associated with the Commonwealth only 'as a matter of external policy', remained neutral throughout the war, whereas Belfast became a prime target for the German bombers. The Union of South Africa, having entered the war by a Parliamentary vote of 80:67, harboured an influential body of Afrikaner (Boer) opinion which for ideological reasons hoped for a German victory. And in India the declaration of war, made independently by the Viceroy, showed the Nationalists how far they still were from their goal of complete self-government. This did not prevent recruitment to the Indian Army, which played a major role in the Middle and especially the Far East, but by the time the war ended Gandhi and his followers were irreconcilable to any continuing British presence in the sub-continent.

The Four Main Phases

The strategy and tactics of a conflict which became much more truly world-wide than its predecessor are complicated and to some extent controversial, but for the present purpose it will be enough to recall its four principal phases as they appeared to the British people at the time.

The first phase was that of the Anglo-French alliance, which was expected to follow the pattern of the earlier war. But nothing was done to help Poland, which was overrun by the German armies in their first *Blitzkrieg* and partitioned with Russia. There followed a period of continued inactivity on the Franco-German border, whilst the Russians fought the 'Winter War' against Finland to secure their flank, and the Germans (on 9 April 1940) launched a rapidly successful surprise attack on Norway and Denmark. Dissatisfaction with the conduct of the war then led to the replacement of the Chamberlain regime by an all-party coalition under Churchill, who took office on the evening of the very day when the Germans had opened their main campaign at dawn by attacking two more small neutrals, Belgium and Holland; this was the prelude to attack on France itself. The Germans had now perfected the *Blitzkrieg*—a lightning advance by tanks and mechanized infantry under the protection of low-flying aircraft. In three weeks the British Expeditionary Force was being skilfully rescued from Dunkirk, but had lost all its equipment; in five weeks Paris had fallen, and Mussolini had brought Italy into the war; in six weeks the French had surrendered and the British Commonwealth stood alone.

Whilst troops from Australia, New Zealand, South Africa, and India helped to preserve Britain's second military base in Egypt, a Canadian army corps was for a time the only completely equipped element in the garrison of the island itself, where the situation for twelve months after the Dunkirk evacuation remained very precarious. Since London lay so close to the likely zone of invasion, a German landing might quickly have inflicted a *coup de grâce*. The preliminary struggle for command of the air over southern England, known as the Battle of Britain, was won by a narrow margin, with the help of technical superiority, over the larger forces of the *Luftwaffe*. From September to May the heavy bomber-attacks on London, Manchester, Coventry, and nearly all the principal ports were a further challenge, to which the response in terms of heightened morale was magnificent; but if they had continued much longer, the material destruction would have been very hard to withstand in view of the simultaneous pressure of the enemy submarine blockade upon all imported resources. And May 1941 brought disquieting news of a second evacuation of British forces from the European mainland—this time from Greece, to which British forces had been diverted from a highly successful campaign against the Italians in Libya and Abyssinia in a vain attempt to try to stem the tide of the German advance south through the Balkans.

The third and longest phase of the war therefore began with a sense of relief, when Britain's isolation was ended at midsummer by Hitler's reversion to his original prime objective, the wresting of 'living space' from Russia. But although this enormous extension of the war was followed within six months by another, when the Japanese attack on Pearl Harbor brought in America, which had hitherto backed the British war-effort only as an unfailing source of supplies (see p. 260), Britain's predicament was still very grave. In 1941, and again in 1942, the German armies drove deep into Russia, whose resistance had to be sustained by the diversion of American and British munitions, transported partly in the heavily attacked Arctic convoys. The Japanese overran every British possession in the Far East, including the newly constructed naval base at Singapore, where 60 000 British, Australian, and Indian troops were taken prisoner. The Battle of the Atlantic—Churchill's name for the unremitting struggle against the submarine—had not yet reached its climax, and in June 1942 the fluctuating campaign in north Africa brought a signal victory to the German general Rommel, when 33 000 men surrendered at Tobruk. The Strategic Air Offensive, which in May 1942 mounted the first 'thousand-bomber raid' on Germany, was indeed believed to be having great effects, but we now know that it had no decisive impact on German morale or material resources before the later part of 1944.

Nevertheless, November 1942 brought what seemed to British eyes the turning-point in our fortunes, though from the standpoint of world history greater significance must be attached both to the operations by which the Americans had already contained the Japanese advance across the Pacific Ocean and to the Russian victory at Stalingrad in February 1943, which prepared the way for the gigantic counter-offensives on the eastern front. For Montgomery's victory over Rommel at El Alamein gave our Eighth Army and its leaders great prestige, and it led on to a series of successful campaigns, in which British and American forces cleared the entire north African coastline, crossed to Sicily and southern Italy, received the submission of a new Italian government, and by 1944 were gradually making their way up the peninsula in the face of stubborn and skilful German resistance. Since 1943 was the year in which the British war effort, in terms of fully mobilized manpower, reached and passed its peak, it was fortunate that the late summer brought decisive victory in the Battle of the Atlantic, enabling the island to receive an uninterrupted flow of men and munitions from the New World for the re-establishment of the western front.

The success of the 'D-day' landings on 6 June, 1944, was recognized as the starting-point of the last phase of the war. After three months France (which was invaded also from the south-east) had been virtually cleared of the enemy and the Allied armies were in Belgium; but at that stage the Supreme Commander, General Eisenhower, who had hitherto allowed Montgomery a free hand on the left flank, prescribed a more cautious strategy of parallel advances into Germany by the British and Canadian armies on the left and his more numerous American compatriots on the right of the line. Eisenhower may have decided wisely, for the British suffered considerable losses in an ultimately unsuccessful airborne landing at Arnhem in Holland, the

Americans a more serious set-back by a German counterattack in the Ardennes; but when the Western Allies joined hands with the Russians at the beginning of May 1945, the British had reached the Elbe and the Americans had overrun south Germany and penetrated some distance into Czechoslovakia and Austria.

There remained the war in the Far East, where in the same month British and Indian forces had substantially completed the reconquest of Burma. But the main thrust against the Japanese was through the American capture of a long series of bitterly contested island positions, which culminated in June in the fall of Okinawa within 400 miles of Japan itself, already devastated by air raids. Two months later the dropping of the atomic bomb (see p. 263) made further resistance there impossible.

A People's War

The principle of conscription, adopted before the outbreak of hostilities, was applied to successive age-groups of the male population, and at the close of 1941 Britain was the first western power to apply it also to the younger women, who (unless they had children to take care of) performed non-combatant duties with the armed forces or various forms of civilian war-work. At its already mentioned peak in 1943 British war production was eight-and-a-half times as large as it had been in the first three months of the war; by then it engaged a bigger share of the total national resources than had ever been committed to war by any modern state. This was likewise a people's war through conscription of property, which an Emergency Powers Act on 22 May 1940 placed formally at the disposal of the State. In practice, the war years saw the transfer of one-tenth of the national income from the rent and dividends accruing to property-owners to the payment of salaries and wages. High salaries were heavily mulcted by surtax, additional to income tax at 10s. (50p) in the pound. Weekly wages, too, were brought increasingly within the scope of the latter tax—hence the introduction in 1943 of the PAYE system to facilitate its collection. But for wage-earners as a whole it was more significant that the years 1940 and 1941 witnessed a fall of 90 per cent in the number of unemployed.

A strong levelling influence was exercised by the comprehensive system of rationing; this extended from heavily subsidized basic foodstuffs to luxuries such as chocolate, provided the same extras for all babies, clothed everyone in garments of the same 'utility' quality, and restricted the supply of furniture and other household goods to cases of proved necessity. A rather similar influence was exercised in the

Sheltering from air attacks in a tube station—January, 1941.

long run by evacuation from large towns to areas less exposed to bombing, though the big government scheme at the outbreak of the war aroused bitter resentment among rural householders and teachers against the uncivilized standards of behaviour among mothers and children from urban slums. At first, many families returned home when no bombs fell, but there were two further waves of evacuation in the winter of 1940–1 and during the flying-bomb attacks on London three years later (see p. 262). By the end of the war 60 million changes of address had been registered, a considerable proportion of them being those of middle-class people driven from their homes by bombs—which were no respecters of persons. Britain had become to some extent a melting-pot of classes, people of different kinds being thrown together and looking for help to emergency social services which some of them had never expected to patronize.

During the twelve months in 1940–1, when Britain stood alone, an exhilarating sense of national unity and confidence was very wide-spread. This owed something to centuries of immunity from ultimate disaster; more to the 'miracle of Dunkirk' and the spectacle of the

Battle of Britain, in which 'so much was owed by so many to so few'; and most of all to Churchill's resolute and resourceful leadership. The public response may be gauged by the mushroom growth of the Home Guard, the first of whose members (eventually numbering 1½ million) arrived within four minutes of the first broadcast appeal for volunteers, or by the spontaneous enthusiasm with which the King and Queen, sometimes in company with Churchill, were received when they visited scenes of recent devastation in the poorest quarters of the great cities. Although such exaltation of spirit did not survive the immediate crisis, the war years as a whole were marked by punctilious fulfilment of what were often hum-drum duties by Home Guard sentries, Air Raid Wardens, fire-watchers in all the premises untenanted at night, and the 1 million members of the Women's Voluntary Services.

During the first winter of the war the Chamberlain government, now reinforced by Churchill's return to his old post at the Admiralty, was bitterly criticized by Labour for the lack of military preparations, albeit the pre-war Opposition had done nothing to promote them. From May 1940 until May 1945—when a 'caretaker' Conservative administration took over, pending the general election in July— political controversy was muted. Nearly half the seats in Churchill's very small War Cabinet were allotted to representatives of Labour: Attlee, the Party leader, was eventually deputy Prime Minister (though Churchill nominated a Conservative successor in the event of his own sudden decease), and Ernest Bevin exerted great influence on home affairs in his capacity as Minister of Labour. But Churchill dominated all his ministers and to a considerable extent the High Command, though its leading members—much abler men than their predecessors in 1914–18—were strong enough to withstand his wilder proposals. Even in June 1942, when a long series of military reverses was crowned by the fall of Tobruk, nine-tenths of the House of Commons voted in support of Churchill's conduct of the war. On the Home Front the internment of Mosley and 762 other members of the BUF was a popular move, taken for security reasons, and after Russia's entry into the war even the Communists in principle supported the war effort, although Bevin claimed that strikes among the South Wales miners were fomented by Trotskyists.

In social development, however, a landmark was reached in December 1942 with the publication of a 'Plan for Social Security', which Sir William Beveridge, an economic pundit who had been the first director of Labour Exchanges, had prepared at the request of one of the Labour members of the War Cabinet. Its detailed exposition of the finances of a national insurance system mattered far less at the time than its appeal for 'the destruction of Want, Disease, Squalor, Ignorance and Illness'. Spread all over Europe by the BBC, the Beveridge Report envisaged a new social era, in which the British social services would be a model for other nations. Churchill and the more conservative of his colleagues were unenthusiastic about any such development, paying no heed to the first sample poll of voters' intentions at a future election, which in August 1943 already showed a significant 10 per cent lead for Labour over the Conservatives.

Nevertheless, the later years of the war were marked by some important social legislation. In 1943 Bevin drove a Catering Wages Act through Parliament, to give permanent help to a body of workers which he knew from his own early experience as a publican's pot-boy was too disorganized to obtain proper pay and conditions of employment. In 1944 a Town and Country Planning Act sought to establish full social control over the rebuilding of Britain, which when hostilities ended must face the problem of destruction or more or less serious damage incurred by two houses out of every seven. Early in 1945 the House of Commons approved the introduction of Family Allowances of 5s. (25p) a week for each child after the first; this became law under the Caretaker administration. But a special significance attached to the Education Act of 1944, the work of a very progressive Conservative minister of the younger generation, R. A. Butler. This provided a new framework for education, which (as we shall see later) lasted for many years; what made an immediate impact on the public mind was the promise that full-time schooling would be extended to fifteen as soon as the war ended, and later to sixteen years of age, and that some form of secondary education would in future be provided both universally and gratuitously.

Thus the wastage of human life, which could not be made good like the material damage done by war, might be compensated to some extent by a better nurturing of the generation which must fill the gap. In the absence of trench warfare, this war was, indeed, less lethal for us than its predecessor: the armed forces of the United Kingdom had only one-half as many killed and one-sixth as many wounded. (Our Russian allies, on the other hand, and the Germans on the eastern front suffered casualties on an unparalleled scale.) But the obduracy of the Battle of the Atlantic meant that twice as many British merchant seamen as before lost their lives, and these 36 000 civilians must be added to the 60 000 who perished under attack from the air, as compared with 1100 in the First World War. Moreover, during the periods of severe bombing the civil population of both sexes and all ages was exposed to risks and strains comparable with those faced by combatants—which made this in yet another way a people's war.

A War of Technologies

The shorter casualty lists of the Second World War were attributable in part to advances in medical science which were brought into widespread use to cope with the emergency. Surgery was facilitated by elaborate arrangements for blood transfusions; psychiatry came into its own in the treatment of what was formerly known as shell-shock; and penicillin—resulting from an initial discovery by Alexander Fleming as far back as 1928—was only the most famous of the many new life-saving drugs made available to every hospital. The mobilization of scientists in general to help the war effort also meant that there was increased application of what was called 'operational research' to such questions as the dietary value of rationed foodstuffs or the possibility of producing our own equivalent for nylon, first supplied from the United States in 1941. But what was, of course, of supreme importance was the achievement of an ascendancy over the enemy in the technology of armaments.

This was not only a matter of inventive talent but also of painstaking organization for mass production. Since a tank had nearly 7000 parts, composed of more than five times as many pieces of material, it was a long way from the making of a blueprint for a new design to the setting-up of the machinery for its manufacture, whilst a new aircraft involved still greater complexities of construction. Accordingly, the fortunes of war varied very much as the result of developments in the weaponry available to either side.

Broadly speaking, in the first half of the war the Germans had a big advantage, because their armaments were re-created under Hitler and built up at top speed as a threat to possible opponents. Hence the remarkable successes of the *Blitzkrieg*, which dominated every campaign until the German mechanized warfare encountered the distances and climatic severities which protect Russia from effective invasion. Hence, too, the ability of the *Luftwaffe* in the autumn of 1940 to bomb London on fifty-seven nights in succession. But in the preceding summer, when control of the daylight sky would have made an invasion attempt possible with a great preponderance of armoured forces, the defeat of the German pilots in the Battle of Britain was partly due to technical advantages now accruing to the other side. The development of 'radio detection and ranging' by R. A. Watson-Watt in 1935 had resulted in the construction of a network of Radar stations, which gave invaluable warning of enemy movements in the air. In addition, the *Spitfire* fighter, which became available in the nick of time, easily outpaced the newest of the German aircraft.

Britain drew increasingly upon American technical resources. In March 1941 the Lend-Lease Act removed all financial barriers to the

Oxford Street, London, after German bombing—September, 1940.

flow of munitions across the Atlantic, and when America entered the war a second generous decision directed their main effort in manufacturing as well as fighting to the defeat of the Germans before the more bitterly hated Japanese. Thus a new American heavy tank played a vital role at El Alamein. D-Day would have been impossible without the provision of landing-craft from American sources, and there was also some American contribution to the three British technical masterpieces which supported the assault—'Mulberries' (artificial harbours), 'Gooseberries' (breakwaters constructed from blockships), and 'Pluto' (the pipe-line under the ocean', conveying the indispensable oil-supply from the Isle of Wight, and later from Dungeness, to the coast of France). And aircraft built in America enabled Britain to play a full part in the later stages of the strategic bomber offensive. In 1943 the RAF and the American Army Air Force between them bombed Germany five times as heavily as in 1942, whilst in the course of 1944 they acquired a mastery in the air which at long last broke down the enemy arms manufactures by methods that included incendiary raids of great intensity on city centres, as at Dresden. By the end of the war ten German civilians had perished in air attacks for each one killed in Britain.

Nevertheless, there were at least three respects in which the Germans came near to recapturing their lead in technology. By 1944 they had fitted many of their submarines with a captured Dutch invention, the *schnorchel*, a tube through which the batteries could be recharged without resurfacing, and were also preparing to use a novel fuel mixture to produce deadly bursts of speed. Secondly, in the last winter of the war they began the employment of jet-fighters, a revolutionary change which, if introduced a little earlier, might have held up the Allied bomber offensive; for our own jet-engines, pioneered by Frank Whittle in 1941, were not yet operational. And thirdly, between June 1944 and March 1945 they conducted a wholly new form of air offensive, chiefly against London, with the unmanned weapons known as 'V1' and 'V2'. The former was a small pilotless aircraft carrying a ton of explosive, which was both visible and audible for some while before the stopping of the engine indicated the moment of its vertical descent; the effect on morale was considerable. The latter was a rocket which carried about the same weight of explosive in its warhead; it came into use when interception in the air and the overrunning of the launching sites had brought the V1 flights almost to an end. Altogether, the two weapons added about 15 per cent to civilian deaths from air attack and about 50 per cent to the number of houses destroyed or damaged. The V2 was received more fatalistically by the public, but its potentialities caused the government to plan for an eventual total evacuation of London. For, pending the capture of the launching-pads, there was no means whatever of combating a jet-propelled missile which descended upon the target area from a height of fifty miles.

The Nuclear Denouement

Although it was the New Zealand genius, Rutherford, who in 1919 split the atom, and James Chadwick, his colleague at the Cavendish Laboratory in Cambridge, who in 1932 discovered the neutron, the early development of nuclear physics was the work of scientists of many nationalities, not least the Germans. By the 1930s it was widely realized that nuclear fission might be able to release an amount of energy beyond the dream or nightmare of Man for purposes of good or ill, though the initial expense would be enormous. Accordingly, in the first years of the war German progress in this field was a cause of alarm, especially when it became known that the enemy attached great importance to obtaining supplies of heavy water from Norway for experimentation. In fact, however, Britain was put in the lead as early as 1940, thanks to an exposition by two refugee scientists who had been working in Paris under Joliot, the almost equally eminent son-in-law of the Curies, and research was continued in several British universities. Finally, in August 1941, Churchill's scientific advisers convinced him that plans for producing an atomic bomb before the war ended were sufficiently realistic to justify official supervision and support; this was provided through the 'Directorate of Tube Alloys', a name which hid the existence of a special division of the DSIR.

A year later the gigantic task of production was transferred by agreement to the United States, where British and American nuclear scientists were given every facility for their investigations under conditions of military security in a purpose-built town at Los Alamos in the Arizona desert. They employed uranium from Canada, which was the third partner in the venture. By the summer of 1944 the very few political leaders who were in the secret—a group which did not include the American Vice-President, or Attlee and most of the other members of the British War Cabinet—could foresee that a trial bomb would be ready for explosion within twelve months and that lethal use could then follow immediately. A plea from a number of the most eminent nuclear scientists, that it should be used only in the very last resort and after the fullest warnings had been given, was brushed aside by Churchill and Roosevelt, and would have evoked even less sympathy in Truman, who succeeded to the Presidency on Roosevelt's sudden death in April 1945.

News of a successful trial reached the two western Allied leaders while they were negotiating with Stalin at the Potsdam Conference over the future of Germany. Within three weeks an ineffective, enigmatic warning to Japan was followed by the dropping of the first atomic bomb on Hiroshima on 6 August. Two days later a second bomb (based on plutonium in place of uranium) fell on Nagasaki, and on 14 August the Japanese surrendered. Although the death-roll of about 70 000 in Hiroshima and 40 000 in Nagasaki had been exceeded in the great fire-raid on Dresden and in its successor against Tokyo in March, the world recognized at once that the enormous potential now latent in a single bomb meant the shrinking into comparative insignificance of all other existing weaponry.

In retrospect this denouement to the six years' war gains in significance. Scant consideration had been given to the effects of contaminated fallout; this cruelly prolonged the sufferings of some innocent Japanese civilians and opened up the prospect that future wars would directly penalize generations unborn at the time of their declaration. No one foresaw that the technology of fission would quickly be replaced by that of nuclear fusion, resulting in a hydrogen bomb many times more powerful than its atomic predecessor. Nor did the many scientists who looked forward eagerly to the development of nuclear energy for purposes of peace suppose that the technical difficulties of explosion risks and disposal of radio-active waste, daunting as they proved to be, might be less of a menace to mankind than the fact that the spread of nuclear know-how for peaceful uses would place its adaptation for war in more numerous and less responsible hands.

Even at the time, the decision to drop the first atomic bomb had great political significance. The primary reason was the obvious one—the desire to save the Allied forces from a loss of life which might prove terribly severe if the Japanese, notwithstanding their tentative offers of surrender, were to continue their immensely stubborn resistance when the campaign reached their home islands. But another reason was the desire to forestall Russian intervention in the Far East. As it was, the dropping of the bomb was followed immediately by the entry of Russian forces into Japanese-occupied Manchuria, which entitled Stalin to some territorial gains at Japan's expense, but not to share in its post-war occupation and political re-orientation. Thus the stage was already being set for the Cold War.

But the decision was also significant in the development of Anglo-American relations, for no British authority was called into the final consultations. At the time of the Quebec Conference in August 1943 Britain had been accorded a right of veto on the use of the bomb, and the close co-operation of the two countries in its development was then envisaged by President Roosevelt as continuing after the war, when an equal partnership in nuclear investigations would help Britain to recover her strength. But by 1945 'The balance of power . . . in the atomic project lay too heavily with the United States for the British to be able, or to wish, to participate in this decision.'[1] The sombre language of the British Official History seems to point forward to the McMahon Act of 1946, by which Congress directly forbade any further pooling of information on atomic matters: America was already losing much of its wartime interest in the 'special relationship' with Britain.

Churchill, by whom those relations had been fostered sedulously, had resigned office on 26 July, when to his great surprise the election result almost exactly reversed the result of ten years before. Thus the enormous problems confronting post-war Britain, some of which still face the present generation, were first tackled by Attlee's Labour administration with the support of a 2:1 majority in the House of Commons.

[1] J. Ehrman: *Grand Strategy Volume VI* (1956), p. 299.

SINCE 1945: A DIFFERENT BRITAIN

28 Recovery, affluence, and the swinging years—1945–77 in outline

The men and women returning from war service faced a changed, and rapidly changing, world. The actual transition from the heroic tasks of war to the hum-drum activities of peace was, indeed, smoothly accomplished, with rationing and government controls of many kinds being retained for some years to ensure fair shares at fair prices so long as almost everything was still in short supply. Perhaps the biggest immediate surprise to many people was that there was no return to the bad times that had followed both the Napoleonic Wars and the First World War, a prospect which had caused some to dread, as a humorist put it, 'peace breaking out'. Instead, Britain moved on from the years of recovery to those of affluence, with high wages backed by extensive new social services, and with increased leisure made possible and also more enjoyable by the rapid advances of technology.

But the more thoughtful saw that our situation had other aspects. The independence of India, conceded in 1947, proved to be the first main stage in Britain's gradual loss of influence over the self-governing states of the Commonwealth and of control over the former colonial empire. She was no longer a 'Great Power' as compared with the super-powers of the USA and Soviet Russia; the former 'workshop of the world' played no part in the stupendous technical achievements which enabled Russians and Americans in keen competition to make an entry into outer space.

Moreover, in Britain as in many other countries the affluent society brought with it its own problems of increased crime—especially among the young—drug addiction, and violence. The affluent society had its counterpart in the permissive society, which reacted against accepted standards in music, art, and literature, no less than in morals and discipline, including self-discipline. Some of the young sought escape by hitch-hiking along the road to Katmandu. Teddy Boys, Hippies, the Flower People, and various anarchic student groups attracted attention for a time by their total rejection of the affluent society and its money-making code of ethics. Yet this was the society by which they had themselves been bred and sustained and to which most of them in the end returned. Indeed, by the 1970s protests against the affluent society attracted less attention, because most people's minds were preoccupied with the struggle to preserve the affluence. The 'swinging years' of affluence and permissiveness gave way to years when the political leaders caused the economic expectations of the public to swing uneasily between hope and fear.

1945–51: Labour in Power; Nationalization

The general election of July 1945 had given the Labour Party a large majority in the House of Commons (as we have already seen), which it interpreted with good reason as a mandate for sweeping changes, including the nationalization of key industries. The Bank of England, which had long been the servant of the government, was taken over first. The coal-mines, the railways (with other forms of transport), the electric power stations, and the gasworks followed. Finally a Bill was passed for taking over the iron and steel industry, after the resistance of the House of Lords had been quelled by a new Act of Parliament, reducing the duration of its veto to a single year.

These measures were intended by Attlee and his Cabinet to make an important contribution to their central task of putting Britain on to its feet again, a task which the havoc wrought by bombs and the wartime sacrifice of overseas investments and export trade made extremely difficult. A huge American (and Canadian) loan and the still huger benefits received from the American Marshall Aid programme enabled our economic life to revive, so that by 1951 London's South Bank could even produce a small-scale copy of the exhibition held in Hyde Park a hundred years before. But at least two events had by then shown clearly that Britain's status in the world had changed beyond recall. In 1947 Attlee—a man of shrewd and incisive judgement, who had served in the Gallipoli campaign during the First World War—had ordered an immediate abandonment of Britain's responsibilities in the Indian Peninsula. And in 1949 Britain's financial position as the centre of the Sterling Area, which included the entire Commonwealth apart from Canada, had suffered a major shock when it became necessary to devalue the pound from 4·03 dollars to 2·80 dollars.

Nationalization, coming at a time when the war had accustomed the public to government controls of every kind and when post-war reconstruction clearly called for drastic measures, made remarkably little stir. On the one hand, there was little denunciation of this important step towards putting into effect the central socialist doctrine—the need to transfer control of the means of production, distribution, and exchange from private enterprise to the State. On the other hand, there was little exultation on the part of the workers liberated from private capitalism; instead, the boards of government appointees who now ran the industries which had been nationalized found the unions as uncompromising as ever in their demands. Accordingly, when the Conservatives came back into office in October 1951, they had little difficulty in holding up the nationalization of iron and steel and also of road haulage, and it was not until the troubled 1970s that later Labour administrations contemplated further advances in this field.

The Social Services

The Labour government had a greater impact upon the general public through its wide extension of the social services, where it built upon the existing edifice of health and unemployment insurance, the proposals of the Beveridge Report, and the family allowances enacted just before it took office. The two basic measures were both passed in 1946.

The National Insurance Act required everybody to pay regular contributions towards a nation-wide provision for old age, for the bereavement of women and children, and for the incidence of sickness or unemployment. Normal needs were met in this way, and in any critical situation further help was available as 'National Assistance'. The National Health Service Act aimed at the creation of a universal system to cope with ill-health and to improve health conditions in general through doctors (including specialists as well as general practitioners), hospitals, and eventually health centres; medical and dental treatment, together with drugs, dentures, and spectacles, would be free of charge to all comers. Doctors and dentists were to be paid by the State according to the number of their patients; the hospitals were all brought under the control of Regional Boards, with the exception

Mobile child welfare clinic at work near Aberdeen.

of the great teaching hospitals which had a special position in the training of doctors.

It was sometimes claimed that the State now looked after everybody 'from the cradle to the grave'. Maternity services were improved, and births usually took place in hospital. The majority of children under one year of age were brought to Infant Welfare Centres, where they were weighed and examined, and where the mother could make arrangements for getting milk, orange juice and other foods free or at a reduced price. Children had slightly better chances than before the war of admission to nursery schools or nursery classes, and from the time of their entry into the regular school system at five, they would come under the care of the school doctor, nurse, and dentist; they would also receive free school milk and could partake of heavily subsidized school dinners. In adult life, too, fuller provision was made for various categories of people in need of special help—institutions for the mentally defective and the physically disabled; books in Braille and training of the blind for employment; and other training schemes of many kinds to enable those who had been injured in the war to become partly self-supporting.

The old, however, were the section of the community which felt most keenly the imperfections of the new system. They were often unaware of the claims they were entitled to make. They were all too often to be found in the wards and waiting-rooms of hospitals, because geriatric institutions were slow to develop (see p. 308). And the physical deterioration which inevitably accompanies old age meant that they were the first to feel the pinch, when the enormous cost of the health service led to the introduction of small standard charges for dental treatment and spectacles, though the elderly were exempted from the concurrent charge for prescriptions. Aneurin Bevan, the Welsh coalminer who had created the service, resigned from the Cabinet in disgust, but it is fair to remember that the government was involved in other heavy social expenditure at this time, above all on the housing needs of the people, which were obviously even more acute in 1945 than in 1919 (see p. 312).

The Welfare State

The establishment of the National Health Service is perhaps the most striking example of the ways in which the State now made available to all its citizens a standard of well-being hitherto reserved for a minority. In a sense the State had always aimed at welfare, for governments which believed in *laissez-faire* expected the efforts of each individual to achieve the maximum of welfare for himself and his dependants. But now the advance of social democracy meant that the powers of the State were used to the full to raise the standard of life of all those who, whether as individuals or families and for whatever reason, were depressed below the national average.

The social services were an instrument for levelling-up, financed by an increase in taxation which was also an instrument for levelling-down. It was not until 1960 that income tax fell to 7s. 9d. (38p in the pound, and five years later it was rising again. With the addition of death duties, surtax, and the heavy rates levied on large or luxurious houses, one section of the population, belonging to the categories of salary-earners and rentiers, found themselves to be worse off than before the war. Their salaries did not rise much faster than prices, and some investments never recovered after the war years; their way of life was greatly affected by the final disappearance of resident domestic servants; and they were reluctant to recoup themselves for the rise in taxation by taking full advantage of free national services. State schools, for example, no longer charged fees; yet many professional families spent money they could no longer afford to meet the rising costs of a public-school education for their children.

In general, however, the Welfare State was characterized by the fact that about three-quarters of all the households constituting the nation were better off than their type of household had been before the war. Prices rose, and the wage-earner too had heavier taxes to pay; but the social services took care of many of his former burdens, and the trade unions—which as early as February 1946 had been freed from the shackles of the Trade Disputes Act—saw to it that real wages more than kept their value. This was helped by the maintenance of full employment, which was now accepted as a prime objective by all political parties. Apart from a fuel crisis, which brought industry almost to a standstill for a few weeks in the severe winter of 1946–7, the number of unemployed seldom reached the half-million mark for more than two decades. On the contrary, work was so plentiful that a rise in the birth-rate was accompanied by a marked increase in the number of married women with jobs outside the home, whilst immigrants from the West Indies, Pakistan, and other Commonwealth countries were readily absorbed, particularly into the less attractive occupations.

Thus the Welfare State brought many good things within the grasp of the great majority of the British people. They enjoyed more leisure, and travelled much more—package tours by air took them to the Costa Brava, Greece, and even more exotic places. They spent more freely on labour-saving equipment for their homes, on furniture, and on entertainment of all kinds—including the novelty of a television receiver. What had once been the privileges and amenities of the upper and middle classes became for the first time widespread, bringing with them a more settled outlook and a decline of extremist political opinions. Indeed, it was often difficult to say clearly how the policies of the two main political parties differed. In 1948, for example, the Conservatives accepted with little fuss the Labour government's final electoral reform, which abolished a few anomalies—such as the separate representation of universities and the restriction of the vote to persons who had been resident for six months in the constituency. Twenty years later, Wilson's reduction of the age of enfranchisement to eighteen evoked scarcely a murmur from the Party which had once sought to conserve the franchise in a minimum of experienced and otherwise well-qualified hands.

1951–64: Conservatives in Power; the Affluent Society

In October 1951, when the Labour Party lost the election, Churchill returned to office. Four months later, Elizabeth II succeeded to the throne at the early age of twenty-five, and when her coronation in the following year coincided with the first scaling of Mount Everest (by Hilary and Tensing) romantics were encouraged to look for the dawn of a second 'Elizabethan Age'. Instead, it was the unromantic Age of the Affluent Society, characterized by the ability of a worker and his family to own a car, and to load it with consumer goods of every kind on their weekly spending spree to a supermarket, of which there were rapidly expanding chains. Hire purchase and the luxury advertising by which it was stimulated enjoyed periods of record growth, especially after the enactment in 1954 of a strongly contested measure which set up ITV as a rival to BBC television, with a budget based on the profits from advertising, now introduced directly and forcibly into the home.

In the eyes of most people the Keynesian system of a managed economy—though they did not know it under that name—had solved the main social problem, for there were jobs available for all and wages continued to rise faster than prices. In these circumstances it was all too easy to ignore disquieting signs that Britain was ceasing to pay her way in the world—a subject to which we shall return in the final chapter of this book. The average man was well content to dismiss as a passing misfortune the recurrent periods of 'Stop–Go', when the government found it necessary to check private expenditure by a sudden increase of taxation, a rise in Bank rate, and the reduction of hire-purchase facilities. In 1955 the Conservatives won an increased majority under Eden, who had succeeded Churchill a few months before, and again in 1959 under Macmillan, who was later to remind the electorate that they had 'never had it so good'.

The Decline of Empire Continues

All the European overseas empires declined and vanished after the Second World War, but Britain's (which was much the largest and most valuable) did so with a particularly impressive absence of controversy. This is partly attributable to Attlee's action to forestall any conflict over the future of India, but also to a process of transition which greatly softened the blow to British pride. Thus India and Pakistan both became Dominions under the Crown, each with its governor-general; then republics which nevertheless accepted the wearer of the crown as Head of the Commonwealth; and finally, after events had gradually shown the British people that this Headship did not give them even a moral claim to any continued leadership,

Pakistan's abandonment of Commonwealth membership passed almost unnoticed.

In 1956, however, Eden's downfall came about as the result of our single attempt at imperial self-assertion in the old style, when British and French troops tried to regain control of the Suez Canal, which the Egyptians had nationalized. Although the action had considerable backing from British public opinion, it had to be ignominiously abandoned in the face of its condemnation as aggression by the outside world—including even the countries of the Commonwealth, apart from Australia and New Zealand. The following year Ghana was the first of the African colonies to achieve independent status. Thereafter the number of independent members of the Commonwealth grew with amazing rapidity, but the British public seemed to avert its gaze from the spectacle of the lowering of the Union Jack at one outpost of empire after another in all parts of the world. In 1957, too, the decision was taken to bring to an end compulsory National Service, which had continued since 1945, and it became possible to foresee that the United Kingdom would eventually give up all defence commitments 'east of Suez'.

'Seven Lean Years'?

In the early 1960s it was beginning to look as though the comfortable years of affluence, like the seven good years in Joseph's interpretation of Pharaoh's dream, might be followed by at least as many years of leanness. There seemed to be some deep-seated trouble in the economic system, which showed itself in the balance of payments (see p. 330) and could not be put right by such palliatives as the 'Stop–Go' interventions of the government. Inflation, unemployment, and trade union difficulties were beginning to threaten.

One factor of growing importance to Britain was the successful establishment of the Common Market among six countries of western Europe, which had first united for the production of coal, iron and steel, and then more fully through the Treaty of Rome of 1957. In 1960 Britain had replied by setting up a European Free Trade Association, but its seven members constituted a much smaller market, which also lacked the protection of a common external tariff. Macmillan had in any case intended this to be a stepping stone to the Common Market, but in January 1963 General de Gaulle—always resentful of Britain's supposed 'special relationship with America'—firmly barred the way. The consequent ten-year delay before Britain's eventual admission to the Common Market was one factor in the continued deterioration of our economic position, to be considered in detail later on (see p. 275).

For the present outline it is enough to note that it had not improved when, in the autumn of the same year (1963), sudden illness obliged Macmillan to resign the premiership in favour of a fellow-Scotsman, formerly 15th Earl of Home. The election was delayed until the autumn of 1964—by which time the deficit on the balance of payments was alarming—and then sustained a narrow defeat at the hands of the Labour Party, which had been out of office for so long.

1964–70: The First Wilson Ministry

The new Prime Minister, Mr Harold Wilson, belonged to a new type of political leader, which was also represented by Mr Edward Heath, who, the following year took Home's place in charge of the Opposition. Both of them came from comparatively humble homes, but the educational ladder now made it easy for men of such outstanding ability to reach the older universities, which in turn gave them an altogether easier access to a political career than had been available to Lloyd George or Ramsay MacDonald. Neither man achieved as much as he set out to do in an increasingly difficult national situation, but Wilson was a born debater, whose intellectual resourcefulness won him numerous evanescent triumphs both in the House of Commons and on television.

Three grave problems arose at this time, which were still unsolved in 1978, suggesting to reflective minds that Britain's increasingly weak position was not the result of economic forces alone but of a whole complex of causes—and therefore not to be remedied quickly by either of the great political parties. One problem was that of Rhodesia (the former Southern Rhodesia), which had the special status of a self-governing colony, ruled by a long-established minority of white settlers. They refused to accept the prospect of a transfer to rule by the native majority, which was the policy pursued by Britain in other parts of Africa, and which had already led to the secession of the rich and powerful Union of South Africa from the Commonwealth in 1961. When the Rhodesian premier, Ian Smith, issued a unilateral declaration of independence (UDI) in November 1965, Wilson shrank from the use of force against our own kith and kin. The alternative was the use of argument, to which Smith proved quite impervious, and an economic blockade by the United Kingdom, the Commonwealth, and the United Nations, which supporters of the white Rhodesians found many means of circumventing. In 1978 it still seemed possible that the Zimbabwe of the Africans' ambitions would be created only at the expense of a civil war involving many non-African interests.

The other two continuing problems arose near home, and were likewise related to the reduced strength of the United Kingdom. Coloured immigration from the Commonwealth countries, welcome in a time of economic expansion, had been checked by law in 1962, but by then immigrant families were numerous, and inevitably conspicuous, in certain districts of London, the industrial Midlands and Yorkshire. In 1965 and 1968 the Wilson government passed two Race Relations Acts, which aimed at preventing discrimination against fellow-citizens of another race or colour; in the two key matters of housing and employment, this was to prove increasingly difficult. The remaining problem also had a racial aspect, for Northern Ireland contained a large Catholic, Irish-nationalist minority, which the Protestant majority had been able to hold in economic and (to some extent) political subjection because the province was a minor part of a strong and wealthy United Kingdom. By the later 1960s, however, it no longer seemed so hopeless for the irreconcilables of the 'Irish Republican Army' to wage an underground war for a united Ireland. In August 1969 serious disturbances in Londonderry and Belfast caused the Wilson ministry to authorize the intervention of the British Army. This led on in due course to the suspension by the Heath ministry of provincial self-government; there followed a long-continued failure to enforce law and order upon either the Catholic or the Protestant extremists.

Crime and Violence

Before turning to the economic crisis which engaged most of Wilson's attention, we may note that in 1965 a free vote of the House of Commons abolished capital punishment. Liberal opinion on both sides of the House had agitated for this reform for many years, but there is something paradoxical in the fact that the law was being made more humane in this and many other less dramatic aspects at a time when law-breaking confronted society with new dangers. The IRA was soon to bring terrorism across the Irish Sea to London and Birmingham. As economic conditions worsened, peaceful picketing during strikes often became an excuse for mob violence. By 1969 even student unrest had taken violent forms, both at the cosmopolitan London School of Economics and at the brand-new University of Essex, and unrest spread to many other universities.

During most of this period—beginning in the mid-1950s and going on up to our present date in the late 1970s—there was a very considerable increase in crime, often ignored or glossed over by the Left, sometimes exaggerated or sensationalized by the Right. What was particularly disturbing was the way in which society generally came to accept crime—especially the appalling situation in Northern Ireland, where 2000 lives were lost in ten years without a settlement being reached.

In Britain itself crimes increased from 500 000 in the mid-1950s to over 1 million by the mid-1960s, and to over 2 million by the mid-1970s. This was not due simply to increase in population, for crime increased much more rapidly—although increased population and the crowding of people together must add to frustration and tension which could lead to law-breaking. The vast majority of crimes are offences against property, whereas crimes of violence against the person—which get the publicity—account for a small percentage of the crime recorded by the police. Nevertheless, crimes of violence have significantly increased in recent years: from 37 800 in 1969, to 52 400 in 1972, to 77 700 in 1976. Homicides went up from 476 to 565 between 1972 and 1976; there was increasing use of firearms; and at Hull prison in 1976 there was one of the worst gaol riots ever known in Britain. There has also been a great increase in vandalism, from 41 000 cases in 1972 to 123 000 cases in 1977. Official figures too, only refer to crimes known officially to the police; there are other crimes never reported.

But to explain this great increase in crime is another matter. Why is crime more pressing now than formerly? And why is the problem of crime common to many countries at the same time? Many suggestions have been made—the war; the growth of drug-taking; deprivation—poor housing and amenities; the effect of TV; the motor car; the affluent society; the decline in religion and family influence; the lack of discipline and punishment. Yet there is no general agreement, and it has been stated that there is little scientific evidence to support precise attributions. It may be so, but many readers will incline to the view expressed recently (June 1978) by a chief constable that the great increase in crime is not due to chance, especially when one considers how the TV highlights physical superiority and prowess, violence and crime, whilst showing teachers as weak intellectuals, the police as bullies, and magistrates as old fools.

The Economic Crisis

And now back to Wilson and economic crisis. The deficit in the balance of payments when Wilson took office was too large to be overcome by the 'Stop–Go' measures which had been tried on previous occasions, so he added a 15 per cent surcharge on imports of manufactured and semi-manufactured goods; this continued for two years, despite the justified protests of the other members of EFTA. Loans were also obtained from the central banks of the United States and other foreign countries, which feared the effect that a devaluation of the pound might have on world trade in general. Other measures were taken of a long-term character. A National Board for Prices and Incomes was to hold in check the upward trend, which was already seriously inflationary; a commission was appointed to study the special position of the trade unions, which exercised so powerful an influence on the rising level of wages; and this government reorganized the National Economic Development Council (alias 'Neddie'), set up by its predecessor as a forum for discussion and planning between the State and the two sides in industry.

The big new device, however, was the establishment of a Department of Economic Affairs, which for some years seriously rivalled the authority of the Treasury. By September 1965 it had published a National Plan, showing how by 1970 a 25 per cent increase in national production could be achieved, which would set right the balance of payments and enable Britain to meet its debts. The details of this elaborate project were never wholly clear, but it did show that the Labour government recognized the danger of the situation—a bleak contrast to the many years during which the public had anticipated increasing affluence rather than any risk of national poverty.

In March 1966 the electorate gave Wilson a secure majority of ninety-seven, which enabled him in the following year to pass an Iron and Steel Act, which brought the major part of another key industry into public ownership, as Labour had long intended. But in the summer following the election a seamen's strike helped to precipitate a further crisis over the balance of payments. The National Plan fell into the background; instead, there was a new attempt to restrict demand, by means of a standstill on wages, prices, and dividends. In addition, a Selective Employment Tax was introduced, to discourage the taking on of more workers in 'service industries' (including building) which did not directly further exports. The intention was to bring about a transfer of labour to the export industries which were the mainstay of the nation's livelihood, but one immediate effect was a small increase in unemployment.

Devaluation

From the moment when he took office Wilson—who had been a teacher of economics in Oxford before the war—was adamant in rejecting all suggestions, whether from colleagues or civil servants, that the pound would have to be devalued again. He persisted in this attitude until 18 November 1967, when a dock strike was the final blow which led to the announcement of a 14 per cent devaluation of the pound, from 2·80 dollars to 2·40 dollars. The object was, of course, to be able to sell our exports more cheaply and to cut down on imports, which must be bought more dearly. But the Prime Minister did not scruple to assure the public, in a television speech which was long remembered against him: 'It does not mean that the pound in your pocket has been devalued.'

Thus the jettisoning of the National Plan was followed by a second *volte-face*, and for a time the minds of the older generation at least turned back to the alarming situation of 1931. There was a big reduction in public expenditure, both on the social services and on our military commitments overseas, albeit the promised total withdrawal of United Kingdom forces from 'east of Suez' would make the Commonwealth less meaningful and no longer centred unmistakably on Britain. The Budget of 1968 followed up with increases in indirect taxation and other measures designed to curtail personal expenditure. But Wilson kept his nerve, blunting the force of criticism both by the ingenuity of his arguments and by his astonishing personal resilience. The public seemed to swallow its feelings of disappointment that a return to Labour rule had not meant an increase in welfare and affluence, and in 1969–70 the state of the economy had improved sufficiently for the government to indicate (not for the first or last time in recent years) that Britain had turned the corner.

Accordingly, the Labour Party was widely expected to win the election of June 1970, but three days before polling the trade figures for May recorded a trade deficit of £31 million, which (again not for the first or last time) implied that the government in office had been over-optimistic about its achievements. Whatever their motivation, the electors gave the Conservatives a majority not much smaller than Labour had received four years before.

1970–77: The Uncertain '70s

Any account of a decade written while it is still in progress is bound to be marked by uncertainty, since it is only in retrospect that we can pick out the events which had most significance. But these years are also uncertain in a more important sense: for election results, opinion polls, and the discussions in the mass media all suggested that the British people was to an unusual degree unconvinced that any political party or leader could point the way out of its accumulated difficulties.

The Conservative government of 1970–4 takes Britain into the Common Market

The Conservatives under Mr Edward Heath embarked on a policy of 'less government', leaving the economy as far as possible to the presumably beneficent workings of private enterprise. This did not last long, however, for early in 1972 unemployment passed the million mark, and even before this the country was alarmed by the bankruptcy of such famous firms as Rolls Royce and Upper Clyde Shipbuilders. An attempt was made to grapple with inflation, first by a statutory standstill on prices and wages, and then by the setting up of a Prices Commission and a Pay Board, which were intended to damp down advances in both these closely interrelated parts of the economy. But Heath, whose political outlook was straightforward and less disposed to compromise than that of most politicians, considered that the biggest problem was that of the mounting power of the trade unions, which he vainly sought to curb.

However, we must notice first Heath's one great success: he took Britain into the European Economic Community or Common Market. He had played the leading part in the first negotiations under Macmillan, and the way was now opened by the retirement of General de Gaulle, who had rebuffed a second approach by the Wilson government just after the devaluation. Heath negotiated with much more conviction than Wilson, and secured the consent of Parliament in October 1971, when thirty-nine Conservatives voted against the government and sixty-nine Labour members rallied to its support. On New Year's Day 1973 Britain became one of the Nine, and although Heath's decision was later challenged, as we shall see (p. 335), it was not reversed. Passing mention must also be made of another measure which has proved permanent. In 1971 the pound was decimalized by general agreement, 100 new pence replacing the traditional 240 pennies or twenty shillings.

Confrontation with the Trade Unions

The war years had brought a rise in trade union membership from 6 to 8 million, and with Bevin as Minister of Labour there had been a corresponding rise in their position in the state. During the period of post-war recovery they co-operated with the Attlee government by accepting voluntary wage restraint in order to keep prices stable and help the revival of exports. Even after the return of the Conservatives to power in 1951, harmony was to a great extent preserved by accepting that the unions had a right to be consulted on all economic questions, and in a time of general prosperity the pressure by which they now kept their members' wages ahead of the rise in prices aroused little resentment. Two features of trade union activity were, however, bitterly resented. One was the increasing number of unofficial strikes, which the official leaders of the unions could not control. The other, possibly related, feature was the infiltration of some unions by Communists, to which public attention was drawn when it was proved in court that they had secured control of the very important Electrical Trades Union by rigging the election of its officers.

By 1964 trade union membership had risen to 10 million—almost one-fifth of the entire population—and for at least four reasons this formidable organization was disinclined to accept any crisis measures which Wilson's newly formed Labour administration might propose at its expense. The prime function of a trade union had always been to raise wages. After so long a period of prosperity it was hard to believe that the economic crisis was more than a passing trade depression. It was nearly always possible (and on some occasions reasonable) to argue that whatever measures a government proposed bore more hardly on the wage-earner than on other elements of the community. And among the wage-earners themselves there was the further complication that any wage concession made on the grounds of social justice to those who earned least was an incentive to fresh demands from those who expected always to earn more, either because their occupation was highly skilled or because their union was strong enough to keep ahead.

It was—and indeed is—especially difficult for any Labour Party government to take effective steps to control wages, however grave the economic plight of the nation may be, because those trade unions which are officially affiliated to the Party have about nine times as many members as the Party has in its local groups. In January 1969 the Wilson government published a White Paper with the optimistic title *In Place of Strife*, on the basis of which a Trade Union Reform Bill was prepared. This would have enabled the Secretary of State for Employment, if it was thought national interests were at stake, to hold up any unofficial strike for twenty-eight days and to require an official strike to be approved in advance by a ballot of the union concerned. In June the TUC called a special conference, which rejected by a majority of more than 20:1 any regulation entitling the Minister to impose sanctions. The Bill—which had also been openly opposed by the Home Secretary, Mr Callaghan—was then abandoned, despite the efforts of the Employment Secretary, Mrs Barbara Castle.

It is clear from the above recital that the Conservative government of 1970 was almost bound to make a further attempt to curb the trade unions, even if it had not been faced with industrial action (a slowing-down of the electrical supply and a postal strike) as soon as it tried to limit wage increases to about 8 per cent. Accordingly, after nearly two whole months of embittered discussion, an Industrial Relations Bill of 170 sections became law in August 1971. This defined the legal rights of employers and employees, often to the advantage of the latter, but the key feature was the setting-up of an Industrial Court with the status of a High Court, staffed by High Court Judges and lay experts, and able to sit at any time and anywhere in Great Britain. Besides dealing with the grievances of individuals, the Court could forbid strike action for a 'cooling off' period of sixty days and order a trade union to ascertain its members' views by a ballot.

In January 1972 a coal-miners' strike was marked by an unusual degree of violence, when picketing was extended from the mines to the power stations, so that industry was slowed down by lack of electricity. But in an age which was increasingly sensitive to all evidences of inequality, the hardships of their work gained much public sympathy for the miners, who eventually obtained a wage increase of about 21 per cent. This made nonsense of the government's previously mentioned limit of 8 per cent; it also gave a menacing demonstration of the ability of a trade union in an essential service to hold the whole community to ransom. Against this background it becomes a little easier to understand how it was that the unions could flout the decisions of the new Industrial Relations Court in a year when the state of the economy was such that it was decided (in June) to allow the pound to float—or sink. The dockers refused to accept the Court's decision in a dispute about the new container traffic to the docks; five of them were sent to prison, which led to a dock strike. A second dispute concerned the rights of a member of the big engineering union (AUEW), which was fined £61 000 for contempt of court, and went on to incur a still heavier fine in the following year. And the prestige of the Court was reduced still further when it required the railwaymen to hold a ballot on the 'work-to-rule' measure by which they were pressing a wage-claim. The vote was 6:1 in favour of continuing the pressure, which within a fortnight of the ballot gained them an additional £2.2 million.

A final showdown between the Heath government and the unions arose from the oil crisis, which began with the Arab–Israeli war of October 1973, when the Arab oil producers imposed a boycott on oil supplies. There followed a drastic curtailment of oil imports, and their increased cost affected industrial output and the balance of payments; but neither the miners, nor the workers in the power stations, nor the drivers and stokers on the railways were prepared to abate their claims. On 13 November the government declared a state of emergency, and on New Year's Day power supplies were husbanded by requiring all factories, workshops and offices to work a three-day week. The miners, whose ban on overtime from 12 November was the direct cause of the emergency, had the support of the TUC, which promised ministers that a generous settlement with the miners would not lead to other exceptional claims. Heath, however, felt by February that the time had come for a challenge on the question, 'Who rules Britain?' On 5 February the miners announced an all-out strike, and on the 7th the government announced a general election.

The result was probably influenced to some extent by the adroitness with which Wilson diverted the attention of the electorate from the intransigence of the miners to the general problems facing the economy. Nevertheless, the fact that the Labour Party won three more seats than the Conservatives must also mean that Heath's uncompromising appeal to patriotism and the defence of the constitution was no longer in harmony with the times.

Return to Labour rule: the Social Contract

When Heath had failed in an attempt to form a coalition with the Liberals, Wilson became the head of a minority government, which ended the three-day week, came to terms with the miners, and dismantled many of the existing economic controls. Wilson proposed to rely instead upon the workings of a 'Social Contract', consisting of a package of measures agreed between the Labour Party and the TUC in the previous year—yet another demonstration of trade union power, functioning now as a determinant of ministerial policy. The aim of the Contract was to curb inflation, partly by strengthening the control of prices, for which purpose the Price Commission was retained, but above all by the practice of voluntary restraint on the part of the unions in the matter of wage increases. In return, the Pay Board and other statutory controls on pay were abolished in July, and the same month saw the demise of the Industrial Relations Court as the result of the repeal of the law of August 1971.

In October the second election put Labour forty-three seats ahead of the Conservatives, but its overall majority was only three. This rather indecisive result was probably attributable, not to doubts about the Social Contract (whose effectiveness had still to be tested) but to a completely different problem, which in this year began to have serious effects in a number of constituencies.

Devolution

Both Scotland and Wales had strong cultural traditions of their own, which from time to time led to modest political demands, such as the disestablishment of the Anglican Church in Wales, campaigned for by Lloyd George in the 1890s and finally achieved in 1919. It was curious that the Scots and Welsh—like the Bretons in France and the Basques in Spain—should raise the nationalist issue at a time when the European powers were coming closer together in the EEC. Yet the economic difficulties from which the whole United Kingdom was suffering now presented nationalist politicians with a plausible argument for withdrawing Scottish and Welsh affairs from English mismanagement by setting up some more or less autonomous form of national assembly; the Scots, however, demanded rather more than the Welsh, as befitted an ancient kingdom with a modern asset in the form of North Sea oil. In the October election the Scottish National Party advanced from seven seats to eleven, came second in forty-two constituencies, and had 30 per cent of the total Scottish vote. In Wales Plaid Cymru advanced from two seats to three, and had 10 per cent of the total vote. The Conservatives having already suggested that Scotland should be given an Assembly, the Labour government now judged it expedient to formulate its own plans for both countries.

Accordingly, in 1976 a Bill was introduced for setting up elected Assemblies, in Edinburgh for Scotland and in Cardiff for Wales. The Scots would have certain legislative powers and a Cabinet responsible to the Assembly, any dispute with the authorities at Westminster being referred to the Judicial Committee of the Privy Council. The Welsh would have executive powers only, their Assembly being run on the committee system. Both Assemblies would administer such services as local government, schools, health, housing, roads, and the environment, to which they would apportion a block grant from the Treasury. But the two peoples would retain their existing representation at Westminster, where responsibility for the overall interests of the United Kingdom would remain. There was, however, much misgiving about the Bill, both political parties being split on the issue; some thought the Bill went too far and others—including a newly formed Scottish Labour Party—not far enough. It passed its Second Reading in December 1976, but was subsequently abandoned owing to the defeat of the government's timetable proposals.

New Bills were, however, introduced in November 1977—separate Bills for Scotland and Wales—incorporating some changes, but still based on four guiding principles, which the government announced as being basic to these and the previous Bill. These principles were: to respect the diversity and traditions of Scotland and Wales; to maintain the economic and political unity of the United Kingdom; to preserve the sovereignty of Parliament; and to secure fairness to the whole UK. Provision was also made for a referendum in Scotland and in Wales on the Bills, when enacted. There was still, nevertheless, deep unease about the proposals. In May 1978 a by-election at Hamilton did something to clarify the situation. The Scottish National Party failed to win an expected victory, the Labour Party, in fact, nearly doubling its majority. This meant the rejection of the SNP idea of a separate Scottish state, and a decline it its prospects at any forthcoming general election. But the Labour victory would also mean a strengthening of the government's devolution policy, and the possibility—in the more distant future—of a SNP move towards independence through the Edinburgh Assembly rather than through Westminster.

The Labour government holds on; the Jubilee Celebrations

The 1970s continued on their uncertain way. The political leadership was changed in both main parties, Heath being displaced in 1975 by Mrs Margaret Thatcher, the first woman to become a Party leader in Britain, and Wilson retiring with dramatic suddenness in March 1976. His final victory had been the modification of the terms of membership in the EEC and their approval by 2:1 in Britain's first referendum. Wilson's successor, Mr James Callaghan, had been employed in the Inland Revenue and on war service as a petty officer in the Navy. When he took over, Labour had just lost its exiguous majority in the House of Commons as the result of the secession of two MPs to the new Scottish Labour Party, but he was able to hang on to office by bargaining for Liberal support, although by-election results went in favour of the Conservatives. The long-continued depression in world trade was now affecting many other countries, but inflation was particularly severe in Britain; the pound fell in 1976 as low as 1·55 dollars; and in the following June unemployment rose to 1 600 000. By that time the Social Contract had gone the way of earlier specifics, such as the National Plan, the Prime Minister having to content himself with a promise from the TUC that wage claims would not be made more than once in twelve months.

In 1963 the Labour Party had condemned the Conservative record since 1951 as 'Twelve wasted years'. But in the view of at least one recent economic critic, 'The same phrase would have been an even more apposite description of 1964–76.' Living standards were admittedly higher in 1976 than in 1964, yet even in that respect the big

Mrs Margaret Thatcher, leader of the Conservative Party—first woman leader of a British political party.

Margaret Bondfield, first woman cabinet minister (Labour government of 1929–31).

advance had come earlier on. 'Judged by all the other main criteria of economic policy—unemployment, the rate of inflation, the balance of payments position—the situation was far worse in 1976 than in 1964.'[1] In the autumn of 1977 it was still possible to believe that prosperity lay just round the corner, but there was no clear reason to suppose that a change of government would be greatly conducive to that longed-for result.

The year 1978 did see an easing of economic pressures: inflation reduced at last to single figures, and reductions in taxation. But the winter of 1978–9 brought another wave of IRA bombings, while the government's attempt to limit wage increases to 5 per cent led to many demands for much higher rises. A wave of strikes followed, most serious was that of the lorry drivers which threatened vital supplies. It seemed that the Labour government of Mr Callaghan might be faced with a confrontation with the unions similar to that which had met Mr Heath's Conservative government in 1974.

The subject of 'paying our way' will be taken up again in our final chapter. The next three will be concerned with technology, the needs of a changing population, and questions of the environment, as to all of which the years since 1945 have seen much progress. It may therefore be appropriate to remind the reader that 1977 was also the year of the Silver Jubilee of Queen Elizabeth II, when spontaneous popular celebrations of many kinds showed a general awareness that the disappointments of the recent past had been accompanied by what an older generation would have called many blessings.

---

[1] M. Stewart: *The Jekyll and Hyde Years* (1977), p. 1.

29 Technology triumphant

The life of the present generation has been enormously enriched by the triumphs of technology—the result of an increasingly rapid and fruitful application of scientific knowledge to Man's needs and desires. This process has, indeed, been going on since the days of the first 'industrial revolution', but the growth of science in recent years has accelerated to such an extent that nearly three-quarters of all the scientists the world has so far known are working today, and nearly two-thirds of the whole existing body of scientific knowledge consists of discoveries made since the Second World War.

This chapter will illustrate the impact of modern technology on British life, emphasizing the share of our own scientists and technologists. But the movement is of course world-wide, and the most spectacular results so far achieved involved expenditure which only the two world-powers could afford. The rival space-exploration programmes of the Americans and the Russians were followed with enormous interest, which culminated in 1969, when television cameras showed an American astronaut step out to be the first man on the Moon. But Britain has played only a small part in rocket and satellite development, though since 1975 she has been a founder-member of the European Space Agency, which hopes eventually to shoot up a 'spacelab' from an American launching-site.

The New Mass Market

A great deal of modern invention responds directly to the public taste. The self-service store and the supermarket both suit the type of customer who is not too concerned about prices and exact quantities, likes to do his or her shopping quickly, and does not especially enjoy the fuss of giving orders to the shop people. In 1947, only ten self-service establishments were officially known to exist; now they are numbered by the thousand. The name 'supermarket' came from America in the late 1950s: between 1961 and 1964, the number in Britain rose from 750 to about 1600. As for what is in the shops, the emphasis is on new materials and on new methods of preparation, which would not have made the same appeal in an earlier age, when taste was governed much more by tradition and class prejudice. One striking new development, which highlights the prosperity of young wage-earners, is the profusion of clothes, records, sports gear, etc., designed specifically to attract teenage custom.

The development of synthetic fibres, such as nylon and terylene, and of plastics, such as polythene, fills the shelves with a great range of standardized clothing and utensils, shirts and other garments, tooth-brushes and ballpoint pens, buckets and washable imitation wallpaper and tiles—all completely different in composition from the goods of a few years before and quite often cheaper and more attractive. Where soap once reigned supreme, a wide range of chemical detergents now vie in offering to make each housewife's wash whiter than her neighbour's. Most striking is the standardization in foodstuffs, where variety used to be almost infinite. Whatever is not canned is factory-frozen, and then kept by the retailer in his newest major appliance—the deep-freeze. In addition, new machinery applies a host of new materials to wrapping and packaging processes, so that even such a homely product as the baker's loaf is more often than not factory-produced.

Of course there are disadvantages in modern methods, particularly perhaps where food is concerned. 'Factory farming', for example, means the artificial speeding-up of natural processes—hens living out a short life in batteries to produce a quick output of eggs and chickens, calves artificially fed for early veal. Fruit and vegetables are subjected to chemical treatments, not all of which are harmless, though they may help preservation or appearance. Cynics say that foods which are not in some way treated before they reach the purchaser are becoming quite rare.

Nevertheless, to visit a supermarket on a Friday evening, when the weekly pay packet is being spent, gives perhaps the clearest impression of the way in which our society has recently developed. Modern invention provides for the masses, and the masses are able to take full advantage of the provision. Food is picked out to suit family likings, not merely to stay the pangs of hunger. Clothes are bought for all kinds of leisure activities, not as they once were for work and a 'Sunday best'. There are sweets and toys for the children, and each week some new amenity is bought—perhaps on hire-purchase—for a considerable proportion of the 9 million newly built homes, whose very existence has helped to raise standards of furniture and equipment throughout post-war Britain. To some of the older generation who have not forgotten the depressed areas in the 1930s, it seems at times like a waking dream.

Advances in Medicine and Chemistry

Medicine is one of the cases in which it is easy for everyone to appreciate the results of modern research. The isolation of viruses, the discovery of new drugs, and the progress made in microbiology—to all of which important contributions have been made in British laboratories—have significantly increased our knowledge and control of disease. Substitute parts for use in the human body, such as the artificial hip-joint, are constructed with increasing success, and experiments and pioneer operations essay the still more delicate task of replacing diseased organs by transplantation from another body.

The chemical industry in Britain produces a whole range of new drugs, including antibiotics such as penicillin—which started what has been called the Golden Age in the treatment of disease by chemical agents—sulphonamides, drugs against malaria, the anti-histamines, and new anaesthetics and vaccines. It also produces the raw material for many of the manufactures on display in the supermarkets, from plastics, which can be moulded into almost any shape, to the synthetic fibres (such as terylene) and the latest dyes, which together provide the base for so many textiles. In addition fertilizers, insecticides, and new plant-controlling chemicals of many kinds play a part in agriculture as important as —though less obvious to the onlooker than—that played by tractors, of which Britain now has one to every thirty-two acres of arable land.

It is sometimes claimed that modern society depends on the chemist almost in the same sense as Victorian society depended on the engineer. In 1975 the chemical industry provided 11 per cent of British exports and was still growing fast. But, like the unhealthy factories produced by Victorian engineering, modern chemicals have their drawbacks—the tendency for human beings to rely overmuch on the curative properties of drugs, which often have undesired side-effects, and the threat to the countryside when the insufficiently controlled application of chemicals upsets the balance of Nature.

The Development of Industry in General: Steel

Big industrial corporations, such as the General Electric Company and Imperial Chemical Industries, each of which has more than 200 000 employees, now devote a great deal of money and man-power to research and development. The government supervises and guides fundamental studies through the Agricultural, Medical, Science, and Natural Environment Research Councils. Public money also finances, directly or indirectly, programmes of modernization in the

Steel works at Port Talbot, South Wales.

nationalized industries, which is all the more important because their number is increasing. The government by 1977 had major holdings in British Petroleum, British Leyland, and Rolls Royce, and was planning to take into public ownership a large part of the aircraft and shipbuilding concerns.

The great ironmasters played such a dominant role in the early phases of the growth of machine industry, and steel-making has become so fundamental to all modern economic development, that special interest attaches to the British Steel Corporation, created as a result of Wilson's nationalization measure of 1967. Six years later the

BSC embarked upon a ten-year programme of modernization and expansion. Technical changes include the replacement of the open-hearth process by the basic oxygen method for the bulk production of steel and by the use of the electric arc for specialized requirements. The BSC also plans to concentrate bulk production at a few main sites such as Port Talbot, which has a deep-water harbour for the importation of the iron-ore. But in spite of new investment amounting to more than £500 million, Britain is not likely to recover quickly from its present modest position as the seventh-largest steel producer, for in the present time of depression world production exceeds world demand.

Aircraft

The successes of the British aircraft industry during the Second World War continued in the 1950s with the production of such outstanding aircraft for civil use as the *Comet*, *Viscount*, and *Britannia*. In 1965 nearly one-half of the jet or turbo-prop aircraft in service or on order in any part of the world were powered from British sources. On the military side disappointments had been rather frequent and extremely expensive, but Britain still had a big lead in the production of vertical-take-off-and-landing or jump-jet fighters. Other widely used British aircraft are the *VC 10* and the *BAC One-Eleven*. Though the aircraft industry is by British standards a big one—it employs more people than shipbuilding and marine engineering together—the home market is very small, the costs of production are extremely high, and American and other foreign competition is very severe. But besides constructing aircraft Britain has an extensive sale of aero-engines, and is also a producer of helicopters, guided weapons, space vehicles, and a wide range of equipment and apparatus for aircraft and airfields.

British Airways and Air France together have designed and built a technological marvel in the *Concorde*, which in January 1976 inaugurated the world's first supersonic passenger service to South America and the Persian Gulf and a few months later to Washington, though environmentalists at first prevented landings in New York on the score of noise. Concordes have a cruising speed of 1350 m.p.h. but their development cost the fantastic sum of £1154 million, which is reflected in the purchase price of £20 million. Sales are also held up because they have to compete against two rivals—the US 'special performance' Boeing 747 jumbo-jet and the Russian TU 144.

A more definite commercial success has been achieved by the Hovercraft, a British invention with a simple basic concept: the ability of a jet engine to maintain a cushion of air beneath a disc, which can therefore be propelled at a height of a few feet above the surface of the

Concorde.

water. They were first used on river estuaries, and between the mainland and the Isle of Wight. In 1966 a cross-Channel ferry service was inaugurated, which is about three times as fast as by ship and now takes nearly one-third of the traffic. The Hovercraft is produced for export as well as home use.

Electrical and Electronic Engineering; Radio and Television

These two forms of engineering are very different from those in which Victorian Britain led the world (see p. 84); they change more rapidly and are the product of a world-wide competition in inventiveness. Electrical engineering concerns the manufacture of a wide range of equipment for producing and distributing electric power, from generators to cables. Then there are the domestic electrical appliances which are now deemed indispensable by most households, from fires to toasters, from the deep-freeze to the hair-drier. The electronics industry, too, is a manufacturer of up-to-date large-scale equipment—for the Post Office and other telecommunications networks or for the computers and other instrumentation used in big business. It also services the most advanced forms of scientific research, as in the case of the radio astronomer's study of radio emissions from outer space. Thus at Jodrell Bank the University of Manchester possesses one of the world's largest fully steerable radio telescopes, with a 250-foot reflector, known to the public on account of its successful tracking of earth satellites and space flights. But the small-scale consumer goods produced by the electronics industry interest us most, for they include such luxuries as high-fidelity audio equipment, as well as radio and television sets to be found in almost every home.

In our own day the inventions which minister most directly and widely to leisure enjoyment are certainly radio and television. The former benefited greatly from the American introduction of the transistor, which since 1948 has provided a much smaller and cheaper substitute for the valve. Hence the highly sophisticated portable radio, whose carrier need never for a moment be alone with his thoughts—unless, indeed, the thoughts of his neighbours become overpoweringly hostile! In addition, radio reception has been improved by the setting-up of a network of VHF (Very High Frequency) stations, and the content of the broadcast varied through the institution of local radio stations. The BBC set up the first of these in 1967, and they have grown to twenty in ten years, but independent local radio stations are now almost as numerous.

Television has a greater hold on the general public. In 1976 there were nearly 18 million licences issued—about half of them for the colour TV, first introduced by the BBC in 1967—and it was estimated that 95 per cent of the population saw television in their homes. Two very different organizations are concerned. The BBC, besides producing all radio programmes except those of the local independent stations, produces its own TV programmes. The IBA or Independent Broadcasting Authority is the successor to an Authority which was set up when the independent television began in 1954, and its function is to control, and operate transmitting stations for, programmes produced by commercial companies. The five biggest among the fifteen companies—Thames, ATV, Granada, Yorkshire and London Weekend—enjoy large revenues from the sale of advertising-time, so that their sumptuously produced serials have had even larger sales on the world market than the more sober output of the BBC. The Companies are also joint owners of Independent Television News. Both the BBC and the IBA belong to the European Broadcasting Union, which provides for exchange of programmes and for intercontinental television, received via satellite.

Towards automation: assistant engineer at the control desk of a nuclear reactor (Hinkley Point, Somerset).

Automation and Computers

No other contemporary industrial change seems likely to prove so significant in the long run as the growing use of computers and the drive towards automation. The words were rarely heard only a few years ago; in any case, a 'computer' was a person, not a thing. Modern computing machines make calculations by means of electronic devices which are capable of handling data with a speed and precision that could not be matched by a whole army of human beings. In this country they were first developed in Cambridge and Manchester in 1948–50, but since then their design and performance have become much more complex and refined. They are used for a great many purposes in science and in business, from the rarefied mathematical calculations required for rocket propulsion and space travel down to the financial problems of a single firm. Nevertheless, a great deal of research is still in progress to find out how best to formulate the programmes on which a computer acts, and to plan for new fields where it can be brought into operation.

The development of automation in industry depends very much upon the installation of computers, which makes it possible to devise systems of control so that the processes of production can be continued automatically without any human intervention. Automation has been introduced to a greater or lesser extent in many big industrial undertakings: a hall full of machinery with no one apparently in control is already a not uncommon sight. But the initial expense of introducing methods of automation is so high that its effect on the labour market in this country—though not in America—is still small. At present it merely accentuates the well-established tendency for the part of the working population engaged in actual manual labour to diminish.

In the long run, however, automation seems bound to create redundancy. Hours of work will then become much shorter—some prophets say that it will be a privilege to be allowed to work at all—whereupon a large part of the inventive capacity of the community, to say nothing of its educational activities, will go over to making due provision for the enjoyment of extended leisure.

Energy: the Sources of Power for Industry

Every technical advance described in this chapter has depended for any large-scale development upon the newer sources of power which, since the early days of the great industrial changes, have replaced the power derived from the physical strength of Man and his domesticated animals and from his devices for harnessing the wind and running water. One marked phenomenon of the last quarter-century has been the rapid increase in the extent to which we depend upon oil as the primary source for our consumption of energy. In 1950 its share of the whole was 10 per cent and in 1975, 42 per cent. The crude oil is now processed in twenty-two refineries, including those in Wales, Scotland, and Northern Ireland; the largest is at Fawley, near Southampton, with excellent facilities for tankers and an annual capacity of 18·9 million (metric) tonnes. The products refined from the petroleum (literally 'rock oil') are these: fuel oil, of which (in 1975) 42 per cent went to the generation of electricity and other large quantities to the steel and chemical industries and to paper-making; diesel oil for ships and 'derv' for diesel-engine road vehicles; petrol or motor spirit; kerosene; and finally bitumen.

Yet in 1975, 36·9 per cent of Britain's energy consumption was still derived from coal, which accounted for two-thirds of the fuel consumption of the electric power stations. Another important use was in coke ovens for steel-making. Some coal also went to factories where manufacturing processes required steam. But diesels had ousted coal from the railways, whilst there was also a big drop in the use of coal for domestic heating, which now takes less than one ton in ten. The quantity of coal mined annually has fallen during the last thirty years from 183 to 124 million tons (the decline is even more striking when we remember the peak production year—1913—before the First World War: then the mines produced 287 million tons, exported 94 million, and employed over a million workers). But the industry retains the solitary advantage that it exploits a native resource which will not quickly be exhausted, and of which new reserves are continually being discovered.

The labour force in the mines has declined from 700 000 to 244 000 since the National Coal Board took charge in 1947, it being the policy of the Board to increase productivity by installing advanced machinery, including machines which cut and load coal automatically on to conveyors. The Board has also sought to close down small, uneconomic units and to concentrate upon the development of the more productive collieries. Its ten-year programme of capital investment envisages the maintenance of the annual production of deep-mined coal at about 120 million tons and an increase to 15 million tons in the amount derived from open-cast mining, which is one of the post-war innovations.

The Gas Council and Area Gas Boards, set up at the time of nationalization, dealt with gas produced in the traditional way by the coking of coal. This was supplemented to some extent by production from oil-based installations, and in 1964 the first shipload of natural gas (liquefied before shipping) arrived in the Thames from Algeria. But the 17·1 per cent of Britain's energy consumption which now comes from gas comes entirely from natural gas, a matter to which reference will be made later (p. 296). Here it will be sufficient to note that rather more than half serves the purposes of industry and commerce; the rest is used domestically for heating and cooking.

Apart from the tiny 0·6 per cent derived from hydro-electric installations, the remaining source for our energy consumption is nuclear power, which contributes 3·4 per cent. A part of Britain's research into problems of atomic energy has been directed to military purposes, including its own atomic and hydrogen bombs and the construction of the four *Polaris* nuclear submarines, with an indefinite underwater cruising range and thermonuclear warheads in their sixteen missiles. But when the Atomic Energy Authority was set up in 1954 there were high hopes that, even without full American co-operation (see p. 264), research stations like Harwell, linked with experimental reactors such as Windscale or Dounreay, would produce big economic results. In 1956 our first nuclear power station, at Calder Hall in Cumbria, began to generate electricity for the national grid, and it was believed that steam-power for generators could be produced more cheaply in this way than by the use of coal or oil. By 1964 nuclear power stations were providing 3 per cent of our electricity; twelve years later a total of sixteen stations provided 9 per cent. Their cost has proved unexpectedly high, and the proposed substitution of the fast breeder reactor, which releases up to sixty times as much energy from the uranium, might prove altogether too hazardous for a congested island population.

Gas and Oil from the Sea-Bed

The island population has, however, found its geographical position extremely fortunate in relation to the extraction of natural gas and petroleum from under the shallow though turbulent waters of the North Sea, where only Norway has a larger share than Britain. The exploitation of gas began first, in 1965; ten years later, six major gasfields were in operation, and others were expected to be in use by 1980. Pipelines have been constructed to bring the gas ashore, the first at Easington in Humberside in 1967, and another at Bacton in Norfolk. Most of the old gasworks have disappeared from the landscape, and private consumers have had their appliances converted to take the new gas. The overall result is that in the five years 1970–75 the gas supply has more than doubled.

The first discovery of oil in the British sector of the North Sea was made in 1969; six years later, oil began to be brought ashore by tanker. The work carried on from the rigs involves considerable hardship and danger, albeit these platforms of steel and concrete are designed to

Natural gas terminal at Theddlethorpe, Lincolnshire.

withstand winds and waves of the utmost anticipated velocity and height. Submarine pipelines are also required; one has been built, for example, to link the Forties field with Cruden Bay, north of Aberdeen, and others are under construction to join adjacent fields to terminals on the Orkneys and Shetland. In 1975 a British National Oil Corporation was established, with its headquarters in Glasgow; besides providing for State participation in the industry, this new body was to exercise a tighter official control over exploration, development, and the installation of pipelines and refineries.

By the middle of 1976 five fields were producing, including the Forties field (mentioned above) which is one of the largest offshore oilfields in the world as known today; other fields have been discovered in our area of the North Sea, and yet others may await discovery. Production was 1·1 million tonnes in 1975; it was expected to cover up to one-third of the nation's needs in 1977; and according to the Secretary of State for Energy (who made the above forecast in December 1976) Britain was well on the way to being self-sufficient in oil by 1980.

Thus, if all goes well, the development of the North Sea oilfields will enormously strengthen our economic position. But caution is needed; apart from the obvious danger of counting our chickens before they are hatched, it is important to remember that these particular chickens will be regrettably short-lived. On the best showing, our seabed oil will make us self-sufficient for one complete generation. This is a world-wide problem: the Earth holds strictly limited and irreplaceable quantities of coal, oil and natural gas, all of which are being used up at a rapidly accelerating pace through the growth of population and of aspirations to a higher standard of living. Britain shares with the rest of mankind in the urgent need to conserve existing sources of energy and to search for new ones. In spite of its disappointments nuclear research may point a way, but hopes are also directed to the harnessing of the tides (as in the Severn barrage) or of the waves, to the use of the heat stored up in the centre of the Earth, or to the possibility of tapping in some direct way the life-giving energy of the Sun.

30 Provision for a changing population

The Continued Growth of the Population

As we saw in an earlier chapter (p. 20), a great increase in population was in part a cause and in part a result of the big industrial changes in eighteenth-century Britain. The growth accelerated further during the Victorian period (see p. 173), but it then slowed down, so that in the 1930s a fall in total numbers began to be seriously anticipated. However, this anticipation has proved to be wrong, as is clearly shown by the diagram (p. 299). Although estimates for 1981–2001 indicate that the increase in population is now being much more slowly achieved, the importance of the growth since the Second World War requires a brief examination of its causes.

Three factors may be distinguished. One is the increased expectation of life. The combined effect of better living conditions, great advances in medical science, and the provision of comprehensive health services has been to add twenty years to the average prospect of life for the child born now, as compared with children born in the first decade of the century. This improvement may be stated in a different way: although the proportion of older people is all the time increasing, the *total* death-rate has remained steady (at twelve per thousand) for more than forty years. Three of the critical periods in human life which are now much more commonly survived are the frailties of infancy, childhood's liability to infectious diseases, and the risk to women in childbirth. Maternal mortality, for example, has been reduced to one-thirteenth of what it was a generation ago.

A second factor has been the rise in the birth-rate, though it never looked like returning to its mid-Victorian level of thirty-five live births a year for each thousand of population. In 1938 it had fallen to 15·1, which largely explains the gloomy prognostications made in that decade. But just after the war there was a pronounced 'bulge in the birth-rate' (20·7 in 1947), and in spite of a temporary decline in the mid-1950s, it was not until the uncertain '70s that it fell below the level of 1938. The rise in the post-war years must largely reflect the increase of economic opportunity, which encouraged earlier marriage—the proportion of women marrying before the age of twenty-five was twice as great as it had been a generation earlier—and made a bigger family less burdensome to the parents. The family allowance for the second and subsequent children will also have played some part. As for the present decline, this may be attributable to economic uncertainties as well as to recent changes in birth control practices (the Pill) and in the legal availability of abortion.

Population of the United Kingdom* (Annual Abstract of Statistics 1976)

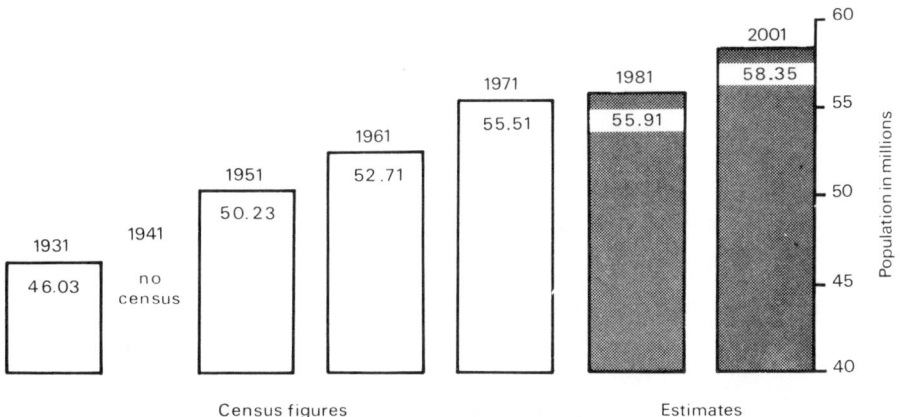

* The UK population figures include Northern Ireland, and therefore are larger than the totals in Table 1, Appendix II, which are for Great Britain only.

The third obvious factor in the growth of the population is the influence of migration into, and out of, our island. In the nineteenth century so many people left Britain for the United States and the Dominions, as already related (pp. 159–60), that the inward flow of foreigners, attracted by the economic and political freedom of British society, was completely outweighed. But after the First World War the Americans restricted immigration by a quota system, whilst as early as 1925 the impulse to move overseas from Britain was stated in a government paper to have been reduced by 'the cumulative effect of the various schemes of social insurance'.[1] In addition, the movement inwards began to increase. During the world economic depression of the early 1930s a good many British settlers were returning home, whilst by 1940 250 000 refugees from political persecution had crossed

[1] Report of Inter-Departmental Committee (Cmnd. 2608).

over from the Continent. One consequence is that present-day Britain contains an Anglo-Jewish religious community of 410 000 members, which is one of the largest Jewish communities in Europe.

By 1951 the migrations of two decades had added half a million to the total population. Then followed a period in which the renewed flow of emigrants to Canada, Australasia, and elsewhere was more than counterbalanced by the attraction which life in Britain with its advanced social services proved to possess for families from the British West Indies, Pakistan, India, and the former African colonies. This reached its climax in 1960–2, when net immigration amounted to 388 000 persons in three years, of whom about three-quarters were from Commonwealth countries. It was then found necessary to impose various legal controls on immigration, whilst in still more recent years the state of the economy has made emigration increasingly attractive to enterprising families. Thus in 1975 emigrants exceeded immigrants to the extent of 7300 leaving the United Kingdom for other Commonwealth countries, 5400 for other member states of the EEC, and 29 100 for the United States and elsewhere.

Changes in its Composition

The growth of population since 1945 is especially important because of the accompanying changes in the groups of which it is composed. The coloured immigrants and their children—most of whom are now United Kingdom citizens by birth—have in various respects proved difficult to assimilate. Two other causes of anxiety, real or unreal, are the 'brain-drain', supposed to result from the emigration of the best elements in the population, and the differential birth-rate, which is alleged to cause the least capable to multiply most rapidly. Finally, there are the basic problems arising from the changing age-structure of the whole community.

As far back as 1958 an ugly outburst of racial rioting at Notting Hill in West London drew attention to the animosities which easily arose out of the settlement in Britain of so many fellow-citizens from Commonwealth countries who differed from ourselves (and often also from each other) in appearance, language, social customs, and—in many cases—religion. But the well-established liberal tradition in such matters prevented any official action from being taken, whilst opportunities of work and housing caused large coloured quarters to grow up, not only in London, but also in big provincial cities, such as Birmingham, Wolverhampton, Nottingham, Bradford and Bristol. Finally, an Act was passed in 1962 to restrict immigration from the Commonwealth—also in principle from the Irish Republic—unless

Notting Hill Carnival—a multi-racial event in contemporary London.

the prospective immigrant had a job to go to or alternative means of support. With the addition of further legislation in 1968 and 1971, the inflow from the Commonwealth was reduced first to about one-quarter of its previous dimensions and eventually to 'a trickle'; but as late as 1976 (the year when the *Annual Register* employed this phrase) public opinion was disturbed about the reputedly large numbers of family dependants whom the law allowed immigrants to send for from their former home countries.

At the same time steps were taken to try to integrate the newcomers more effectively with the rest of the population. The Race Relations Acts of 1965 and 1968 set up a Race Relations Board and a Community Relations Commission to promote fair play between the various racial groups, white and coloured, and to prevent discrimination—by legal action if necessary—in matters of employment, housing, and services of all kinds. In 1976 these bodies were replaced by a single Commission for Racial Equality, but the situation remained very difficult. By 1973 the population of New Commonwealth (i.e. coloured) origin in Britain was officially estimated at 1 189 300 or more than 2 per cent of the whole, and it included 319 000 British-born children. Thus repatriation, as demanded by a lone-wolf Conservative politician, Mr Enoch Powell, and by small, militant groups of neo-Fascists, would be prodigiously expensive at Powell's proposed rate of £1000 a head and, in the case of the above-mentioned children, legally as well as morally impossible. On the other hand, the heavy incidence of unemployment among young coloured people had helped to bring about a serious increase in crimes of violence, whilst the disorders attending upon the annual West Indian carnival at Notting Hill were an unwelcome reminder for the general public of the fact that whole districts had been taken over by an imperfectly assimilated though colourful population. Although only about one-third of the immigrants had settled in Greater London, they attracted more attention there than in the provinces, both from the news media and from the neo-fascist National Front, which was set up in 1966. Soon after he became prime minister, Mr Callaghan made a timely appeal in the House of Commons that rising passions should not be allowed to destroy Britain's reputation as a tolerant, cohesive and unified society.

The term 'brain-drain' refers to the loss through emigration of some proportion of the engineers, doctors, and professional scientists who have been born and educated in this country, largely at the public expense. In the case of medical practitioners it was stated in the House of Commons ten years ago that the annual loss was of the order of 300–350, tempted to go abroad at the height of their careers by better salaries and greater opportunities. But it is not clear how far the loss is made good by the number of professional men and women who return disillusioned from their foreign experiences and by immigrants, such as the doctors from other parts of the Commonwealth, who help to staff the Health Service.

The influence of the differential birth-rate is likewise uncertain. The least able and most feckless groups are alleged to have the largest families, whereas the most intelligent are the most careful to practise a strict limitation. This would mean a decline in average intelligence for the nation as a whole, which might also explain the decline and fall of earlier civilizations. It is true that size of family increases as one goes down the social scale, and that intelligence tests produce lower average results from children of large families than from those of small ones. But experts disagree. Is social status to be equated with intelligence, it may be asked, and is the kind of intelligence measured by intelligence tests necessarily the most valuable asset to society?

The changing age-structure of the population is a more definite cause for anxiety, since the number of elderly people and children, the two big dependent groups, is very large in comparison with those in the 16–65 age-group on whom they depend. The proportion is about forty non-workers to every sixty workers. Machinery has, of course, greatly reduced the input of human labour now needed to produce any given quantity of goods and services. On the other hand, each individual now has much higher expectations than before—and, as we have seen, the total number of individuals to be provided for is still on the increase.

In the late Victorian period, when literally millions of the Queen's subjects lived on the very margin of subsistence—the sort of 'living' that Charles Booth described (see p. 180)—the increase of numbers (which was going on at a great pace all the time) may have meant much to each family concerned, but there was no special problem for the community in squeezing more people in. It is very different now-adays, when each child born in the United Kingdom can expect to receive something like equal treatment. In the long run he or she represents a claim on the working population for all kinds of amenities, from well-designed housing and travel facilities to pure air and uncontaminated water. These are matters to which reference will be made in the next chapter of this book. Here we will only notice that, if all babies born today are potential car-owners, their demands on the motor industry must follow a long period during which they are provided by the community with school desks, the books to put into them, and the basic education without which they could not even aspire to become learner-drivers.

Changing Schools

After the Second World War the large increase in the number of children to be educated—including those who stayed on at school because of the raising of the leaving-age to fifteen—would in any case have made it imperative to build more schools and train more teachers. But it was also an age of rising expectations, in which each child needed to be taught to play a part in an increasingly complex economic system, in which qualified scientists and technologists would be enormously in demand, and in which the future citizen also needed to learn how to make proper use of more abundant leisure. Of course, other organizations were concerned here besides the schools; youth club activities, for example, expanded to such an extent that by 1972,

Edwardian education: Standard II receives an object lesson on oranges.

68 per cent of all young people were believed to have been members at some time. But the bulk of the work fell upon the educational authorities, whom the post-war bulge in the birth-rate seems to have taken by surprise.

Between 1945 and 1960 attendance at publicly maintained primary and secondary schools rose from about 5 million to nearly 7 million. Not only were buildings too small and teachers too few, but the difficulties were accentuated by the fact that much more provision was needed for the sixth forms of the grammar schools, because the abolition of fees by the Act of 1944 encouraged pupils to stay longer. This in turn led to heavy pressure upon admission to universities. However, a big though belated programme of educational expansion brought several thousand new schools into existence and made improvements to many of the older ones, educational expenditure as a whole being almost trebled in the ten years 1953–63. This was a considerable achievement, even after allowance is made for rising prices; it meant that, out of our total effort expressed in terms of the GNP (gross national product), the proportion devoted to education

Education today: a Junior School class.

rose from more than 3 to over 5 per cent. The latter figure compared favourably with the efforts made in most countries, the United States and Soviet Russia being among the important exceptions.

In 1972, the year when the leaving age was raised to sixteen, a ten-year programme was announced for England and Wales, together with parallel developments for the separately administered educational systems of Scotland and Northern Ireland. Expenditure was to be increased on nursery schools, school buildings of all kinds, and the provision of a higher ratio of staff to pupils. By 1975, indeed, the programme had been scaled down because of the nation's economic difficulties, and also because the authorities—to their surprise—had now to budget for the educational consequences of the fall in birth-rate (see p. 298). But in that year Britain had about 38 000 schools attended by over 11 million children, of whom 10¼ million were being educated at the public expense.

What did they learn? The content of primary education had been fairly fully developed through long experience. But Butler's Act of 1944 set up a new tripartite system of secondary education in grammar schools, secondary modern schools, and technical schools. The entry into the different types of school was settled—in practice, once and for all—by each child's performance in the 'eleven-plus' examination. The technical schools were very few; the grammar-school places were hotly competed for, on grounds which included their traditional prestige; and the result was that the secondary modern schools seemed often to shape their curricula mainly to the supposed needs of the 'also-rans'. Moreover, there was a good deal of evidence that children from careful middle-class homes got grammar-school places that their intellectual merits did not deserve, because they could express themselves better in many kinds of test than more intelligent late-developers from a working-class background.

Early experiments showed the advantages of an alternative system, under which all children of secondary-school age in any neighbourhood would attend a single comprehensive school. Its large size would enable it to offer a very wide range of subjects to suit all tastes and—in principle—every opportunity of transfer from group to group in accordance with varying rates of individual development. But the large size also provided a strong argument for critics, who pointed out the loss to the community if its intellectually ablest children were to suffer a lifelong handicap through immersion in huge institutions designed first and foremost to meet the needs of the less-gifted majority. Be that as it may, the comprehensive system fitted in with the more democratic and egalitarian outlook of a new age, so that it gained ground rapidly with the London and other major urban education authorities.

The Labour government of 1964–70 required all local authorities to accept the comprehensive school as the basis for their educational planning, and although some areas and individual schools have offered a stout legal resistance, by 1977 the proportion of children in England and Wales who attended comprehensive schools had risen in ten years from 14 to 80 per cent. The big city comprehensives usually have an age-range of 11–18; others have middle and senior schools, or there may be an age-range of 11–16, followed by a Sixth-Form College. More than 800 secondary modern schools and a few secondary technical schools still survived, together with 407 grammar schools. These included many Direct Grant schools, which faced the alternative of joining the comprehensive system or forfeiting their grant and becoming wholly independent of State support, as are the public schools. They were encouraged to make the latter choice by seeing the prosperity which the public schools have enjoyed—in spite of rising costs—during the thirty years in which state education has become increasingly democratic.

The Expansion of Higher Education

One obvious link between the schools and higher educational institutions is the dependence of the former upon the latter for the teaching staff without which they could not function at all, however up-to-date the buildings might be. After the Second World War there was an acute shortage of teachers, especially in mathematics and natural science, because qualifications in those subjects opened the way to so many posts in industry and research. Marriage also removed a high proportion of women teachers from the schools within a very short time after they had completed their training. The growth of the universities, to which we shall turn shortly, in time increased the availability of graduates, whilst in 1965 the government took steps to double the number of teachers in training at colleges of education. Ten years later, however, the numbers to be trained had to be cut down in line with the lower estimates of future school-pupils based on the birth-rate, so some colleges of education were closed whilst others became 'liberal arts' colleges, whose courses envisage other occupations besides teaching, or have been merged as education departments in polytechnics. These complicated rearrangements are intended to serve a further important purpose—the development of a system in which every British teacher will have graduated at a university.

The number of universities in Britain has grown in thirty years from seventeen to forty-five, including eighteen which have received their charter since 1960. In 1974–5 they provided for just over a quarter of a million full-time students, of whom one-fifth were postgraduates, and nearly a half were accommodated in residential halls and colleges. Thus the pre-war situation has been transformed out of all recognition, which is indisputably to the national advantage, albeit the cynics point out that more does not necessarily mean better. That there remains an unfulfilled demand for university studies is shown by the success of the Open University, which was set up in 1971 to enable persons who lack the normal academic qualifications and opportunities for regular study to obtain university degrees notwithstanding. At the end of five years some 50 000 students were following the courses provided, which employ television, radio, instruction by correspondence, and attendance at summer schools.

Apart from the universities, the biggest expansion in higher education has been achieved through the polytechnics, of which England and Wales now have thirty, their counterpart in Scotland being the Central Institutions and in Northern Ireland the Ulster College. These provide courses in almost all subjects and at all levels, including many of the 'sandwich courses' in which part-time study is combined with work in industry. Although polytechnics and similar centres for advanced study cannot confer their own degrees, many of their courses are approved for degrees and other academic qualifications conferrable since 1964 by a new Council for National Academic Awards. One important result is to stimulate technological studies, in which Britain has for several generations appeared to lag behind her continental competitors.

Provision for the Aged

It is natural that the middle age-groups in the community, on whose directly productive work we all depend, should be willing to finance the enormous educational developments which have just been outlined, for this is plainly an investment in the nation's future. It is also natural that they should be less ready to finance equally big developments for the benefit of the aged, for this would be the payment of an uncertain debt to the nation's past. The Health Service plus the provisions of National Insurance result in a long average period of retirement, which normally begins at sixty-five for men and at sixty for women. This in itself represents great social progress, but thirty years have passed without an effective handling of the further problem of the integration into the community of this constantly increasing class of 'Senior Citizens'. Indeed, this American term, now employed by our own Central Office of Information, would strike many of them as intensely ironical, since they are all too often allowed to feel that they no longer belong anywhere.

In 1971, 19 per cent of men and 12 per cent of women remained at work for a time after retiring-age, a proportion which is encouraged to rise by those enterprising firms which experiment with light employment for pensioners. But to a great extent the energies of elderly people, who find themselves suddenly retired from an occupation for which they are not yet physically unfit, have little outlet beyond the running of their own homes. The only collective provision for their needs is through about 7000 social clubs of all kinds and sizes and the rather more systematic activities of Old People's Welfare Committees under the auspices of the National Council of Social Service.

As regards the aged and infirm—a category into which even the most able-bodied of the elderly must eventually fall—the geriatric wards of hospitals are still unable to cope with more than a small fraction of their need for help. Since 1945 about 2500 small homes have been opened by local authorities; these provide for 1·5 per cent of the over-sixty-fives—a meagre amount, which is however extensively supplemented by the efforts of churches and many private organizations. Local authorities also try to keep old people in their own homes as long as possible by building one-room flats and bungalows adapted to their needs. Finally, there are services designed to mitigate the plight of the many who must continue to live alone when they can no longer look after themselves completely. These include 'meals-on-wheels'—a subsidized portion of ready-cooked food, brought round by the WRVS; the ministrations of Local Authority 'home helps'; and especially that of the district nurses, who on an average spend more than half their time in work of this sort.

Pensioners are the first to suffer from each rise in the price level. In April 1975, for example, when state retirement pensions were increased by 16 per cent, the voluntary organization known as 'Age Concern' estimated that, nevertheless, retired persons would be worse off by October than they had been two years before. Moreover, the older the pensioner becomes, the harder it is in most cases for him to be articulate about his needs or to make new contacts of any kind. The mobility of our modern way of life accentuates this difficulty, because an increasing proportion of the old find themselves to be living on in neighbourhoods from which their relations and younger friends have long since vanished—to a new housing estate or possibly to work in another town. Really lonely old people, those who have no one to look to for assistance on the basis of family or friendship, are therefore more numerous than ever before. As these senior citizens are still increasing, we have here one of the biggest problems in giving reality to the concept of citizenship in the welfare state.

31 Control of the environment

New Brooms Sweep Clean?

The rising expectations which followed the war, the triumphs of technology, and the changing structure of the population have all had a big impact upon the physical conditions of life on our island. England now has 923 persons to accommodate in every square mile, and although the Scots and Welsh are less thick on the ground, the entire United Kingdom is one of the very few countries in the world where the average density of population approaches 600 per square mile. In comparison with some of our more disciplined neighbours we continued rather longer with *laissez-faire* policies as regards land-use and development; and whilst successive governments have been busy catching up in this respect, they have also become involved, along with the rest of the civilized world, in the attempt to solve the increasingly complex problems of pollution.

It is therefore interesting to see that, almost exactly a century after the establishment of the first small-scale Local Government Board (p. 165), a Department of the Environment was brought into existence to meet the needs of the present day. It is headed by a Secretary of State, whose responsibilities range from the control of housing and local government, through all-purpose planning of the environment, to its protection from pollution and the conservation of natural resources. To a great extent, however, these wide powers are exercised by delegation to, and supervision of, subordinate bodies, the most important being the elected local government authorities. Just as each school has closer day-to-day relations with the Local Education Authority than with the Department of Education and Science, so the individual citizen is chiefly brought into contact with the Department of the Environment through policies and plans which are enforced by his local council.

Here too, recent years have brought drastic changes in a system which had survived with little alteration since the last decades of the nineteenth century (see pp. 166–7). It had been under review since the 1950s, criticism being directed at the multiplicity of authorities and anomalies of size, such as the fact that Rutland, having returned two knights of the shire to the Model Parliament of 1295, continued to rank as a modern county on the same level as Lancashire with a hundred times its population. In 1963 London was reorganized as a two-tier authority, composed of the Greater London Council and thirty-two Councils of London Boroughs, redefined to represent equal populations. But there were two exceptional arrangements; the ancient Corporation of the City, with a resident population of less than 6000, was to remain and be treated as a borough, and education in the twelve central London boroughs was entrusted to a special Inner London Education Authority. Six years later the Redcliffe–Maud Commission pointed out that ancient divisions, intended to keep town and country apart, no longer fitted the pattern of life and work and constituted an artificial barrier to the proper planning of development and transport. Instead the Commission proposed that, except in Birmingham, Manchester, and Liverpool, all services should be administered by fifty-eight unitary authorities, dividing the whole of England and Wales (outside London) among them. This was acceptable to the Labour Government, but not to its Conservative successor, which passed the Local Government Act of 1972 and subsequent legislation for Scotland and Northern Ireland.

The upshot has been the institution of a two-tier system for England and Wales, based on fifty-three counties (in which the old county boroughs have been merged) and 369 districts, formed out of the boroughs and districts already in existence, to whose councils only the smaller services are assigned. But in six 'metropolitan counties' comprising densely populated urban areas—Greater Manchester, Merseyside, South Yorkshire, Tyne and Wear, West Midlands, and West Yorkshire—the second tier is made up of 'metropolitan districts'; these have a minimum population of 200 000 and are responsible for certain of the large-scale services.

The casual observer notes that, even in England, old names like Rutland have disappeared and new ones emerged, such as Avon and Cumbria. In Wales and Scotland changes of nomenclature are more radical, so that the less erudite of the natives—to say nothing of the tourists—sometimes have difficulty in placing Gwynedd, Clwyd, Grampian, and Strathclyde. The student of administration has graver doubts as to whether the sacrifice of time, money, and tradition will be justified in the long run by a marked improvement in the detailed control of the environment. And those who look for guidance in such matters to the vagaries of party politics draw their conclusions from the fact that, in the summer of 1977, a different solution was being put forward by Labour pundits, who would put an end to county councils, institute twelve regional authorities, and give wider powers to a reduced number of district councils.

The Housing of the People

This was a problem with which local authorities had grappled during the inter-war period, but in 1939 slum clearance and the reduction of overcrowding were nowhere completed tasks and in Scotland they were at most half-done. Then came the enormous destruction of housing in the Second World War, which made it necessary to rebuild the central areas of a number of cities, such as Coventry, Plymouth, and Bristol; to undertake big schemes in almost every part of the metropolis; and to replace a considerable proportion of house property in Manchester, Liverpool, Birmingham, Glasgow and many smaller urban centres—not to mention villages, which were often bombed in error.

The consequence was that ten years after the end of hostilities the number of slum houses still in occupation was estimated at 1 million. Since then large slum areas have been cleared; this has involved the rehousing of over 3 million people, as for example in the notorious Gorbals district of Glasgow, where the old tenements on the south bank of the Clyde have been replaced by high-rise flats interspersed with smaller blocks, all of modern design. Nevertheless, the deterioration of old buildings and stricter definitions of what constitute slum conditions combine to produce a situation in which the local authorities in regions of early industrialization still have a slum problem to face. In 1975, for example, 60 000 houses were demolished or closed, which meant that local authorities had to provide elsewhere for the people who were displaced.

By degrees, however, public and private enterprise between them have met the general demand for new homes of a higher standard than before the war, both in lieu of what was destroyed and to provide for the rise in population and requirements. In 1954, when Macmillan had charge of housing in the last Churchill government, the number of new dwellings (i.e. houses and flats) erected in one year reached 300 000, and by 1975 the total was nearly 9 million—a post-war dwelling for two families in five throughout Britain. Nearly half are nowadays provided by public authorities and nearly half by private interests, with a small balance of 5 per cent by housing associations. Almost four-fifths of all households occupy a separate house; more than one-half of all dwellings are owned by the occupiers; and the total number of dwellings, both owned and rented, corresponds fairly closely to the total number of households. Not every problem has

High-rise flats—residential council blocks in Roehampton.

been solved, however. Older houses still need modernization to bring them up to contemporary standards. New housing designs have their defects, such as those complained of by people, especially the elderly, living in isolation on the top floors of near-skyscrapers. Both mortgage repayments and 'fair rents' present special difficulties in a time of prolonged economic crisis.

Land Use and Development

Housing competes with agriculture, industry, facilities for transport and the needs of open-air leisure activities for a share of space in our crowded island. The Town and Country Planning Act of 1944, which began the practice of state control over areas of land which had already been developed but needed redevelopment (as in the case of bombed sites), has had more far-reaching successors. Today large-scale planning of this kind is among the most important functions of the county councils, as is its detailed implementation for the district councils, though the Department of the Environment may intervene at either level by sending its inspector to hold an inquiry. Under the Community Land Act of 1975 local authorities will eventually be the suppliers of all land for private development; already, the owner of land requires planning permission before he can develop it.

Regional Economic Planning Councils—eight in England plus comparable councils in Wales, Scotland, and Northern Ireland—advise the Ministry of the Environment over the broad strategy of land use, which determines where factories or commercial activities should be concentrated. This is particularly important for the north and west, which suffer from depression and unemployment; the Industry Act of 1972 made financial aid available to firms moving into these Assisted Areas, which are graded in three categories according to the urgency of their needs. Three years later a National Enterprise Board was set up, which invests public funds in the development or restructuring of concerns which are expected in due course to become remunerative.

A considerable part of the planning and building effort of the nation has gone into carrying out the New Towns Act of 1946, which entitled the government—after consulting the local interests affected—to designate any area of land as the site for a new town. Its establishment would then become the task of a Development Corporation, financed from public sources and empowered to acquire land and provide houses, factories, offices, and essential services. Twenty-nine such towns have been designated, of which twenty-one are in England (eleven of them to relieve the congestion of London), two in Wales, and six in Scotland. In spite of their artificial origins, which meant that they started without the traditions and special local atmosphere accumulated by older settlements, the new towns are said to be 'generally recognized as one of the most successful post-war experiments, both socially and industrially, and as a profitable long-term investment'.[1]

Yet here too—as in the case of tall blocks of flats and new types of education—time has revealed some disadvantages. By 1977, Stonehouse, the sixth of the Scottish new towns, was being 'de-designated', for it was felt that the very success of the new towns as a whole had contributed towards devitalizing the city centres in the older urban areas. Instead of draining population into new towns—and into some older ones (such as Aylesbury and Basingstoke) which had been helped to expand under the Town Development Act of 1952—the government now intended to bring back homes and industry to city centres; these were very largely deserted outside office hours, which was uneconomic and a temptation to vandals.

[1] Central Office of Information; Britain: An Official Handbook (1977 edition) p. 168.

The Greenfaulds area of Cumbernauld New Town, Scotland.

South-east England has special problems of its own. Rather more than 7 million people live in Greater London, which provides an enormous amount of administrative, commercial, and industrial employment. But the population of inner districts declines, whilst the rising number of those who commute to work from outer London creates complex difficulties of transportation. Decentralization of government departments—the Post Office Savings Bank transferred to Glasgow, for instance, and part of the Inland Revenue to South Wales; a ban on the building of new offices in central London; and the direction of industry away from the metropolis are methods which have been tried to alleviate the almost intolerable pressure. But the south-eastern region as a whole continues to attract population, because of its climatic advantages and amenities for residence and because of the greater variety of jobs and opportunities of all kinds.

Public control of development in any region involves endless difficulties and conflicts of interest. Nevertheless, it does much to mitigate the effects of the constant necessary encroachment of building of one sort or another upon what is left of our empty spaces. The fitting-together of housing estates, shopping centres, and factory areas is obviously a matter for experts; but we can all of us appreciate the relevance of good advance-planning in such matters as the location of swimming-pools, sports grounds, and stadia, or in the preservation of a 'green belt' round the heavily built-up inner nucleus of a town.

One very striking development since 1949 has been the institution of National Parks. There are now seven in England and three in Wales, covering 9 per cent of the total area, as well as five Scottish districts under the control of National Park Directions. These national parks, and the 'forest parks' controlled by the Forestry Commission, are areas in which farming and similar activities continue but where amenities are carefully preserved—sometimes by subsidies to private landowners—and public access is made as easy as possible. Some of the finest and wildest parts of the country are included, such as the Lake District, Snowdonia, and Loch Maree in the north-western Highlands, and there are extensive footpaths like the 250-mile Pennine Way.

Road Traffic

As we saw in an earlier chapter (p. 236), even before the war road traffic was increasing to an extent which brought the railways into difficulties. Since the war their plight has become worse, but we may first consider the roads, where one very important new feature is the presence of private motor cars in numbers which show that they are now possessed by average working families. In 1949–70 they increased from 2 to 11½ million (plus 1 100 000 motorcycles) and were still increasing as fast as the state of the economy allowed. By 1975 the number of motorized vehicles of all kinds licensed to use the roads was 17½ million—a total which created all-too-familiar bottlenecks at certain times and places and a general pressure with which the pre-war road network could not possibly have coped.

To deal with the problem, a long-term scheme was started, based on the diversion of the bulk of the fast-moving, long-distance road traffic to new motorways, characterized by greater width, fewer curves, and better surfaces. The programme for this began to take shape in the 1950s, and by 1975 major routes had been opened in most parts of the country, so that it is possible to travel all the way from Exeter to Carlisle, for example, by motorway. The needs of the motorways also stimulated the execution of the largest British bridge-building programme for over a century, including a new suspension bridge over the Firth of Forth in 1964, followed two years later by a bridge over the Severn estuary giving better access to South Wales. Existing main roads have also been improved, such as the A1 from London to Edinburgh, which Telford had offered to redesign soon after the Battle of Waterloo, and even the one-vehicle-wide Highland roads with their occasional passing-places have in many cases been replaced by modern thoroughfares. As far north as Fort William one now finds

Viaduct carrying the South Wales motorway into London.

the by-pass brought into use, which has been employed to save the historic High Streets of so many ancient cities farther south from being flooded with through-traffic.

But in spite of all that has been done, the roads are still a constant source of dangerous frustration, and the number of deaths in road accidents (6350 in 1975) is a tragic comment on the failures of our society. Nor is it only vehicles in motion which cause trouble; they also cause congestion and confusion when they stop, crowding into what were once quiet streets and squares and creating demands for further parking space which are a constant headache to town-planners. Proposals have been made for severely penalizing or even totally prohibiting the use of private motor cars in the central areas of large towns. This, however, is a mere palliative, if we accept the daunting prospect suggested by the Buchanan Report in the early 60s, namely that within the next half-century the number of road vehicles of all kinds to be somehow accommodated in our island will rise to approximately 40 million.

It is natural for most of us to think of road traffic primarily in terms of the public or private transport of which we ourselves make daily use. But a high proportion of road vehicles, including the largest and heaviest, serve the needs of industry and commerce. At the present day a calculation based on weight and distance shows that 66 per cent of all freight is carried by road, as compared with 17 by rail, 14 by coastal shipping, and 3 per cent by canal or pipeline. Every new growth of

Hovercraft.

industry brought about by modern technology therefore creates a road problem; likewise each major addition to the dock facilities required for our exports and imports. We have seen (p. 155) how docks were built and extended to meet nineteenth-century requirements; in the same way our own generation must provide for an enormous influx of oil, for such novelties as container and roll-on/roll-off traffic, and even for hovercraft services. Accordingly, big dock developments have been taking place at Tilbury, Liverpool, and Bristol. Bristol West Dock, which was opened by the Queen in Jubilee Year, is of particular interest, having the largest entrance lock in Britain and discharging its traffic by a road link of less than a mile on to one of the new motorways.

The Railways

No evidence of modern progress was viewed by Victorian eyes with more complacency than the great railways (see p. 121), but in our own day their ubiquity has helped to make them one of the most problematic features of the environment. In the London Passenger Transport Area and a few provincial conurbations they suffer like the roads from overcrowding; but their main trouble has been the opposite one—reduction of traffic. In addition to heavy competition from road transport, they lose passengers and light freights to the air services. Accordingly, the nationalization of the railways after the war was followed by a long period of decline, in spite of a big modernization plan introduced in 1955, providing for stage-by-stage electrification of the more important lines, the replacement of steam-locomotives by diesels, and other improvements. For these cost more money than the value of the traffic they attracted, so that by 1962 the deficit totalled £150 million.

In the following year, however, Dr Beeching's *Report on the Reshaping of British Railways* marked the beginning of more drastic changes. This expert from private industry pointed out that one-third of the lines carried only 1 per cent of the passenger traffic, and in spite of the outcry from aggrieved localities, he had many of these lines closed down, at any rate as regards passenger services. On the other hand, Beeching saw that main-line services could be made competitive, partly by providing fast and frequent passenger trains between the principal cities, and partly by speeding up goods traffic with the help of new types of wagon, computer-operated marshalling yards, and express container-services. Since October 1976 the Western Region has had 'high-speed trains' which can keep up 125 mph, and in 1978 Glasgow was to be brought within four hours of London by the 'advanced passenger train', reaching 155 mph. Nevertheless, it is likely that the canny Scottish businessman, borne through the countryside in conditions of extreme efficiency and comfort, will still be making two uncomfortable reflections. One, that rail travel inside the metropolitan area will present him with contrasting conditions of overcrowding and inconvenience; the other, that in spite of much higher fares and freight charges British Rail continues to operate at a loss, and that its staff of a quarter of a million is by no means backward in stating and enforcing its wage demands.

In 1973, the year in which Britain joined the EEC, the British and French governments signed a Channel Tunnel treaty. This was a project with a long history—both I. K. Brunel and Robert Stephenson were among the great railway engineers who had once been interested—which in its modern form would have brought a double benefit to the railways: there would be a through service for passengers and freight between the British and French networks, and vehicle-ferry trains for the short distance under the Channel. The scheme was officially abandoned in 1975, chiefly because Britain's economic difficulties made it impossible to face the cost of reconstructing the rail routes feeding in to the tunnel on our side, but it has since been resuscitated by the EEC.

Air Services

To some extent the need for the long-discussed Channel Tunnel has been reduced by the meteoric rise of air transport. In every part of the world passengers and freight are conveyed by air to an extent which before the war was scarcely envisaged outside the pages of science fiction. Inside Britain not only the major centres of population and industry but even the remoter areas, such as the Highlands and Islands of Scotland, now have some share of regular air services. The continents are brought so close to each other that it has proved practicable for an enterprising television star named David Frost to twinkle in New York all through the week and in London every weekend. As for holidays, the European Grand Tour, which occupied an eighteenth-century 'milord' for many months, can be performed in a short series of hour-long air hops (though the cultural profit is doubtless smaller); or winter warmth on southern Mediterranean shores can be reached from London almost as quickly as Brighton was by its well-wrapped-up visitors of December 1879 (see p. 192–3). In 1962 the number of passengers entering or leaving Britain by air slightly exceeded that of passengers by sea; thirteen years later it was almost twice as great.

The principal airlines were converted into two public corporations, British Overseas Airways (1940) and British European Airways, added in 1946. In 1972 these became divisions of British Airways, which operates the largest route network in the world, almost half a million miles, with 170 destinations in eighty countries. Charter traffic is conducted mainly by independent companies, and British Airways still makes an annual loss of about £16 million—about a quarter of that incurred by the railways. The Civil Aviation Authority, which was set up at the same time as British Airways, is ultimately responsible for the enforcement of safety regulations and flight controls, apart from the management of seven big airfields (Heathrow, Gatwick, Stansted, and four in Scotland) by the British Airports Authority, set up by statute in 1966.

Problems of Pollution

High speed on a motorway; smooth, fast travel on an advanced passenger train; supersonic flight in Concorde—these are three of the recent triumphs of technology in which we might all find satisfaction and a sense of progress. But technology has its dark side also—the shrinkage of the unspoilt Nature, which Man used to have freely at his disposal; the industrial accidents and disasters, reported so often by the media; and the pollution, which is only beginning to receive the attention it deserves. One might perhaps adapt a striking phrase from Mr Heath and describe pollution as 'the unacceptable face' of technology. What are we to do with the waste products which arise from the technical processes of modern manufacture, when their proper disposal is expensive and time-consuming? They are got rid of in the cheapest possible way—as smoke, as effluents, in slag heaps, or in rubbish pits—with results which justify the claim, 'Most pollution comes from getting rid of waste at the lowest possible cost'.

Whilst the rapid advances of technology, culminating in nuclear installations, render the problem more urgent and more dangerous, it arises also from the growth of population. As long as the people of Britain were few in relation to the habitable area of the island, waste products could without difficulty be absorbed by the soil, the rivers, and the surrounding seas. It was only in the eighteenth century that London, as we have seen (pp. 7–8), became a huge metropolis with serious problems of pollution, which assumed an even graver character as people pressed into the new industrial areas. Since then the continued growth of the population has presented each generation with new pollution problems—down to the spoiling of the countryside, or such parts of it as have not already been built over, by the noise and debris of the unappreciative traveller, who did not matter when travellers were few. Today, even so remote and impressive a sight as a prehistoric 'Pictish broch' may be completely spoilt for the sensitive tourist by the rusty tin cans which record the visit of some modern vandal.

Legislation in these matters is plentiful, and the work of the NERC, already mentioned (p. 288), has been supplemented since 1970 by that of a Royal Commission on Environmental Pollution, which issues reports at frequent intervals. One instance of successful action is the banishment from urban life of the smoke-laden fog, alias 'smog', which Dickens was so fond of describing and which, as recently as December 1952, was deemed responsible for the deaths of several thousand Londoners. The Clean Air Act of 1956, making it possible to establish compulsory smoke-free zones, increased winter sunshine in central London by 70 per cent in ten years, and similar results have been achieved in other cities, such as Glasgow. The Water Act of 1973 provides pure water supplies, by methods which include the enforcement of stricter standards in local authority arrangements for the disposal of sewage. Fish swim again in the Thames; fewer coastal beaches suffer from contamination; and it required an unprecedentedly dry season in 1976 to show that the quantity as distinct from the quality of the water supply needed further measures of conservation. The Litter Act of 1958 introduced the imposition of a fine for leaving your unwanted property behind you on any land to which the public has free access, and if deliberate dumping becomes a habit the Civic Amenities Act of 1967 provides a cure by enabling the miscreant to be put behind bars for three months at a time. Lastly, we may notice the comprehensive Control of Pollution Act (1974), which codifies and amplifies existing legislation to reduce pollution in all three elements (land, water, and air), giving local authorities new powers and duties, such as the right to establish 'noise abatement zones'. In addition, this Act concerns itself with yet another environmental problem of mounting significance, namely the need to recycle waste containing materials of which the global supply may soon be in danger of exhaustion.

But many of these problems tend to outrun our efforts to catch up with them. During the term which Prince Charles spent in Wales as a university student, he found time to point out that 'in South Wales nearly an acre disappears under mine wastage every three days'; in England and Scotland, too, almost any one of his future subjects could point to beauty spots degenerating into eyesores. And whilst the effects of mining are an example of environmental troubles which date back to the early days of industrial development—and which were for a long time ignored by those in authority—some of the industries which are now developing fastest confront us with new hazards. The application to soil and crops of new chemical preparations, which kill off some pests and noxious growths but provide an unexpected stimulus to others, constitutes a large-scale threat to Nature, just as the chemicals in our food and medicines may upset the balance of Nature in the human body. Our increasing dependence upon the oil industry involves two separate hazards—the pollution of the urban environment by the accumulated fumes from internal-combustion engines of all kinds, and that of the coastline by the wrecking of a giant tanker or, still worse, by an uncontrolled blow-out from a North Sea oil-rig. Most ominous of all, there are the dangers of nuclear fall-out and nuclear waste, for the problems arising from the much-disputed development of nuclear power stations are overshadowed by those of nuclear armaments, where the environment at risk extends to the whole biosphere.

Leading scientists have urged the setting-up of a national 'Doom-watch' to prevent us from destroying ourselves. But in their extremer forms these environmental problems are an international concern, for which both the UN and the EEC have programmes. Industrial pollution, for example, transcends national boundaries—deposits from British factories, for instance, are clearly traceable above the snow-level in the mountains of western Norway—so the Council of Ministers of the Nine made a good start when they laid down the principle in November 1974 that the polluter pays the cost of damage done.

32 Paying our way

How we are to pay our way is the central problem of life and work in contemporary Britain. And in considering this problem—in other words, in looking at the national economy as a whole—the first thing to be borne in mind is that Britain is not self-supporting. Most countries nowadays depend to some extent upon international trade, but Britain does so to an exceptionally great extent. As a crowded population on a small island with only modest natural resources, we have to produce goods and services for the outside world in order that we may buy the necessary foodstuffs and raw materials and some hardly less indispensable machinery. So long as we are able to do this, we can prosper; if the ability begins to fail, then we face decline.

The profusion of goods in the shops and supermarkets and the crowds of shoppers show that plenty of individuals are well able to pay their way. But what about the nation as a whole? An individual may be living on inherited wealth, social insurance, or credit—which really means that someone else produces the goods for him. To some extent and for a limited period a nation can do the same—perhaps by using up the capital accumulated by an earlier generation or by raising foreign loans. But the capital is a wasting asset, and foreigners will not lend unless there is a good prospect of eventual repayment; so in the long run prosperity depends upon carrying out successfully the complicated process of modern production and exchange.

British prosperity in the first two decades after the Second World War had a genuine basis in industrial and commercial achievement. But even then minor economic crises, leading to 'Stop–Go' policies practised by Conservative and Labour governments alike, suggested that there was some inherent weakness in our situation. Our foreign creditors certainly began to think so, although to most British people the disappearance of the mass unemployment of the inter-war years was proof enough of the fundamental soundness of the economy.

The Managed Economy

In the nineteenth century the working of the economic system had been left almost entirely to *laissez-faire*, that is to say, to the unfettered activity of each capitalist or businessman. Even in the difficult period between the wars the orthodox opinion had been that it was a mistake to try to help matters by government financial aid or expenditure on public works, since this would divert resources from private enterprise, which would itself use them as profitably as possible. But this view was challenged with increasing success by the economist J. M. Keynes, who urged that the way to meet a depression was for the government to increase rather than reduce its expenditure. In January 1931 he told radio listeners, 'The best guess I can make is that, whenever you save five shillings, you put a man out of work for a day.' Five years later his theory of the Managed Economy was fully stated in *The General Theory of Employment, Interest and Money*; this only later and after the impact of war found official acceptance in a White Paper on Employment Policy, published by the Churchill government in 1944 and fully endorsed by its Labour successor.

Keynes maintained that employment was determined by effective demand—the amount of money available for purchasing goods and so stimulating production, which in turn increases the number of jobs. In order to stave off unemployment, a government should take such measures as reducing taxation, lowering bank rate, buying back official securities, and/or paying out wages on public works—all of which would add to effective demand. In the post-war years Keynesian economics was not the only explanation advanced for the long-continued prosperity; heavy government expenditure on armaments—such as the USA and Britain engaged in on account of the Cold War—and even the booming American motor industry, providing the wherewithal for America to spend and lend overseas, were also held responsible. But the need for effective demand attracted most attention, especially as our social services gave the government a particularly convenient and powerful instrument for maintaining it.

But in the later 1960s it was becoming evident that the government's ability to manage the economy in the Keynesian fashion was very imperfect. The effects of its measures were imprecise; one measure might counteract another; and a mistimed measure might be worse than useless. Moreover, the evil to be combated was not the same as before the war; at first it was inflation, and then, from 1970–1 onwards, inflation and unemployment *at the same time*. In April 1971 *The Observer* commented on the conjunction: 'Nobody has a sovereign cure for either ... Looming and lowering over everything else is the unsolved problem of the management of the economy.'

The Vital Role of Exports in Paying Our Way

When one buys something in a shop, the money paid for it represents an equivalent in goods or services which the shopkeeper accepts in its place. This is obviously more convenient to both sides than exchange by barter. The same principle applies to international trade, though complicated by the fact that we pay for imports in foreign currencies, whilst selling exports in terms of our own money. Either side may supplement its exports by also providing services to the other country or by being in a position to claim interest or capital repayment on an existing debt (see p. 197). But a satisfactory 'balance of payments' in our dealings with the whole body of our foreign customers and suppliers, though expressed in terms of money, depends primarily on our ability to keep the outward flow of exports roughly commensurate with the inward flow of imports. Although wine, tobacco, and other much-desired luxuries form a part of our imports, the essentials are one-half of our food supply and most of our industrial raw materials, excepting coal, salt, and the offshore gas and oil. British exports, on the other hand, consist to the extent of 85 per cent of manufactures, many of which are not essentials and nearly all of which are also obtainable by our customers from competitors abroad. Gone are the days when foreigners had to 'buy British' or go without, though fond memories may still colour our commercial attitudes. Markets abroad have now to be held or regained with goods of an acceptable quality, availability, and price. As Sir Harold Wilson said when he was Prime Minister, 'We stand or fall as a nation on the sharpness of the cutting-edge we can develop in production and exports.'

The Importance of the Price—

A sharp cutting-edge means, above all, competitive prices. An unduly rapid rise in the price-level, what we call inflation, has been the common experience of most western countries in recent years. Unfortunately, the rise in Britain has been rather greater than elsewhere: retail prices rose by fully one-third in 1965–70, and they went on rising. The rise in prices was opposed by governments of both parties: numerous conferences were held, many eloquent speeches delivered, and various measures directed to the holding down of prices. Besides the Prices and Incomes Board (p. 276), mention may be made of the legislation against trade monopolies and retail price maintenance agreements, which built upon the work of the Monopolies and Restrictive Practices Commission, set up in 1948. But the impracticability of any measure for holding down wages caused events to move all the time in a vicious circle.

One of the worst-paid major groups of wage-earners, such as the railwaymen, would demand a rise on the basis of actual need, and the general public's sense of social justice would help them to get it. Other groups would then present their claims, partly at least because each in turn feared to lose its established position on the wages ladder as compared with workers less skilled than their own group or less well organized. Under conditions of full employment the simplest way out for employers was to concede the claims, add the extra wages bill to their costs of production, and raise the price of their product accordingly. When prices had all gone up, claims of social justice started the process all over again, with the same ultimate results. However sensible it might be to call a halt, the enormous power of the trade unions blocked the way.

As there were so few unemployed, the workers were in a strong bargaining position, and could generally see to it that wages rose faster than prices. Given the increasing circulation of money in wages and salaries (which rose in proportion), it was easy for the employer to sell all he made on the home market at prices which even enhanced his profit margin. But this would not apply to foreign markets, where British prices must compete with foreign prices. Our export prices might, indeed, be artificially reduced by lowering the value of the pound, which is what Wilson presumably meant when he invited the House of Commons in November 1967 to notice 'the opportunities of export-led expansion resulting from devaluation'. Experience has shown, however, that foreign markets have many ways of protecting themselves against any undue influx of goods which have been cheapened in this manner, whilst the advantage to us of selling in a devalued currency is counterweighed by the disadvantage of having to buy our imports in the currency of those who sell them. Thus in the long run the prices charged for British goods abroad must be directly competitive with what the foreign producer charges. His wage-rates and profit-margin may be equally high or even higher than in Britain, but his prices may be kept lower by greater productivity.

—and the Influence of Productivity

Any industrial concern in which the most up-to-date machinery is used to the best advantage may increase wages and at the same time increase output per head to an extent which more than compensates—that is one of the main ways in which America built up its prosperity. This efficient pattern is still characteristic of some British industries: as recently as 1964 British motor-works were able to export more than one-third of a record output of 1 870 000 cars. But our general position in this important matter has deteriorated; incomes have increased much more rapidly than production. In the

1950s, for example, the annual rate of increase for incomes (about three-quarters of which came from employment) was about 6 per cent, but the rate of increase for the product of employment was 2–2½ per cent. Other industrial countries of western Europe did better.

Percentage Growth of Output Per Person Employed, 1950—61

West Germany	4·9	Sweden	3·3
Italy	4·2	Belgium	2·6
France	3·9	Britain	2·0

Since the percentage growth in the United States was slightly below our own, it was possible to derive some comfort from the consideration that Britain, like America, had a relatively high productivity rate before 1950; but the position of the Americans is not comparable with our own, because their well-being does not depend on exports. It is far more important for us to find the contributory factors to this slowing-down of growth. Lack of initiative on the part of owners and managements is certainly one, an attitude which was encouraged by heavy taxation and governmental interference as well as by the distraction of the leisure interests which are so abundant and so accessible in the modern world. A second, related factor has been the costly delay in switching capital and attention from the old, declining staples, such as cotton textiles, to the new engineering industries with brighter prospects. This in turn has produced the handicap of obsolescent machinery and a small amount of capital equipment in relation to the number of employees.

The employees, for their part, contribute to the slowing-down of industry by wildcat strikes, absenteeism, and a generally less disciplined attitude to their work than they had to show in the days when there was always an unemployed man ready to take over the job. To some extent this attitude is mitigated by the policy of the trade union officials, who are not more prone to resort to strikes in Britain than in other countries, including America. But very little attempt has been made by them to change the workers' traditional addiction to restrictive practices, such as the banning of the most up-to-date machinery; the workers' addiction was established when hands were always more plentiful than jobs for them to do. The overmanning which now results attracts less attention than striking but, as recently as 14 September 1977, *The Times* presented as 'the best available guess' that with existing machinery our industry is overmanned by a factor of about 30 per cent, which with the best machinery available would rise to about 50 per cent.

This helps to explain the catastrophic fall in Britain's share of the world's manufactured exports—from one-third in 1900 to about one-quarter in 1950, followed by a further fall of 12 per cent in fourteen years. In the eight years 1953–61 wage costs per unit of output rose seven times as fast in Britain as in other main exporting countries, which prompted the National Economic Development Council to observe: 'Unless prices and costs go up considerably more slowly than in the past, it is unlikely that the United Kingdom can maintain her competitive position in world markets.'

The Role of Invisible Exports in the Balance of Payments

If the balance of a country's payments was made up by merely reckoning exports against imports, the balance would have been unfavourable in our case throughout the last one-and-a-half centuries. But we have long been accustomed to have a favourable balance on invisible trade, which more than makes up for the excess of imports.[1]

One such invisible export is the provision of insurance, banking, and other financial services, where Britain was first in the field and foreigners still find it convenient to use the widespread facilities we can offer. Secondly, there are payments of interest, profits, and dividends arising out of all kinds of British overseas investments. A third item which used to be very important was the earnings of our mercantile marine all over the seven seas. It is still the third-largest in the world in active employment, but has been overhauled by other nations to such an extent that we spend more on using their ships to carry our goods than they do on using ours for theirs. However, in the six most recent years the loss here has been turned into a small favourable balance by the profits from civil aviation. Lastly, we may notice that in all but one of those six years there has also been a favourable balance on travel and tourism—a marked contrast to the days when the British could well afford to travel abroad because the exchange rates were in our favour, whereas for the same reason many foreigners were deterred from visiting the island.

These invisible exports are set off to some extent by what are sometimes called invisible imports. These include military expenditure, such as that incurred for the 55 000 men of BAOR and RAF Germany, and the considerably larger sums disbursed in aid of various kinds to Commonwealth and other underdeveloped countries. In the former case the expense is justified because of the protection afforded us by NATO, and in the latter because of the contribution it makes to

[1] See Appendix II, Table 5.

the growth of a healthy world economy, by which we all benefit. But another large item on this side of the account is the sum required for the repayment of short-term loans, such as the emergency help Britain obtained in 1964–5 and from the International Monetary Fund in 1976 (see p. 338), and the service of the huge loan from the United States and Canadian governments to set us on our feet again after the war. Both interest and capital payments on this loan, totalling £67 million, were suspended in 1964 and again in 1965—a desperate expedient on our part, as additional interest charges are incurred for each year's delay.

We may now sum up the history of the balance of payments for the first two decades after the Second World War. For the first half-dozen years it fluctuated rather wildly, as we might perhaps expect, but from 1952 to 1959 (inclusive) the balance stayed on the right side, except for a deficit in 1955. Then came a large deficit in 1960, a small one in 1961, and in 1964 the alarmingly large deficit of £393 million. This did not mean that an over-all national bankruptcy impended, for Britain's total external assets exceeded her external liabilities by an amount estimated at nearly £2 billion, which rose to £2·7 billion by 1969.[1] What it did mean, however, was that on the basis of *current* activities we were no longer making ends meet.

Hence the sterling crisis which confronted Wilson when he came into office in the autumn of 1964; his struggle to avoid devaluation, which he was three years later forced to accept; and his partly successful attempts to cope with the resulting situation, down to his defeat at the election of 1970. But it was increasingly evident that the British economy was handicapped by persistent high inflation, for which neither Wilson nor his Conservative successor, Heath, could find a cure.

The Problem of Inflation

Just as the depressed economy of the 1920s and 1930s was characterized by the problem of unemployment, so the more resilient society of the post-war era has been characterized by difficulties arising from inflation. Whereas in the former period it could be claimed that the low level of wages prevented goods from being sold, in the latter period an increasingly high level of wages has raised prices to an extent which produces a dangerous depreciation in the value of money. To preserve a proper equilibrium between the supply of goods and the supply of money has always been difficult, even in the days when the precious metals were a universally accepted standard of value; for any sudden increase in their availability could cause prices to soar.

[1] *United Kingdom Balance of Payments* (HMSO 1970).

In modern times the use of gold and silver ingots and coins has of course been supplemented (though not completely replaced) by more sophisticated devices. Cheques drawn on bank accounts, bank loans, quickly realizable bonds and building society shares, hire purchase agreements, and the handy credit card are examples of the many methods by which purchases are nowadays facilitated. In 1959, indeed, a Committee of economic experts under Lord Radcliffe went so far as to say, 'Bank notes are in effect the small change of the monetary system', but they are not only the oldest regular substitute for bullion, they are also under the direct control of the government. A large part of the notes issued by the Bank of England to provide our currency is known as the 'fiduciary issue', whose trustworthiness was originally based on the Bank's holding of gold but nowadays on government and other securities. In 1954 this issue was fixed by law at £1575 million, but by 1967 it had been raised to £3000 million. It might be supposed that this represented a failure on the government's part to hold down inflation; yet the Radcliffe Report seems to have doubted whether it was the government's duty to inconvenience the public by trying to limit the currency in circulation when inflation was due to many other causes.

Economists argue as to whether it is cost or demand which brings about the inflation of prices. They distinguish between 'cost-push' inflation, where cost pushes up the price, and 'demand-pull' inflation, where it is pulled up by demand. Since inflation has been experienced in recent years by so many differently situated countries, it is likely that both factors contribute to the result. So far as Britain is concerned, we have already seen how costs rise through inefficient management, high wages, and low productivity. As to the pull of demand, the ten years 1959–69 provide clear evidence. In that period total personal income in this country was almost doubled, whilst the output of goods increased by approximately one-third. Since there was more money to be spent, prices rose; and there was little competition from cheap imports, because our exports were insufficient to stimulate trade in return.

Every shopper is aware of inflation affecting almost every purchase, although comparison with the past is rendered more difficult by the decimalization of the currency on 15 February 1971 and the gradual adoption of international weights and measures, which the Metrication Board has been promoting since 1969. In any case, the most striking comparisons can only be made by those who, from their clear recollections of the pre-war era, are in a position to weary their grandchildren with accounts of the 'seven-and-sixpenny' shirt which they wore when they entertained grandmamma to a 'three-and-sixpenny' table d'hôte meal—both prices in shillings for what would now require the equivalent number of pounds. But a little research in works of reference will show the rising cost of an article which may be assumed to differ less in quality than shirts or restaurant meals, namely the type of brain which reaches the topmost level in the civil service. In the forty years from 1900 to 1940 the salary of the Permanent Secretary to the Treasury rose from £2500 to £3500; since then it has taken less than forty years to reach £20 175.

High salaries, whether in the public service or in private enterprise, are much more vulnerable than weekly wages to the mounting demands of the tax-man. But trade unions, as we have seen (p. 327), have exerted enormous pressure to keep their members' 'take-home pay' (from which tax has already been deducted) ahead of the rise in prices. In so far as wages are in this way insulated from the effects of inflation, some people are tempted to suppose that inflation does very little harm. It is, however, directly harmful in at least three ways. Firstly, so long as our inflation rate is higher than that of other countries, British exports are too dear to be competitive. Secondly, all those pensioners whose pensions are not price-indexed, people who live on savings, and others whose income is fixed (or alterable only at long intervals) suffer undeserved losses. And thirdly, society as a whole loses some of its stability, since there is no incentive to save and a fear that the currency might eventually collapse completely, when almost everyone would be most disagreeably affected.

This grave and complex problem sorely taxes the ablest minds, and even members of parliament have been heard to admit that they do not know the answer. The Labour government of 1964–70 failed with its Prices and Incomes policy. The Industrial Relations Act of its Conservative successor was likewise a failure. As for the Labour regime which took its place in 1974, it would be difficult to count the occasions on which it has announced the impending reduction of inflation to a yearly 10 per cent—a rate which had not been achieved by the autumn of 1977.

Britain and the Common Market

In the course of the 1970s inflation affected all the industrialized countries of Europe, but seldom to the same extent as in Britain. It is therefore relevant now to examine in a little more detail our relations with the Common Market, mentioned briefly in an earlier chapter (pp. 272 and 278); for it was reasonable to suppose that, by joining a flourishing trading bloc, whose members—like Britain—devoted about one-half of their total output to industrial goods, we too should be able to achieve greater financial stability.

Since 1957 the European scene has been dominated by the activities of the European Economic Community, which grew out of an earlier united authority for coal, iron, and steel, the ECSC, which had functioned at Luxemburg since 1952. In March 1957, the Treaty of Rome set up a similar supranational authority of much wider scope, as France, West Germany, Italy, Belgium, the Netherlands and Luxemburg now bound themselves to form a single economic unit through the step-by-step establishment of a Common Market and the harmonizing of their economic, investment and social policies. Complete internal free trade was duly achieved, together with the building of a common tariff wall against the rest of the world. This could be breached by various forms of association and reciprocal arrangements—or by such an act of exceptional generosity as the Lomé Agreement of 1975, giving duty-free access to the Market for the exports of forty-six underdeveloped countries, about one-half of which are in the Commonwealth. To sum up, the general result was the growth of a thriving economy among the Six; in spite of recurrent difficulties about agricultural policy and about the eventual political implications of their union, the new system was seen to confer solid benefits which none of the states concerned would lightly abandon.

The history of Britain's relations with the EEC suggests a lack of foresight on the part of our rulers. Only an observer was accredited to the coal, iron, and steel authority, because we were confident it would prove a fiasco. Britain was concerned in the early negotiations leading up to the Treaty of Rome in 1957, but eventually held back. One reason for so doing was the difficulty of adopting a common tariff against outsiders, in view of the long-standing preferences given to member states of the Commonwealth: but trade with the Commonwealth was in any case relatively on the decline. The other main reason was the feeling that the inclusion of agricultural commodities in the common system would be incompatible with the retention of subsidized prices for our own agriculture. In 1965–6 these subsidies were costing Britain £244 000 000, and this very large figure was likely to rise.

Instead, Britain took the lead in the establishment of the European Free Trade Association, sometimes known as the 'Outer Seven'. The other signatories of the Stockholm Convention of January 1959 were the three Scandinavian powers, Austria, Switzerland, and Portugal. Basic differences included the facts that the freedom of trade, which EFTA set out to achieve by the end of 1966, concerned industrial products only; that EFTA had no common tariff against outsiders;

and that it was in any case a much smaller economic unit than the EEC. Indeed, the members of EFTA had a bigger total trade with the EEC countries than with each other.

Only a year later, Britain gave colour to the suggestion that EFTA was merely designed to increase her bargaining power by directly applying to join the Common Market. Long and hard negotiations took place, much harder than they would have been if Britain had applied for membership in the beginning. After the rebuffs in 1963 and 1967, already mentioned (pp. 272 and 278) a further British application was made; this had much support from within the EEC, and negotiations were reopened in 1970. Up to the last moment, there were difficulties about the amount of Britain's contribution to the common budget, imports of New Zealand dairy produce, and imports of Commonwealth sugar, but in June 1971 agreement was reached on terms for British entry to the Common Market.

The general arguments for entry were both economic and political. It was thought that joining a larger market would lead to an expansion of British trade, and that Britain would be in the position to share in—and to assist—a further development of the European economy. When Denmark, Norway, and the Irish Republic, also applicants for membership, together with Britain, had joined the Common Market, it would have a population of 250 million and be the most important trading area in the world. In the years following the formation of the Market, trade between the original six members had greatly increased—by about five times—and, at the same time, the trade of the six with the outside world had also increased considerably. Gross National Product increased a good deal faster in the Common Market countries than in Britain, and inside the Community there could be co-operation in scientific and technological research, especially as regards nuclear energy, space, air travel and computers, areas of research too expensive for any one of the countries acting alone.

Economically, Britain stood to gain, inasmuch as our trade with the industrialized countries of western Europe had grown more rapidly in recent years than that with some other traditional British markets; in particular, we now exported twice as much to Western Europe as we did to the Commonwealth. Politically, the diminution of our national sovereignty would be counterbalanced, in so far as Britain might eventually acquire a new sphere of influence in Western Europe to make up for a visibly shrinking sphere of influence among the nations of the Commonwealth. In particular, Britain might have a role to play in preserving harmony between France and the rising power of West Germany, which on no account must relapse into isolation.

In January 1972, Mr Heath duly signed at Brussels the Treaty of Accession raising the membership of the new Europe from the Six to the Ten.[1] In the following month, however, the European Communities Bill passed the House of Commons by a majority of no more than 309:301, and disagreement was not silenced when Britain, on New Year's Day 1973, became a legally bound member of the three communities—EEC, ECSC, and 'Euratom' (for the common development of atomic research). A year later the in-coming Labour government listed seven 'objectives' for renegotiation; these were achieved to a sufficient extent for Wilson—who had shown all his debating skill in opposing Heath's measure—to declare that membership of the EEC now had his support. He submitted the matter to the first referendum ever held in Britain, which produced a pro-Community majority of two to one—all the more decisive because every county voted Yes, with the solitary and remote exceptions of Shetland and the Western Isles.

The years following Britain's accession to the EEC were difficult ones. Britain was sometimes regarded as the half-hearted spoil-sport of the Community; and indeed there was considerable impatience among ordinary British people with what seemed remote European discussions. Pessimists could even suggest that there was no real agreement among members as to the shape and content of the ultimate goal of political union. The fundamental economic difficulty—especially in times of economic recession—was that some member countries were much stronger and richer than others, and did not wish to risk their relative prosperity. They feared, for example, that they would be paying for strikes and inflation in Britain. Nevertheless, attempts were made to set stages for economic and monetary common action, while in 1976 it was decided that there should be direct elections to the European Parliament, planned at first for 1978. Possible enlargement of the Community also lay ahead: Greece, Spain, and Portugal were applying for membership.

Britain, after her accession, had been gradually phased-in over five years; she paid lower contributions, and her tariffs on trade were progressively reduced, while the common external tariff was completed. Agriculture and fisheries presented problems. Over fisheries there was continuing friction, with regard to coastal limits and conservation of fish, and British opposition led to the breakdown of EEC negotiations in 1978. The application of the Common Agricultural Policy (CAP) was particularly difficult. Its aims were admirable:

[1] Operative as the Nine, because in September 1972 the Norwegians held an advisory plebiscite which rejected membership.

stable market conditions, a fair return to farmers, and a reasonable price to the consumer. But it soon appeared that considerable adjustments would be needed. There was serious over-production of dairy products, resulting in the so-called 'butter-mountain', for example. Financial help to dairy farmers proved very expensive; inflation and unstable currencies increased the cost of the monetary compensation amounts (MCAs) used to maintain price stability. Britain began to feel she was subsidizing Continental farmers (possibly inefficient ones), and getting little in return; there were far more farmers across the Channel. Britain's Milk Marketing Board (with its dependent doorstep milk-delivery) was threatened by EEC proposals, but in a poll in 1978—required by EEC rules—British farmers voted 99 per cent to keep the Board. Relations with the Commonwealth were also affected by Britain's EEC membership. The Lomé Agreement of 1975 (referred to above) gave duty-free access to the Market, and its beneficiaries included more than a score of the African, Caribbean and Pacific members of the Commonwealth. But in other cases there could be hardship. New Zealand was faced by special problems in exporting her meat and dairy products, and by 1978 had pressing economic difficulties—a trade deficit and inflation.

What came to be especially important to Britain was the method of financing the EEC. Its financial resources were drawn from the product of the common external tariff; and, in the future, a part was also to come from a proportion of the VAT raised in each country. By 1978 Britain was having to face up to full contributions—the phasing-in was coming to an end. As Britain was a large importing country—and was also likely to have a large VAT contribution to make—some calculations showed Britain, actually one of the poorer members, as likely to be the largest contributor. (It was this which led to a strong speech by Mr Callaghan in November 1978, criticizing the arrangements. There was a 'correcting mechanism'—but presumably it was thought to be insufficient.) Another pressing issue at this time was that of the common monetary system towards which the EEC was moving. But Britain was hesitant; she was weighing the advantages of a flexible exchange rate under her own control against those of the stability hoped for from a fixed rate inside the Community.

It was still too soon to say whether the economic advantages of Community membership would outweigh political disadvantages, which in many eyes were increased by the prospect of a directly elected European parliament. High food prices continued to be blamed on politics framed in Brussels. Our membership had certainly not produced any sudden or dramatic improvement in our economic situation, but it is fair to bear in mind that the 1970s—unlike the period in which the Common Market made its rapid early advances—were almost everywhere a time of deepening economic difficulty. In 1975, other members of the Community took less than half in value of our total exports to the developed countries of the world, whilst they supplied just over half of our total imports calculated on the same basis.

Britain's Economic Troubles Continue

It is extremely difficult to find landmarks in the monotonous continuity of the economic scene during recent years. Inflation mounted under Wilson and Callaghan as it had mounted under Heath; unemployment increased, in spite of government subsidies to stimulate employment through training, re-training, and job creation. Vain hopes were pinned to the operation of trade cycles, whose course the government's economic advisers plotted for the years 1950–73. No upward turn being apparent by 1977, the public resigned itself to a situation in which neither government nor opposition had any practical policy for control of the economic system. Instead they were waiting for world conditions to improve. The 1970s had brought little if any growth to the British economy, but in 1977 production was still falling in France and West Germany also, and it was clear that the world had not emerged from recession.

Unemployment fortunately kept well below the totals of the dark days in the 1930s, and there was no return to the privations suffered then. The unemployed were paid substantial benefits—free of tax—so that unskilled workers with large families might be quite as well off without work as with it; and the relief regulations were so much less stringent than in the old days that occasional unscrupulous individuals seemed to live opulently on the Dole. A much more important characteristic of the age was the general appearance of affluence; bustle and business in the shops, restaurants, and pleasure resorts; and the evidence that many people still found it possible to save. In 1975, for instance, record deposits were reported by the building societies.

Nevertheless, Britain was in fact continuing to live beyond her means. One ominous sign was the serious financial difficulties in which such large concerns as Burmah Oil, British Leyland, and Ferranti became involved; they were kept going with public money, which meant an increasing degree of public involvement. The social contract was eroded by the wage claims of powerful trade unions, such as the seamen, dockers, miners, and railwaymen, so in August 1975 the government tried to reinforce it by a voluntary agreement that for the next twelve months no one should receive a pay rise exceeding £6 a week, whilst salaries of £8500 and above should be completely frozen. But the Cabinet itself was split as to the causes of inflation and unemployment, one member arguing that they were not attributable to pay-rises but to the fact that underpaid workers were set to produce over-priced goods with out-of-date equipment.

In September 1976 the failure to pay our way resulted in an acute crisis, when the pound had fallen to $1·637 and seemed likely to plunge further. The Chancellor of the Exchequer, recalled from London airport on his way to a meeting of Commonwealth finance ministers in Hong Kong, succeeded in obtaining the largest credit ever granted to any country by the International Monetary Fund; but the price was the acceptance of a right of surveillance over our economic affairs which would once have been utterly unthinkable. In the same September the number of unemployed in the United Kingdom— seasonally adjusted to exclude school-leavers and students— reached 1 318 000 or 5·6 per cent of the work-force. Twelve months later the corresponding figures were 1 450 000 and 6·1 per cent, and in the meantime the TUC had formally abandoned the Social Contract, though agreeing with the government that wage claims should be restricted to minimum intervals of one year and marked by self-restraint. How this would work out in practice was anybody's guess.

In place of speculation, we may again sum up. Ever since the Second World War, there has been a strong tendency for people in Britain to regard a high standard of living and even affluence as something to which they are entitled by right, and not in virtue of their individual effort and productivity. Our invisible exports still produce a credit balance, but the manufactures we try to sell abroad are not made or marketed efficiently enough to hold their own in a highly competitive world—thus there is constant pressure upon the exchanges and balance of payments. As people demand more of the good things of life, they agitate for more money; but as they fail to produce more goods, the value of their money falls. This inflation is a standing menace to the community; it could lead to a breakdown of the economic system and place our political liberties in jeopardy from a dictatorship either of the Left or of the Right. Is there a way out?

Pouring Oil on Troubled Waters

According to a statement by the Secretary of State for Energy in December 1976, North Sea oil would save $2000 million in the following year and bring Britain well on the way to self-sufficiency by 1980. Assuming a production rate in that year of 95–115 million tonnes, the proven reserves on the British Continental Shelf would last for about

North Sea oil—Britain's economic salvation?

ten years, but 'The total reserves of the designated areas could amount to 4500 million tonnes.'[1] In August 1977, a disquieting report that the Argyll oilfield, from which the first tanker-load had been obtained twenty-six months before, was already running down gave place quickly to news of further discoveries.

Since Norway was the only country in Western Europe with comparable prospects of wealth from oil, it seemed reasonable to look forward to a period of some decades during which paying our way would be relatively easy and the economy might be reconstructed on a permanently sounder basis. This offered perhaps the best underlying justification for a more hopeful financial outlook in the autumn of 1977. The *Daily Telegraph*, not given to optimism under a Labour government, announced as its front-page heading, 'City sees end of Recession'. In October, when the crude unemployment figures had reached 1 600 000, the Labour Prime Minister himself invited the Party Conference to lift its eyes and see the brightening horizon.

But in fact renewed difficulties lay ahead in 1979,[2] when wage demands and a wave of strikes once more brought into sight the dangers of inflation and unemployment.

[1] *Britain 1977: An Official Handbook*, p. 259.
[2] See p. 285.

Epilogue

Every book must, for practical reasons, be brought to an end, but there is no ending to history—the flow of events goes on and on. Our book is finished, but we cannot say that the making of modern Britain is complete, for Britain continues to change, even as we write. What, then, is 'Modern Britain'? Young or old, we commonly use the term to mean the Britain we are actually experiencing. This book, however, has used it in two other senses: firstly, to describe the Britain which arose from the coming of the machine; and secondly, to describe the different Britain which began to take shape at the end of the Second World War. All three of these 'modern Britains' have their place in a time-span which is very short—barely two out of the twenty-five centuries which separate us from Herodotus, 'the father of history'. Family tradition can even bridge the gap between persons who figure in the very first chapters of our story and its readers—or writers.[1] Yet in such a comparatively brief stretch of time greater changes have taken place than in all those earlier centuries of the historical record, a process of 'modernization' breath-taking in its speed and completeness.

The early industrial revolution, as we know, wrought many dramatic changes in the face of the country. One of these was marked by a classical Latin quotation, *Perrupit Acheronta Herculeus labor*, inscribed at the mouth of the tunnel from which the first canal emerged to carry the coal out of the mine and across the countryside to Manchester.[2] The inscription is appropriate for more than one reason. There and then the coal was being brought into the light of day and the service of Man by the truly Herculean labours of miners and canal-navvies. In a wider, symbolic sense the efforts of workers and the enterprise of their employers were opening up the dark underworld (or 'Acheron') of the past and creating a new industrial society. The development of coal and iron, machinery, textiles, steam power, and railways; the growth of population and of political and social reform; and the eventual reaction against capitalism by Karl Marx and many later thinkers—all

---

[1] One of the present authors, for instance, can recall how his great-grandmother spoke of her father's personal recollections of his uncles, the Hunters—the eighteenth-century Scottish doctors mentioned on p. 11.

[2] See p. 52, footnote.

this is the story of the Industrial Revolution. But the citation of Horace is appropriate for yet another reason. A classical education was as characteristic of eighteenth-century Britain—not merely of public schools like Eton, attended by the nobility and gentry, but of every tiny local grammar school—as is a strictly 'modern' curriculum of our twentieth-century comprehensives.

However strong its attachment to the past, the quiet, rustic Britain of Parson Woodforde developed into the busy, industrialized Britain of Victorian times. Compare the Parson's account of life in his Norfolk parish in 1776 with the bustling scene on Paddington Station as the painter Frith saw it in 1862. The transformation is tremendous: in what could have been the lifetime of an individual, a country of villages had become the workshop of the world. And throughout Victoria's reign the process continued—growth of industry, wealth, and population. One such industrial revolution might seem to be enough; it had produced a new Britain, and changes on such a scale could hardly be repeated. However, since 1945 another new Britain has made its appearance. Developments which began in late-Victorian and Edwardian times had been greatly accelerated by the two world wars. The regime of steam-power, with its railways and steamships, was followed by that of electricity and the internal combustion engine, culminating in air travel as an everyday experience. A phenomenon of almost equal significance was the new economic climate of full employment, which enabled Britain to achieve not only a Welfare State, with social services of every kind, but also an affluent society with a general standard of material living hardly dreamed of between the wars.

But this time there is one very big difference from the era of change inaugurated by such men as Arkwright, Watt, and Stephenson. Britain is no longer far ahead of the rest of the world in working out either the new technologies themselves or the social changes to which they give rise. On the contrary, a declining economic position *vis-à-vis* other countries has much to do with the difficulties and dangers discussed in our closing chapters. Some of the virtues of Victorian society— industriousness, thrift, self-control, respect for law and order, and pride in one's work—seem to have diminished. But since the outside world is under no obligation to supply us with a power and prosperity beyond our deserts, we are in the long run dependent upon our own disciplined exertions. We can, however, take courage from the past: a nation which rose so notably to earlier challenges has it in it to do the same again.

Appendix I
Social history in contemporary verse

1. *The publication of* THE VILLAGE *by George Crabbe in 1783 marked a revival of realism in the attitude of poets to the lives of humble people, with their long hours of work and, even in the wretched poor-house (a less highly organized predecessor of the Victorian workhouse), the 'doleful hum' of compulsory spinning.*

> The Village Life, and every care that reigns
> O'er youthful peasants and declining swains;
> What labour yields, and what, that labour past,
> Age, in its hour of languor, finds at last;
> What form the real picture of the poor,
> Demand a song—the Muse can give no more.
>
> Go then! and see them rising with the sun,
> Through a long course of daily toil to run;
> See them beneath the dog-star's raging heat,
> When the knees tremble and the temples beat;
> Behold them, leaning on their scythes, look o'er
> The labour past, and toils to come explore;
> See them alternate suns and showers engage,
> And hoard up aches and anguish for their age.
>
> Theirs is yon house that holds the parish-poor,
> Whose walls of mud scarce bear the broken door;
> There, where the putrid vapours, flagging, play,
> And the dull wheel hums doleful through the day;—
> There children dwell who know no parents' care;
> Parents, who know no children's love, dwell there! ...
> The lame, the blind, and, far the happiest they!
> The moping idiot and the madman gay.
> Here too the sick their final doom receive,
> Here brought, amid the scenes of grief, to grieve ...
> Here, sorrowing, they each kindred sorrow scan,
> And the cold charities of man to man.

2. THE BOROUGH *(1810) gives Crabbe's account of the tiny seaport of Aldeburgh in Suffolk, his native town, where he struggled in vain to establish himself as a doctor or apothecary, for which he had been educated. The descriptions of a Friendly Society and of local schools are typical of the everyday scenes pictured in the twenty-four letters composing the poem.*

Of manufactures trade, inventions rare,
Steam-towers and looms, you'd know our Borough's share—
'Tis small: we boast not these rich subjects here,
Who hazard thrice ten thousand pounds a year;
We've no huge buildings, where incessant noise
Is made by springs and spindles, girls and boys ...
Still common minds with us in common trade,
Have gain'd more wealth than ever student made.

The poor man has his club; he comes and spends
His hoarded pittance with his chosen friends;
Nor this alone—a monthly dole he pays,
To be assisted when his health decays;
Some part his prudence, from the day's supply,
For cares and troubles in his age, lays by;
The printed rules he guards with painted frame,
And shows his children where to read his name.

To every class we have a school assign'd,
Rules for all ranks, and food for every mind:
Yet one there is, that small regard to rule
Or study pays, and still is deemed a school;
That, where a deaf, poor, patient widow sits,
And awes some thirty infants as she knits;
Infants of humble, busy wives, who pay
Some trifling price for freedom through the day.
At this good matron's hut the children meet,
Who thus becomes the mother of the street ...
Though deaf, she sees the rebel heroes shout—
Though lame, her white rod nimbly walks about.

To learning's second seats we now proceed,
Where humming students gilded primers read ...
'Reading made Easy', so the titles tell;
But they who read must first begin to spell:
There may be profits in these arts, but still
Learning is labour, call it what you will.
'But is it sure that study will repay
The more attentive and forebearing?'—Nay!
The farm, the ship, the humble shop have each
Gains which severest studies seldom reach.

3. *Shelley's* MASK OF ANARCHY, *of which these are the central stanzas, was written on his receiving news in Italy of the Peterloo Massacre (August 1819). It was sent to the Radical periodical,* THE EXAMINER, *but though it advocated no more than passive resistance, this 'flaming robe of verse', as Leigh Hunt called it, remained unpublished until 1832.*

What is freedom?—ye can tell
That which slavery is, too well—
For its very name has grown
To an echo of your own.

'Tis to work and have such pay
As just keeps life from day to day
In your limbs, as in a cell
For the tyrants' use to dwell,

So that ye for them are made
Loom, and plough, and sword, and spade,
With or without your own will bent
To their defence and nourishment.

'Tis to see your children weak
With their mothers pine and peak,
When the winter winds are bleak—
They are dying whilst I speak. ...

'Tis to let the Ghost of Gold
Take from Toil a thousandfold
More than e'er its substance could
In the tyrannies of old. ...

And at length when ye complain
With a murmur weak and vain
'Tis to see the Tyrant's crew
Ride over your wives and you—
Blood is on the grass like dew.

4. THE LAY OF THE LABOURER, *like the better-known* SONG OF THE SHIRT, *was written by Thomas Hood in the early 'forties, when nearly 10 per cent of the entire population were paupers and agricultural wages for eighteen southern counties averaged 8s. 5d. a week.*

A spade! a rake! a hoe!
A pickaxe, or a bill!
A hook to reap, or a scythe to mow,
A flail, or what ye will—
And here's a ready hand
To ply the needful tool,
And skill'd enough, by lessons rough,
In Labour's rugged school.

To hedge, or dig the ditch,
  To lop or fell the tree,
To lay the swarth on the sultry field,
  Or plough the stubborn lea;
The harvest stack to bind,
  The wheaten rick to thatch,
And never fear in my pouch to find
  The tinder or the match.

To a flaming barn or farm
  My fancies never roam;
The fire I yearn to kindle and burn
  Is on the hearth of Home;
Where children huddle and crouch
  Through dark long winter days,
Where starving children huddle and crouch,
  To see the cheerful rays,
A-glowing on the haggard cheek,
  And not in the haggard's blaze!

To Him who sends a drought
  To parch the fields forlorn,
The rain to flood the meadows with mud,
  The lights to blast the corn,
To Him I leave to guide
  The bolt in its crooked path,
To strike the miser's rick, and show
  The skies blood-red with wrath.

A spade! a rake! a hoe!
  A pickaxe, or a bill!
A hook to reap, or a scythe to mow,
  A flail, or what ye will—
The corn to thrash, or the hedge to plash,
  The market-team to drive,
Or mend the fence by the cover side,
  And leave the game alive.

Ay, only give me work,
  And then you need not fear
That I shall snare his worship's hare,
  Or kill his grace's deer;
Break into his lordship's house,
  To steal the plate so rich;
Or leave the yeoman that had a purse
  To welter in a ditch.

Wherever Nature needs,
  Wherever Labour calls,
No job I'll shirk of the hardest work,
  To shun the workhouse walls;

Where savage laws begrudge
  The pauper babe its breath,
And doom a wife to a widow's life
  Before her partner's death.

My only claim is this,
    With labour stiff and stark,
By lawful turn, my living to earn,
  Between the light and dark;
My daily bread and nightly bed,
  My bacon, and drop of beer—
But all from the hand that holds the land,
  And none from the overseer!

5. *A contrasting picture, from the same period as the preceding one—the meeting of the Maidstone Mechanics' Institute at Park House, the home of Tennyson's friend Edmund Lushington, on 6 July 1842, which he used as the setting for* THE PRINCESS *(1847).*

Sir Walter Vivian all a summer's day
Gave his broad lawns until the set of sun
Up to the people: thither flocked at noon
His tenants, wife and child, and thither half
The neighbouring borough with their Institute
Of which he was the patron.

There moved the multitude, a thousand heads:
The patient leaders of their Institute
Taught them with facts ... and here were telescopes
For azure views; and there a group of girls
In circle waited, whom the electric shock
Dislink'd with shrieks and laughter: round the lake
A little clock-work steamer paddling plied
And shook the lilies: perch'd about the knolls
A dozen angry models jetted steam:
A petty railway ran: a fire-balloon
Rose gem-like up before the dusky groves
And dropt a fiery parachute and past:
And there thro' twenty posts of telegraph
They flash'd a saucy message to and fro
Between the mimic stations; so that sport
Went hand in hand with Science; otherwhere
Pure sport: a herd of boys with clamour bowl'd
And stump'd the wicket; babies roll'd about
Like tumbled fruit in grass; and men and maids
Arranged a country dance ...

                              And overhead
The broad ambrosial aisles of lofty lime
Made noise with bees and breeze from end to end.
Strange was the sight and smacking of the time.

6. *An extract from Tennyson's hymn to Victorian prosperity, written for the opening of the International Exhibition at South Kensington in 1862. There were twice as many exhibitors as in 1851, which seems to justify both Gladstone's Free Trade budgets and the poet's elaboration of what he calls the 'myriad horns of plenty at our feet'.*

> Lo! the long laborious miles
> Of Palace; lo! the giant aisles,
> Rich in model and design;
> Harvest-tool and husbandry,
> Loom and wheel and enginery,
> Secrets of the sullen mine,
> Steel and gold, and corn and wine,
> Fabric rough, or fairy-fine,
> Sunny tokens of the Line,
> Polar marvels, and a feast
> Of wonder, out of West and East,
> And shapes and hues of Art divine!
> All of beauty, all of use,
> That one fair planet can produce.

7. *W. H. Davies, before he found success as the author of* THE AUTOBIOGRAPHY OF A SUPER-TRAMP *(1908), experienced for many years the hardships of existence in doss-houses on 8s. a week. His verses therefore show London, then the richest city in the world, as it appeared to the generally inarticulate 'submerged tenth' of its population.*

> My song is of that city which
> Has men too poor and men too rich;
> Where some are sick, too richly fed,
> While others take the sparrows' bread:
> Where some have beds to warm their bones,
> While others sleep on hard, cold stones
> That suck away their bodies' heat.
> Where men are drunk in every street;
> Men full of poison, like those flies
> That still attack the horses' eyes.
> Where some men freeze for want of cloth,
> While others show their jewels' worth
> And dress in satin, fur or silk;
> Where fine rich ladies wash in milk,
> While starving mothers have no food
> To make them fit in flesh and blood;
> So that their watery breasts can give
> Their babies milk and make them live.
> Where one man does the work of four,
> And dies worn out before his hour;
> While some seek work in vain, and grief
> Doth make their fretful lives as brief.
> Where ragged men are seen to wait
> For charity that's small and late;
> While others haunt in idle leisure,
> Theatre doors to pay for pleasure.

8. THE DEAR OLD VILLAGE, *John Betjeman's modern version of Crabbe, should not be taken too seriously. Nevertheless, there is a sting in its tail.*

Behind rank elders, shadowing a pool,
And near the Church, behold the Village School,
Its gable rising out of ivy thick
Shows 'Eighteen-Sixty' worked in coloured brick.
By nineteen-forty-seven, hurrah! hooray!
This institution has outlived its day.
In the bad times of old feudality
The villagers were ruled by masters three—
Squire, parson, schoolmaster. Of these, the last
Knew best the village present and its past.
Now, I am glad to say, the man is dead,
The children have a motor-bus instead,
And in a town eleven miles away
We train them to be 'Citizens of To-day'.
And many a cultivated hour they pass
In a fine school with walls of vita-glass.
Civics, eurhythmics, economics, Marx,
How-to-respect-wild-life-in-National-Parks;
Plastics, gymnastics—thus they learn to scorn
The old thatch'd cottages where they were born.
The girls, ambitious to begin their lives
Serving in Woolworth's, rather than as wives;
The boys, who cannot yet escape the land,
At driving tractors lend a clumsy hand.
An eight-hour day for all, and more than three
Of these are occupied in making tea
And talking over what we all agree—
Though 'Music while you work' is now our wont,
It's not so nice as 'Music while you don't'.
Squire, parson, schoolmaster turn in their graves.
And *let* them turn. We are no longer slaves.

9. MRS CANUTE, A REFORMER—*a final tailpiece, from* THE COLLECTED POEMS OF WILLIAM PLOMER, *1973.*

Oh for my non-permissive youth!
I shall not rest, as I had planned,
Till I have built Tabusalem
In England's mad, unbuttoned land.

Appendix II
Social history in figures

The tables which follow show the growth of total and selected urban populations; the spread of the franchise; the expansion of some key industries and forms of transport; changes in the composition of the Balance of Trade; the place of trade unionism, of industrial disputes, and of unemployment in the history of the Work Force; and the general rise in Real Wages. The trend of the figures provides a commentary upon the generalizations made in the text, and they may also be used in a more detailed way to throw additional light upon the situation of British society in any given short period.

Any use of statistics is, however, beset by difficulties and uncertainties which have been disregarded in our highly simplified presentation. The interested reader is therefore referred for more exact and scientifically organized information to the sources on which we gratefully acknowledge our dependence:

B. R. MITCHELL with PHYLLIS DEANE, *Abstract of British Historical Statistics* (CUP).

B. R. MITCHELL and H. G. JONES, *Second Abstract of British Historical Statistics* (CUP)—a continuation, covering 1938–65.

B. R. MITCHELL, *European Historical Statistics 1750—1970* (Macmillan)—for Britain this uses mainly the same materials, but with European measurements and valuable international comparisons.

D. BUTLER and ANNE SLOMAN, *British Political Facts 1900—1975* (Macmillan)—relevant statistical material is in sections IV, X, XI, and XII.

Table 1   Population of Great Britain (in thousands)

Year	England and Wales	Scotland	Total
1760 (est.)	6665	1265	7930[a]
1801	8893	1608	10 501
1811	10 165	1806	11 971
1821	12 000	2092	14 092
1831	13 897	2364	16 261
1841	15 914	2620	18 534
1851	17 928	2889	20 817
1861	20 066	3062	23 128
1871	22 712	3360	26 072
1881	25 974	3736	29 710
1891	29 003	4026	33 029
1901	32 528	4472	37 000
1911	36 070	4761	40 831
1921	37 887	4882	42 769
1931	39 952	4843	44 795
1951	43 758	5096	48 854
1961	46 072	5178	51 250
1971	48 750	5229	53 979

[a] Mitchell's *Abstract*, p. 5, gives five estimates for England and Wales in 1760, ranging from 6 736 000 to 6 480 000; the population of Scotland had been enumerated by parish ministers in 1755, and is therefore less uncertain.

Table 2   Urban populations: the fifteen largest towns in 1801 and their later growth (in thousands)

Year	Greater London[a]	Bath	Birmingham[b]	Bristol	Edinburgh (including Leith)	Glasgow	Hull	Leeds	Liverpool	Manchester (excluding Salford)	Newcastle upon Tyne	Norwich	Plymouth (including Devonport)	Portsmouth	Sheffield
1801	1117	33	71	61	83	77	30	53	82	75	33	36	40	33	46
1811	1327	38	83	71	103	101	37	63	104	96	33	37	51	42	53
1821	1600	47	102	85	138	147	45	84	138	135	42	50	55	47	65
1831	1907	51	144	104	162	212	52	123	210	194	54	61	66	50	92
1841	2239	53	202	124	166	287	67	152	299	252	70	62	70	53	111
1851	2685	54	265	137	194	363	85	172	395	338	88	68	90	72	135
1861	3227	53	351	154	203	443	98	207	472	399	109	75	113	95	185
1871	3890	53	435	183	242	568	122	259	540	446	128	80	118	114	240
1881	4770	52	546	207	295	673	154	309	627	502	145	88	123	128	285
1891	5638	52	634	222	332	766	200	368	631	575	186	101	139	159	324
1901	6586	50	760	329	394	904	240	429	685	645	215	112	178	188	381
1911	7256	50	840	357	401	953	278	446	746	714	267	121	194	231	455
1921	7488	69	919	377	420	1034	287	458	803	730	275	121	210	247	491
1931	8216	69	1003	397	439	1088	314	483	856	766	283	126	208	249	512
1951	8348	79	1113	443	467	1090	299	505	789	703	292	121	208	234	513
1961	8172	81	1106	436	474	1056	303	511	747	661	269	120	204	215	494
1971	7452	84	1015	427	454	897	286	496	610	544	222	122	239	197	520

[a] 'Greater London' was not legally defined until 1963. It grew up through the movement of population into suburbs surrounding an inner area, which from 1889 to 1965 constituted the 'County of London' and reached its maximum of 4½ million inhabitants in 1901.

[b] Birmingham and the other major provincial cities have extended their boundaries into the neighbouring county (or counties) on several occasions since 1801.

Table 3   Extension of the franchise

Year	Number of voters	Population	Percentage enfranchised
		(in thousands)	
1831	439	16 261	2·7 (male, 5·6)
(Act of 1832)			
1833	717	16 720	4·3 (male, 8·8)
1866	1162	24 600	4·7 (male, 9·8)
(Act of 1867)			
1868	2230	25 200	8·8 (male, 18·3)
1883	2920	30 300	9·6 (male, 19·9)
(Act of 1884)			
1885	4931	30 960	15·9 (male, 32·7)
1913	7356	41 660	17·7 (male, 36·9)
(Act of 1918)			
1918	19 456	42 369	45·9 (male, 58·0; female, 35·4)
1927	21 117	43 969	48·0 (male, 59·5; female, 37·1)
(Act of 1928)			
1929	28 080	44 395	63·3
1945	32 836	47 650	68·9
(Act of 1948)[a]			
1950	33 269	48 650	68·4
1966	35 964	53 025	67·8
(Act of 1969)			
1970	39 342	53 903	73·0

[a] This Act did not enfranchise new groups, but made it easier to exercise the franchise (see p. 270). The subsequent decline in the enfranchised percentage of the total population reflects the 'bulge in the birth-rate', referred to on p. 298.

Table 4   The growth of industry

Year	Raw cotton[a] Consumption in 000 metric tons	Coal[a] output in 000 metric tons	Pig-iron[a] output in 000 metric tons	Railways[b] length in km	Mercantile marine[a] net capacity in 000 tons (British measure)
1800	24				1699
1805	27		248 ('06)[c]		2093
1819	56				2211
1815	37	16 200 ('16)[c]	330 ('18)[c]		2478
1820	54	17 700	374		2439
1825	76	22 300	591	43	2327
1830	112	22 800	688	157	2202
1835	144	28 100	1016	544	2360
1840	208	34 200	1419	2390	2768
1845	275	46 600	1537	3931	3123
1850	267	50 200	2285	9797	3562
1855	381	65 487	3270	11 744	4349
1860	492	81 327	3888	14 603	4659
1865	328	99 726	4882	18 439	5760
1870	489	112 203	6059	21 558 ('71)[c]	5691
1875	557	135 445	6467	23 365	6153
1880	617	149 327	7873	25 060	6575
1885	589	161 908	7534	26 720	7430
1890	755	184 528	8031	27 827	7979
1895	755	192 704	7827	28 986	8989
1900	788	228 794	9104	30 079	9304
1905	822	239 918	9762	31 456	10 736
1910	740	268 676	10 173	32 184	11 556
1915	876	257 269	8864	32 623 ('13)[c]	12 429
1920	783	233 215	8164	32 707	11 361
1925	730	247 078	6362	32 849	11 983
1930	577	247 796	6291	32 632	12 454
1935	572	225 819	6527	32 450	10 486
1940	630	227 898	8337	32 094	10 412
1945	325	185 709	7221	31 984	10 341
1950	461	219 780	9788	31 353	11 103
1955	354	225 107	12 670	30 693	11 282
1960	278	196 712	16 016	29 579	12 088
1965	230	190 508	17 740	24 025	11 698
1970	176 ('69)[c]	152 790 ('69)[c]	16 653 ('69)[c]	19 481 ('69)[c]	13 574 ('69)[c]

[a] All tonnages are for the United Kingdom.

[b] Length of railways is for Great Britain, except in 1835 and 1845, when Ireland is included.

[c] Indicates a year other than the fifth.

Table 5 The balance of trade (in £ million)

Year	Excess of imports over exports	Earnings from investment overseas	Other gains from invisible trade	Transfers of bullion and specie	Resulting balance[a] on current account
1820	−7·4	+2·6	+13·4	−5·4	+3·2
1825	−26·5	+5·7	+17·8	+5·4	+2·4
1830	−12·0	+3·9	+12·2	−3·5	+0·6
1835	−11·4	+7·8	+15·5	+0·8	+12·7
1840	−29·8	+7·1	+19·5	+0·9	−2·3
1845	−19·0	+9·7	+19·6	−1·0	+9·3
1850	−19·6	+9·4	+21·8	−1·0	+10·6
1855	−25·9	+12·9	+34·7	−7·8	+13·9
1860	−45·5	+18·7	+48·0	+2·5	+23·7
1865	−51·2	+24·1	+68·4	−6·4	+34·9
1870	−57·5	+35·3	+76·8	−10·5	+44·1
1875	−90·5	+57·8	+89·6	−5·6	+51·3
1880	−121·1	+57·7	+96·4	+2·6	+35·6
1885	−98·5	+70·3	+90·7	−0·2	+62·3
1890	−86·3	+94·0	+99·6	−8·8	+98·5
1895	−126·5	+93·6	+87·8	−14·9	+40·0
1900	−167·0	+103·6	+109·1	−7·5	+37·9
1905	−155·9	+123·5	+120·1	−6·2	+81·5
1910	−152	+187	+125	−7	+153
1913	−146	+210	+129	−12	+181
1920	−386	+200	+395	+43	+252
1925	−393	+250	+188	+10	+54
1930	−386	+220	+194	−5	+25
1931	−407	+170	+134	+133	−70
1932	−286	+150	+86	−17	−67
1933	−258	+160	+103	−201	−196
1934	−284	+170	+117	−142	−139
1935	−275	+185	+108	−56	−38
1936	−346	+200	+127	−227	−246
1937	−431	+210	+176	−99	−144
1938	−388	+200	+122	+74	+8
1946	−103		−127		−230
1950	−51		+358		+307
1955	−313		+158		−155
1960	−406		+141		−265
1965	−237		+187		−50
1970	−25		+758		+733
1975	−3204		+1531		−1673
1976	−3571		+2166		−1405

[a] The balance on current account excludes all *capital* values, e.g. of overseas investments.

Table 6 The work force

Year	Membership[a] of trade unions (in thousands)	Days lost[a] through stoppages (in thousands)	Number registered as unemployed (monthly average, in thousands[b])	Percentage of unemployed workers[c]
1872	c. 400			
1882	c. 600			
1894	1530	9510		6·9
1896	1608	3560		3·3
1898	1752	15 260		2·8
1900	2022	3090		2·5
1902	2013	3440		4·0
1904	1967	1460		6·0
1906	2210	3020		3·6
1908	2485	10 790		7·8
1910	2565	9870		4·7
1912	3416	40 890		3·2
1914	4145	9880		3·3
1916	4644	2450		0·4
1918	6533	5880		0·8
1920	8347	26 570		2·4
1922	5625	19 850	1543	15·2
1924	5544	8420	1130	10·9
1926	5219	162 230	1385	12·7
1928	4806	1390	1217	11·2
1930	4841	4400	1917[d]	14·6
1932	4443	6490	2745[d]	22·5
1934	4570	960	2159[d]	17·7
1936	5295	1830	1755[d]	14·3
1938	6053	1330	1791[d]	13·3
1940	6613	940	963	6·0
1942	7867	1527	123	0·8
1944	8087	3714	75	0·5
1946	8803	2158	374	2·5
1948	9319	1944	310	1·5
1950	9289	1389	314	1·5
1952	9583	1792	414	2·0
1954	9556	2457	285	1·3
1956	9763	2083	257	1·2
1958	9626	3462	451	2·1
1960	9821	3024	377	1·6
1962	9887	5798	467	2·0
1964	10 079	2277	404	1·6
1966	10 261	2398	361	1·5
1968	10 193	4690	586	2·4
1970	11 179	10 980	577	2·6
1972	11 353	23 909	835	3·8
1974	11 756	14 750	585	2·6
1976	11 515	3284	1304	5·8

[a] Figures include Northern Ireland and (down to 1914) small numbers for southern Ireland.

[b] In 1940–6 the figures include Northern Ireland.

[c] At first a percentage of trade union members only, in 1922–38 of all insured workers, and since 1939 of all persons registered as unemployed.

[d] The proportion of unemployed who were 'temporarily stopped' varies between 1 and 37 per cent; in the 1930s it averaged 21·6 per cent.

Table 7   Wages and prices

Year	Wages index[a] (1914=100)	Cost of living index[b] (1914=100)	Resulting index[c] of real wages	Purchasing power of the £ (1900=20s.)
1860	58	113	51	
1866	66	114	51	
1870	66	110	60	
1874	80	115	70	
1880	72	105	69	
1885	73	91	81	
1890	83	89	93	
1895	83	83	100	
1900	94	91	103	20s.
1905	89	92	97	19s. 4d.
1910	94	96	98	18s. 1d.
1914	100	100	100	17s. 5d.
1915	108			14s. 2d.
1920	283			7s.
1925	196	175	112	9s. 11d.
1930	191	157	122	11s.
1935	185	143	130	12s. 2d.
	(1955=100)	(1953=100)		
1939	39			10s. 10d.
1941	48			8s.
1943	54			7s. 2d.
1945	59			6s. 10d.
1947	66			6s. 2d.
1949	64	79	(80)	5s. 7d.
1951	74	89	(81)	5s.
1953	85	100	(85)	4s. 8d.
1955	100	106	(94)	4s. 5d.
1957	113	114	(99)	4s. 1d.
1959	122	118	(103)	4s.
1961	138	123	(112)	3s. 10d.
1963	150	131	(114)	3s. 7d.
1965	175	141	(125)	3s. 5d.
1967	189	151	(125)	3s. 2d.
1969	221	166	(133)	2s. 10d.

[a] No allowance is made for periods of unemployment.

[b] Calculated from the retail prices affecting (or believed to affect) working-class households.

[c] This calculation (based on the two preceding columns) gives only a very rough indication of the changes in the value of wages. The figures from 1949 onwards show no more than the general trend, since the price level rose between 1953 and 1955.

Appendix III
Books for further reading

GENERAL WORKS (FOR ALL CHAPTERS)

W. H. CHALONER and R. C. RICHARDSON, *British Economic and Social History—a bibliographical guide* (Manchester UP).

J. F. C. HARRISON, *Society and politics in England 1780–1960: A Selection of Readings and Comments* (Harper and Row, NY).

R. L. JAMES, *Documents of the Industrial Revolution 1750–1850* (Hutchinson).

E. R. PIKE, *Human Documents Series,* 5 vols (Allen & Unwin): from Adam Smith to Lloyd George.

R. W. BREACH and R. M. HARTWELL, *British Economy and Society* 1870–1970—*Documents—Descriptions—Statistics* (OUP).

B. R. MITCHELL and P. DEANE, *Abstract of British Historical Statistics* (CUP): from 1801.

B. R. MITCHELL and H. G. JONES, *Second Abstract of British Historical Statistics* (CUP): supplementary.

D. BUTLER and A. SLOMAN, *British Political Facts, 1900–1975* (Macmillan): also contains a selection of economic facts, conveniently arranged.

I VILLAGE LIFE IN THE EIGHTEENTH CENTURY

Introductory

R. BAYNE-POWELL, *English Country Life in the Eighteenth Century* (Murray): pp. 96–111—an account of Woodforde.

Authorities

G. M. TREVELYAN, *English Social History* (Longmans): c. XIII—country-house life.

C. HOLE, *English Home Life, 1500–1800* (Batsford): Part II—illustrations of domestic interiors, etc.

Contemporary

J. WOODFORDE, *The Diary of a Country Parson* (OUP): selections, edited by J. Beresford.

J. BOSWELL, *Journal of a Tour in the Hebrides* (Dent).

A. J. YOUNGSON (editor), *Beyond the Highland Line* (Collins): three journals illustrating the very different kind of life in Scotland.

2. TOWN LIFE IN THE EIGHTEENTH CENTURY; LONDON

Introductory

R. J. M. MITCHELL and M. D. R. LEYS, *A History of England* (Longmans): pp. 455–66—houses and furniture.

K. BARNE, *Elizabeth Fry* (Methuen).

D. LINDSAY and E. S. WASHINGTON, *A Portrait of Britain, 1688–1851* (OUP): cc. 11 and 12—life in Johnson's England.

Authorities

A. S. TURBERVILLE (editor) *Johnson's England*, 2 vols. (OUP): Vol. I, c. VII—London, by M. D. George; c. VIII—provincial town-life, by G. D. H. Cole; pp. 329–34—philanthropy, by J. L. and B. Hammond.

M. D. GEORGE, *London Life in the Eighteenth Century* (Kegan Paul): Introduction and cc. I, II and IV—the life of the poor.

P. PRINGLE, *The Romance of Medical Science* (Harrap): c. VIII—vaccination.

Contemporary

D. DEFOE, *A Tour through England and Wales,* 2 vols. (Everyman): Letter V, on London; notices of other towns, as indexed.

3. EIGHTEENTH-CENTURY PEOPLE AT WORK

Introductory

C. R. FAY, *Great Britain from Adam Smith to the Present Day* (Longmans): Introduction.

T. K. DERRY and M. G. BLAKEWAY, *The Making of Britain, 2* (Murray): cc. 17 and 18.

Authorities

L. W. MOFFIT, *England on the Eve of the Industrial Revolution* (King): for the period 1740–60, especially in Lancashire.

J. H. PLUMB, *England in the Eighteenth Century* (Penguin Books): cc. I and II—for the period 1714–42.

B. A. HOLDERNESS, *Pre-Industrial England* (Dent).

Contemporary

A. E. BLAND, etc. *English Economic History Select Documents* (Bell): pp. 482–500.

4. WHAT WAS THE INDUSTRIAL REVOLUTION?

Introductory

T. K. DERRY, *Britain Since 1750* (OUP): c. I.

Authorities

T. S. ASHTON, *The Industrial Revolution, 1760–1830* (OUP): cc. I and II.

J. L. and B. HAMMOND, *The Rise of Modern Industry* (Methuen): cc. I–IV—origins; cc. V–XI—main aspects of industrial change.

W. H. B. COURT, *A Concise Economic History of Britain from 1750 to Recent Times* (CUP): c. I—population.

G. T. GRIFFITH, *Population Problems of the Age of Malthus* (CUP): cc. I, II, X, XI.

M. C. BUER, *Health, Wealth and Population in the Early Days of the Industrial Revolution* (Routledge): cc. IX–XVI—health factors.

Contemporary

ADAM SMITH, *Wealth of Nations* (Everyman).

5–6. HOW THE GREAT CHANGES CAME

Introductory

FAY, op. cit., c. VII.

H. HAMILTON, *History of the Homeland* (Allen & Unwin): c. XV—commerce and the flag.

Authorities

P. MANTOUX, *The Industrial Revolution in the Eighteenth Century* (Cape):Pt. III, c. II.
COURT, op. cit., c, V.
R. SAW, *The Bank of England* (Harrap): cc. I–VIII—on the period 1694–1821.
Johnson's England: Vol I, pp. 256–9—banking.

Contemporary

C. R. FAY, *Huskisson and His Age* (Longmans): c. XI—mater t for the Truck Act of 1831.

7. THE REVOLUTION IN TEXTILES

Introductory

M. and C. H. B. QUENNELL, *A History of Everyday Things in England*, 4 Parts (Batsford):
Part III, c. III.

Authorities

MANTOUX, op. cit. Pt. II, c. II and p. 225–39—for Arkwright.
ASHTON, op. cit. pp. 70–8.
A. P. WADSWORTH AND J. DE L. MANN, *The Cotton Trade and Industrial Lancashire,
1600–1780* (Manchester UP): cc. XXI–XXIII—machine spinning.
E. LIPSON, *A Short History of Wool* (Heinemann): c. VII.
S. LILLEY, *Men, Machines and History* (Cobbett): c. VI.

Contemporary

J. GALT, *Annals of the Parish* (Everyman): cc. XXIX–LI—the development of the
factory system, etc. in a Scottish parish, 1788–1810.

8. THE REVOLUTION IN TRANSPORT: ROADS AND CANALS

Introductory

G. D. H. COLE, *Persons and Periods* (Penguin Books): pp. 78–98.

Authorities

W. T. JACKMAN, *The Development of Transportation in Modern England*, 2 vols. (CUP):
Vol. I, c. IV—roads; c. V—canals.
Johnson's England: Vol. I, c. VI.
C. HADFIELD, *British Canals* (Phoenix House): pp. 1–141.
S. and B. WEBB, *The Story of the King's Highway* (Longmans): pp. 114–91.

Contemporary

G. E. MINGAY (editor), *Arthur Young and his Times* (Macmillan): pp. 145–58—Young on
canals and roads.

9. THE REVOLUTION IN FARMING

Introductory

QUENNELL, op. cit.: Part III, c. I.
C. S. and C. S. ORWIN, *Farms and Fields* (OUP): pp. 61–85.

Authorities

J. D. CHAMBERS and G. E. MINGAY, *The Agricultural Revolution 1750–1880* (Batsford).
LORD ERNLE, *English Farming Past and Present* (Longmans): cc. VIII–XI.
J. L. and B. HAMMOND, *The Village Labourer, 1760–1832* (Longmans): cc. III–V
—enclosures.

Johnson's England: Vol. I, c. X—by C. S. Orwin.

E. HALÉVY, *A History of the English People in 1815* (Benn): pp. 192–224—the system of large estates.

M. D. GEORGE, *England in Transition* (Penguin Books): c. V—the village in transition.

T. C. SMOUT, *A History of the Scottish People 1560–1830* (Collins): cc. XII–XIV—land-ownership, improvements, and the Highland Clearances.

Contemporary

J. BYNG, VISCOUNT TORRINGTON, *The Torrington Diaries* (Eyre & Spottiswoode): selections edited by C. B. and F. Andrews—enclosures (index).

BLAND, etc. op. cit.: pp. 528–41.

MINGAY, op. cit.: quotations from Arthur Young.

10–12. COAL, THE STEAM ENGINE, AND IRON

Introductory

G. S. RANSHAW, *Great Engines and their inventors* (Burke): cc. I and II; c. III—Trevithick.

Authorities

T. S. ASHTON and J. SYKES, *The Coal Industry of the Eighteenth Century* (Manchester UP): cc. II, III, IX, X.

W. H. B. COURT, *The Rise of Midland Industries* (OUP): Bk. II, cc. I–III, VI—coal, iron, power.

A. RAISTRICK, *Dynasty of Ironfounders: The Darbys and Coalbrookdale* (Longmans).

MANTOUX, op. cit.: Pt. II, c. IV, pp. 385–390—Boulton.

T. S. ASHTON, *Iron and Steel in the Industrial Revolution* (Manchester UP): cc. II, III, IV, VI.

LILLEY, op. cit.: c. VI.

W. O. HENDERSON, *J. C. Fischer and his Diary of Industrial England 1814–51* (Frank Cass).

13. POTTERY AND SHIPPING

Introductory

S. E. ELLACOTT, *The Story of Ships* (Methuen): pp. 47–66.

Authorities

R. H. THORNTON, *British Shipping* (CUP): cc. I–V.

B. CABLE, *A Hundred Years History of the P. & O.* (Nicholson): cc. I–XVII.

G. M. YOUNG (editor), *Early Victorian England,* 2 vols. (OUP): Vol. I c. VIII—the mercantile marine 1830–65.

MANTOUX, op. cit.: pp. 391–7—Wedgewood.

Johnson's England: Vol. I, pp. 232–4—pottery.

14. THE FACTORY TOWNS

Introductory

QUENNELL, op. cit.: Pt. III, c. V.

Authorities

J. L. and B. HAMMOND, *The Town Labourer, 1760—1832* (Longmans): c. III.

Early Victorian England: Vol. I, c. IV—life in the new towns.

HALÉVY, op. cit.: pp. 289–95—Luddism.

A. REDFORD, *Labour Migration in England,* (Manchester UP) cc. III, IV.

Contemporary

J. T. WARD (editor), *The Factory System* (David and Charles): source materials.

B. DISRAELI, *Sybil* (World's Classics): description of industrial conditions in early 'forties based on official reports.

15. WOMEN AND CHILDREN: THE FACTORY ACTS

Authorities

1. PINCHBECK, *Women Workers and the Industrial Revolution* (Routledge): cc. IX and XI—work in factories, mines, and the metal trades.

J. L. and B. HAMMOND, *Lord Shaftesbury* (Constable): cc. II–IV, VII–XI.

A. HUTCHINS and A. HARRISON, *A History of Factory Legislation* (King): cc. II–IV.

M. G. JONES, *The Charity School Movement* (CUP): pp. 142–54—Sunday Schools.

Contemporary

W. A. BARKER, etc. *Documents of English History, 1832–1950* (Black): II—industrialism.

BLAND, etc. op. cit.: pp. 502–25, 592–614—factory legislation.

16. BRITAIN AFTER WATERLOO

Authorities

A. BRYANT, *The Age of Elegance* (Collins): cc. VIII–X—the rulers and the ruled; the underworld.

D. THOMSON, *England in the Nineteenth Century* (Penguin Books): cc. I and II—Britain in 1815; the forces of change.

E. L. WOODWARD, *The Age of Reform, 1815–1870* (OUP): pp. 1–38—England in 1815.

J. BUTT (editor), *Robert Owen* (David and Charles): especially sections 1 and 2.

Contemporary

W. COBBETT, *Rural Rides,* 2 vols. (Everyman): visits to twenty-seven counties.

17. THE COMING OF THE RAILWAYS

Introductory

O. S. NOCK, *The Railways of Britain Past and Present* (Batsford).

O. S. NOCK, *British Trains Past and Present* (Batsford).

J. THOMAS, *The Story of George Stephenson* (OUP).

E. GARNETT, *The Master Engineers* (Hodder and Stoughton): the Brunels.

Authorities

JACKMAN, op. cit.: Vol. II, c. VII.

J. H. CLAPHAM, *An Economic History of Modern Britain,* 3 vols. (CUP) Vol. I, c. IX.

C. H. ELLIS, *British Railway History, 1830–76* (Allen & Unwin): pp. 77–149—covering the period 1830–45.

R. B. LLOYD, *Railwayman's Gallery* (Allen & Unwin): c. II—the navvy.

Contemporary

R. S. SURTEES, *Plain or Ringlets?* (Methuen): cc. XXXIII and LXI—a novelist's picture of railway stations in the 'fifties.

18. THE COMING OF FREE TRADE

Introductory
A. BRYANT, *English Saga* (Collins): pp. 84–119.

Authorities
FAY, op. cit.: cc. II–IV.
COURT, op. cit.: pp. 310–16—origins of the free trade policy.
WOODWARD, op. cit.: pp. 68–70, 114–19, 159–61, 172–5.
J. MORLEY, *Life of Richard Cobden* (Unwin): cc. VI–XVI.

Contemporary
BLAND, etc. op. cit.: pp. 692–711—the Corn Laws.
N. McCORD (editor), *Free Trade* (David and Charles): documentary sources.

19. TRADE UNIONS AND CO-OPERATIVE SOCIETIES

Introductory
W. CITRINE, *British Trade Unions* (Collins): pp. 1–37—history, with illustrations.
QUENNELL, op. cit.: Part IV, pp. 155–7—co-operatives.

Authorities
G. D. H. COLE, *A Short History of the British Working-Class Movement, 1789–1947* (Allen & Unwin): Pt. I, cc. V and VI, Pt. II, cc. III, V, VI and VIII.
FAY, op. cit.: cc. XIX and XX.
S. and B. WEBB, *A History of Trade Unionism* (Longmans).
W. H. CHALONER, *The Social and Economic Development of Crewe* (Manchester UP): c. IX—a local co-operative movement, 1845–1923.
J. F. C. HARRISON, *Robert Owen and the Owenites* (Routledge).

Contemporary
G. WALLAS, *The Life of Francis Place* (Allen & Unwin): c. VIII—extracts from Place's writings about the repeal of the Combination Acts.
E. C. GASKELL, *Mary Barton* (Everyman): a novel by a resident describing industrial life in Manchester in 1842–3.

20. THE WORKSHOP OF THE WORLD

Introductory
A. WILLIAMS-ELLIS, *Men Who Found Out* (Howe): c. V—Faraday; c. VIII—Lister.
A. WILLIAMS-ELLIS and E. COOPER-WILLIS, *Laughing Gas and Safety Lamp* (Methuen): Davy and Faraday.
QUENNELL, op. cit.: Part IV, c. II—the farmer and his work.

Authorities
J. D. CHAMBERS, *The Workshop of the World, 1820–1880* (OUP).
J. DEARDEN, *Iron and Steel To-day* (OUP): cc. I–VII—history of techniques.
CLAPHAM, op. cit.: Vol. II, pp. 17–72—iron and steel; shipbuilding.
COURT, op. cit.: pp. 161–84—Victorian agriculture and industrial enterprise.
ERNLE, op. cit.: pp. 358–382.
G. E. FUSSELL, *The English Rural Labourer* (Batchworth): cc. VIII–XI.

Contemporary
S. SMILES, *Self-Help* (Murray).
J. RUSKIN, *Unto This Last* (Everyman): four essays on the nature of wealth which aroused great controversy in 1860–2.

21. NEW TRENDS IN GOVERNMENT

Introductory

T. K. DERRY (editor), *Oxford Junior Encyclopaedia Vol. X, Law and Society*: articles on Parliamentary Elections, History of Local Government, etc.

F. G. KAY, *Royal Mail* (Rockliff).

Authorities

K. B. SMELLIE, *A Hundred Years of English Government* (Duckworth).

J. T. WARD (editor), *Popular Movements 1830–1850* (Macmillan): parliamentary reform, Chartism.

J. A. R. MARRIOTT, *England Since Waterloo* (Methuen): pp. 98–9, 350–54, 417, 491–2—parliamentary reform.

H. J. LASKI, W. I. JENNINGS, and W. A. ROBSON (editors), *A Century of Municipal Progress, 1835–1935* (Allen & Unwin): c. II—the social background, by J. L. Hammond; c. III—the municipal revolution of 1835, by W. I. Jennings.

A. BRIGGS, *History of Birmingham*, 2 vols. (OUP): Vol. II, c. IV.

E. T. CRUTCHLEY, *G.P.O.* (CUP).

Contemporary

J. L. GARVIN, *The Life of Joseph Chamberlain* (Macmillan): Vol. I, pp. 179–214—some contemporary material for the reforms in Birmingham.

R. H. TAWNEY (editor), *The Life and Struggles of William Lovett*, 2 vols. (Bell): on the struggle for the 1832 Reform Act (c. IV) as well as for the history of Chartism.

22. TOWN LIFE AND HEALTH

Introductory

C. WOODHAM-SMITH, *Lady-in-Chief* (Methuen): Florence Nightingale.

P. PRINGLE, *The Romance of Medical Science* (Harrap): cc. IX and XI.

QUENNELL, op. cit.: Part III, c. V—sanitation; Part IV, c. VI—public health.

Authorities

J. L. and B. HAMMOND, *The Bleak Age* (Penguin Books): cc. V and XII—towns and public health; cc. VI and XIII—parks, etc.

F. S. TAYLOR, *A Century of Science* (Heinemann): cc. III and IV.

H. WILLIAMS, *A Century of Public Health in Britain* (Black): pp. 263–301—the architects of social medicine.

Contemporary

P. QUENNELL (editor), *Mayhew's Characters* (Kimber): pp. 85, 157, 169—examples of London poverty.

C. KINGSLEY, *Two Years Ago* (Macmillan): novel describing a cholera outbreak in a Cornish village.

P. KEATING (editor), *Into Unknown England* (Fontana/Collins): selections from Charles Booth, William Booth, etc.

23. VICTORIAN ASPIRATIONS

Introductory

A. BOTT, *Our Fathers* (Heinemann): lavishly illustrated social history of 1870–1900.

A. BOTT and C. CLEPHANE, *Our Mothers* (Heinemann): as above.

QUENNELL, op. cit.: Part IV, c. XI—amusements and holidays.

D. M. STUART, *The English Abigail* (Macmillan): cc. VIII and IX—domestic service.

Authorities
Early Victorian England: Vol. I, pp. 90–103—the daily round in a country house.
TREVELYAN, op. cit.: Vol. I, pp. 8–9 and Vol. II, pp. 517–18—growth of coastal resorts.
Contemporary
F. A. WALBANK, *England Yesterday and To-day* (Batsford): pp. 1–23—extracts from representative Victorian novels.

24. THE EDWARDIAN ERA

Introductory
H. PELLING, *Modern Britain 1885–1955* (Nelson): c. 3.
P. MAUGER and L. SMITH, *The British People 1902–1968* (Heinemann): a simple and straightforward account, which includes foreign affairs and is lavishly illustrated.
T. L. JARMAN, *Socialism in Britain* (Gollancz): cc. 1–7.
P. R. THOMPSON, *The Edwardians: the Remaking of British Society* (Weidenfeld and Nicolson).
R. CECIL, *Life in Edwardian England* (Batsford).
Authorities
R. C. K. ENSOR, *England 1870–1914* (OUP): cc. XI–XV.
S. NOWELL-SMITH (editor), *Edwardian England 1901–1914* (OUP).
T. L. JARMAN, *Landmarks in the History of Education* (Murray): pp. 209–13 on education and the Industrial Revolution, and cc. XIV–XVIII on its development in England.
Contemporary
J. H. BETTEY (editor), *English Historical Documents 1906–39* (Routledge).
R. H. GRETTON, *A Modern History of the English People 1880–1922* (Secker): the volume covering 1899–1910 was published in 1914 and presents the period as seen by the contemporary newspaper reader.
C. F. G. MASTERMAN, *The Condition of England* (Methuen): by a Liberal politician, writing in 1909.

25. DISAPPOINTMENTS OF WAR AND PEACE, 1914–39

Introductory
L. C. B. SEAMAN, *Life in Britain between the Wars* (Batsford).
M. YASS, *Britain between the Wars* (Wayland): excellent illustrations.
N. BRANSON, *Britain in the 1920s* (Weidenfeld and Nicolson).
N. BRANSON and M. HEINEMANN, *Britain in the 1930s* (Weidenfeld and Nicolson).
Authorities
D. THOMSON, *England in the Twentieth Century* (Penguin Books): cc. 1–6.
B. H. LIDDELL HART, *The War in Outline* (Faber).
E. L. WOODWARD, *Great Britain and the War of 1914–1918* (Methuen).
A. MARWICK, *Britain in the Century of Total War* (Penguin Books): cc. 3–5.
C. L. MOWAT, *Britain between the Wars 1918–1940* (Methuen).
W. ASHWORTH, *Economic History of England 1870–1939* (Methuen): cc. XI–XVII.
B. W. E. ALFORD, *Depression and Recovery: British Economic Growth 1918–1939* (Macmillan).
J. SYMONS, *The General Strike* (Cresset).
Contemporary
C. L. MOWAT, *Great Britain since 1914* (The Sources of History Ltd/Hodder and Stoughton): pp. 98–160 on diaries, memoirs, and other contemporary writings.
H. LLEWELLYN SMITH (editor), *The New Survey of London Life and Labour* (King): Vol. I.

26. THE CHANGING PATTERN OF LIFE AND WORK

Introductory

V. OGILVIE, *Our Times—A Social History 1912–1952* (Batsford).

QUENNELL, op. cit.: Vol. 5—everyday things from 1914 to 1968.

W. SHEPHERD, etc. *The Wonderful Story of British Industry* (Ward Lock): cc. 3, 5 and 8—light industry, the chemist, the scientist in the factory.

E. HOLT, *The Farmer* (ESA).

Authorities

A. J. P. TAYLOR, *English History 1914–1945* (OUP): cc. V and IX.

CLAPHAM, op. cit.: Vol. III, pp. 511–54—an Epilogue on the War and its consequences.

G. D. H. COLE and M. I. COLE, *The Condition of Britain* (Gollancz): the 1930s.

Report on the Education of the Adolescent (HMSO 1926): the Hadow Report.

Contemporary

R. GRAVES and A. HODGE, *The Long Week-end: A Social History of Great Britain 1918–1939* (Faber).

J. B. PRIESTLEY, *English Journey* (Heinemann/Gollancz): a tour of inquiry in the autumn of 1933.

M. MUGGERIDGE, *The Thirties* (Hamish Hamilton).

A. G. STREET, *Farmer's Glory* (Faber): Parts I and III—farming in 1906–31.

27. THE SECOND WORLD WAR: DIVIDING-LINE FOR BRITAIN

Introductory

T. L. JARMAN, *Democracy and World Conflict—A History of Modern Britain 1868–1970*: c. 10.

R. C. K. ENSOR, *A Miniature History of the War* (OUP): includes exact dates of all principal events.

Authorities

C. FALLS, *The Second World War* (Methuen).

H. PELLING, *Britain and the Second World War* (Fontana).

MARWICK, *Britain in the Century of Total War* (Penguin Books): c. 6.

A. CALDER, *The People's War* (Cape).

W. K. HANCOCK and M. M. GOWING, *British War Economy* (HMSO).

M. M. GOWING, *Britain and Atomic Energy 1939–45* (Macmillan).

Contemporary

W. S. CHURCHILL, *The Second World War*, 6 vols. (Cassell).

W. H. BEVERIDGE, *Report on Social Insurance and Allied Services* (HMSO): the 'Beveridge Report'.

28. RECOVERY, AFFLUENCE, AND THE SWINGING YEARS—1945–77 IN OUTLINE

General

A. F. HAVIGHURST, *Twentieth Century Britain* (Harper and Row, NY): cc. X–XII.

R. K. WEBB, *Modern England* (Allen & Unwin): c. 13.

T. O. LLOYD, *Empire to Welfare State* (OUP): cc. 10–13.

A. MARWICK, *The Explosion of British Society, 1914–1970* (Macmillan): pp. 97–186.

T. L. JARMAN, *Socialism in Britain* (Gollancz): cc. 12–14.

M. BRUCE, *The Coming of the Welfare State* (Batsford).

P. GREGG, *The Welfare State* (Harrap): economic and social history, 1945–66.

A. SAMPSON, *The New Anatomy of Britain* (Hodder and Stoughton).
M. STEWART, *The Jekyll and Hyde Years* (Dent): politics and economic policy since 1964.
The Annual Register (Longman): a narrative history, year by year.
Keesing's Contemporary Archives: fortnightly bulletins of current events.
Official
COI (CENTRAL OFFICE OF INFORMATION), *Social Services in Britain* (HMSO).
COI, *Britain and the European Community* (HMSO): with chronology of relevant events, 1945–75.
COI, *The European Community—Facts and Figures* (HMSO).
Our Changing Democracy: Devolution to Scotland and Wales. Cmnd 6348. Supplementary Statement, Cmnd 6585 (HMSO).

29. TECHNOLOGY TRIUMPHANT
General
I. M. KRANZBERG and C. W. PURSELL (editors), *Technology in Western Civilization*, Vol. 2 (OUP): the twentieth century.
L. BAGRIT, *The Age of Automation* (Penguin Books).
Encyclopaedia Britannica Book of the Year: articles in each annual issue.
Official
COI, *Britain 1977—An Official Handbook* (HMSO): c. 19 Promotion of the Sciences.
COI, *British Industry Today* series (HMSO): reference pamphlets on Aerospace, Energy, Shipping, etc. with photographs.

30. PROVISION FOR A CHANGING POPULATION
General
R. K. KELSALL, *Population* (Longman).
D. WEIR (editor), *Men and Work in Modern Britain* (Fontana/Collins).
E. BUTTERWORTH and D. WEIR, *Social Problems of Modern Britain* (Fontana/Collins).
M. THOMAS and J. PERRY, *National Voluntary Youth Organisations* (PEP).
Official
Census 1971: Summary Tables (HMSO).
Report of the Population Panel. Cmnd 5258 (HMSO).
COI, *Education in Britain* (HMSO).
The Youth Service and Similar Provision for Young People (HMSO).
COI, *Care of the Elderly in Britain* (HMSO).

31. CONTROL OF THE ENVIRONMENT
General
P. G. RICHARDS, *The Reformed Local Government System* (Allen & Unwin).
J. B. CULLINGWORTH, *Town and Country Planning in Britain* (Allen & Unwin).
C. LAMBERT and D. WEIR, *Cities in Modern Britain* (Fontana/Collins).
W. H. COX, *Cities: the Public Dimension* (Penguin Books).
Official
COI, *Britain 1977—An Official Handbook* (HMSO): c. 8 Planning and the Environment.

COI, *The New Towns of Britain, Housing in Britain, Town and Country Planning in Britain*: reference pamphlets (HMSO).

Inland Transport in Britain (HMSO): with motorway map.

Reports of Royal Commission on Environmental Pollution, 1–5. Cmnd 4585, 4894, 5054, 5780, 6371 (HMSO).

32. PAYING OUR WAY

General

S. POLLARD, *The Development of the British Economy 1914–50* (Arnold).

G. D. N. WORSWICK and P. H. ADY, *The British Economy in the 1950s* (OUP): cc. I, VII, and XIV.

V. BOGDANOV and R. SKIDELSKY (editors), *The Age of Affluence 1951–1964* (Macmillan): c. 4—by P. Oppenheimer.

A. D. YOUNGSON, *British Economic Growth 1920–66* (Allen & Unwin): c. VI.

B. HOOBERMAN, *An Introduction to British Trade Unions* (Penguin Books).

The Annual Register (Longman): the balance of payments, as indexed each year under 'United Kingdom, Economic and Industrial Affairs'.

Official

United Kingdom Balance of Payments 1966–76 (HMSO).

Report of the Committee on the Working of the Monetary System (HMSO): the Radcliffe Report, 1959.

POLITICAL EVENTS	AGRICULTURE, INDUSTRY, AND COMMERCE	COMMUNICATIONS	CONDITIONS OF WORK; TRADE UNIONISM	SOCIAL CONDITIONS, PUBLIC HEALTH, ETC	SIGNIFICANT LITERATURE
1760					
1760 GEORGE III.		1760 Metcalf began road-making. 1761 Worsley Canal opened. 1762 Grand Trunk Canal begun.			1760–1803 Period of the *Woodforde Diary*.
1763 Seven Years War ended.	1764 Watt began to improve the Newcomen engine. 1767 Spinning-jenny invented.		1763–9 Spitalfields silk weavers' riots.		
	1769 Watt's steam engine and Arkwright's water-frame patented.	1768 Forth and Clyde Canal begun (Smeaton).		1769 First dispensary opened.	1768–71 Period of Arthur Young's *Tours*.
1770	1770 Bankers' clearing house established.			1771 The Adelphi completed.	
	1775 Spinning-mule invented.	1773 Turnpikes Act.	1775 First law to release bondsmen from Scottish mines.	1774 Howard's work for prisoners begun.	
1775–82 War of American Independence.			1779 Truck Act for the lace industry.		1776 Adam Smith: *Wealth of Nations*. 1781–94 Period of the *Torrington Diaries*.
1780				1782 Sunday Schools instituted by Raikes.	
1783–1801 Pitt's First Ministry.	1784 Puddling process patented. 1785 Power loom; first steam-driven spinning factory. 1786 Threshing machine invented. 1786 Commercial treaty with France.	1784 First mail coaches.		1785 John Hunter established his museum of anatomy.	
			1788 First Child Sweeps' Act.		1788 *The Times* founded.
1789 French Revolution.					

POLITICAL EVENTS	AGRICULTURE, INDUSTRY, AND COMMERCE	COMMUNICATIONS	CONDITIONS OF WORK; TRADE UNIONISM	SOCIAL CONDITIONS, PUBLIC HEALTH, ETC	SIGNIFICANT LITERATURE
1790					
1793–1815 Wars against French Revolution and Napoleon.	1793 First Board of Agriculture. 1793 Whitney's cotton gin.	1793 Telford engineer of the Ellesmere Canal.		1795 Law of Settlement modified. Start of Speenhamland system. 1796 Vaccination introduced.	
1797 Unlawful Oaths Act.			1799, 1800 Combination Laws.		1798 T. R. Malthus: *Essay on Population.*
1800					
1801 Union with Ireland.	1801 General Enclosure Act.	1801 Trevithick's steam carriage.	1802 Health and Morals of Apprentices Act.	1801 First census.	
1804–6 Pitt's Second Ministry.	1802 Gaslight used at Soho Works.	1802 West India Dock opened.		1808, 1811 'British' and 'National' Schools began.	
1810					
1811 THE REGENCY.		1812 The *Comet* on the Clyde.	1811–16 Luddism.		1811 Jane Austen: *Sense and sensibility.*
1812–27 Liverpool Ministry (Tory).	1813, 1833 East India Company's trade monopoly abolished. 1815 Corn Law.	1814 Stephenson's *Blücher* engine. 1815 MacAdam, surveyor-general at Bristol.	1815 Davy's safety lamp.	1817 Elizabeth Fry's work for prisoners begun.	
1819 Peterloo; The Six Acts.	1819 Gold standard adopted.		1819 Owen's Factory Act.	1819 Stamp duties restricting newspapers reach their maximum.	
1820					
1820 GEORGE IV.			1824 Repeal of Combination Laws.		1821–32 W. Cobbett: *Rural Rides.*
1823–7 Huskisson at the Board of Trade.	1825 General reduction of the tariff; free trade with Ireland. 1828 Neilson's 'hot blast' patented.	1825 Stockton–Darlington Railway. 1826 Menai Suspension Bridge.		1825 Society for the Diffusion of Useful Knowledge. 1828 London University founded. 1829 Metropolitan Police established.	1828 E. Elliott: *Corn-Law Rhymes.*

1830

1840

1850

	Political / Economic	Industry & Transport	Labour	Social & Public Health	Literature & Culture
1830s	1830 WILLIAM IV. 1830–41 Grey and Melbourne Ministries (Whig-Liberal). 1832 Parliamentary Reform Act. 1835 Municipal Reform Act. 1837 VICTORIA. 1839–48 Chartism.	1830 Liverpool–Manchester Railway. 1837 Electric telegraph first patented. 1839 Nasmyth's steam hammer.	1830 Revolt of farm labourers. 1831 General Truck Act. 1833 Althorp's Factory Act. 1833–4 Owen's GNCTU.	1831 Cholera epidemic: first local boards of health. 1834 Poor Law Amendment Act.	1837 C. Dickens: *Oliver Twist*.
1840s	1841–6 Peel Ministry (Conservative). 1844 Bank Charter Act. 1846 Repeal of Corn Laws. 1849 Repeal of Navigation Laws.	1840 Penny Postage.	1842 Coal Mines Act. 1844 Factory Act restricting women's labour. 1847, 1850 Ten Hours Acts.	1842 Report on sanitary conditions. 1844 Rochdale Pioneers (First co-op). 1848 Public Health Act. 1850 Libraries Act.	1840 *Punch* founded. 1845 B. Disraeli: *Sybil*. F. Engels: *Conditions of the Working Class*. 1848 E. C. Gaskell: *Mary Barton*.
1850s	1851 Great Exhibition. 1853–66 Gladstone's free trade Budgets. 1855, 1862 Limited liability introduced. 1856 Bessemer steel. 1854–6 Crimean War.	1850 First British clipper built. 1851 Dover–Calais cable laid.	1851 Amalg. Soc. of Engineers founded.	1853–61 Repeal of the 'Taxes on Knowledge'. 1855 *Telegraph* founded, the first London daily paper at 1d.	1851–64 H. Mayhew: *London Labour and the London Poor*. 1855 A. Trollope: *The Warden*. 1857 T. Hughes: *Tom Brown's Schooldays*.

POLITICAL EVENTS	AGRICULTURE, INDUSTRY, AND COMMERCE	COMMUNICATIONS	CONDITIONS OF WORK; TRADE UNIONISM	SOCIAL CONDITIONS, PUBLIC HEALTH, ETC	SIGNIFICANT LITERATURE
1860					
	1860 Cobden–Chevalier commercial treaty with France.			1861 Post Office Savings Bank.	1861 I. M. Beeton: *Household Management.*
				1863 North of England CWS.	
		1866 Regular cable service established between Britain and North America.		1865 Lister's first use of antiseptics.	
1867 2nd Parliamentary Reform Act.		1867 Agricultural Gangs Act.			1868–79 Period of the *Kilvert Diary.*
1868–74 Gladstone Ministry (Liberal).		1869 Suez Canal opened.			
1870					
				1870 Forster's Education Act.	1871–2 G. Eliot: *Middlemarch.*
				1871 Bank Holidays introduced.	
1874–80 Disraeli Ministry (Conservative).	1875 Decline of British agriculture began.	1876 First telephones.	1875 Disraeli's trade union legislation.	1875 Public Health Act.	
	1879 Gilchrist-Thomas steelmaking process.				
1880					
		1883 Electrification of tramways began.		1882 Married Women's Property Act.	
1884 3rd Parliamentary Reform Act.	1884 Parsons' steam turbine.			1884 Foundation of Fabian Society and of university settlements (Toynbee Hall).	1887 First English translation of Marx's *Das Kapital.*
1888 County Councils.			1889 London dock strike.		1889 C. Booth: *Life and Labour of the People.*
1890					
		1892–4 Modern bicycle came into use.			1890 W. Booth: *In Darkest England, and the Way Out.*
1894 Subordinate local councils established.	1894–6 First important industrial combines (origin of ICI, etc.).				1894 R. Blatchford: *Merrie England.*
		1896 Motor cars freed from 4 m.p.h. speed limit.	1897 Workmen's Compensation Act (Chamberlain's).	1896 *Daily Mail* first published.	1898 B. Shaw: *Plays Pleasant and Unpleasant.*

1900					
1901 EDWARD VII.	1900 First important artificial silk factory.	1900 Central London Railway.			
	1903–5 'Tariff Reform' campaign.	1901 First transatlantic wireless message.		1902 Balfour's Education Act.	1905 H. G. Wells: *Kipps*.
1905–15 Campbell-Bannerman and Asquith Ministries (Liberal).		1903 First aeroplane flight (in America).			1906 J. Galsworthy: *A Man of Property*.
		1905 First London motor-buses.	1908 Coal Mines (8 Hours) Act.	1908 Old Age Pensions.	
			1909 Trade Boards; Labour Exchanges.	1908 Boy Scout Movement began.	
1910					
1910 GEORGE V.			1910–12 Big strike movement.	1911 Lloyd George's Insurance Act.	1912 *The Miners' Next Step*.
1914–18 1st World War.	1913 British coal output at its maximum.		1913 Nat. Union of Railwaymen founded.		
1917 Russian Revolution.			1915 Shop stewards first instituted on the Clyde.		1918 *Labour and the New Social Order*.
1918 Representation of the People Act.		1919 First transatlantic flight.		1919 Sex Disqualification (Removal) Act.	1919 J. M. Keynes: *The Economic Consequences of the Peace*.
1920					
				1920 First municipal housing estates.	
		1922 First British Broadcasting Company.	1921–40 Unemployment exceeds 1 million.		
1924 First MacDonald Ministry (Labour).				1925 Widows' and Orphans' Pensions.	
	1925–31 Pre-war gold standard restored.		1926 General Strike.		
1928 Equal Franchise Act.					1929 *We Can Conquer Unemployment* (Liberal Party 'Orange Book').
1929 Local Government Act.					

POLITICAL EVENTS	AGRICULTURE, INDUSTRY, AND COMMERCE	COMMUNICATIONS	CONDITIONS OF WORK; TRADE UNIONISM	SOCIAL CONDITIONS, PUBLIC HEALTH, ETC	SIGNIFICANT LITERATURE
1930					
1931–40 'National' Ministry.	1932 Tariff system reintroduced: Ottawa Conference.		1932 Unemployment reaches its climax at 3 million.	1934 Assistance Board.	1930 H. Ll. Smith: *New Survey of London Life and Labour*. 1931 *Report of the May Committee on National Expenditure*.
1936 EDWARD VIII; GEORGE VI. 1939–45 2nd World War.		1936 BBC television service begun.			
1940					
		1944 Jet propulsion of aircraft.		1944 Butler's Education Act.	1942 The Beveridge Report.
1945–51 Attlee Ministry (Labour).	1946–7 Nationalization of the Bank of England, coal mines, and railways. 1947 Agriculture Act.		1946 Trade Union Act abolishing restrictions imposed after General Strike.	1945 Family allowances begun. 1946 National Insurance Act. 1946 National Health Service. 1947 Town and Country Planning Act. 1948 National Assistance Act.	1948 W. S. Churchill: *The Second World War*, Volume I (Book I, From War to War).
1950					
1951–64 Conservative Ministries.				1952 First post-war university charter.	
1952 ELIZABETH II.	1954 Atomic Energy Authority.	1955 ITV services began.			
	1956 Restrictive Trade Practices Act.				
1957 British H-bomb.		1959 First motorway.			

1960 ————

1962 Commonwealth Immigration Act.	1960 EFTA Agreements. 1962 Nuclear power stations in regular service.	1962 Satellite communication via Telstar.	1965 Trade Unions Commission.	1964 Comprehensive school policy officially adopted.
1964 Wilson Ministry (Labour).	1967 Iron and Steel Act—£ devalued to $2.40.	1969 American Moon landing.		1965 *The National Plan.*
				1969 *In Place of Strife.*

1970 ————

1970 Heath Ministry (Conservative).	1973 Britain joins EEC.	1972 British Airways established.	1972 Unemployment exceeds 1 million.	
1972 Local Government Act.	1975 First North Sea oil.	1976 First Concorde flights.	1974 Control of Pollution Act.	
1974 Labour Ministry.			1976 Commission for racial equality.	
1976 Devolution Bill.				
1977 Silver Jubilee.				

Index

Figures in bold refer to Illustrations